MEN
CONFRONT
PORN
OGRAPHY

Books by Michael S. Kimmel

Absolutism and Its Discontents: State and Society in
Seventeenth Century France and England

Changing Men: New Directions in Research and
Masculinity (editor)

Men's Lives (editor, with Michael Messner)

MEN
CONFRONT
PORN
OGRAPHY

EDITED BY
MICHAEL S. KIMMEL

CROWN PUBLISHERS, INC., NEW YORK

For Kate and for Iona,
"sexual intellectuals"

Published by Crown Publishers, Inc.,
201 East 50th Street, New York, New York 10022

CROWN is a trademark of Crown Publishers, Inc.

Manufactured in the United States of America

Library of Congress Cataloging-in-Publication Data

Men Confront Pornography / edited by Michael S. Kimmel.
p.   cm.
1. Pornography—Social aspects—United States.   2. Men—United
States—Attitudes.   I. Kimmel, Michael S.
HQ471.G84   1989
363.4'7—dc19   89-1341
                                                                                CIP

ISBN 0-517-56931-0

10 9 8 7 6 5 4 3 2 1

First Edition

Contents

Porn as Therapy?: The Psychology of Pornography

Enter the Academics: Social Science Research on Pornography

Gay Male Porn: Does Sexual Orientation Make a Difference?

What Is To Be Done Now?

Notes and References   320

Contributors   338

Preface

In an article in *The Village Voice* in 1982, feminist film critic B. Ruby Rich issued a challenge to her male readers: "Finally, here's a proper subject for the legions of feminist men: let them undertake the analysis that can tell us why men like porn (not, piously, why this or that exceptional man does *not*), why stroke books work, how oedipal formations feed the drive, and how any of it can be changed." The contributors to *Men Confront Pornography* take this challenge seriously and confront the issue of pornography in men's lives: the extent to which it shapes and informs our feelings and perceptions about our own sexuality, about women's sexuality, and about the relations between women and men.

I have brought together many different men in this book to give expression to the range of men's voices about their experiences and their positions about pornography. I've included essays with which I don't agree in order to expand the discussion among men, which parallels the debate among women. I believe that such an inclusive policy will allow this book to find a wider audience than simple partisanship and therefore could help more men raise the issue of pornography in their own lives.

One of the central themes in the feminist debate about pornography is that pornography is *political*, not necessarily in the narrow legislative or electoral sense, but in that it brings the hidden, private world of male sexual pleasure into the public arena of political discussion. I share this assumption: The personal *is* political, and the personal pleasures that millions of American men take in pornography require public debate. If pornography informs our sexuality—what we do, what we dream about doing, what we want to do but dare not admit—then men can be held accountable for what happens in our heads when we are thinking about sex or having sex. Even if there is no single "politically correct" sex, that doesn't mean that what we do in bed, and what happens in our heads, is not political.

That men should confront the role pornography plays in our sexual lives seems especially important in the era of sexual backlash in which we live. In the face of AIDS hysteria, the Moral Majority's antisex crusades, marked increases in homophobia and antigay violence and discrimination, as well as efforts to turn back the clock on abortion, sex education, and women's health-care information, influential segments of our nation are becoming profoundly *erotophobic*—exhibiting an irrational hatred and fear of the erotic. More than ever, it is imperative to hold fast to the proclamation of a universal right to sexual pleasure—particularly as that right now comes with a moral imperative to be sexually responsible. We all—women and men, straight and gay—have a right to pleasure, *as well as* an obligation to be sexually responsible. If men can confront the role of pornography in our lives, we can better claim our rights and accept our responsibilities.

As I have worked on this book, I've been constantly challenged to explore the questions raised by the feminist debate about pornography. Conversations and correspondence with Tim Beneke, Bob and Joann Brannon, John Gagnon, Janet Goldstein, Cathy Greenblat, and Peter Lyman have been particularly helpful. I am grateful to *Changing Men*, the profeminist men's magazine, whose editors, Mike Biernbaum and Rick Cote, first allowed me to invite men to think about pornography for a special issue of the magazine. Several friends have provided the intellectual and emotional support that makes writing possible; I am especially grateful to Angela Aidala, Claire August, Judith Brisman, Donna Carroll, Barbara and Herb Diamond, Martin Duberman, Pam Hatchfield, Wray Herbert, Ed Kimmel, Sandi Kimmel, Martin Levine, Mary Morris, and Mitchell Tunick. My own essays in this volume have benefitted from critical readings by Bob Brannon, Kate Ellis, Frances Goldin, Cathy Greenblat, Iona Mara-Drita, and Jane von Mehren.

This book would not have been possible without the pioneering efforts of the women who first brought the politics of pornography to the center of public debate. The writings of Susan Brownmiller, Pat Califia, Lisa Duggan, Andrea Dworkin, Kate Ellis, Amber Hollibaugh, Judith Levine, Catharine MacKinnon, Gayle Rubin, Ann Snitow, Carol Vance, and Ellen Willis have been provocative and challenging, and have invited—no, compelled—me to enter the debate and examine the questions they have raised. I also acknowledge a significant debt to the members of the "Sex, Gender, and Consumer Culture" seminar at the New York Institute for the Humanities for five years of stimulating conversations.

My agent, Frances Goldin, has believed in this project from its beginning and has given me enormous support. And my editor, Jane von Mehren, had the enthusiasm to take on such a risky project and the patience and careful editorial eye to allow the book to take shape. I am sincerely grateful to both of them.

I also want to thank my students in my course "Sex and Society," at SUNY at Stony Brook, as well as students in earlier classes on sexuality at Rutgers and at New York University. Their honest discussions and thoughtful research have helped all of us disentangle this complex and difficult issue. I am proud to include a paper by one of my former students, Chris Clark, in this collection.

The two women to whom this volume is dedicated have been the most important influences on my thinking about sexuality. In different ways, each has pushed me to think and feel in new and often unexpected ways and stretched what I thought were the limits of the erotic-as-theory. Our conversations have been among my life's greatest turn-ons.

M. S. K.
New York City

Introduction:
Guilty Pleasures-Pornography in Men's Lives

by

MICHAEL S. KIMMEL

*Representation of the world, like the
world itself, is the work of men; they
describe it from their own point of view,
which they confuse with the absolute
truth.*

Simone de Beauvoir,
The Second Sex (1970)

Men look at pornography, but we do not *see* it. We read pornography,
but it is not literature. We watch pornographic films, but we are indifferent to narrative content or cinematic technique. Men *consume* pornography, using pornographic images for sexual arousal, usually without
considering the relationship between what's in the pictures or stories and
the sexual pleasure we seek. What matters with pornography is its utility,
its capacity to arouse. Its value appears to be contained in its function.

Pornography is not just men looking. It is men producing images for
men to consume. And consume it we do. In 1984, for example, 200
million issues of 800 different hard- and soft-core magazines were sold in
the United States alone, generating over $750 million.

And most of the images produced by men to be consumed by men are
images of women. In 1970, the President's Commission on Obscenity
and Pornography found that ninety percent of all pornographic material
is geared to male heterosexuals and ten percent is geared to male homosexuals, and that consumers of pornography are "predominately white,
middle-class, middle-aged married males." Though today more women
are both producing and consuming pornography, and men always appear
in gay male pornography, the percentages probably remain comparable;
I'd estimate that now male heterosexual pornography might compose

eighty percent of the market, with that for gay men constituting fifteen percent, and for women, the remaining five percent.

As men have been producing pornography for other men to watch, read, and look at, women have begun, with the rise of the women's movement in the 1960s, to talk about pornography, about how they feel about seeing other women's bodies portrayed in pornography, about how pornography makes them feel about themselves, about their sexuality, about other women, about men. The debate about pornography has split the women's movement in painful disagreement, dividing women on issues as fundamental as the nature of women's oppression, the organization and expression of sexuality, and the forms of political resistance to women's oppression.

To some women, pornography is, in the words of Susan Brownmiller, "the undiluted essence of anti-female propaganda." To these women, pornography graphically illustrates the subordination of women in our culture. And what is particularly objectionable about pornography is that it renders this brutal subordination so that men can experience sexual arousal and pleasure from it. Pornography, as John Stoltenberg puts it, "makes sexism sexy." And they feel it is a major cause of men's violence against women—especially rape. As Robin Morgan wrote, "Pornography is the theory, rape is the practice."

Other women are distrustful of feminist-inspired efforts to combat pornography. Some have claimed that pornography has helped them to break away from traditional passive definitions of women's sexuality and to claim a more active, vital sexuality. Some women are even attempting to create their own pornography about lustful women who act on sexual feelings and initiate sexual encounters.

What have men had to say about the pornography debate? Frankly, very little. In large part, men's response to this debate has been a deafening silence. Perhaps it is the sheepish silence that conceals a guilt of the pleasures taken from pornography. Perhaps it is the frightened silence of the culpable child caught with his hand in the cookie jar. Perhaps it is the angry silence that seeks to protect privileges now threatened by women's interference. Perhaps it is the bored silence of a nonissue, of men who know that antipornography feminists are not going to put *Playboy* out of business. Of course, for many men, there is silence about the question of pornography because there is no question: Pornography is a vital part of many men's sexuality, and the feminist debate may threaten that privilege. Silence is a refusal to acknowledge the debate.

Perhaps all these; perhaps more. I think that men have been the silent spectators in the debate about pornography because, quite simply, we don't know what to say. Even among those men who, in general, support women's efforts to carve out more meaningful and equal lives, there has been a stunning silence. Here, it is a silence born of confusion about the role of pornography in our own lives, and a more general confusion about how we experience our sexualities, a confusion that remains fixed in place because of our inability to talk frankly and openly with other men about our sexualities, and that is compounded by a paralyzing fear that whatever we say about something as volatile as pornography will reveal us to be less than "real men." Men are frightened to raise the subject, inarticulate when we try.

But men must try. Men need to raise the issue, to examine the role of pornography in our lives. A lot is at stake: Although most pornographic images are *of* women, pornography is, at its heart, *about* men. It is about men's relationships with sexuality, with women, and with each other. It is about women as men want them to be, and about our own sexual selves as we would like them to be. Whether or not pornographic images determine our sexual behaviors, there is little doubt that these images depict men's fantasies about sexuality—both women's sexuality and our own.

This book contains essays by men who have attempted to shatter this silence, who examine various parts of the role of pornography in men's lives, and who confront different elements in the debate about pornography. In the remainder of this essay, I will try to map out some of these elements and suggest the ways in which the various contributors address these questions.

I. Sexuality, Masculinity, Pornography

Sexuality as a Social Construction

Sexuality is the source of enormous confusion. Sex evokes conflicting and often contradictory emotions: profound guilt at moments of exuberance and pleasure; simultaneous feelings of vulnerability in sexual surrender to another and the power and control that often accompanies another's pleasure. The moments of most intense intimacy and connection are also moments of loss and abandonment. In sex, we are often at once in full possession of all our senses and in danger of utter annihilation. As Japanese novelist Shusako Endo recently wrote in *Scandal*, "our erotic behavior expresses our profoundest secrets, the ones we ourselves aren't aware of."

Confusion itself is frightening, accompanied by anxiety, threat, instability, uncertainty. Often, when confused, we retreat to a more comfortable, secure place, like the past, when we could be certain about a situation. Recourse to tradition—"it's always been like that and always will be"—is an attempt to hold in check a confusion that threatens inherited certainties. And when we are confused about our sexuality, we often retreat to biology: "It's in my genes," we want to say, believing our sexual attitudes and behaviors are the emanation of biological impera- tives, the "natural" expression of inner needs and drives. It's more com- fortable to think that what we do sexually has to do with biological imperatives, since such a posture allows us to avoid responsibility for our behavior.

Biological arguments maintain a privileged status in popular wisdom about sexuality. But what they reveal about physiological functions, they obscure about the relations among people. Biological arguments assume that what exists is supposed to exist as a result of evolution. They ob- scure the ways in which social relations involve assumptions about, and are based upon, the power of some people over others. Biological argu- ments claim that such power imbalances are inevitable and "natural" and not subject to challenge or change. That which is *normative*—constructed and enforced by society through socialization of the young and through social sanctions against deviants—begins to appear as *normal*, that which is designed by nature. This is a sleight of hand; the normative is not necessarily normal but is the result of a long and complex set of social conflicts among groups. "It is precisely through the process of making a power situation appear as a fact in the nature of the world that tradi- tional authority works," writes anthropologist Maurice Bloch. And in this way, we can see how the biological perspective is irretrievably conserva- tive and resistant to change from social movements whose purpose is to transform sexuality, especially the women's movement and the gay and lesbian movement.

In contrast to these biological arguments, many social scientists un- derstand our sexuality to be a *social construction*, a fluid assemblage of meanings and behaviors that we construct from the images, values, and prescriptions in the world around us. The social-constructionist perspec- tive examines variability and change in sexual behaviors and attitudes. Specifically, sexuality varies (1) from culture to culture; (2) within any one culture over time (historically); (3) depending upon the context in which it is presented; and (4) over the course of an individual's life.

Anthropological evidence suggests enormous variability in sexual be- haviors and attitudes. In fact, it is through this dramatic variation in sexual behaviors that we have learned how cultures define the erotic and shape the ways in which the erotic is enacted. For example, Alfred Kin- sey found, in his famous studies of sexual behavior in the 1940s and 1950s, that eighty-five percent of American men had never had sex in any way other than the "missionary position." By contrast, anthropolo- gist Clyde Kluckhohn found that position to be preferred in only ten percent of the Native American cultures he surveyed. In some cultures people are only sexual at night, in others only during the day. In some cultures, sex can only take place inside the couple's dwelling, while in other cultures it must take place outdoors, away from the family's food supply. Although we may believe that kissing is expressive and required foreplay, the Siriono of the Brazilian Amazon jungle believe that kissing is a disgusting practice that contaminates the mouth. If our sexuality were biologically programmed, it would be a scientific invariant, like gravity: If gravity fails to work once, the entire theory must be revised.

The ways in which people are sexual and the meanings we attach to our behaviors change dramatically over time. Think, for example, about the progressive dissociation between sex and reproduction in the United States. Since the nineteenth century, sexuality has been progressively cut loose from its yoking to reproduction and the family, so that, today, the pursuit of sexual pleasure, independent of marriage, is both possible and, for many people, desirable. The progressive disentangling of sex and reproduction has been propelled by social changes such as urbanization, which provides the first historical possibility of sexual encounters with relative strangers; by medical advances such as reliable birth control; and by technological changes like the automobile, which provides an opportunity to get away from the family as well as a place to engage in sex itself. A general trend of secularization of social values has loosened the hold of religion, long the chief buttress of the sex-reproduction complex. Although academic research continues to discuss sexuality in relation to marriage, tabulating surveys whose categories are often coded as "premarital, " "marital," and "extramarital" (sometimes with a special category for homosexual sex as "nonmarital"), Americans continue to have sex in ways that may, or may not, have anything to do with the institution of marriage.

Sexuality also varies through any individual's lifetime. What turns us on when we are adolescents may not turn us on when we are in our mid-fifties. As men age, for example, they may become open to more sensual behaviors, such as cuddling and extended foreplay, while women often report that their explicitly sexual sensations increase in their late thirties and early forties. It may be convenient to explain such developments as simple biological maturation of different anatomical creatures, but men and women in other cultures do not "mature" sexually in this way, nor have they always "matured" in this way in the United States.

The reliance on biological maturation processes, to discuss sex as a force of nature, ignores the ways in which men's and women's sexuality are related to one another. That "his" sexuality shifts toward the sensual just when "her" sexuality takes a sharp turn toward the steamingly sexual indicates more than simple divergence of biological patterns. In part, this may have to do with the institution of marriage. Marriage domesticates sex, which means that sexuality is increasingly brought into the domain reserved to women: the home. When men feel that sex is no

longer dangerous and risky, and therefore exciting, their sexual repertoire expands to include a wider range of sensual pleasures. By contrast,
when women feel that sex is no longer dangerous and risky, and therefore threatening, they are freed to explore more explicitly sexual pleasures. (That women feel threatened by the same danger and risk that
men find exciting further illustrates the power differences between
women and men. The fact that fear and sexual excitement often produce
the same physiological responses may confuse men, who may mistake
that fear for passion.)

Finally, our experience of the erotic depends on the social context in
which it takes place. We may find it convenient to think that some
behaviors are simply sexy and cannot do anything but bring about sexual
arousal, while other behaviors are simply never arousing, no matter what
the context. But does this correspond with our experience? Take, for
example, pictures of the genitals. How many anatomy students find their
textbooks arousing? Scientific books and soft-core pornography may
show the reader the same body part, but they usually don't produce the
same outcome. What about a representation of the genitals involved in a
sexual act, or even preparing for a sexual act? Compare a pornographic
film loop with a clinical explanation of how to put on a condom to
practice safer sex. So much for representations, which obviously require
a sexual context for the images to be sexually arousing.

But what about the real thing? One might argue that the mere sight of
the other's nakedness is uniformly arousing. Yet sexual arousal is actually
quite rare at places where nudity is approved, such as nudist colonies and
art classes. And the touching of another's genitals might seem to be
"naturally" arousing, but neither physician nor patient ordinarily experiences much sexual arousal during gynecological or prostate examina-
tions. Few, if any, women are aroused by breast self-examination, few
men by self-examination for testicular cancer.

If sexuality is socially constructed, it both changes and it can be
changed. The repertoire of sexual behaviors available to women and men
can be expanded, and the associations of the erotic with various forms of
domination can be reevaluated and, perhaps, recontextualized. Of
course, such processes take time, but the social-constructionist position
opens us to the possibilities of transformation, including the responsibility to account for our own sexuality. If what we do and what we think do
not simply bubble up into consciousness or behavior because of our
genetic programming, we can be held accountable for them. For men,
this is especially important when it comes to pornography, which is one
of the major sources of sexual information that young males have about
sexuality, and thus a central mechanism by which our sexuality has been
constructed. Men can no longer hide behind pornography as "harmless
fun."

What Makes Sex Sexy?

If sexuality is not constructed out of thin air, but carefully proscribed by rules and values that govern our behavior, then there is a relationship between what happens in the real world and what we do in bed. Some social scientists have adopted sociologists John Gagnon and William Simon's term "sexual scripts" to refer to "the plans that people have in their heads for what they are doing and what they are going to do," as well as devices interpreting what people have done in the past. Through our sexual socialization, we learn our scripts as an actor might learn a part in a play; we learn such things as motivation (why some things should make us feel sexy and why others should not), scenery construction, cues, props, costumes, and what we should do if we forget our lines. (Like actors in the play, we are both handed a script that was created by forces external to us, and we have some power to transform the script slightly to accommodate our own interpretation. This is why what is considered normal sexuality is so strikingly similar in any particular culture and why there are individual idiosyncratic variations on the normative theme.) Sexual scripts provide us with the answers to the fundamental questions of any narrative: Who is an appropriate sexual partner? Whom do we desire? What do we want to do with that person? When do we like to have sex? Where? How should we have sex? Who does what to whom? And finally, and most critically: Why should we have sex?

Although these questions appear rather simple, arriving at the answers in our culture is an extremely complex process. Sexual desire is filtered through so many layers that "pure" lust—unconnected to a person's history—is rarely, if ever, the reason for a sexual encounter. The major organizing principle of sexual desire, the axis around which it revolves, is gender. It is through our experience of our masculinity or our femininity that we come to know ourselves as sexual beings. When we are sexual, we regard our behaviors and the meanings we attach to those behaviors as the confirmation of our gender identity, as badges that we are "real" men or women.

One way to illustrate this is to look at what happens when the confirmation of one's gender identity through sexual behavior breaks down, when people experience sexual problems. (I'll discuss only masculinity here, though sexual problems such as anorgasmia are also experienced by women in gendered terms.) Sexologists and therapists agree that if a man experiences one of the three most common sexual problems—erectile dysfunction, premature ejaculation, or low sexual interest—he almost invariably interprets this problem in gender terms, not in sexual terms. "I don't feel like enough of a man," he might say, or, "If I can't (get it up, keep it up, want to keep it up), I'm failing as a man." He'll almost never describe a desire to experience more sexual pleasure, to feel stronger desire, or to last longer simply because it feels good. Sexual performance is a confirmation of gender scripts.

It is equally unlikely that, when sex is successful, a man will interpret that in terms of satisfaction of purely sexual desire. Instead, it will confirm his status as a man, generate pride in his successful ability as a lover. The relationship is mutually reinforcing: We construct a sexuality through gender, and we confirm gender through sexual behavior.

The rules of masculinity, like sexuality, vary from culture to culture and within any culture over time. The meaning of masculinity also varies in our culture by class, race, ethnicity, and age. Though it is appropriate to speak of multiple masculinities, we can also identify some elements that, if they are not held by all men in our culture, at least define the dominant form of masculinity, the model to which middle-class white men aspire and against which others are measured. Social psychologists Robert Brannon and Deborah David summarized the rules of masculinity into four basic axioms:

1. "No Sissy Stuff": Masculinity can allow no behaviors or attitudes that even remotely hint of anything feminine. Masculinity is demonstrated by distance from the feminine.
2. "Be a Big Wheel": Masculinity is measured by success and status in the real world, by one's capacity as a producer. We measure masculinity by the "size of our paycheck" or the recognition we receive from others.
3. "Be a Sturdy Oak": Men must be confident, secure, reliable, inexpressive, and utterly cool, especially during a crisis.
4. "Give 'Em Hell": Exhude a manly air of violence, aggression, daring. Masculinity is demonstrated by taking risks, by "going for it."

These four rules of masculinity are given expression in men's sexual behavior. Men learn their sexual scripts beginning in childhood, from the scraps of information they find surrounding them in our society, including misinformation from peers and even *dis*information from adults who are frightened of youthful sexuality. One of these sources of information is, of course, pornography, which, as Alfred Kinsey found, is one of the most-often cited sources of a boy's first information about sexuality. In fact, one of the reasons masculinity and sexuality are often so entangled is that they become salient issues simultaneously. During adolescence, young boys struggle to master the rules of masculinity at the same time that they become aware of their emergent sexualities. What, then, do adolescent males learn about sexuality and how is this connected with their emerging definitions of themselves as men?

As adolescents, we learn that sex is secret, morally wrong, and wonderfully pleasurable. The association of sexual *pleasure*, achieved alone or in the company of another, with feelings of *guilt* and shame occurs early and often in a man's development and is reinforced by family, friends, school, religion, and media images of sexuality. Perhaps this guilt reinforces the demand that real men be constantly in control and produces the demonstration of masculinity in the separation of emotion and pleasure, in emotional detachment. (This is profoundly different for women, who also experience sexual guilt but often attempt to resolve it by inextricable connection of sexual pleasure and emotional commitment.)

In locker rooms and playgrounds, men learn to detach their emotions from sexual expression. Detachment requires sexual self-objectification and the development of a secret sexual self that performs sexual acts and indulges in "guilty pleasures." That men use the language of work as a metaphor for sexual behavior—"getting the job done," "performance," "achieving" orgasm—illustrates more than a passing interest in turning everything, including sexual pleasure, into a job where performance can be evaluated; it reinforces detachment so that the body becomes a sexual machine, a performer instead of an authentic actor. The penis is transformed from an organ of sexual pleasure into a "tool," an instrument by which the job is carried out, a thing, separate from the self. Men have developed a rather inventive assortment of nicknames for their penises, including the appropriation of real first names, like "John Thomas" and "Peter." (Can we imagine a woman calling her vagina "Shirley" or her clitoris "Sally Ann"?) Many men have elaborate conversations with their penises, cajoling, pleading, or demanding that they become and remain erect without orgasmic release. The penis can become the man's enemy, ready to engage in shameful conspiracy—getting an erection "inappropriately" or failing to get one when it is appropriate. Is it any wonder that "performance anxiety" is so pervasive an experience for American men?

As a result, sex for men often requires emotional detachment, which allows sexual pleasure to be pursued as an end in itself. But sex is also to be hidden, a covert operation, private, and we have few skills by which we can share the experience with others. Masturbation teaches men that sex is phallocentric, that the penis is the center of the sexual universe. And the "tools" of masturbation, especially sexual fantasy aided by pornography, teach men to objectify the self, to separate the self from the body, to focus on parts of bodies and not whole beings, often, even, to speak of one's self in the third person.

Male "sexual socialization" emphasizes how real men are supposed to have sex. Passivity is prohibited, and males must constantly seek to escalate the level of sexual activity. With young women, the adolescent male feels pressure to continue the sexual encounter; he is the aggressor, since, as one man once remarked in a group discussion of male sexuality,

"It only counts if I put it in." And the young woman must play the feminine role of "gatekeeper," determining the level of sexual intimacy appropriate to the situation. As a result, neither can fully experience the pleasures of the moment. No sooner does he arrive at a particular level of sexual intimacy—touching her breast, for example—than he must begin to strategize how to advance to the next level. There is simply no time to pause and think about how soft and warm and lovely her breast might feel, how different from his own, how pleasurable to touch her. To stop would expose him as less than manly. And she cannot allow herself to take much pleasure in his hand caressing her breast, because she must now determine if it is all right with her for him to continue (she knows he will try) and to calculate how to thwart his efforts if she doesn't want the encounter to go further. It is as if each is living in the future tense, thinking only of how to escalate or how to prevent plea-sure. Neither can fully experience the pleasures of the journey to sexual intercourse. And this dance is a pantomime; we perform it as a dumb show, believing ourselves to be without scripts and incapable of asking for help or even talking about what feels good and why. Men find it difficult to ask for directions when they're lost in their cars. How, then, could they ask for directions around the foreign territory of another's body?

How do men maintain the sexual distancing and objectification that they perceive is required for healthy functioning? In an early nightclub routine, comedian Woody Allen offered a brilliant rendition of a typical male strategy. After describing himself as a "stud," Allen remarked:

> While making love, in an effort [pause] to prolong [pause] the mo-ment of ecstasy [pause] I think of baseball players. All right, now you know. So the two of us are making love violently, and she's digging it, so I figure I better start thinking of baseball players pretty quick. So I figure it's one out, and the Giants are up. Mays lines a single to right. He takes second on a wild pitch. Now she's digging her nails into my neck. I decide to pinch hit for McCovey [pause for laughter]. Alou pops out. Haller singles, Mays takes third. Now I've got a first and third situation. Two outs and the Giants are behind by one run. I don't know whether to squeeze or to steal [pause for laughter]. She's been in the shower for ten minutes already [pause for laughter]. I can't tell you any more, this is too personal [pause]. The Giants won.

Readers may be struck by several themes: the imputation of violence, how her pleasure leads to his decision to think of baseball players in the first place, the requirement of victory in the ball game, and the sexual innuendo contained within the baseball language. The text also provides a startlingly honest relevation of male sexual distancing. Here is a device that is so successful at delaying ejaculation that the narrator is rendered utterly unaware of his partner. "She's been in the shower for ten minutes already," Allen remarks, as if he's just noticed. Other men have told me that they have silently recited multiplication tables, fantasized about other sports, and even thought about subjects as diverse as laundry, cleaning the bathroom, or watching television as strategies for feeling less, so they can delay orgasm and hence be perceived as more successful lovers. Sexual adequacy seems to be measured by the time elapsed between penetration and male orgasm, and the sexual experience itself is transformed into an endurance test in which one is competing against the clock. Pleasure, if present at all, is almost accidental. Surely such behaviors are not biologically programmed! And no wonder that male sexuality, whether with women, with men, or with ourselves, often bears more than a passing resemblance to Thomas Hobbes's description of man's life in the state of nature: "solitary, poor, nasty, brutish, and short."

Although this discussion has concentrated on heterosexual males, a similar model could be constructed for gay men. From the research on gay male sexuality now available, we can understand that what's true for straight men is equally true for gay men. Straight men and gay men have far more in common about their sexuality than we might at first suppose. Boys, whether they become straight or gay, are socialized similarly; there is no "anticipatory socialization" for homosexuality. In addition, the modern gay male culture, since the Stonewall riots of 1969, has thrown out the old equation of gay man as "failed man," which was casually equated in a homophobic culture as "false woman," since gay men and women are penetrated in sex.

From this new perspective, gay men are "real men" and gender may be a more fundamental source of behavior and attitudes than sexual orientation. (This despite the fact that most gay men, when asked about the origins of their homosexuality, respond in *gender* terms, not in terms of sexual attraction: "I knew I was different from other boys," a statement of gender nonconformity, is a far more common response than "I was attracted to other boys.") For much of the 1970s and 1980s gay men often aspired to "hypermasculinity" and demonstrated that gays were as capable of objectification, phallocentrism, distancing, and the separation of emotion from physical sensation as straight men. "Tricking" for gay men was an exaggerated version of "scoring" for straight men. That gay men have, at least until recently, had much more sex and with more partners than straight men has been the source of envy as well as anger among straight men. As sociologist Martin Levine has commented wryly, "Straight men might have as much sex as gay men, if women would only let them."

Pornography, a central source of material that instructs young men about the relationship between their sexuality and their masculinity, shows men what it means to be a real man having sex. Pornography is an important part of the male sexual script, which, in turn, is a vital confirmation of masculinity. It is therefore essential to respond to the recent politicization of pornography if we are to understand our sexuality and what it means to be a man in our culture.

II. The Politicization of Pornography

In 1888, an anonymous writer for the *London Sentinel* passed by a London bookshop and observed a fourteen-year-old boy reading a passage from the newly translated novel *La Terre (The Earth)*, by Emile Zola, which was displayed in the shop's window. Outraged, the writer barged into the shop and demanded that the book be removed from the shelf because "the matter was of such a leprous character that it would be impossible for any young men who had not learned the Divine secret of self-control to have read it without committing some form of outward sin within twenty-four hours after."

This little tiff a century ago raises the two central themes that have framed the current political debates about pornography—themes that are brought to the center of Western cultural discourse by the availability of cheap written materials and, more recently, by cheap mechanisms of photographic reproduction. The first of these concerns the definition of pornography, specifically the difference between the obscene and the pornographic. What is "leprous" and what is merely scabrous? And by what and whose standards are such words and images to be judged? The second issue concerns the relationship between images and behavior: Does pornography cause changes in its consumers' behavior, leading them to commit "some form of outward sin" after using it? In particular, does pornography change men's attitudes toward women, celebrating and championing misogyny? In so doing, can it be said to cause violence against women? Does it, at the very least, desensitize consumers to the brutality of sexist culture, inuring us to a world in which violence against women is routine?

These two themes express different politics, different ways in which the debate over pornography has been framed. The first is, of course, the right-wing assault against obscenity, a critique of explicitly sexual images and undermining traditional authority, especially within the family. Dirty pictures are said to lead young minds—especially the minds of adolescent males—into a fantasy realm where they are not subject to the traditional demands of parental obedience, homework, and church attendance:

> The boy's mind becomes a sink of corruption and he is a loathing unto himself. In his better moments he wrestles and cries out against this foe, but all in vain; he dare not speak out to his most

intimate friend for shame: he dare not go to parent—he almost fears to call upon God. Despair takes possession of his soul as he finds himself losing strength of will—becoming nervous and infirm; he suffers unutterable agony during the hours of the night, and awakes only to carry a burdened heart through the day.

So wrote Anthony Comstock, in the Report of the New York Society for the Suppression of Vice in 1887. Pornography in this view portrays a world of sexual plentitude and therefore encourages the pursuit of sexual pleasure outside the confines of traditional marriage; obscene materials have the ability, Comstock wrote, to "poison and corrupt the streams of life, leaving a moral wreck, a physical deformity, an enervated system, and carrying the seeds of destruction far into the social fabric." It is thus to be combatted in the same way as one would combat the individual's right to sex education, birth control, abortion, divorce, the ERA, homosexuality, premarital sex, and women's right to enter the labor force as men's equals.

A century after Comstock, Patrick Fagan, director of the Child and Family Protection Institute, a Washington-based, right-wing policy analysis center, repeated this position:

> Pornography can lead to sexual deviancy for disturbed and normal people alike. They become desensitized by pornography. Sexual fulfillment in marriage can decrease. Marriages can be weakened. Users of pornography frequently lose faith in the viability of marriage. They do not believe that it has any effect on them. Furthermore, pornography is addictive. "Hard-core" and "soft-core" pornography, as well as sex-education materials, have similar effects. Soft-core pornography leads to an increase in rape fantasies even in normal males.

(Note that Fagan equates hard-core pornography and sex education information.)

A conservative contemporary antiporn activist in Kansas City confesses that he has seen how pornography "has destroyed people's lives." Although it is "not the cause of all the world's evils, [pornography] does have a catalytic effect on somebody who already has other problems." And who doesn't already have other problems?

Political campaigns against pornography have historically been framed by public concern over obscenity, the proliferation of increasingly explicit sexual images. "Art is not above morality," proclaimed Comstock as he campaigned furiously against smut. In both Europe and the United States, antiobscenity campaigns led to the censorship of dozens of books now hailed as great literature. Works by Gustave Flaubert, Oscar Wilde, Emile Zola, James Joyce, and D. H. Lawrence constitute only some of the more celebrated cases earlier in this century; recent antismut crusades have removed books such as *The Joy of Sex; Our Bodies, Ourselves;* John Irving's *The World According to Garp;* Kurt Vonnegut's *Slaughterhouse Five;* and John Updike's *Rabbit Run* from the library shelves in many communities.

The liberal response to the right-wing assault against sexuality and individual freedom has always been to assert the primacy of an individual's right to freedom of expression over any community's right to squash that freedom in the name of collective decency. Community standards shift too easily and unpredictably to compromise the fundamental right of individuals to control what they see and what they say, according to the liberal position. Few liberals are what one might call "propornography," and many are deeply offended by the content of some materials, but they see the freedom of the individual as a cause to be defended despite their own discomfort.

Conservatives have historically remained unconvinced. After the President's Commission on Obscenity and Pornography in 1970 found little evidence of social collapse from the use of pornography and issues of freedom of expression to be worth upholding, President Nixon rejected his commission's report, arguing that "pornography is to freedom of expression what anarchy is to liberty; as free men willingly restrain a measure of their freedom to prevent anarchy, so must we draw the line against pornography to protect freedom of expression." Few liberals were convinced by an argument that promoted censorship in the name of preventing censorship. And so the debate continued.

In the 1980s, the right-wing crusade against pornography has been carried forward by a zealous former attorney general representing an administration gravely troubled by the erosion of traditional values symbolized by unrestrained sexual expression. The second President's Commission on Obscenity and Pornography, which came to be called the Meese Commission, held a series of hearings across the nation, in which women who were victims of sexual assault, spouse abuse, and marital rape also testified about being victims of pornography. The commission also heard testimony about pornography's links with organized crime and its casual role in the rise of divorce, abortion, and teenage sexuality and the decline in marital fidelity and church attendance.

The feminist challenge to pornography, mounted in the late 1970s and continuing today, has radically shifted the terms of this debate. Earlier discussions pitted the community's right to censor speech it didn't like against an individual's freedom to consume that which the community didn't like. The current feminist debate makes few, if any, claims for community morality. They are less concerned with the corruption of young boys' morals, or the erosion of the traditional nuclear family; some, in fact, support the dismantling of the family as an institution that fundamentally oppresses women. And they are less concerned than conservatives with the community's right to censor speech; as far as they are concerned, the community of male domination has made the silencing of women's speech a foundation in the building of its culture. What feminists *are* interested in is the harm done to women.

It is ironic that as the right wing is challenging pornography because it undermines the patriarchal family, casting sexuality as a threat to male domination, women are challenging pornography because they believe it reinforces male domination. In their view, pornography depicts women in submissive positions, enjoying rape and torture, and thus graphically illustrates male domination; in fact, it makes sexual torture of women a turn-on. Antipornography feminists challenge pornography because it maintains the subordination of women in society.

Feminist writers such as Susan Brownmiller, Andrea Dworkin, Susan Griffin, Catharine MacKinnon, and Robin Morgan have also confronted the traditional liberal idea that pornography is protected by the First Amendment right of freedom of speech. Their argument is that pornography is not freedom of expression but itself a form of censorship: Pornography silences women, suppresses the voices of women's sexuality, constrains women's options, and maintains their subordination in a male-dominated world. We live, they argue, in a culture in which simulated (or real) rape, mutilation, torture, or even murder of a woman are routinely presented to men by men, with the intention (and effect) of making men experience desire, of turning men on, of eliciting erection. It is impossible to frame the debate in terms of freedom of speech versus community standards; now the conflict is between men's free speech and women's free speech.

If a man's freedom of speech requires the silencing of women, there is only partial freedom and surely no justice. Pornography "is not a celebration of sexual freedom," writes Susan Brownmiller, "it is a cynical exploitation of female sexual activity through the device of making all such activity, and consequently all females, 'dirty.'" Pornography is "designed," she continues, "to dehumanize women, to reduce the female to an object of sexual access, not to free sensuality from moralistic or parental inhibition." Pornography does not represent a liberating breath of free sexuality in the normally stale and fetid air of conservative censoriousness; it is only the sexualization of that traditional patriarchal world. Pornography is not rebellion; it is conformity to a sexist business-as-usual.

Along the same lines, Andrea Dworkin and Catharine MacKinnon completely reframed the political debate by arguing that if pornography stifles free speech, then it ought to be subject to legal challenge because it prevents women from obtaining the equal rights guaranteed by the Constitution. If pornographic images suppress women's right to free speech, then these obstacles can be legally removed. Their coauthored municipal ordinance was passed by city councils in Minneapolis and Indianapolis (although the former was vetoed twice by the mayor and the latter struck down by a federal judge as unconstitutional), and introduced in several other city and county legislatures around the nation (by a two-to-one margin, such an ordinance was passed by referendum in Bellingham, Washington, in November of 1988). It is a remarkable document that completely shifts the terms of the debate, and it raises, for men, some profound questions about men's sexuality.

The intent of Dworkin and MacKinnon's civil-rights ordinance, often called the Minneapolis Ordinance, can best be understood by analogy. Imagine the following scenario: What if photographs of the sexual mutilation of black women and men and the lynching of black men by whites in the South during the 1920s were sold on virtually every newsstand in the nation, intended to arouse white consumers to erotic fantasies under the pretense that this is "what blacks really want"? When blacks say they do not like Jim Crow laws, they "really mean" that they do, and so the racist subordination of black people can continue unabated—fueled, in fact, by these images. (I believe it's possible that the sexualization of the violence against blacks—the rape of black women by whites, the genital mutilation of black men before lynching them—does, in fact, reveal an eroticization of oppression that makes the analogy even more powerful.) How long, antipornography feminists ask, would blacks in this country put up with such humiliation? How long would they stand for the sexualization of torture and murder? How long would the government allow magazines that publish such images to remain "protected" as free speech?

The feminist campaign against pornography rests on three levels of harm said to be caused by pornography. First, they argue that pornography *is* violence against women. The offscreen activities that lead to the production of a pornographic movie often involve the coercion of the woman into scenes of humiliation, rape, and degradation. For example, Linda Marchiano, who under the name Linda Lovelace starred in *Deep Throat*, the most successful pornographic movie in history, claims that she was forced, often at gunpoint, to perform the sexual acts that were filmed for male consumption. *Deep Throat* is not fiction; it is a documentary of a sexual assault. "Every time someone watches that film," Marchiano writes in her autobiography, *Ordeal*, "they are watching me being raped."

This blurring of the distinction between "art" and reality, and the actual coercion recorded in pornographic material, is far more common than we might believe, many women claim. But even so, women who are not pornographic models are also injured by pornography, humiliated and degraded. Just as every joke that makes fun of a black or a Jew hurts all blacks and Jews, so too does pornography hurt all women. In an interview recently, Susan Brownmiller commented:

> I find any crotch shot in *Playboy* or *Penthouse* absolutely humiliating. People say, "Well, what are you humiliated by? You've spread your legs and looked at yourself in the mirror; that's what you look like." Well, yeah, I know that's what I look like, but why should it be in a magazine on the newsstand? To me, the issue of privacy is really significant. Where are the images displayed and for what ultimate purpose? If they're displayed for men in business suits to jerk off on, then there's something wrong with the image.

Susan Griffin's moving analysis, *Pornography and Silence*, underscores the psychological costs of sexual objectification in pornography. Griffin speaks of the necessity for women to create a false self, to become "the pornographic ideal of the female." The constant barrage of images of violence against women does great violence "to a woman's soul. In the wake of pornographic images, a woman ceases to know herself. Her experience is destroyed." The new self-image she constructs is of the adorable plaything of pornography; silenced by pornography and denied a real voice, she speaks with the false voice of the pornographic sex symbol. Pornography maintains sexual inequality by injuring some women directly, and silencing all women. As one woman commented: "I want a legal remedy that will give relief to women who are harmed by the *practice* of pornography. I want a legal remedy that's going to stop looking at the pictures, stop calling them fantasy, stop calling them representations and images and depictions and start viewing them as *documents, presentations*, and the *reality* of women and men in this culture."

A second level of argument is that pornography *causes* violence against women. Pornography provides a how-to manual for woman-hating, they argue, and it makes sexism sexy in the process. As Dworkin writes, pornography "functions to perpetuate male supremacy and crimes of violence against women because it conditions, trains, educates, and inspires men to despise women, to use women, to hurt women. Pornography exists because men despise women, and men despise women in part because pornography exists." Pornography thus causes rape and battery by convincing men that when their dates/wives/lovers say no they really mean yes, and that if they force women to have sex against their will they will eventually love it. "The point about pornography is that it changes men," Dworkin noted in an interview. "It increases their aggression toward women. It changes their responses." Here, antiporn feminists refer to the same evidence as the right-wing would-be censors: Convicted rapists often confess to having used pornography, and many men accused of other forms of sexual crimes or deviance also have, in their homes, large quantities of pornographic materials. To antiporn feminists, these men are not the sexual deviants the right-wingers see, but rather overconformists to the rules of misogynist masculinity. What might sound like an abdication of responsibility if spoken by a man ("Pornography made me do it!") appears to the antiporn feminist as an insight into social-science causation.

Finally, these women argue that even if it were not violence itself, and even if it did not cause violence against women, pornography would inure consumers to the culture of violence that surrounds us. Repeated exposure to pornographic images "desensitizes people to the abuse of women," Catharine MacKinnon noted in an interview. Viewers become "numb to abuse when it is done through sex." Underscoring this position, Chief Justice Nathaniel T. Nemetz, of the British Columbia Court of Appeals in Canada, argued that pornography precludes gender equality: "If true equality between male and female persons is to be achieved," he wrote in his opinion on *R. v. Red Hot Video*, "it would be quite wrong to ignore the threat to equality resulting from the exposure to male audiences of such violent and degrading material, given that it has a tendency to make men more tolerant of violence to women and creates a social climate encouraging men to act in a callous and discriminatory way toward women." Even against some evidence from social-scientific experiments that seem to contradict this view, antiporn feminists hold fast to their convictions. "Does one need scientific methodology in order to conclude that the anti-female propaganda that permeates our nation's cultural output promotes a climate in which acts of sexual hostility directed against women are not only tolerated but ideologically encouraged?" asks Susan Brownmiller.

As some women have reframed the political debate about pornography, they've been confronted not only by liberals who advocate a sexual laissez-faire, but by other women who oppose what they see as an impulse to censor and who claim that pornography can be a vital element in a woman's reclaiming of a vital sexuality. Others are fearful of the censorship implications of the antiporn position. Writers such as Lisa Duggan, Barbara Ehrenreich, Kate Ellis, Ann Snitow, Carole Vance, and Ellen Willis have been involved in the Feminist Anti-Censorship Taskforce (FACT), which was created to expand the political debate and especially to engage with antiporn feminists who had organized Women Against Pornography (WAP). (I'll use these acronyms for convenience, even though not all antiporn feminists are associated with WAP and not all anti-antiporn feminists are associated with FACT.)

In part, the pornography debate among feminists recapitulates old divisions between radical feminists on the one hand and socialist feminists on the other. To radical feminists, the context in which all political struggle takes place is male domination, the violent subordination of women by men. It permeates all interpersonal relationships, and it is institutionalized in governmental and community organizations. The goal of radical feminists has been to protect women who have been the victims of male violence and to create institutional mechanisms to prevent future abuse. To socialist feminists, by contrast, feminism involves the claiming of a rebellious sexuality, extracted from the contradictory images that consumer society provides.

Feminists disagree about the context in which pornography is produced and consumed. To WAP, that context is sexist violence. Pornography eroticizes this violence and therefore reassures men that sexist violence is all right. In the ideal world that these women construct, there would be no pornography, because all sexual relationships would be based on mutual respect for the other's integrity, in contrast to the pornographic world fueled by inequality and domination. "We will know that we are free when pornography no longer exists," Andrea Dworkin writes in her powerful book *Pornography: Men Possessing Women.*

To FACT, on the other hand, pornography's context includes not only sexist violence but also sexual repression and sexual scarcity. Not only does sexism lead to violence against women, but it leads to bad sex and too little of it. In Western culture, we can't have as much sex as we want—civilization, as Freud understood, would be impossible if we did. To FACT, feminism is an empowering drive to affirm women's sexuality, to claim appetite, and leads not to the elimination of images but to their proliferation, as women become more articulate about their sexuality. Feminism is thus about the capacity to transform experiences of powerlessness and oppression into sources of liberation. And, they claim, the inherent contradiction of sex—the fusion of omnipotence and powerlessness through surrender—is a chief vehicle of the transformation of powerlessness into pleasure. Their vision of utopia is one in which women can claim their sexuality based on a belief that desire is not exclusively a male prerogative. In a society of sexual plenty there might be no need for pornography, because the pornographic need is fed by scarcity and repression. Antiporn feminists, by contrast, claim that the *form* is male. "There can be no equality in porn, no female equivalent, no turning of the tables in the name of bawdy fun," writes Susan Brownmiller. "Pornography, like rape, is a male invention, designed to dehumanize women, to reduce the female form to an object of sexual access, not to free sensuality from moralistic or parental inhibition." (Brownmiller is obviously thinking only of heterosexual male pornography, since some gay male pornography uses gender equality as a springboard to erotic fantasy.)

FACT questions the claim that pornography is violence against women, causes violence, or inures consumers to a culture of violence. To members of FACT, the antiporn feminist position seems to rest on a crude behaviorism: If I see it in pornography, I will fantasize about it. If I fantasize about it, I will want to do it. If I want to do it, I will do it, even if it means doing it against someone's will. WAP claims that fantasy reflects those experiences and desires that men currently entertain; sexual fantasy resembles the world as men want it to be. FACT uses a more psychoanalytic explanation, that fantasy is a transformation of past experiences, in which loss can be recaptured. To them, fantasy is about structuring fears in order to gain control over them, transforming the darker regions of sexuality into potentials for pleasure.

And FACT also disputes the contention that pornography inures us to the culture of violence that defines women's daily lives. Repeated exposure to fantasy images of violence does not always have this effect in nonsexual situations. How many times have you seen a murder enacted on television? One thousand? How about a car crash in which someone is obviously injured? Ten thousand? Imagine strolling down the street and witnessing a real murder or a real car wreck. Do you think you'd feel numb, unable to respond because you've been anesthetized to the real pain that those real people are feeling? FACT's position is that people can tell the difference between genuine screams and set-ups, between blood and ketchup. The troubling phenomenon of insensitivity to violence is more closely and obviously connected to fear than to media images.

Most women agree, however, that pornography expresses male hostility to women's political gains over the last two decades. As women advance in real life, they are pushed back in men's fantasies. Here is antipornography activist and sociologist Diana Russell:

> The great proliferation of pornography since 1970—particularly violent pornography and child pornography—is part of the male backlash against the women's liberation movement. Enough women have been rejecting the traditional role of being under men's thumbs to cause a crisis in the collective male ego. Pornography is a fantasy solution that inspires non-fantasy acts of punishment for uppity females.

And here is FACT member, writer Ellen Willis:

> The aggressive proliferation of pornography is . . . a particularly obnoxious form of sexual backlash. The ubiquitous public display of dehumanized images of the female body is a sexist, misogynist society's answer to women's demand to be respected as people rather than exploited as objects. All such images express hatred and contempt, and it is no accident that they have become more and more overtly sadomasochistic. . . . Their function is to harass and intimidate, and their ultimate implications are fascistic.

(Note that the key difference here is that Russell claims an explicit relationship between these images and men's behavior, while Willis explores the impact of these images on women and makes no claims that the images translate into behavior.)

But there is more common ground among women with differing political views on pornography. Perhaps most critically, we must understand how *pornography is gendered speech*, how form is related to content, and how both form and content are and have been so ineluctably male. So here is one place where men come in. Our culture is so suffused with sexism that it is often invisible to us. And the eroticization of others' pain and terror is important for all men to examine: Why do depictions of rape turn so many of us on? Women are challenging men to stop eroticizing violence against women, and help protect women who consider themselves victims of pornography from further abuse. Moreover, the seeds of liberation are often found among the contradictory images that our culture produces: Sexual liberation is a vital element in the feminist challenge to sexism, precisely because women's sexual desire has so long been suppressed under the blanket of "natural" passivity. Women are now challenging men to develop healthy and exuberantly erotic relationships with women as equals. How will men respond?

Men have only recently begun to enter the debate about the politics of pornography, examining the ways in which pornography has informed the construction of male sexuality and the political implications of that construction. Men enter the debate from several different perspectives. Some of the essays assembled here speak personally about the ways in which pornography has affected individual men. Allan Creighton, for example, writes of his pain and guilt over the ways in which we have been trained to view women and sexuality in our culture. David Steinberg, on the other hand, explores the ways in which pornography has enabled men to recover damaged identities and assert more healthy sexualities. Several writers, like Phillip Lopate, Scott MacDonald, and Timothy Beneke, examine the connection between personal experiences with the pornographic and larger cultural meanings.

Men have entered the debate about pornography as political men, committed to various political causes and activated by a concern about women's pain and anger at the violent reality of many women's lives. John Stoltenberg writes as a man committed to the political vision of radical feminism, while others, such as Joel Kovel, Richard Goldstein, Todd Gitlin, and Fred Small, offer a range of analyses that all stem from a progressive political critique of consumer capitalism.

Academic men have entered the debate in two ways. A theoretical exploration by Harry Brod indicates careful and clear thinking on a complex and often confusing topic. Jeffrey Masson writes as a psychoanalyst unafraid to take on the darker regions of the psyche and the Freudian establishment in the process. Men have also performed social-scientific research experiments to examine the effects of pornography. The essays here by Edward Donnerstein and Daniel Linz, and by Dolf Zillmann and Jennings Bryant, summarize some of the most influential social-science research about the effects of pornography on male viewers. Berl Kutchinsky, who conducted the pioneering experiments on the effects of pornography in Denmark, summarizes the results of his research.

Several of the men included here write about the ways in which sexual orientation figures into the debate about pornography. Jeff Weinstein, John Stoltenberg, Scott Tucker, Chris Clark, and Thomas Waugh all wrestle with the question: Is gay male pornography, in which there are no women and the sexual encounter is between two people who are gender equals, different from heterosexual pornography?

For some men, thinking about pornography or performing research on its effects is not sufficient to support the feminist campaign against pornography. The Dworkin-MacKinnon ordinance in Minneapolis was introduced in the city council by Van F. White, who explains his perspective as a black man viewing pornography. A leaflet by Men Against Pornography explains the group's political position. Sociologist William Simon challenges these organizing efforts as misguided, although he is critical of right-wing censorship positions as well.

These men confronting pornography do not exhaust the range of men's responses to the debate about pornography. Indeed, they are but a first attempt to explore the ways in which pornography is one of the means by which men come to know women, to explore sexuality, and to know themselves as sexual beings. The pornography debate must be enlarged and extended if we are to understand more adequately the role sexuality plays both as a cornerstone of male supremacy and, in its liberatory capacity, as one of the chief weapons we may have to assist in the dismantling of gender inequality and in the creation of a world in which we all—women and men, gay and straight—can be equal in desire.

Pornography and the Construction of Male Sexuality: Personal Voices

SMUT

by

JULES FEIFFER

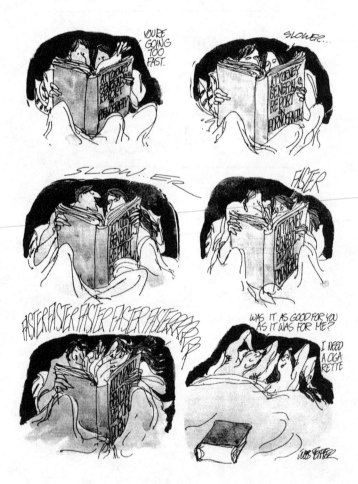

Renewing Sodom and Gomorrah

by

PHILLIP LOPATE

Every few years, on the front page of the *Times*, a plan is announced by a consortium of merchants and industrialists and bankers to transform Forty-second Street into a squeaky-clean thoroughfare. One recent proposal calls for glass-enclosed atriums (the Ford Foundation, sponsoring the project, is big on atriums), "bridges crisscrossing 42nd Street, and escalators moving through a complex set of spaces making up the display area," which would include "a ride that would simulate movement through the layers of a slice of New York from underground to a skyscraper top." They are also getting smarter: they are not going to knock down all the movie houses, just the less "historical" ones, and then turn those allowed to survive into what the planners genteelly term "legitimate playhouses" (a throwback to the old prejudice that Theater was the more respectable art, and Film the bastard).

Every time such an article appears my whole day is ruined. Because I think that if I ever get up the courage to marry and have a family, how will I be able to show my children Forty-second Street if there is no Forty-second Street? And if I lack the nerve and turn into a seedy old bachelor, then I will need Forty-second Street all the more, in those golden waning years.

All of Manhattan tilts toward that magnetic field of neon. Ever tried ambling through the streets of New York without any destination? I know that I am always pulled toward that glittering needle—at first into the triangle around Times Square, with the three-card-monte sharks and the Bible screamers and the sad-eyed camera stores bobbing me around until I wind up on *the* street, West Forty-second, between Seventh and Eighth avenues. Then I don't know where to start to turn my head and

look. Heaven for a film lover is ten marquees that change bills every day.
Forty-second Street comes close.

It was here I used to rush to at eleven in the morning, cutting classes
in college to see *Rules of the Game* with my legs dangling over the Apollo
balcony. And here I caught up with all the flicks that opened and closed
fast and nobody else would show: with the last great Westerns of Raoul
Walsh and Howard Hawks, with Otto Preminger's melodramas, like
Hurry Sundown and *In Harm's Way*. And the show in the balcony was as
interesting as the one on the screen. First you saw concessionaires hawk-
ing ice cream and caramel popcorn in between (and sometimes during)
films, those sad sacks in white Good Humor uniforms climbing up the
balcony steps; then the reefers would be passed around in back, along
with criticism of the characters: "That girl is *dumb!*" "Why don't she just
get out of there?" (This during a scene with a psychotic killer stalking a
coed, what could be better?) The chorus in the audience started direct-
ing advice and taunts—"You better run, girl! I wouldn't stay in that house
by myself, that's for damn sure."

Meanwhile some vagrant in the pit was snoring too loudly, having
come into the theater only to escape the cold and rainy street, and was
two-thirds through his second double bill with his head between his
knees as an usher approached and rudely shook him awake. Shortly
after, a fight would start between pit and balcony, the Guelfs and the
Ghibellines, because some joker from on high had been throwing popcorn at the patrons below. All manner of threats were exchanged. Then
someone tossed lit cigarettes from the balcony, each one a dying fire-
cracker, drawing the attention of everyone in the theater. Meanwhile,
the glories of late Hollywood-studio *auteur* style, outdoor night se-
quences all bluish black with just a few klieg highlights, tracking shots
around corrals, men in white sheets, Jane Fonda making love to a saxo-
phone, who can figure out what's going on? "*Shut up!*" someone yelled. It
turned out to be me. I was appalled at myself and sank deeper into my
seat. What a way to see a movie!

All that's changed, you'll say; I'm just being sentimental. The Apollo
stopped showing art films years ago and now it's kung fu and sex from
one end of the street to the other. Or as the article puts it, "violent or
pornographic movies." But you know, even if I never walked into another
Forty-second Street movie house again, which is highly unlikely, it
would still do me good to take in the street periodically for health reasons, like a sauna. Such concentrated steaminess. Do planners know
how hard it is to achieve a visual clutter so extreme that it makes the
simple traversal of one city block as adventurous as running a gauntlet?
Sure, there are hustlers, thieves, prostitutes, cripples, derelicts, winos,
molesters, droolers, accosters—I'm not denying it. Would you prefer to

cement over the whole beehive with a dipsy-doodle exhibition hall and kick out those people so they'll congregate on another block and make a new heaven and hell somewhere else, maybe not as bright and never as satisfyingly central?

The politics of such civil plans are transparent. What's objected to here is not movie houses and pinball parlors but the people who go into them, who are the wrong class and the wrong color. No need to dwell on the racism and antagonism to down-and-out poor people that is the real message behind urgent appeals to "clean up" Times Square. But I wonder if this city knows how lucky it is to have a raunchy street so famous and so densely compacted. We are told that tourists can ride escalators in the new Forty-second Street and visit a gallery with an object or two on loan from each of the city museums; whoopee-do. Don't they know that tourists, even the straightest, come to New York City partly because they've heard that we've got a real Sodom and Gomorrah? They want to see something that they can go back home and tell their neighbors was "dis-*gusting!* I mean—vermin!" Not that I see it that way, but it's nice to know that people who like to feel that way can go to a place and be shocked by it every time.

I remember once taking my then mother-in-law from out of town on a tour of New York City. She was very proper, and I wanted to protect her sensibilities—I was much younger then—so when we were within sight of that dangerous street I turned westward a block early. Imagine her disappointment as I took her down Forty-third Street, by the esteemed grey *New York Times* headquarters. Nothing but loading trucks and offices.

Supposing, though, that I *had* taken her on a tour of the strip—or, to leave my ex-mother-in-law out of it, supposing for purposes of this essay that we not evade the issue, but go into the topless bars and massage parlors, porno movies and bookstalls. I don't pretend to have an encyclopedic knowledge of these dens, but as an occasional imbiber, I will be happy to pass on what I know, in the interests of social science.

Stand outside any pornographic movie theater in a large city on a quiet afternoon, and watch who goes in. You will probably see a smattering of old men, widowers and inactive pensioners; some young blacks and Hispanics, mostly unemployed; a core of neatly dressed manual and clerical workers, black and white (the pornography parlor being one of our few models of racial integration); and a small number of middle-class businessmen.

Why do men go to pornography shows? The most obvious answer is that they are looking for a sexual satisfaction that is missing in their own lives. It is safe to say that the majority of people in this country, single or married, do not have happy sex lives. In lieu of the real thing many will accept images, experiences once removed.

The patrons of pornography may be divided into two types: occasional and regular. The occasional customer may approach pornography as an annual cleansing of the senses. Some unhappily married men use it as a kind of mental adultery; others may even be happily married or involved with someone, but feel the need from time to time to check into the Hotel of Erotic Dreams, to see what they have been missing. (Not always does pornography win out over real life; the man may run home to his wife or lover with a new sense of how lucky he is.) There are also inexperienced young men who look to pornography for education. If it implants false or, as the antipornography groups say, with some justice, "perverted" notions of sexuality, it also conveys demonstrations of a range of lovemaking possibilities—assuming, as marriage manuals have done, a teaching function that the society is too prudish to undertake.

However, the novice, the married man on moral holiday or the bachelor aesthete like me are all marginal. The industry would die on its feet if it had to rely on these occasional clients. What keeps pornography alive are the repeaters. The look they give as they approach the movie ticket-taker and slip five dollars across the booth opening is that of a pinched lab rat who has finally spotted a straight run of several hours within the maze. They are looking for mental space as much as for Eros.

Once inside, they take their seats quietly in the darkened hall (they are the most docile of spectators, and the most solitary) with as much seat and row distance as possible from other spectators. Very rarely do they venture a brotherly word to their neighbor. Each is there to be swept away in the great flood.

Men go to pornography for excitement, but also, I think, to be put in touch with their sadness. They know that before the experience is over, the connection between their own desire and the lusty bodies dangled before them will have been missed. Elegiac is the mood that often settles on a pornography audience. They go in search of something they don't have, that they half remember perhaps having had. The aged hero in Kawabata's novel *The House of Sleeping Beauties* is overtaken by sensual memories and regrets while contemplating the sleeping form of a young woman in a brothel for men too old to do anything else. So the watchers of pornography often seem to be using the spectacle before them as a meditation screen from which to contemplate the missed opportunities of a lifetime. All the bodies in a film are as good as "asleep" in the sense that they cannot be roused to respond to us. Even when the entertainment is live, the convention that the performer herself cannot be made love to means that, for all the provocative come-ons of the artiste, the customer must remain as though in a stupor, interpreting but not interacting. At most, he may touch himself but not the other. This is the essential pathos behind all pornographic spectacle.

Some people have objected to the fact that these pornography parlors are "nothing more than masturbation halls." An *Equal Times* exposé reports that there are "naked women dancing in the peep show 'carousel' or performing 'live lesbian sex' on stage while men jerk off and the janitor comes around time and time again with the Lysol bucket." Is there something wrong with masturbation? Would it have been better not to use the Lysol? The problem cannot be that the customers are wrong to masturbate in public places, since everyone knows that these particular public places are employed for that purpose, and decent citizens need not go in there in the first place. The only thing these men can be faulted for is not having strong enough imaginations to produce erotic images on their own, so that they could jerk off at home and save some money.

No, I will be told, the objection is not that they are masturbating, but that they are masturbating off of women exploited as sexual objects.

Let us first ask who is being exploited. The woman on the film screen is certainly undisturbed by the jets of sperm her beauty has inspired. She contracted to do the film months ago. When the entertainment is live, the performer may indeed feel grossed out by some of her male customers' responses, but it is a job she chose, and if she quits there will be many others to take her place. The job may be horrible, or it may be like any other job, depending on the performer's point of view; in either case, the antiporn forces are not in the business of organizing female workers in the pornography industry to improve their conditions. No, their concern is not so much with the exploitation of the particular woman performing the simulated (or real) sex act, but with collective womanhood, all of whom are claimed to be affected by the reproduction of degraded images of females as sex objects.

There is much to be said for and against this argument. Better polemicists than I have got their feet stuck in these bear traps, and I suspect that I would not be any more successful at disentangling the justice and logic on both sides. Feminists themselves are divided on these issues. On the one hand, the injustice and pain caused by sexual roles in our society merit angry opposition. On the other hand, there is the case for the defense of imagination, however barbaric. There are the rights of communities to set standards of decency, versus rights of minorities to seek private pleasures; the understandable desire of parents to control the intake of the young, balanced against the protection of free speech; the intuitive connection felt by many between pornography and violent crimes against women, and the lack of hard evidence to support this hypothesis. Finally, there is the pragmatic question: Is it practical to wage war against pornography, knowing that it will probably always be with us? What would you propose in its stead?

*   *   *

I confess I myself see nothing terribly wrong with pornography; but then, I have never felt myself to be victimized by it. I would only question, from the discredited (and hitherto largely ignored) standpoint of the pornography customer, whether the stuff is being accurately described in the first place.

For instance, regarding the matter of sex objects, it needs to be pointed out that men no less than women have shallow, thinglike personalities in pornographic presentations. There is precious little characterization of a novelistic sort in pornography. Part of the promise of pornography is that people can engage in pleasure without having to deal with each other's personalities. In such an arena, where there are no *dramatis personae*, only nerve ends receptive to pleasure, one could as easily say about the performers that, rather than being reduced to sexual objects, they have been elevated into embodiments of the physical life, like dancers. Everything personal has been extinguished, except during the minimal "frame" establishing a situation, the scant dues paid to narrative. With pornography at its purest—the loop—even the remotest suggestion of a story is removed and we are left with a continuously repeating reel of sex acts. All pornography follows, like Schnitzler's *Ronde*, a circular form. Its theatrical paraphernalia—the G-strings, the whips, the dildos, the boas—belong to a spectacle inherently repetitious.

Pornography is a sort of utopian kingdom, where the women are always ready and the men are always hard and they go at it for what seems like forever, and when they come they don't need to rest, they start again with someone else; and so they spend their lives screwing and have no worries about money or leaking radiators or family illnesses. Gone are psychological scars, fears of not impressing the other, needs for special treatment. There is no rejection in this utopia, no "He's not my type" or "She's too bland" or "I don't think he's intelligent enough for me." Everyone will do. No sooner met than made. Pornography transcends all of life's hesitations and doubts.

A milkman rings the doorbell and is met by a housewife in a negligee. She offers him a cup of coffee, the milk "accidentally" spills on her, she runs into the kitchen to wash off her slip, he peeks at her naked breasts through the doorway, she sees him staring and gives him a look of indignation that slides irresistibly into melting hunger. The next moment they are in the bedroom (oh, those sudden transitions of lowered resistance—you keep thinking you must have missed something), and the rest is—unmemorable.

Most pornography shows consist of what the trade calls "sucking and fucking." To watch people going at these activities for any length of time is a numbing experience. At first one is titillated, then aroused, maybe even stirred, excited, at the edge of one's seat. Then the effect wears off.

If pornography is a timeless world freed from social responsibilities, it is also a static one. The problem it has always faced as entertainment is how to build interest. The progression may go from a blow job to straight intercourse to lesbian sex to a threesome to an orgy or whatever, but the attempt to create an ascending curve of sexual stimulation will usually not keep up with the descending curve of involvement. The last scenes are generally anticlimactic, in more ways than one. Here the physiology of male arousal and pornographic spectacle may be at odds. The first close-up of genitals and penetration can be rapturous; by the tenth one feels as though one were taking a turkey-basting course.

It may be the nature of all utopias to be boring. But I am convinced that pornography is meant to be boring. Men bring to it their painfully aroused libidos in the hope not only that they will be turned on but that they will be turned off. Not enough has been made of pornography as a depressant and anti-aphrodisiac. The thoughtful, slugged look in the eyes of customers leaving such exhibitions shows that they have indeed rid themselves of some of their annoying sexual energy. For some of these men it is a way of looking the devil of unsatisfied sexual desire in the face and outstaring it, the reward for which is a hard-won indifference.

Not only is the stylized picture of sexuality represented in pornography unreal, but I would argue that those who frequent it *know* it is unreal. Pornography is like science fiction about a planet on which nothing can grow or develop because nothing important is at risk. The orgasm? It would be inappropriate to apply a Maileresque search for bigger and better orgasms to this more standardless, unteleological planet. The orgasms in pornography are not graded, they are simply presented matter-of-factly in rough interchangeable sequence. Since there are no sexual dysfunctions that we are allowed to see, no failures to lubricate or premature ejaculations ("Cut! Take two!"), the sense of vulnerability and uniqueness in sexual communion is lost, which is perhaps why D. H. Lawrence hated pornography. There is nothing at stake. One watches it, like a slow baseball game between two teams already eliminated from the pennant race, for a moment of awkward surprise.

In many ways, the experience of pornography resembles dream life. Both place us before a stream of images in which the normal laws of social reality are suspended. No sooner desire a thing than it begins to occur. Taboos of incest, class, color, age, gender, number, genus and species fall with a fluttering fluidity. All that has been repressed pops out. It is not surprising that hostility and violence also make their appearance; but as in dreams, they are only part of what happens, not the whole. As with dreams, too, the pornography watcher suspends criteria of quality, knowing that there will be a great deal of dross for every moment of magic.

To try to separate the broad stream of pornography into good and bad is a little like attempting to screen out uninteresting from interesting dreams, pleasant from horrible ones. That is why I think the effort to defend pornography by pointing to legitimate specimens of erotic art is misguided. As soon as the style becomes too brilliant it ceases to be pornography; it becomes "literature" or "art cinema." Pornography may be a sort of art-making activity too, but the sublimity that it does momentarily attain is never far from its sludgelike mediocrity. And it is this very medocrity from which it draws its secret energy.

I don't want to leave this subject before reporting one final experience: a visit to a topless-bottomless bar. One night, in a benign mood, rounding out a pleasant evening with my older brother, I had suggested we stop in one of those clip joints on Eighth Avenue and Forty-second Street. It was a sort of long-delayed rite of whoring together, something we had never had the courage to do while growing up; and I knew it would go no farther this night than sitting at a bar being soaked for expensive drinks, which is essentially what happened, and staring at some female flesh. I expected to be disappointed; but it is in the nature of such ventures into the underworld that you want to know, *in what way* will I be disappointed?

It was a small, surly room, much like an off-off-Broadway theater between productions, perhaps because of the unfinished wooden flats used for dance platforms and the uncertain lighting. On one platform stood a young woman, completely naked, scratching her nose. She looked as though she had just stepped out of a bath and was trying to remember where she had put her glasses. From time to time she would remember to sway vaguely to the beat of the disco music, but mostly she just stood there like a figure model waiting to be told it was time to take a break.

She was a mildly pretty brunette with a ski-jump nose and Slavic features, and I imagined her growing up in one of those goulash-and-paprika restaurants in the East Eighties, where everyone spoke Magyar and the middle-aged men with thinning hair got dressed up on Sundays and told jokes to her chubby mother, who worked the espresso machine, and once a year they all went on a boat ride.

On the other platform, a black woman was shaking for all she was worth, definitely earning her salary. She did an odd trick, which was to put her fingers by her crotch and snap them as if igniting a match—a metaphor. She tried winking and talking sexy to the deadbeat customers, but they—we—were like lobotomy cases with blue stigmata of electroshock on our foreheads.

Crossing in front of her, a much more haggard woman with a see-through nightie and battle-scarred face and bony legs approached us at the bar and asked if we would buy her a drink, "for thirty dollars." We could drink it "inside" if we liked and have some fun. We declined and she went on to another customer.

At a table near the door, the manager (or was he the bouncer?), a heavyset man round like a bowling ball in a shiny black suit, was talking to another man about something he had in his eye. He lowered the skin under his eyelid and showed the other man—a boil or a sty. Then, oblivious to the black woman, who was shaking her hips and trying to maintain at least some semblance of erotic illusion, he got up on the same platform, standing with his back to the audience, to use the tall mirror behind her. He worried his eyelid this way and that, trying to see himself in the dim mirror light. "See, it's all red," he called over to his friend. "I told you it was swollen!"

The man with the carbuncle sharing the platform with the topless dancer was that intrusion of the mundane into the lewd that always strikes me as the essence of Forty-second Street. I don't find it dehumanizing, but rather, all too human. It depends on what your definition of human is.

Confessions of a Feminist Porn Watcher

by

SCOTT MACDONALD

For a long time I've been ambivalent about pornography. Off and on since early adolescence I've visited porn shops and theaters, grateful— albeit a little sheepishly—for their existence; and like many men, I would guess, I've often felt protective of pornography, at least in the more standard varieties.[1] (I know nothing at all about the child porn trade which, judging from news articles, is flourishing: I've never seen a child in an arcade film or videotape or in a film in a porn movie house; and though I've heard that many porn films involve women being tortured, I don't remember ever coming in contact with such material, except in Bonnie Klein's *Not a Love Story*, a film polemic/documentary on the nature and impact of porn films.) On the other hand, I've long felt and, in a small way, been supportive of the struggle for equality and self-determination for women; as a result, the consistent concern of feminist women about the exploitation and brutalization of the female in pornography has gnawed at my conscience. The frequent contempt of intelligent people for those who "need" pornographic materials has always functioned to keep me quiet about my real feelings, but a screening of *Not a Love Story* and a series of responses to it have emboldened me to assess my attitudes.

As I watched *Not a Love Story*, the film's fundamental assumption seemed very familiar: pornography is a reflection of a male-dominated culture in which women's bodies are exploited for the purpose of providing pleasure to males by dramatizing sexual fantasies which themselves imply a reconfirmation of male dominance. And while one part of my mind accepted this seemingly self-evident assumption, at a deeper level I felt resistant. The pornographic films and videotapes I've seen at theaters and in arcades *are* full of narratives in which women not only do what

Reprinted from *Film Quarterly* 36(3), Spring 1983: 10–17. Copyright © 1983 by the Regents of the University of California. All rights reserved. Used by permission of the Regents.

men want and allow men to do what they want, but effusively claim to love this particular sexual balance of power. Yet, given that males dominate in the culture, why would they pay to see sexual fantasies of male domination? Wouldn't one expect fantasy material to reveal the opposite of the status quo? Further, if going to porn films or arcades were emblematic of male power, one might expect that the experience would be characterized by an easy confidence reflective of macho security.

For me, however—and, I'm guessing, for many men who have visited porn arcades or film houses—these periodic visits are always minor traumas. While there is an erotic excitement involved in the decision to attend and in the experience itself, this is mixed with considerable amounts of fear and embarrassment. From the instant my car is carrying me toward pornography, I feel painfully visible, as if everyone who sees me knows from my expression, my body language, whatever, precisely where I'm going. The walk from the car to the door—and later, from the door to the car—is especially difficult: will someone drive by and see me? This fear of being seen has, in my case at least (as far as I can tell), less to do with guilt than with a fear of being misunderstood. Even though the frequency of my experiences with pornography has nothing at all to do with the success of my sex life—I'm at least as likely to visit a porn arcade when I'm sexually active as when I'm lonely and horny—I always feel the power of the social stigma against such experiences. Unless the people who see me have been in my situation, I'm sure they'll deduce that my visit to the arcade reflects my inadequacy or some inadequacy in the person I'm living with, that either I "can't get any" or I'm not satisfied with what I can get. As a result, I try to look at ease during the walk to the door: any evident discomfiture on my part, I warn myself, will only fuel whatever laughter my presence has provoked.

Once inside an arcade or a theater, this anxiety about being seen continues, though with a different slant: will I run smack into someone I know? Of course, anyone I would run into would be unlikely to misunderstand the meaning of my presence; but such a meeting would interfere with what seems to me the most fundamental dimension of going to a porn arcade or movie house: the desire for privacy and anonymity. Meeting someone I know would, I assume (this has never happened to me), force us to join together in the phony macho pose of pretending that our interest in the pornographic materials around us is largely a matter of detached humor, that we've come for a few laughs.

The concern for privacy determines the nature of the interaction of the men (I've seen women at porn theaters, but never in porn arcades) involved with porn. Of course, theaters are constructed so as to impede the interactions of members of the audience (I always feel a pressure not to look at people on my way out), but the structure of arcades makes some interaction between strangers almost inevitable. In retrospect, the nature and apparent meaning of this interaction always seems rather poignant. Because of our shared embarrassment about being in this place together and, perhaps, because of our awareness that our presence is a sign of an erotic impatience our casual stances belie—for whatever reason, the men I've seen in porn arcades seem to allow themselves a detached gentleness with each other. For my part—and, judging from my limited observation, I'd guess my experience is pretty standard—I move in an unthreatening way; I am careful not to make eye contact with anyone. When eye contact is unavoidable, I put my mind on erase. When I walk out of a porn arcade, I take with me no functional memory at all of the particular faces I saw there, though each visit has confirmed my feeling that in general the faces are those of quiet middle-class men pretty much like me.

I've always assumed that, essentially, those of us who co-exist with each other for a few minutes in porn theaters or arcades share the embarrassing awareness that we're there for the same thing: to look for awhile at forbidden sexual imagery which excites us and, finally, to masturbate. In my experience, the masturbation itself seems less important as an experience than as a way of releasing the excitement created by the imagery. Even though most men seem to look rigorously frontward in porn theaters and even though porn arcade booths are designed so as to provide enough security for masturbation, the idea of being seen masturbating has always seemed so frightening to me (and, I assume, to others: I've never seen or heard anyone masturbate in an arcade) that I've never felt free to get deeply involved in the act the way I can when I have real privacy. Usually at a porn arcade I keep myself from masturbating for ten or twenty minutes, until I'm ready to leave; the act itself rarely takes more than fifteen or thirty seconds, and as soon as it's over, I'm on my way to my car. I move quickly because, often, despite my confidence that the other men I see have much the same experience I do, I leave terrified that someone will enter the booth I've just left, see the semen on the floor—impossible in the dimly lit booths—and yell after me. I've never masturbated in a theater (though on rare occasions I've seen others do so), but only later, outside the theater, in the privacy of a car or a men's room.

Since the reason for braving the kinesic complexity of the porn environment is exposure to the pornographic materials themselves, it's important to consider what these materials really are. Over the years I've developed what I hope is a generally accurate sense of the motifs that dominate standard porn fare directed at heterosexual men; and I've thought a good deal about why these particular motifs seem so pervasive. I'm speaking of "motifs" here rather than of "films" because the films seem centered (both in terms of the time allocated to specific imagery and in terms of the viewing gaze) on specific configurations, "acts." Even though there's always a skeletal narrative, this is so obviously a function of the need to create a context for the motifs, that one doesn't need to pay particular attention to it—except insofar as it raises the adrenalin by slightly withholding the awaited imagery.[2] The empty nature of the porn narratives is confirmed by the booths, which, in my experience, have all presented Super-8 films in loops, usually two or three films to a loop. Since each quarter, or whatever the fee is, buys only 30 seconds or so of film (then the film stops until another quarter is deposited), one doesn't automatically see a film from start to finish. The motif structure is also reconfirmed by the announcements on booth doors of the particular acts which are featured in particular booths.[3]

For me the obvious amateurishness of the production values, the acting, and the writing has generally added to the titillating mood, since what the characters do to and with each other is all the more outrageous *because* it's so patently done for the camera. In fact, some acts appear so uncomfortable and pleasureless for the actors that the camera's presence seems the only possible explanation. Our consciousness of the films as films is maintained by the camera angles, the length of shots, the lighting, all of which are usually (or at least this is how I remember them) overtly functional, providing a clear view of the sex acts between the actors and between their close-up genitals. In most films "aesthetics" are rigorously avoided in service of clarity.[4]

The motifs themselves have generally involved a relatively limited number of sexual interactions. Sexual intercourse in a variety of poses is nearly inevitable, of course, but it's rarely the clincher in a film. Judging from my limited experience, blow jobs (especially ending in ejaculation into the woman's mouth or on her face) and anal intercourse seem the present-day favorites. Sometimes they involve more than a pair of partners (two men have intercourse—one vaginally, one anally—with one woman; two women provide a blow job to one man; a woman gives a blow job to one man while another has intercourse with her) and/or a mixture of ethnic backgrounds. While the women involved seem to mirror conventional notions of attractiveness, the men are frequently quite average-looking: nearly any man will do, apparently, so long as he has a large erection.

No doubt the psychology of wanting to view sexual performances on a movie screen is complex, but over the years I've been aware of two general functions of the experience: one of these involves its "educational" value, the other its value as psychic release. When I was younger, my interest was in seeing just what the female body looked like and how it moved. Sexuality, as I experienced it as an adolescent, was something that usually occurred in the dark, in enclosed spaces, and under the pressure of time. Often I was more engrossed in the issue of "how far I was going to be able to go" than with really seeing and understanding what I was doing. In those days (the fifties) there were no porn films or arcades, but newsstands were beginning to stock *Playboy*, *Nugget*, and a variety of other girlie magazines; and my hunger to see women's bodies —and to be able to examine them without the embarrassment of being observed by the women—resulted in periodic thefts of magazines. These thefts were serious extralegal transgressions to me; I was terrified of being caught, arrested and made an example of, until I developed the courage to try buying magazines from drugstore owners. These early magazines seemed a godsend to me, and they provided the stimulation for countless hours of masturbation. But they were also carefully censored: the focus was on breasts, though there were frequent side views of demurely posed buttocks; and all vestiges of pubic hair were, for some strange reason, erased from the photographs. (I didn't realize this until I was 17 and had the shock of my life during a heavy petting session.) One can certainly imagine a culture, like that of the Polynesians, in which the bodies of members of the opposite sex would not be visual mysteries, where we could be at ease with seeing each other. But though that has never been the case here, men continue to grow up under considerable pressure to know "how to handle" women sexually: we're supposed to know what's where and how it works. Looking at girlie magazines may seem (and be) a callous manipulation of female bodies, but its function was never callous for me. I was powerfully drawn to women, but my complete ignorance of them frightened me; the magazines were like a nightlight: they allowed me to know a little more than I otherwise would have and they allowed me the fantasy (I always knew it was an illusion) that I'd "know what to do" the next time I got to see and touch a flesh-and-blood woman.

The functioning of pornographic imagery as a means of allowing men to examine the bodies of the opposite sex seems an important aspect of porn films and videotapes, which are full of extreme close-ups of cocks thrusting into cunts. The ludicrous lack of romance in such imagery is often mentioned in condemnations of pornography, but the function seems more scientific than romantic, more like Muybridge's motion studies than a Hollywood love story. And it seems to me that the value of this visual option continues to be defensible, at least in a limited sense, given this society's pervasive marketing of rigidly defined standards of attractiveness. For one thing, direct sexual experience with a conventionally attractive woman is, or seems, out of the question for many men; and yet it's come to be one of the definers of a life worth living. Pornography provides a compromise by making visual knowledge of such an experience a possibility. Secondly, many men feel supportive enough of women to take them seriously when they complain about the invasion of privacy implicit in the unprovoked leers and comments they continue to endure on the street. I'll go to considerable lengths to avoid intruding in this way, but I have to fight the urge to stare all the time. Some of the popularity of pornography even among men who consider themselves feminists may be a function of its capacity to provide a form of unintrusive leering.

I've become conscious of a second aspect of this first function of pornographic materials, the "educational" function, during the past few years. Feminists have made us aware of the politics of staring at women, but the culture at large—particularly the culture as evident in the commercial sphere—tells us constantly that looking at women is what men are supposed to do. Looking at other men continues to be another matter entirely. Of course, spectator sports, and other forms of physical performance, allow for almost unlimited examination of how bodies function, but knowledge of the naked male body continues to be a tricky matter for heterosexual men. In conventional American life men are probably naked together more often than women: in shower rooms, most obviously. And yet, as is true in porn arcades, the kinesics of the interaction between men in such places are very precisely controlled. Men certainly don't feel free to look at other men; our lives are full of stories about how one guy catches another looking at him and punches him out. Never mind that I've never witnessed such an incident: a taboo is at stake, and potential embarrassment, if not danger, seems to hover on the edge of it. This situation is complicated further by the fact that even if men felt free to look carefully at each other in shower rooms, or wherever, a crucial element of the male body—how it functions during sexual activity— would remain a mystery. Of course, I know what my own erection looks like, but so much stress is placed on the nature of erections that it's difficult not to wonder what the erections of other men look like (and how mine looks in comparison).

One of the things that distinguishes the pornographic materials available in porn movies and arcades from what is available on local news-stands—and thus, implicitly, one of the things that accounts for the size of the hardcore porn market—is the pervasive presence of erections. In fact, to a considerable extent theater and arcade porn films are about erections. The standard anti-porn response to this is to see the porn film phallus as a combined battering ram/totem which encapsulates the male drive for power. And given the characterizations of the vain strutting men on the other ends of these frequently awesome shafts, such an interpretation seems almost inevitable. And yet, for me the pervasiveness of erect penises in porn has at least as much to do with simple curiosity. The darkness of porn houses and the privacy of arcade booths allow one to see erections close-up. The presence of women has its own power, but in this particular context one of the primary functions of the female presence is to serve as a sign—to others and to oneself—that looking at erections, even finding them sexy, does not mean that the viewer defines himself as a homosexual.

A second function of the pornographic experience involves the exact converse of a number of cultural attitudes which feminists have often seen as subtly detrimental to women. Most people now recognize that the constant attention to the "beauty" of the female body, which has been so pervasive in the arts and in commerce during recent centuries, may involve more than a respect and love for women—that it may be a tactic for keeping them more involved with how they look (and to a considerable extent, with pleasing men) than with what they do, or can learn to do. Further, the emphasis on a pristine ideal of beauty, as feminists have often pointed out, has frequently alienated women from their own bodies: real odors, secretions, processes have frequently been seen as contradictory to the Beauty of Womanhood. On the other hand, the same cultural history which has defined women as Beautiful has had, and to some extent continues to have, as its inevitable corollary, the Ugliness of men; women have been defined as beautiful precisely in contrast to men. Now, even if these definitions are seen as primarily beneficial to men, in the sense that not having to be concerned with appearances allows them more energy and time for attaining their goals and maintaining their access to power, I sense that the definition also creates significant problems for men, and especially in the areas of love and sex, where physical attractiveness seems of the essence. In recent years we've seen a growing acceptance of the idea that men, too, can be beautiful. The burgeoning homosexual subculture seems evidence of this, as does the popularity of body building. And yet, just as the pressure to see women as "the weaker sex" continues to be felt in a culture where millions of women dramatize the intrinsic bankruptcy of that notion, many men—I'd guess most men—continue to feel insecure about the attractiveness of their bodies.

Perhaps the most obvious aspect of male sexual functioning which has been conditioned by negative assumptions about male attractiveness is ejaculation. Even among people who are comfortable with the idea that men can be beautiful, semen is often (if not usually) seen as disgusting. Is it an accident that many of the substances that our culture considers particularly revolting—raw egg, snot . . .—share with semen a general texture and look? Accidental or not, I've heard and read such comparisons all my life. I remember the shock and fear that followed my first orgasm. Without knowing it, I had been masturbating in the attic of my aunt's house where I had discovered a pile of girlie magazines. The unexpected orgasm was astonishing and thrilling, but at the end of it, I discovered, to my shock, that my shirt and the magazine were covered with a substance I hadn't known existed. I cleaned myself up (even at that early point I was clear that for my relatives—especially for my mother and my aunt—the mysterious substance would be seen as a form of dirtiness), and I spent the remainder of the day walking around with my arms and hands in odd configurations in front of my shirt in the hope of avoiding detection. From that time on, I was alert to the fact that every indulgence of my desire for sex would produce evidence the discovery of which, I was sure, could be humiliating.

Now, I'm well aware that to accept a mucuslike substance that comes out of one's own body is a different matter than accepting such a substance from another's body. I not only understand, but can empathize with the revulsion of many women to semen. Nevertheless, I suspect it creates the same problems for many men as the widespread squeamishness about menstruation has caused women. There are instances of course—in the midst of passion—where semen is temporarily accepted, even enjoyed by women, but these moments tend to be memorable exceptions. For the most part, even between people who love each other, the presence of semen is at best a necessary evil. Recently I mentioned this idea to a woman friend, who has had sex with many men and is proud of it, after she had indicated her contempt for men who were turned off by women's smells and secretions. "I think it depends on who you're with," she said. "If you care about the person, there's nothing disgusting about his semen." A few seconds later she added, "But who has to lie in it?" and laughed. Many women are concerned about the danger of "bleeding through" during menstruation, presumably because they feel, or fear that men feel, that menstrual secretions make them sexually undesirable; and dozens of products have been marketed to protect against such an occurrence. I feel a similar concern about semen, and must face a very special irony: the fact that it surfaces precisely at the moment of my most complete sexual abandon.

To me, the nature and function of pornography have always seemed understandable as a way for men to periodically deal with the cultural context which mitigates against their full acceptance of themselves as sexual beings. The fantasies men pay to experience in porn arcade booths and movie houses may ostensibly appear to be predicated on the brutalization of women. But from a male point of view, the desire is not to see women harmed, but to momentarily identify with men who—despite their personal unattractiveness by conventional cultural definitions, despite the unwieldy size of their erections, and despite their aggressiveness with their semen—are adored by the women they encounter sexually. Only in pornography will the fantasy woman demonstrate aggressive acceptance when a man ejaculates on her face. As embarrassingly abhorrent as it always strikes me, the hostility toward women which usually seems to hover around the edges of conventional film pornography (in the frequently arrogant, presumptive manner the male characters exhibit, for example), and which is a primary subject matter in some films, seems to be a more aggressive way of dealing with the same issues. In these instances the fantasy is in punishing resistant women for their revulsion. Of course, the punishments—usually one form of rape or another—often end with the fantasy woman's discovery of an insatiable hunger for whatever has been done to her. This frequent turnabout appears to be nothing more than a reconfirmation of the stupid, brutal myth that women ask to be raped or enjoy being raped, but—as sadly ironic as this seems—it could also be seen as evidence that, in the final analysis, men don't mean harm to women, or don't wish to mean harm to women: their fantasy is the acceptance of their own biological nature by women.[5] I've always assumed that porn and rape *are* part of the same general problem, though I've always felt it more likely that porn offers an outlet for some of the anger engendered by men's feelings of sensual aesthetic inferiority, than that it serves as a fuel for further anger. But I'm only speaking from my own experience. I've rarely spoken frankly about such matters with men who use porn.

To try to understand the reasons for the huge business of making and marketing pornographic movies is not necessarily to justify the practice. One can only hope for increasingly definitive studies of how porn functions and what its effects are.[6] But, however one describes the complex historical factors which have brought us to our present situation, the fact remains that in our culture men and women frequently feel alienated from their own bodies and from each other. Pornography is a function of this alienation, and I can't imagine it disappearing until we have come to see ourselves and each other differently. We don't choose the bodies we are born with; natural selection, or God—or whatever—takes care of that for us. And though we can't change the fact of our difference (and regardless of whether we choose to accept and enjoy this difference by being passionate about our own or the opposite sex, or both), surely we can learn to be mutually supportive about our bodies. My guess is that porn is a symptom not so much of a sexual need, but of a need for self-acceptance and respect. If we can come to terms with that need, as it relates to both sexes, my guess is that porn will disappear.

Interview with a Rapist

by

TIMOTHY BENEKE

Regularly beaten by his stepmother and stepbrothers from the age of five, at thirteen he ran away from home and began a life of drug addiction and crime. At twenty, after two painful years of marriage, he separated from his wife and daughter, and felt enormous rage toward women for a year. One night while high on alcohol, pot, heroin, and downers, he went into a pornographic bookstore and watched a twenty-five-cent peep show that portrayed a man raping a woman. "It was," he said, "like somebody lit a fuse from my childhood on up. When that fuse got to the porn movie, I exploded. . . . It was like a little voice saying, 'It's all right, it's all right, go ahead and rape and get your revenge; you'll never get caught.'" That night he attempted his first rape. Within ten days, he had attempted three, succeeded in one, and was contemplating a fourth. He spent six and a half years in a state hospital as a mentally disordered sex offender and has been out for a year. He is twenty-eight.

It is worth noting that while "Chuck" may represent a certain type of sex offender, many, perhaps most, rapists have psychological profiles that differ little from the "average man."

My real mom abandoned me when I was a baby. My first stepmom had three boys; from the time I was five they used to hold me and she used to punch me out for hours. I got beat three or four times a week by my stepmom—every time my dad was gone. I got tied up in my room for two days once. My job when I was younger was always to take care of the house. One time I didn't clean up the house, so they drug me stripped naked all through the living room on my back and I got first-degree rug-burns.

I couldn't eat meat fat as a kid and I refused to eat it. There was a time when my stepmom and two of her sons held me at the table and shoved a plate of fat in my face and made me lick the plate clean. I don't know why they were like that; 'cause I was the youngest, I guess. I used to go to school with big welts on my back from getting hit with a belt; I had black eyes, teeth missin'. Teachers used to see it and the law would let it go. My stepmom walked away a lot of times from child abuse cases. The one time I went to court as a kid, my grandmother begged the court to let her adopt me; the court said no because my father said I got my injuries somewhere else. He didn't want to lose me.

I hated my stepmom and my stepbrothers for beating me; I hated my real mom for abandoning me; I hated my dad for never standing up for me; I hated the laws; I hated the police.

I ran away from home when I was thirteen 'cause I couldn't take it no more. I just got tired of coming home and getting the shit kicked out of me. Up until I was thirteen, I was always pushed and shoved around. When I was thirteen, an uncle of mine who's now dead made a statement that if you back an animal into a corner, he's going to come out. At the age of thirteen, I started coming out, and the way I came out was violence. Every time I got into a fight with some dude or a family member, I always came out on top 'cause I learned how to street fight. I'd go for the kill. It would be no just beatin' them up. I always tried to kill all the people I fought. You mess with me, you better kill me 'cause I'm going to do my damnedest to *kill* you, and if you *don't* kill me, you better watch your back 'cause I'll come back and I will kill you. From thirteen to twenty-one that's the way I believed.

My grandma gave me a few thousand dollars when I ran away from home. When that ran out I started workin' mowin' lawns, odds jobs, sleepin' on park benches, jumpin' freights, drivin' tractors or trucks. I learned how to drive a truck at sixteen. I was in and out of jail a lot for all kinds of things: theft, grand theft, drugs, drunk drivin', assault and battery, gang fights, street wars, concealing a deadly weapon, assaulting a police officer. . . .

I was into drugs at thirteen, dealing at sixteen, intertransporting at eighteen. By the time I was eighteen, I had a $200-a-day heroin habit and had to steal a lot to support it. I was strung out for seven years. I tried every branch of the armed forces and got turned down and that hurt. I wanted to go over to Vietnam and kill gooks and see what it felt like.

I got married when I was eighteen and that was okay at first; but then I found out my wife was bedding down with family members. I would get into bed with her; she'd just lay there and I'd get pissed off and go out and get drunk. One night I came home and caught my wife in bed with my cousin. I almost beat that boy to death. If it weren't for a black friend that was with me, I'd have killed him.

I started hating all women. I started seein' all women the same way, as users. I couldn't express my feelings to nobody. I'd go to work, clock in, and be by myself. I didn't trust anyone, not even the people I partied with. I had a bike and I rode with a lot of bikers, but I didn't talk to half of them. I went by different nicknames and nobody ever really knew me. I'd thought about murder and other ways of getting even with women and everyone who'd hurt me. I was just waiting to explode.

Then one night about a year after I split from my wife, I was out partyin' and drinkin' and smokin' pot. I'd shot up some heroin and done some downers and I went to a porno bookstore, put a quarter in a slot, and saw this porn movie. It was just a guy coming up from behind a girl and attacking her and raping her. That's when I started having rape fantasies. When I seen that movie, it was like somebody lit a fuse from my childhood on up. When that fuse got to the porn movie, I exploded. I just went for it, went out and raped. It was like a little voice saying, "It's all right, it's all right, go ahead and rape and get your revenge; you'll never get caught. Go out and rip off some girls. It's all right; they even make movies of it." The movie was just like a big picture stand with words on it saying go out and do it, everybody's doin' it, even the movies.

So I just went out that night and started lookin'. I went up to this woman and grabbed her breast; then I got scared and ran. I went home and had the shakes real bad, and then I started likin' the feeling of getting even with all women.

The second one was at a college. I tried to talk to this girl and she gave me some off-the-wall story. I chased her into a bathroom and grabbed her and told her that if she screamed, I'd kill her. I had sex with her that lasted about five minutes. When I first attacked her I wasn't even turned on; I wanted to dominate her. When I saw her get scared and hurt, then I got turned on. I wanted her to feel like she'd been drug through mud. I wanted her to feel a lot of pain and not enjoy none of it. The more pain she felt, the higher I felt. As I did it to her, my head was back one night where my wife just lay there like a bump on a log and didn't show any pleasure. That's the one thing that was in my head. She was just layin' there doin' nothin'. It wasn't a victim no more; it was my wife.

I pulled out of her when I was about to come and I shot in her face and came all over her. It was like I pulled a gun and blew her brains out. That was my fantasy. She was the blonde that reminded me of my wife. In my head it was like poppin' caps off. I said, "Later," and just walked off and said, "Bye, Jane." That was my wife's name. The orgasm was a great thrill. In my head I blew Jane's brains out and that made it more of a thrill. I not only raped a girl or raped Jane in my head but I killed Jane. I killed her in my head and that was a beautiful high. When I blowed her away that day, she stayed dead for five years in my head.

It was the most beautiful high I'd ever experienced, better than any heroin I'd ever done. I was just floatin'. It didn't even feel like I was walkin' on the ground when I was walkin' home. I felt like a parachute was on my back and I was just hangin', floatin' in midair. I felt like I'd gotten even with different girls who'd fucked me over. I stayed floatin' until the next morning, and that's when I came down and I was sick, and then I wanted to get caught. I didn't know if she'd turned me in or not. I didn't know if they'd believe me if I said I'd done it. I got dressed and put the same clothes on and went lookin' for my next victim.

With my third victim, I ripped her clothes off and a man saw me and I just happened to turn around and saw him and I ran home. A week later when I was out lookin' for number four, I got busted. I'd had a lot of thoughts of committing suicide. When the cops busted me I had a gun on me and I was going to use the gun and shoot it out so they'd blow me away. I didn't care. I didn't have the heart to pull the trigger and kill myself. But I was killing myself and everything I remembered when I'd go out and rape. . . .

When I got caught a policeman called to me and I said, "Yes, I raped them three girls." When I was rapin' I was asking for help each time I raped—help or to be killed. I didn't trust anybody. In each of my attacks I wore the same clothes and I committed them a block away from each other. During the trial, the judge kept sayin', "We can send you to the hospital or we can send you to prison." I said, "Send me to prison, I don't care."

My sisters asked me why I raped and I told 'em I wanted to hurt you females in my family, just like I'd been hurt. They knew my real mom abandoned me and that my first stepmom beat the hell out of me all the time. And then I got married and she was bedding down all my family members. They understood, but they didn't want to believe it. They said you're just not that way. It took me three years to convince them that I *am* that way. The three girls I attacked represented to me my real mom, my stepmom, and my wife. They all had special features that reminded me of them.

In the hospital I was a loner at first. I kind of enjoyed feeling safe. I was in the best group therapy the hospital had to offer —what they call dry therapy. They sit around and hot-seat you, and for four years they couldn't get me to talk; they couldn't get me to open up. I'd go to staffing and they used to tell me, "If you don't start talking, we're going to ship your ass to prison." And I'd say, "Is that all you've got to say?" They'd say, "Yeah," and I'd say, "Start my paperwork, send me on my way."

We lived in dorms and after two and a half years, this guy sort of picked me out. We started talkin'. We started relatin' a lot. He showed me that everybody wasn't out to hurt me or use my feelings against me. He's the first dude I ever cried in front of. He told me, "Everybody's not out to hurt you, man. You're going to keep on the way you are, and you're just going to go nuts, and they're going to just blow your shit up."

I'd been there about four years the day he got out. He turned to me that day and he started cryin' and I was cryin', and he goes, "You can't let it beat you, man; you can't fight for the rest of your life, you'll always lose."

I sat around for about two months after that tryin' to understand what he was meanin' in what he said. It come to me: Why should I be a loser for the rest of my life? So I just started openin' up to people. I went to group one day and I said, "You know what? I've got to talk." I opened up for four hours' worth of group that day. Everybody liked what I was puttin' out and saw that I was sincere in what I had to say.

A bunch of us were doin' drugs in the hospital and I told the people I was doin' drugs with, "I'm not going to spend the rest of my life in here. I want to go home." And I quit drugs. My friend wrote me a lot, tryin' to talk me into gettin' out and comin' to live in another state. I started makin' friends in group and started workin', started accepting other people's feelings, lettin' them know they could trust me. I call that place a hell-hole, and in some ways it is, but the help's there for people who want it.

When I went home I got harassed by the cops. They remembered me and ran drug tests and looked for track marks. They said, "We heard you was dead." I said, "No, I've just been away." I told them I was locked up for six and a half years and I'm not the same. They looked at me and said, "You don't seem the same anymore." I just grew up. That's all I did, I grew up.

If anything was to cause me to go back, it would be somebody messin' with my daughter. If anybody touches her I will definitely hurt 'em. That kid is my number one. She's my pride. I seen my daughter at Christmas for the first time in almost seven years. I'm supposed to get her this summer. She's got pictures of me all over her bedroom wall. She knows I'm her father. She sees me and she knows who I am.

When I was home I ran into a lot of people that I did drugs with who are still there. I told 'em, "If I ever find out that you turned my daughter on to drugs in any way, I'm going to come back. You *know* I can find you." I told the cops, "If they ever turn my kid on to drugs, you better be ready for a war because that's how it is." I was strung out for seven years and I hate drugs. Drugs, rape, and child abuse are the things I hate most in life, because I've been through 'em. And I hate the law now because since I've been out I want to get into counseling, and they all say, "No, you don't have a license." I said, "I've got the best license in the world—I've been there," and they tell me you've gotta have a Ph.D. or umpteen years in college. . . . I'd like to work with kids. I'd like to keep kids from goin' through what I went through.

I've been out almost a year. At the hospital they had odds against me stayin' out this long. Just before I left they said, "We believe you won't rape, but we're puttin' odds that you'll go kill somebody." They don't think I'll rape again, but they think I'll pull a different crime.

Rape is sick. It hurts because that's what I was. I'm a rapist and I can say it. And I think that's what's going to help me stay out. I can look myself in the mirror and say, "You know what, you're a rapist." Or I can look in the mirror and say, "You ain't foolin' a motherfuckin' soul, man." I've looked in the mirror and talked to myself for hours since I been out. I say, "You ain't foolin' me. I know what's on your mind. I know what you are. I know what games you're playin', what you're not takin' care of." People come in and catch me and say, "You're sick"; but that's what's gonna keep me out. That's what's kept some of my other friends out.

My pants have got a chain and lock design on 'em. A friend asked me what that's for. I said, "It helps me remember. As long as I can remember, I ain't ever going back. When I can't remember, I'm going back." I've got my little family album with my release papers and my court transcript. I read through it once a week or so to help me remember and see what kind of a sick dog I was. It helps me want to fight. I've got my own ways. Even when I slip back, I've got ways of helpin' myself.

When I get pissed off or upset, I grab my handball and just work it out. I get to where I concentrate real hard on a picture of somebody I'm pissed at, and I just keep hitting it at that picture of the guy's face or girl's face—I keep hitting it 'til I can't move no more, 'til I'm physically and mentally drained. There's no one sending me back, not the state, not my old lady, not my family. They're not making me do another five, six, or seven years. I tell 'em, I say, "Hey, you ain't worth it, and I'll be goddamned if I'm going to spend another seven or eight years playin' your game. You can get out of my life."

If I'm hurtin' really bad inside I go talk to a friend because I know if I keep bottling it up, trippin' on it, fantasizing on it, I'm going to slip back into my old ways; I'm going to go out and hurt somebody. That scares the hell out of me. I call up my friends and say, "I gotta talk. This is what's goin' on—I'm going back to that old way of life. Talk to me, help me see my stop signs," and we just rap. Afterward, I feel better. I do different things, walk around and say "hi" to people, I even wave at cops. I just feel better after I talk to people. It's like everything's taken off my shoulders. That's all anybody ever really needs. I believe that. I could take you to the hospital and handpick as many people as you want who'll say the same thing as me. There are guys in there who really go nuts every time somebody commits a rape; they get fightin' mad. I seen 'em come close to jumpin' about half a dozen guys that come in that place for rape.

If there had been no pornographic movies showing rape, would you have raped?

I think I would've hurt a woman in a different way physically. If I wouldn't have committed rape, I'd be in prison for murder right now, because it was goin' that way. I would've killed my next victim or the one after that. I would've killed somebody. I would've killed my stepmother, my mother, and my wife if I'd had the chance.

Pornographic movies have a lot to do with rape. I believe they shouldn't make movies of *any* kind of rape. They just shouldn't show it. Specials are okay because they can tell what can happen in rape, but a TV movie, a porn movie, or a regular movie about rape—they should ban them. You look at these movies and think, "Wow, I wonder what it would be like to go out and rape somebody!" I heard stories in the hospital of people saying society must condone it—they have it on TV and movies. I know five or six guys who saw pictures of rape in a dirty book and believed it was all right to go out and rape; just still snapshots and that justified it to them. It said, okay, go out and rape because it's in a dirty book; there's nothin' wrong with it. That goes for child molesting, too.

What could your victims have done to keep from being raped?

If they'd said, "Okay, go ahead, do anything you want," I don't believe I would've raped. If a girl had said, "Take me, I'm yours," I know I would've turned and walked away. It just wouldn't have been there for me. I didn't want somebody to be passive for me. I wanted somebody to show me the fear and the hurt that I always had to show. It was a turn-on to see 'em scared and me being in control for once.

Rapists want to be in control. Somewhere in their life a woman destroyed their ego. Rape is a way a man rebuilds his ego, rebuilds his manhood. Shit like that.

I don't like what I did to those girls. If I seen a girl getting raped now I'd bust my ass tryin' to catch somebody's butt. I *know* that's the worst thing you can do to a female. I would probably hurt the man severely that raped a girl. I know I destroyed three lives in one way or another and it makes me *sick*. I have nightmares about it and I get freaked out because I get to tripping on it so hard. I know I can't go to my victims and say, "Hey, you know what? I wish I could turn back the hands of time, and know what I know now." That's a fantasy for me. That's bullshit. I wanta work against rape. I've seen the horror of it. I put my victims through hell and I know that women that's been raped get nothing but bullshit reasons and answers when they protest, and they don't need to hear that, 'cause it's not going to make 'em feel better.

When I was inside I worried about my sisters getting raped. I know what I'd want done to the man once he was inside. I got friends in all the prisons in this state, not just the hospital, and I know that wherever he went I could get that guy killed. I would have no remorse in doing it. I remember what my victims went through. I put my victims through a lot of hell. I know one that got a divorce. I feel bad about that. I know if her husband had gotten a hold of me, he would've killed me. I can understand that.

I got friends now that piss me off real bad. We'll be out partyin', and they'll see a girl on the street and say, "I'd like to rape her." I've gotten out of the car and told 'em, "You're a sick motherfucker! That's the worst thing you can do to a girl or a woman!" They don't know I've been in or what I've been in for. It totally freaks 'em out. I've lost a few friends that way.

Do you have more positive feelings toward women these days?

I admire the women nowadays. I think they've got just as much to offer as men do. I think the way they're going through life is really great. I believe in equal rights and all that stuff.

If I see a woman upset I'll go and ask her what's wrong, or if I see she needs help I'll be the first one to ask her. I don't like people hurt. I guess after six years in the hospital I got all my hurt out.

I get scared sometimes around women. I see a nice-lookin' lady and I get to thinkin', man, I'd like to get her in the sack; man, I get scared and I get the hell away from her. When I'm walkin' out on the street at night and a girl passes me, I get scared. I'm afraid that after she passes me someone else will grab her, and she won't see his face but she'll remember mine. I have nightmares of raping again. I'm scared of doin' it again. The girls I rape in my nightmares are always the same ones that I did rape, so it's sort of a torment.

My stepmom now, my second stepmom, she's the best lady I ever met. To me she's my real mom. She gave me birth, in my eyes and in my heart and everything. I just love her to pieces. I'd hurt somebody if they ever hurt her. That's the way I am about her. She gave me something to look forward to. It made me see that women's not just bitches. Some out there are really beautiful and can give you love and respect if you have the right thing in mind. That's all she gave me, that's all I ever asked for. I just never got it when I was younger.

I had a girl friend for a few months and we just broke up two months ago. We used to talk about my rapes and my drug involvement and everything. She says, "It's hard to believe, you just don't seem that way." I got out my records and said, "Well, how good can you read?" She said, "What are you?" I said, "Well, I'm very violent, I'm an ex-junkie, I'm a rapist, and I've got human qualities, too. Those are just my bad qualities. I'm easy to hurt. I love people, I care about everybody. I don't like to see nobody hurt; I cry when I want to cry; when I want to be alone I'm alone. Mostly, I just love people."

She really hurt me. She just said, "I gotta be free. I gotta do what I gotta do," and that hurt 'cause I wanted to marry her. We're still friends. If she needs me I'm there in a flash. The hurt she did to me isn't the same as when the other women hurt me.

Are you able now to forgive people for what they do to you?

I've forgiven a lot of my family for what they did to me. I don't like it but I've forgiven them. Everybody has problems. The way I forgive is to say, "Hey, you've got problems, and I don't like what you did to me, but it's your problem and some day you'll deal with it, but I do forgive you." That's how I learned to forgive my dad for not bein' there when I needed him, how I learned to forgive my cousin who I caught in bed with my wife. I don't like what happened but I forgive him, and I forgive what my girl friend did to me. You'll always remember it and you'll have those feelings of being hurt, but you don't want to do anything about it.

Now there's people I won't forgive for the rest of my life, like my first stepmom and my real mom. It's gonna stay there. I can't forgive my mom for abandoning me when I was just a baby. I don't want nothin' to do with her. She was down here and I refused to see her. I don't ever want to see her.

I ran into my first stepmom one time when I was nineteen and I was walkin' through an alley and she ran up and grabbed me and hugged me. I said, "If you *ever* come around me, if you *ever* touch me, I'll kill you. I'll strangle you with my bare hands!" And I spit on her. If I found out she died today, I'd go down there just to spit on her, and hope one of her sons tried something.

It's like a scar that'll never heal. I pick at it when I see her. I don't want their friendship, their concern, nothin'. Yet, if I see 'em and when I see 'em, I want to always remember what they done to me, so I'll never do it to my kids. I've never hit my kid. As long as I remember what that lady and them boys did to me, there's no way. It's like the decal on my pants. It's a remembrance. The scar's a remembrance. My keepin' my own records is a remembrance. There are scars that I don't want to forget. As long as I don't, I'll be all right.

...Those Little Black Dots

by

TOM CAYLER

I come home from work and I am tired. I wanna take a shower, see the kids, get something to eat and lie down, watch a little TV. Maybe if there's not a ballgame on, I'll read a book, okay? So, there I am, I'm reading this adventure novel and I get to the portion of the book where the hero has got this gorgeous dame writhing above him, biting her lips with pleasure. I mean, how do you even do that? That doesn't feel so good to me.

But I am getting turned on by this. I am getting turned on by this imaginary, illicit, sexual liaison. And I say to myself, "Hey, there's the wife. She is lying right next to you. She is gorgeous, available, warm, loving, naked." But, am I turned on by her? No, I am turned on by these little black dots marching across the page.

Because, see, if I wanted to have sex with her, I would have to put down my book, I would have to roll over, I would have to ask her to put down her book, I would have to say . . . "How ya doin'? Are the kids in bed, is the cat out, is the phone machine on, are the doors locked, maybe we should brush our teeth, is the birth-control device handy." Then I would have to turn on the sensitivity. I would have to ask her what's been goin' on with her, what she's been dealin' with, I mean with the kids, and the house, and the budget, and her mom, and everything like that. I'd have to tell her what was happenin' with me. My problems, my worries. I'd have to hold her, I'd have to stroke her, I would have to tell her how important she is to me, I would have to commit myself to an act which these days I may or may not be able to consummate. You think that is easy? The little black dots, they are easy.

The Politicization
of Pornography:
Responding to
the Feminist Debate

The Roots of Pornography

by

DAVID STEINBERG

It is striking that in the midst of so much vehement debate on the subject of pornography, there is so little discussion of, or attempt to understand, the nature of the pornographic phenomenon itself. The *Hite Report on Male Sexuality* notes that eighty-nine percent of its respondents report some involvement with pornography. Something basic is going on here.

What is it that makes pornography so popular among American men and, increasingly, among American women? Why does it sell? What does pornography accomplish, or seem to accomplish, for the tens of millions of people who are its market?

For myself, and for virtually all the men I have talked to, pornography is essentially a tool for masturbation, a fantasy enhancer. This is important to remember. Pornography is not about partner sex, not about sexual reality, not about our real lovers and mates, not about our real selves. Though women I have talked to consistently fear that their male lovers expect them to look and act like *Playboy* models or porn stars, I believe that the vast majority of men who use pornography are clear about the difference between images and real people, between archetypes and human beings, between the jet-setters and the rest of us.

To be effective, then, pornography must be good masturbation material. It must address our longings, our unfulfilled desires, the sexual feelings that have power in fantasy precisely because they are unsatisfied in our real lives. So what are some of these unresolved sexual issues addressed by men through pornography?

From my point of view, the most important single issue that welds men so forcefully to pornography is that of sexual scarcity. Although attitudes are changing, most heterosexual men still experience sex from the perspective of scarcity. Men seem to want sex more than women. Men try to get women to have sex with them. Or, more subtly: Men seem to respect sexual desire more than women do. Men feel resistance to sexual desire from women, expressed as fear, reluctance, disinterest, even revulsion.

Women, sadly, have been handed (and have generally accepted) the cultural role of being the final defenders of puritan antisex. Sexual desire is evil, they are told, or at least low. Men desire. Women—higher, more spiritual beings than men—are to distrust and defend themselves against male desire and will be severely punished if they do not. Women are not to enjoy being the focus for male desire and certainly ought not desire sex for its own sake.

Women are taught to experience sexual desire only in the context of emotional commitment or expression of affection, not as simple bodily hunger. Lust is, by definition, unwomanly. To be a lustful woman— especially a lustful young woman—still carries slutty connotations that few women want to engage.

Let me be clear that I am in no way blaming women for this situation. Nor am I trying to invalidate the many reasons women are protective of themselves sexually—ranging from fear of pregnancy, to fear of rape, to fear of mother, to fear of losing the respect of other women or of men. I am simply noting that we live in a sex economy that produces an ongoing pool of surplus male desire, a culture that fears even the best of male desire, a world that gives men precious little opportunity to be desired, feel desirable, feel attractive and appreciated for our sexual natures.

A closely related issue, one that is perhaps even more significant emotionally, is that of rejection. Even in progressive, "liberated," "enlightened" circles, and certainly in the dominant culture, men still carry the burden for being the sexual initiators, the desirers, and thus, inevitably, the rejected ones. A difficult, dangerous, and painful job but, as they say, somebody has to do it.

I believe that we are only beginning to appreciate the significance of the emotional work men must do to be able to repeatedly express sexual interest and initiative to those who are being taught to reject us. Warren Farrell, author of Why Men Are the Way They Are, suggests that men's attempts to deal psychologically with rejection have a lot to do with our need to objectify women—that it is less painful to be rejected by an object than by a thinking, feeling human being. I think he's right.

In any case, fear of rejection, and the resulting negative feelings about ourselves as sexual beings and about our sexual desirability, are difficult aspects of sexual manhood all men grapple with, usually with only partial success. The residue is part of the emotional material we take to pornography.

I believe that these issues—sexual scarcity, desire for appreciation and reciprocation of desire, and fear of being sexually undesirable—are the central forces that draw men to pornography. While violent imagery, by various estimates, accounts for only three to eight percent of all pornography, images that address scarcity, female lust, and female expression of male desirability account for at least seventy-five percent of porn imagery.

Pornography is a vehicle men use to help us fantasize sexual situations that soothe these wounds. The central themes are available, lusty sex, focused on *our* desirability, involving archetypal images of the very women who must represent our felt undesirability in real life. When we buy pornographic magazines, take them to the safety and privacy of our bedrooms, and masturbate to their images (or when we masturbate to the images of these same women on screen), we vent the frustrations born of scarcity, the sexual fears born of rejection, and the sexual insecurity born of being so seldom appreciated by women for our specifically sexual existence.

And which images most effectively accomplish this for us? Images of women who are openly desirous of sex, who look out at us from the page with all the yearning we know so well yet so rarely receive from our partners. Images of women hungry for sex *with us*, possessed by desire *for us*. Women hungry to get their hands on our bodies or get our hands on theirs. Receptive women who greet our sexual desire not with fear and loathing but with appreciation, even gratitude. And glamorous women whose mere bestowal of sexual attention mythically proves our sexual worth.

Is it any wonder that such a sexual world is attractive to so many men? The problem, however, is that although the pornographic fantasies may be soothing in the moment, they often contribute to bad feelings about ourselves over time. This depends on the specific images, what we do with them, and how we feel about ourselves to begin with. But in general, the more the imagery of pornography confirms who we are as sexual people, the better we will probably feel about our sexual energies afterward. Conversely, the more we are told that to be sexually desirable we need to be other than who we really are, the worse we will feel.

From this point of view, much of pornography is likely to affect us negatively (although, again, not all—and we do get to pick and choose among the offerings). Michael Castleman, in his book *Sexual Solutions*, notes how seldom pornography includes "any kissing, handholding, caressing, massages, reciprocal undressing, tenderness or discussion of lovemaking preferences." It is sad that pornography speaks so little about softness, vulnerability, uncertainty, intimacy—all of which we know to be important parts of our sexual reality.

But the likelihood that pornography may alienate us from our sexual selves, or the fact that it fails to offer more than temporary relief from our sexual wounds, should not blind us to the very real and valid feelings that attract us to the medium in the first place.

Besides, not all of our attraction to pornography is rooted in pain and fear, and not all of pornography's effects are negative. Pornography is still the medium that most vociferously advocates free and diverse sexual expressiveness, a radical stance in our culture, which is still essentially puritanical and sex-negative. Pornography still serves as an arena for adolescents to get validation and approval for their emerging sexual feelings, whose power far exceeds what society is willing to endorse as proper. Pornography is still an ally for those of us who choose to fight for the full recognition and admiration of our sexual natures in the face of the growing forces of sexual repression.

Pornography is the one arena that is not afraid of the penis, even when erect, that does not find sperm disgusting, that shows pictures of men ejaculating in slow motion, even as other films emphasize the beauty of birds flying or dolphins leaping. And it is in the world of pornography where much of traditional male hatred and fear of vaginas has been redirected toward vaginal appreciation, through what writer Michael Hill calls "graphic and realistic depictions of the cunt as beautiful, tasty, wonderful to smell and touch."

In addition, pornography, for all its *misinformation*, is still an important source of real and useful sexual information as well. The "G" spot and the normalcy of female ejaculation have been introduced to mass culture not by sex therapists but by the porn network. Dozens of magazines, and now a feature-length film, have taught men these important aspects of *female* pleasure. Mass acceptance of oral and anal sex as normal sexual practices has been accelerated by the repeated, indeed casual, depiction of these acts in hundreds of porn films.

Porn films in general offer real learn-by-watching information (the information we should all receive as emerging adults, but don't) on all kinds of sexual practices—as long as we bring a critical eye to tell the fake from the real (there's plenty of both), and the friendly from the nasty (also both well-represented). And if we want to encourage our sexual imagination, going to see a variety of sex loops will give us plenty of food for thought, and plenty of support for what we may feel to be our unique infatuations.

Finally, I think it is important to acknowledge that pornography provides a victimless outlet for the basic sexual rage that seems to sit within so many men, whether we like it or not. This is the rage that sadly gets vented at specific women through rape and other forms of sexual assault. It will not go away from the social psyche, pornography or no pornography.

For all the terrible pain this rage has brought to women, we must understand that at the core of this feeling there is a righteous anger: the anger at having our naturally exuberant, lively, pleasurable sexual feelings twisted, stunted, denied, and used against us. This anger needs to be acknowledged, respected, and redirected away from women, toward its appropriate targets: antisexual religious teachings, sex-phobics in general, the complex of societal institutions intent on denying us all the natural exploration of one of life's greatest miracles.

Respecting the roots of male sexual anger may be as uncomfortable for us as respecting the roots of our attraction to pornography. But both are important to own and affirm. If we can respect the core of what attracts us to pornography, we can begin to find ways to have that core more effectively addressed by the sexual materials we use. On the other hand, if we think that every time we're drawn to pornography we only express the worst of ourselves as men, we will both hate ourselves and become trapped in repeating and self-defeating cycles of guilt and rebellion.

What is needed, in my opinion, is not an attempt to drive pornography underground, socially or psychically. If pornography becomes outlawed (again), it, like prostitution, will only come to represent the notion that sex is dirty, even more strongly than it does today. What is needed instead is the development of sexual materials that take the *best* of the pornographic tradition—sexual openness, exploration, and celebration—and add to these egalitarian values, imagination, artfulness, respect for ourselves, and respect for the power and beauty of sex itself.

We need sexual materials that more fully address our real sexual needs and feelings, materials that help us feel better about ourselves, materials that enable us to resist the antisexual insanity that assaults us every day. We need material with which we can identify without contradicting our best sexual intuitions—photographs and stories whose beauty affirms our own sexual power and worth.

Happily, we can now point to the beginning of such materials. In the past few years, a group of us have developed an erotic theater show, *Celebration of Eros*, a dramatic presentation of poetry and prose with four slide shows set to music, to celebrate the best of our erotic natures. I have also recently edited an extensive hardcover collection of high-quality erotic photography, writing, and drawing, *Erotic by Nature* (Shakti Press/Red Alder Books). Excellent collections of erotic writing by women have recently been edited by Susie Bright (*Herotica*, Down There Press), Laura Chester (*Deep Down*, Faber & Faber), and Lonnie Barbach (*Pleasures: Erotic Interludes*, Doubleday). *Yellow Silk*, a journal of erotic arts whose motto is "all persuasions, no brutality," is in its seventh year of publication. *On Our Backs*, a San Francisco magazine of "entertainment for the adventurous lesbian," is to my knowledge the first explicitly feminist sex magazine anywhere.

We need more. We need what Paula Webster calls "a truly radical feminist pornography-erotica." Recent thinking and writing among the sex radicals of the feminist movement are an encouraging start toward understanding what such a feminist pornography might look like. Hopefully, before too long, when we and our sons and daughters go out to buy some sexual stimulation, we'll all be able to feel good about what we bring home.

Pornography and Freedom

by

JOHN STOLTENBERG

There is a widespread belief that sexual freedom is an idea whose time has come. Many people believe that in the last few decades we have gotten more and more of it—that sexual freedom is something we can carve out against the forces of sexual repressiveness, and that significant gains have been won, gains we dare not give up lest we backslide into the sexual dark ages, when there wasn't sexual freedom, there was only repression.

Indeed, many things seem to have changed. But if you look closely at what is supposed to be sexual freedom, you can become very confused. Let's say, for instance, you understand that a basic principle of sexual freedom is that people should be free to be sexual and that one way to guarantee that freedom is to make sure that sex be free from imposed restraint. That's not a bad idea, but if you happen to look at a magazine photograph in which a woman is bound and gagged and lashed down on a plank with her genital area open to the camera, you might well wonder: Where is the freedom from restraint? Where's the sexual freedom?

Let's say you understand that people should be free to be sexual and that one way to guarantee that freedom is to make sure people can feel good about themselves and each other sexually. That's not a bad idea. But if you happen to read random passages from books such as the following, you could be quite perplexed:

> "Baby, you're gonna get fucked tonight like you ain't never been fucked before," he hissed evilly down at her as she struggled fruit-lessly against her bonds. The man wanted only to abuse and ravish

Adapted from a speech delivered at the Ninth National Conference on Men and Masculinity in Washington, D.C., July 1, 1984. First published in *Changing Men* 15 (Spring 1985). Copyright © 1985, 1989 by John Stoltenberg.

her till she was totally broken and subservient to him. He knelt between her wide-spread legs and gloated over the cringing little pussy he was about to ram his cock into.[1]

And here's another:

"Bitch," he snapped, pulling away from her, yanking his dick out of her mouth. "You're trying to make me come before I'm ready. You know I like to fuck your ass before I come! You inconsiderate bitch!" he spat, knowing how she ate up that kind of talk.[2]

Passages such as these might well make you wonder: Where are the good feelings about each other's body? Where's the sexual freedom?

Let's say you understand that people should be free to be sexual and that one way to guarantee that freedom is to make sure people are free from sexualized hate and degradation. But let's say you come upon a passage such as this:

Reaching into his pocket for the knife again, Ike stepped just inches away from Burl's outstretched body. He slid the knife under Burl's cock and balls, letting the sharp edge of the blade lightly scrape the underside of Burl's nutsac. As if to reassert his power over Burl, Ike grabbed one of the bound man's tautly stretched pecs, clamping down hard over Burl's tit and muscle, latching on as tight as he could. He pushed on the knife, pressing the blade into Burl's skin as hard as possible without cutting him. "Now, you just let us inside that tight black asshole of yours, boy, or else we're gonna cut this off and feed it to the cattle!"[3]

After reading that, you might well ask: Where's the freedom from hatred? Where's the freedom from degradation? Where's the sexual freedom?

Let's say you understand people should be free to be sexual and that one way to guarantee that freedom is to make sure people are not punished for the individuality of their sexuality. And then you find a magazine showing page after page of bodies with their genitals garroted in baling wire and leather thongs, with their genitals tied up and tortured, with heavy weights suspended from rings that pierce their genitals, and the surrounding text makes clear that this mutilation and punishment are experienced as sex acts. And you might wonder in your mind: Why must this person suffer punishment in order to experience sexual feelings? Why must this person be humiliated and disciplined and whipped and beaten until he bleeds in order to have access to his homoerotic passion? Why have the Grand Inquisitor's most repressive and sadistic torture techniques become what people do to each other and call sex? Where's the sexual freedom?

If you look back at the books and magazines and movies that have been produced in this country in the name of sexual freedom over the past decade, you've got to wonder: *Why has sexual freedom come to look so much like sexual repression? Why has sexual freedom come to look so much like unfreedom?* The answer, I believe, has to do with the relationship between freedom and justice, and specifically the relationship between *sexual* freedom and *sexual* justice. When we think of freedom in any other sense, we think of freedom as *the result* of justice. We know that there can't truly *be* any freedom until justice has happened, until justice exists. For any people in history who have struggled for freedom, those people have understood that their freedom exists on the future side of justice. The notion of freedom *prior to* justice is understood to be meaningless. Whenever people do not have freedom, they have understood freedom to be that which is arrived at by achieving justice. If you told them they should try to have their freedom without there being justice, they would laugh in your face. Freedom *always* exists on the far side of justice. That's perfectly understood—except when it comes to sex.

The popular concept of sexual freedom in this country has never meant sexual justice. Sexual-freedom advocates have cast the issue only in terms of having sex that is free from suppression and restraint. Practically speaking, that has meant advocacy of sex that is free from institutional interference; sex that is free from being constrained by legal, religious, and medical ideologies; sex that is free from any outside intervention. Sexual freedom on a more personal level has meant sex that is free from fear, guilt, and shame—which in practical terms has meant advocacy of sex that is free from value judgments, sex that is free from responsibility, sex that is free from consequences, sex that is free from ethical distinctions, sex that is essentially free from any obligation to take into account in one's consciousness that the other person is a *person.* In order to free sex from fear, guilt, and shame, it was thought that institutional restrictions on sex needed to be overthrown, but in fact what needed to be overthrown was any vestige of an interpersonal ethic in which people would be real to one another; for once people are real to one another, the consequences of one's acts matter deeply and personally; and particularly in the case of sex, one risks perceiving the consequences of one's acts in ways that feel *bad* because they do not feel *right.* This entire moral-feeling level of sexuality, therefore, needed to be undone. And it was undone, in the guise of an assault on institutional suppression.

Sexual freedom has never really meant that individuals should have sexual self-determination, that individuals should be free to experience the integrity of their own bodies and be free to act out of that integrity in a way that is totally within their own right to choose. Sexual freedom has never really meant that people should have absolute sovereignty over their own erotic being. And the reason for this is simple: Sexual freedom has never really been about *sexual justice between men and women.* It has been about maintaining men's superior status, men's power over women; and it has been about sexualizing women's inferior status, men's subordination of women. Essentially, sexual freedom has been about preserving a sexuality that preserves male supremacy.

What makes male supremacy so insidious, so pervasive, such a seemingly permanent component of all our precious lives, is the fact that erection can be conditioned to it. And orgasm can be habituated to it. There's a cartoon; it's from *Penthouse:* A man and woman are in bed. He's on top, fucking her. The caption reads: "I can't come unless you pretend to be unconscious." The joke could as well have taken any number of variations: "I can't get hard unless—I can't fuck unless—I can't get turned on unless—I can't feel anything sexual unless—" Then fill in the blanks: "Unless I am possessing you. Unless I am superior to you. Unless I am in control of you. Unless I am humiliating you. Unless I am hurting you. Unless I have broken your will."

Once sexuality is stuck in male supremacy, all the forms of unjust power at its heart become almost physically addictive. All the stuff of our primitive fight-or-flight reflexes—a pounding heart, a hard sweat, heaving lungs—these are all things the body does when it is in terror, when it is lashing out in rage, and these are all things it is perfectly capable of doing during sex acts that are terrifying and sex acts that are vengeful. Domination and subordination—the very essence of injustice and unfreedom—have become culturally eroticized, and we are supposed to believe that giving eroticized domination and subordination free expression is the fullest flowering of sexual freedom.

Prepubescent boys get erections in all kinds of apparently nonsexual situations—being terrified, being in physical danger, being punished, moving perilously fast, simply being called on to recite in class. A boy's body's dilemma, as he grows older, as he learns more about the cultural power signified by the penis and how it is supposed to function in male-supremacist sex, is how to produce erections reliably in explicitly heterosexual contexts. His body gets a great deal of help. All around him is a culture in which rage and dread and hazard and aggression are made aphrodisiacs. And women's bodies are made the butt of whatever works to get it up.

The sexuality of male supremacy is viscerally committed to domination and subordination, because those are the terms on which it learned to feel, to feel anything sexual at all. Its heart pounds and its blood rushes and its autonomic nervous system surges at the thought and/or the action of forced sex, bullying sex, violent sex, injurious sex, humiliating sex, hostile sex, murderous sex. The kind of sex that puts the other person in their place. The kind of sex that keeps the other person *other.*

The kind of sex that makes you know you're in the presence of someone who is palpably a man.

Some of us know how male-supremacist sexuality feels better than do others. Some of us know how that sexuality feels inside because we do it, or we have done it, or we would like to do it, or we would like to do it more than we get a chance to. It's the sexuality that makes us feel powerful, virile, in control. Some of us have known how that sexuality feels when someone else is doing it to us, someone who is having sex with us, someone whose body is inhabited by it, someone who is experiencing its particular imperative and having male-supremacist sex against our flesh. And some of us don't really know this sexuality directly; in fact, our bodies haven't adapted to male supremacy very successfully at all—it is not the sexuality that moves us, that touches us, that comes anywhere near feeling as good as we imagine we want our sexual feelings to feel. We don't recognize a longing for anything like it in our own bodies, and we've been lucky so far—very lucky—not to have experienced it *against* our bodies. Nonetheless, we know that it exists; and the more we know about pornography, the more we know what it looks like.

Pornography and Male Supremacy

Male-supremacist sexuality is important to pornography, and pornography is important to male supremacy. Pornography *institutionalizes* the sexuality that both embodies and enacts male supremacy. Pornography says about that sexuality, "Here's how": Here's how to act out male supremacy in sex. Here's how the action should go. Here are the acts that impose power over and against another body. And pornography says about that sexuality, "Here's who": Here's who you should do it to and here's who she is: your whore, your piece of ass, yours. Your penis is a weapon, her body is your target. And pornography says about that sexuality, "Here's why": Because men are masters, women are slaves; men are superior, women are subordinate; men are real, women are objects; men are sex machines, women are sluts.

Pornography institutionalizes male supremacy the way segregation institutionalizes white supremacy. It is a practice embodying an ideology of biological superiority; it is an institution that both expresses that ideology and enacts that ideology—makes it the reality that people believe is true, keeps it that way, keeps people from knowing any other possibility, keeps certain people powerful by keeping certain people *down.*

Pornography also *eroticizes* male supremacy. It makes dominance and subordination feel like sex; it makes hierarchy feel like sex; it makes force and violence feel like sex; it makes hate and terrorism feel like sex; it makes inequality feel like sex. Pornography keeps sexism sexy. It keeps sexism *necessary* for some people to have sexual feelings. It makes reciprocity make you go limp. It makes mutuality leave you cold. It makes tenderness and intimacy and caring make you feel like you're going to disappear into a void. It makes justice the opposite of erotic; it makes injustice a sexual thrill.

Pornography exploits every experience in people's lives that *imprisons* sexual feelings—pain, terrorism, punishment, dread, shame, powerlessness, self-hate—and would have you believe that it *frees* sexual feelings. In fact, the sexual freedom represented by pornography is the freedom of men to act sexually in ways that keep sex a basis for inequality.

You can't have authentic sexual freedom without sexual justice. It is only freedom for those in power; the powerless cannot be free. Their experience of sexual freedom becomes but a delusion borne of complying with the demands of the powerful. Increased sexual freedom under male supremacy has had to mean an increased tolerance for sexual practices that are predicated on eroticized injustice between men and women: treating women's bodies or body parts as merely sexual objects or things; treating women as utterly submissive masochists who enjoy pain and humiliation and who, if they are raped, enjoy it; treating women's bodies to sexualized beating, mutilation, bondage, dismemberment.... Once you have sexualized inequality, once it is a learned and internalized prerequisite for sexual arousal and sexual gratification, then anything goes. And that's what sexual freedom means on this side of sexual justice.

Pornography and Homophobia

Homophobia is absolutely integral to the system of sexualized male supremacy. Cultural homophobia expresses a whole range of antifemale revulsion: It expresses contempt for men who are sexual with men because they are believed to be "treated like a woman" in sex. It expresses contempt for women who are sexual with women just *because* they are women and also because they are perceived to be a rebuke to the primacy of the penis.

But cultural homophobia is not merely an expression of woman-hating; it also works to protect men from the sexual aggression of other men. Homophobia keeps men doing to women what they would not want done to themselves. There's not the same sexual harassment of men that there is of women on the street or in the workplace or in the university; there's not nearly the same extent of rape; there's not the same demeaned social caste that is sexualized, as it is for women. And that's thanks to homophobia: Cultural homophobia keeps men's sexual aggression directed toward women. Homophobia men acting in concert as male supremacists so that they won't be perceived as an appropriate target for male-supremacist sexual treatment. Imagine this country *without* homophobia: A woman raped every three minutes *and a man* raped every three minutes. Homophobia keeps that statistic at a manageable level. The system is not foolproof, of course. There are boys who have been sexually molested by men. There are men who have been brutalized in sexual relationships with their male lovers, and they too have a memory of men's sexual violence. And there are many men in prison who are subject to the same sexual terrorism that women live with almost all the time. But for the most part—happily—homophobia serves male supremacy by protecting "real men" from sexual assault by other real men.

Pornography is one of the major enforcers of cultural homophobia. Pornography is rife with gay-baiting and effemiphobia. Portrayals of allegedly lesbian "scenes" are a staple of heterosexual pornography: The women with each other are there for the male viewer, the male voyeur; there is not the scantest evidence that they are there for each other. Through so-called men's sophisticate magazines—the "skin" magazines —pornographers outdo one another in their attacks against feminists, who are typically derided as *lesbians*—"sapphic" at best, "bull dykes" at worst. The innuendo that a man is a "fairy" or a "faggot" is, in pornography, a kind of dare or a challenge to prove his cocksmanship. And throughout pornography, the male who is perceived to be the passive orifice in sex is tainted with the disdain that "normally" belongs to women.

Meanwhile, gay male pornography, which often appears to present an idealized, all-male, superbutch world, also contains frequent derogatory references to women, or to feminized males. In order to give vent to male sexual aggression and sadism in homosexual pornography and also to circumvent the cultural stigma that ordinarily attaches to men who are "treated like a woman" in sex, gay male pornography has developed several specific "codes." One such code is that a man who is "capable" of withstanding "discipline"—extremely punishing bondage, humiliation, and fist-fucking, for instance—is deemed to have achieved a kind of supermasculinity, almost as if the sexual violence his body ingests from another man enhances his own sexual identity as a man. (This is quite the reverse in heterosexual pornography, where sexual sadism against a woman simply confirms her in her subordinate status.) Another code common in gay male pornography, one found frequently in films, is that if a man is shown being ass-fucked, he will generally be shown ass-fucking someone else in turn—this to avoid the connotation that he is at all feminized by being fucked. Still another code in gay male pornography is that depictions of mutuality are not sustained for very long without an intimation or explicit scene of force or coercion—so you don't go limp out of boredom or anxiety that you've been suckered into a scene where there's no raw male power present.

There is, not surprisingly, an intimate connection between the male supremacy in both heterosexual and homosexual pornography and the woman-hating and effemiphobia in them both as well. That connection is male-supremacist sex—the social power of men over women acted out as eroticized domination and subordination. The difference is that gay male pornography invents a way for men to be the *objects* of male-supremacist sex without seeming to be its *victims*. In its own special fashion, gay male pornography keeps men safe from male-supremacist sex—by holding out the promise that you'll come away from it more a man.

Needless to say, for heterosexual men who don't buy this, it's repellent and a crock. Needless to say, for homosexual men who *do* buy into this, it can become a really important part of one's sexual identity as a gay man. Because if you think the problem facing you is that your masculinity is in doubt because you're queer, then the promise of gay male pornography looks like forgiveness and redemption. Not to mention what it feels like: communion with true virility.

Now this is the situation of men within male supremacy: Whether we are straight or gay, we have been looking for a sexual freedom that is utterly specious, and we have been looking for it through pornography, which perpetuates the very domination and subordination that stand in the way of sexual justice. Whether we are straight or gay, we have been looking for a notion of freedom that leaves out women; we have been looking for a sexuality that preserves men's power over women. So long as that is what we strive for, we cannot possibly feel freely, and no one can be free. Whatever sexual freedom might be, it must be after justice.

Sexual Justice and the Law

The question is how to get justice. The question is how to effect it.

There are many necessary ways to achieve sexual justice in society. The law ought to be an important one. Justice, after all, is supposed to be among the law's primary functions. But the law has had a very sorry record on that score. Historically, laws have served to perpetuate injustice—slavery, for example—as often as, or more often than, they have served to undo it. And laws about sex have been especially unhelpful, for they tend to serve the interests of the powerful and betray those who are powerless. Rape laws, for instance, have maintained the right of husbands to rape. Obscenity laws have perpetuated a belief in the vileness of women's bodies and protected men from their sexual shame in relation to other men. Sodomy laws have legitimized the persecution of those whose very existence would seem to jeopardize men's hold on the superior status of their sex. If anything, law has functioned to defend male supremacy, to reinforce sexual injustice.

In the fall of 1983, in Minneapolis, a new legal theory was invented that might actually defy male supremacy and materially effect sexual justice. This legal theory was contained in antipornography legislation that would allow civil lawsuits against pornographers on the grounds that pornography is a violation of women's civil rights—because pornography subordinates women as a class and thereby creates sex discrimination. The law was written by two radical feminists who had been co-teaching a course on pornography at the University of Minnesota Law School—Catharine A. MacKinnon, the constitutional-law professor who pioneered the legal definition of sexual harassment as sex discrimination, and Andrea Dworkin, the author of *Woman Hating* and *Pornography: Men Possessing Women.*[4] The ordinance they drafted at the invitation of the Minneapolis City Council would essentially give to those who had been the victims of male-supremacist sex in the form of pornography a cause of action—for the first time, this law would allow a woman to go into court to try to prove that she had been injured or victimized by having pornography forced on her, by being coerced into a pornographic performance, or because pornography was used in some sexual assault on her. The ordinance would also allow a woman to sue traffickers in pornography on the basis of the proven harm pornography does to the civil rights of women as a class. The fact is, these things happen, as became horrifyingly clear in public hearings before the city council during which testimony was given by both victims and victim-service providers. And the fact is, there is nothing yet on the lawbooks that would let anyone to whom these things have happened get any justice whatsoever.

The civil-rights antipornography ordinance has absolutely nothing to do with police action, morals squads, or a censorship board; it would function entirely in the form of complaints and civil suits brought by individual plaintiffs, not through prosecutions brought by the state. Under the ordinance, a woman could not get anyone arrested or put in jail, the police could not conduct a raid, and there could not be a criminal prosecution. What kind of justice, then, could a woman get? If she proved her case in a trial, she could get money damages and removal of the particular pornography from sale in the city. And that's after a court fight.

By making possible certain civil lawsuits against pornographers and traffickers in pornography, this ordinance would actually *extend* civil liberties to victims who are now outside the law; it would grant a right of speech to those victims, a right to speak in a court of law. And though the ordinance is based in laws against sex discrimination, anyone—a woman, a child, a man, or a transsexual—could sue under it if they could prove that they had been a victim of pornography.

Needless to say, what happened in Minneapolis became a national astonishment. Shock waves went out. Many allegedly progressive people had a basic problem with the ordinance: It took a stand against eroticized domination and subordination; it took a stand against male-supremacist sex; it took a stand against the very sexual conduct that makes injustice feel sexy. There was a rather widespread horror at the notion that a woman, a mere woman, might ever enter a courtroom and possibly prove—through cumbersome and expensive litigation—that a particular manifestation of male-supremacist sex had injured her and that her injury had specifically to do with the fact that she was a woman. The new law would let a woman prove that a particular instance of male-supremacist sex had done what male-supremacist sex is *supposed* to do: make her inferior and harm her, make her subordinate, make her suffer the sexual freedom of men. So it became a question of community standards: How much justice could a city tolerate?

Opponents raised an issue of freedom of speech that was really an issue about freedom of sex. Their argument was really an argument for the sexuality that feels its freedom most exquisitely when it is negating someone else's freedom. It was about wanting to keep safe the style of sexual subordination to which they had become accustomed, the sexual freedom that abhors sexual justice, the sexuality that can get hard and come only when it is oblivious to another person's rights. And it was an argument to keep off the public record any acknowledgment that male-supremacist sex is dangerous, especially to women.

Remember the cartoon: "I can't come unless you pretend to be unconscious."

Perhaps most profoundly, the civil-rights antipornography ordinance would help make victims *conscious*—conscious of their civil rights. The existence of this ordinance would have an important effect symbolically in terms of helping carve out social consciousness about what equal rights for women really must mean. Just as the existence of laws against marital rape has a "ripple effect" on people's minds—sending out the message that women are not to be raped in marriage, even to those who don't use the laws against it—this ordinance would be a community's declaration that women have civil rights that pornography may not trample on. And that would have a radical effect: That would shake male supremacy to its core, because that would make male-supremacist sex not feel so sexy.

Linda Marchiano, who as Linda Lovelace was coerced into making the pornographic film *Deep Throat*—the highest-grossing pornographic film in history—would be able to sue under this ordinance. As it becomes law in community after community, more and more victims of pornography can be expected to come forward. At last there will be the possibility of some legal recourse. At last there will be an instrument of justice available to those who are now most silenced by pornographers' freedom of so-called speech.

Pornography and Men

I want to address those of us who live in male supremacy as men, and I want to speak specifically to those of us who have come to understand that pornography does make sexism sexy; that pornography does make male supremacy sexy; and that pornography does define what is sexy in terms of domination and subordination, in terms that serve *us as men*— whether we buy it or not, whether we buy into it or not—because it serves male supremacy, which is exactly what it is for.

I want to speak to those of us who live in this setup as men and who recognize—in the world and in our very own selves—the power pornography can have over our lives: It can make men believe that anything sexy is good. It can make men believe that our penises are like weapons. It can make men believe—for some moments of orgasm—that we are just like the men in pornography: virile, strong, tough, maybe cruel. It can make men believe that if you take it away from us, we won't have sexual feelings.

But I want to speak also to those of us who live in this setup as men and who recognize the power that pornography has over the lives of women: because it can make us believe that women by nature are whores; because it can make us believe that women's body parts belong to us—separately, part by part—instead of to a whole, real other person; because it can make us believe that women want to be raped, enjoy being damaged by us, deserve to be punished; because it can make us believe that women are an alien species, completely different from us so that we can be completely different from them, not as real as us so that we can be men. I want to talk to those of us who know in our guts that pornography can make us believe all of that. We know because we've watched it happen to men around us. We know because it has happened in us.

And what I want to say is simply this: We've got to make some serious changes, and we've got to get busy and *act*. If we sit around and don't do anything, then we become the ones who are keeping things the way they are. If we sit around and all we do is intellectual and emotional dithering, then we stay in the ranks of those who are the passive enforcers of male supremacy. If we don't take seriously the fact that pornography is a radical political issue and an issue about *us*, and if we don't make serious progress in the direction of *what we're going to do about it*, then we've just gone over to the wrong side of the fight—the morally wrong, historically wrong side of a struggle that is a ground swell, a grass-roots *people's* movement against sexual injustice.

We've got to be telling our sons that if a man gets off by putting women down, *it's not okay.*

We've got to be telling merchants that if they peddle women's bodies and lives for men's consumption and entertainment, *it's not okay.*

We've got to be telling other men that if you let the pornographers lead you by the nose (or any other body part) into believing that women exist to be tied up and hung up and beaten and raped, *it's not okay.*

We've got to be telling the pornographers that whatever they think they're doing in our names as men, as entertainment for men, for the sake of some delusion of so-called manhood . . . well, it's not okay. It's not okay with *us.*

Freedom and Equality

Historically, when people have not had justice and when people have not had freedom, they have had only the material reality of injustice and unfreedom. When freedom and justice don't exist, they're but a dream and a vision, an abstract idea longed for. You can't really know what justice would be like or what freedom would feel like. You can only know how it feels *not* to have them, and what it feels like to hope, to imagine, to desire them with a passion. Sexual freedom is an idea whose time has *not* come. It can't possibly be truly experienced until there is sexual justice. And sexual justice is incompatible with a definition of freedom that is based on the subordination of women.

Equality is still a radical idea. It makes some people very angry. It also gives some people hope.

When equality is an idea whose time has come, we will perhaps know sex with justice, we will perhaps know passion with compassion, we will perhaps know ardor and affection with honor. In that time, when the integrity within everyone's body and the whole personhood of each person is celebrated whenever two people touch, we will perhaps truly know the freedom to be sexual in a world of real equality.

According to pornography, you can't get there from here. According to male supremacy, you should not even want to try.

Some of us want to go there. Some of us want to be there. And we know that the struggle will be difficult and long. But we know that the passion for justice cannot be denied. And someday—*someday*—there will be both justice and freedom for each person—and thereby for us all.

Pornography and Censorship

by

FRED SMALL

Writing about pornography[1] I shoulder two burdens: guilt and fear. Each clouds reason and impedes communication. I feel guilty about patriarchy, about the injuries women have for centuries suffered at the hands of men and the oppression against which they struggle today. While I have actively supported their struggle, I have also unwittingly participated in their oppression. This knowledge is painful. I worry about making more mistakes, causing more hurt.

And I am afraid of controversy, afraid of criticism and denunciation by sisters and brothers who share my critique of patriarchy and my commitment to equality. I fear their anger. When Andrea Dworkin says that "any defense of pornography is war" against women,[2] I am discouraged from contemplative and free-ranging discussion. Pornography is so complicated and so vast a subject. My thinking on it has changed more than once and will change again. Dare I cast my thoughts in unchangeable print?

The pain of pornography is not equally shared. As a man, I am not hurt and enraged by pornography in the same way as women. Some will feel I have nothing to contribute, no moral ground to stand on. But I am concerned enough about the dangers of censorship and about my priorities for activism that I offer my thoughts.

I oppose censorship because I believe it threatens our freedom to express unpopular ideas, to create subversive images, to make radical culture. I think that the legislative restrictions proposed for pornography are so vague that they could and would be used against feminist publications. Even if worded more precisely, these restrictions would set a precedent for governmental repression dangerous to us all.

My views on pornography itself are less strongly held. They are tentative, admitting of error, colored by personal experience and inexperience. As an artist I strive to create a new culture that fully respects all women and men as human beings. Pornography has no place in such a culture. I denounce pornography as I denounce all sexist propaganda. But I suspect that pornography is not the central problem of patriarchy, that it is more symptom that disease. I suspect it may account for less direct harm than is sometimes attributed to it. I suspect that strategies other than antiporn activism may be more effective against sexism and violence. Pornography may not be the best target for our rage.

Censorship: Too Blunt and Dangerous an Instrument

Misogynist violence in this country has imposed a state of siege against women. Responding to these intolerable conditions, women and men in Minneapolis proposed an ordinance in 1983 that would permit individuals to sue to prevent the production or sale of pornography as a civil rights violation. Slightly modified, the Minneapolis ordinance has been offered as model legislation against pornography. Initially appealing, this legislation threatens grave dangers.

While proponents of the ordinance argue that its meaning is plain, many people—including widely respected feminist leaders—find its language vague and confusing. It defines pornography as "the graphic sexually explicit subordination of women through pictures and/or words" that satisfies *any one* of nine criteria. These include the presentation of women "dehumanized as sexual objects'" or "in postures of sexual submission" or "as whores by nature" or "being penetrated by objects" or "in scenarios of degradation," or the exhibition of "women's body parts . . . such that women are reduced to those parts."

These terms do not mean what you or I or Catharine MacKinnon or Andrea Dworkin thinks they should mean. *They mean whatever a commissioner or judge or jury or the Supreme Court of the United States thinks they should mean in the political and social climate of the moment.*

Is fellatio "subordination"? Is genital exposure? Is wearing high heels? Is a short story about lesbians making love a "scenario of degradation"? Is the missionary position a "posture of sexual submission"? Does the word "objects" include a speculum demonstrated in a woman's self-help health manual or a dildo described in a lesbian sex guide? Does a documentary on prostitution depict women as "whores by nature"? Does an illustration teaching women how to examine their breasts "reduce" women to their "parts"? Don't ask me. Ask a juror in Attapulgus, Georgia, or Brigham City, Utah, or New York, New York. Ask William Rehnquist.

Advocates of this legislation may believe that they command its destiny, that it will be used forever in the spirit of its creation. Historically, however, censorship is invoked not against the powerful and ideologically dominant, but against the weak, the outlaw, the radical. Ordinance coauthor Dworkin concedes—indeed, she asserts proudly—that this ordinance will be applied against materials produced by and for the gay and lesbian community.[3] She even concedes that it could be used against her own writing on pornography.[4] She is willing to take that chance. I am not. A time when *Our Bodies, Our Selves* is being removed from library shelves under pressure from the Right is no time to devise a new rationale for censorship.

Writers, photographers, artists, models, producers, directors, actors, publishers, clerical workers, magazine distributors, news dealers, and art exhibitors are all potential defendants under this legislation. They can't be sure how its language will be interpreted, either—and they can't afford to find out. Many will refrain from producing, selling, or exhibiting legally protected materials because of the possibility of a ruinous adverse ruling or because the costs of defending a lawsuit would be prohibitive.

Proponents of the ordinance emphasize that its enforcement provisions are civil, not criminal. But civil law can have the same impact as criminal law. When individuals sue for damages or to enjoin publication, the power of the state is invoked. A judge or jury looks at the material and decides if it is "pornography." If the judge issues an injunction, and the defendant refuses to comply, he or she can be sent to jail. The result is censorship: the materials are forbidden, banned by state decree.

Censorship advocates argue that if pornography contributes to violence against women, then censorship is *ipso facto* justified. Research in this area is very new. The studies some find conclusive others find ambiguous or flawed. But even if we assume for the sake of argument that pornography does influence violence against women, censorship is still not the answer. It is too dangerous, and it will not work.

The lethal effects of alcohol on the victims of crimes (including rape and drunk driving) committed under its influence, on alcoholics, and on people close to them are unarguable. But when prohibition was tried it failed utterly, and succeeded only in romanticizing liquor further, feeding organized crime, and breeding public cynicism. Likewise, prostitution is an abhorrent way for human beings to relate to one another. It systematically exploits and brutalizes women and girls forced by economic oppression to engage in it. But its illegality in forty-nine states has done nothing to protect women or to improve sexual relations. Banning porn will not make it unavailable, just illegal—thereby enhancing its allure.

If the state can ban pornography because it "causes" violence against women, it can also ban *The Wretched of the Earth* because it causes revolution, *Gay Community News* because it causes homosexuality, *Steal This Book* because it causes thievery, and *The Feminine Mystique* because it causes divorce. When speech is abridged in order to prevent crime, the precedent is set for censoring any book, magazine, or film documentary that encourages civil disobedience or draft resistance, suggests herbal remedies unapproved by the F.D.A., explains home birth techniques, or approves gay or lesbian sex. Despite its shortcomings, failures, and misapplications, the First Amendment does protect ideas worth protecting. Carving out special exceptions to it will return to haunt us.

Pornography is a concrete, stationary target for our rage against misogynist violence, a horrifying and seemingly intractable problem. It is an issue on which feminists and our old foes, the religious Right, can at last agree, and thus united, win. It is just a start, goes the argument, but at least it's winnable.

But a start to what? After the porn shop is closed down, the Moral Majority's next target will not be the businessmen's club that excludes women or the sweatshop that exploits them; it will be the gay bookstore, another purveyor of "perversion." I am in favor of building coalitions with those who disagree with us on other issues, but people who rail against pornography, abortion, sex education, and gay rights in the same breath are too dangerous to dignify with alliance or embolden with victory. We in the men's movement are all sexual outlaws: sissies, gays, bisexuals, egalitarians, nudists, abortionists, sodomists, pacifists. Let us not arm those who would destroy us.

Pornography: A Picture of the Pain

Revolting as pornography can be, it does not exist in a cultural vacuum. I perceive it as just one band in a continuous spectrum of sexist media. Other media, it seems to me, are equally destructive and more pervasive.

The critics of pornography are right. Pornography is relentlessly sexist, displaying women as objects for men's sexual gratification. It wrenches sex from any human context of affection, understanding, or commitment. It depicts intercourse without reference to either contraception or conception. It generally presents a viciously narrow and rigid physical stereotype of women: young, slim-waisted, large-busted, with virtually no body hair. Often it associates sex with violence. It is patriarchal, produced by a multimillion-dollar, male-dominated industry in which women are exploited and frequently mistreated.

In each of these particulars pornography seems indistinguishable from American mass media as a whole. Advertising (including TV, radio, print, billboard, and shop window display), movies, television, music videos, recorded music (including album cover art), magazines, and written fiction inculcate the same values and perpetuate the same stereotypes. Sexism and violence are epidemic in our society. Sexism and violence run in a seamless continuum from *The New Yorker* to *Esquire* to *Playboy* to *Hustler*. The sole unique feature of pornography is that its sexism and violence involve women, and frequently men, with their genitalia graphically displayed.

Personally, I am no more offended by sexism and violence unclothed than clothed. I am no more offended by *Playboy* than by *Bride's* magazine, no more by *Gallery* than by the mercenary magazine *Soldier of Fortune*, no more by *Behind the Green Door* than by *Porky's*, no more by an s/m video than by *The Texas Chainsaw Massacre*. One of the top-grossing films of all time was also on the the most sexist and violent: *Indiana Jones and the Temple of Doom*, targeted at and enthusiastically promoted to a juvenile audience. The "classic" *Gone with the Wind* panders vicious racist and sexist stereotypes while it celebrates rape.

Among so many media abuses, why does pornography strike us as patently, uniquely offensive? Nearly all of us, women and men, are survivors of deep hurt and humiliation around sexuality and nudity. As children we were reprimanded if we touched our genitals, punished if we engaged in sex play, yelled at if we wandered outside naked. Our questions about sex provoked adult discomfort, hostility, and sometimes violence. Many of us were victims of sexual abuse. Nudity is still taboo in public and in most households. Sex remains largely forbidden, mysterious, charged with cloudy memories of pain and powerlessness. No wonder the depiction of women and men in a sexual context brings intense response, whether revulsion or stimulation. Both may be a distorted measure of reality.

My own observations of pornography do not rise to the level of scientific research. Feminism has taught us, however, that personal experience may be at least as true as what passes for science. My observations suggest that most pornography is not inherently violent, and that explicitly violent pornography is not as ubiquitous as some have alleged.

Playboy: Violence in Disguise?

Playboy, *Penthouse*, and their imitators are commonplace in the United States. They are generally available at newsstands and convenience stores and are advertised in mass-circulation newspapers. These magazines are slightly slicker and subtler than the "hardcore" magazines found in porn shops. They use more sophisticated photography, more "discreet" poses, and more articles on nonsexual subject matter to project a "classier" image than their raunchy brethren. With few exceptions (which are apparently increasing), they avoid explicitly violent imagery in their photographs of women. Antiporn activists argue, however, that the images in these magazines are inherently violent because they depict women as powerless, subservient, and subjugated.

*   *   *

I think the images in these magazines operate differently. Economic and political realities notwithstanding, most men do not perceive women as powerless, in part because women hold the power of rejection. I suspect that a man who whistles at women on the street actually perceives women as having more sexual power than he. We are trained from childhood to believe that real men get sex from women, that if we do not get sex from women we are not men, we are nothing. Women can deny sex to men, thereby denying our manhood, our existence. Men do not want to hurt women. Men hurt women only when they have been fooled into believing with all the force of hallucination that they must hurt women in order to save their own lives. It is a brutal order that robs the humanity of both women and men.

Playboy offers men a dream vacation from this system. In its pages, women are not aloof and rejecting, but welcoming and sexually accessible. *Playboy* delights in showing "nice girls"—The Girls of the Ivy League, The Girls of the Big Ten—wanting sex, wanting us. In these purposefully constructed images, women greet us with flattery and invitation, with airbrushed smiles that speak eager, delighted consent; they are not powerless; they freely surrender their power of rejection; they are not coerced or hurt; they are on our side. They seem to say to us: "I want sex with you. Therefore, you are a man." If the fantasy sounds pathetic or preposterous, it is a measure of male terror and desperation.

The fabricated leters to these magazines, sold separately in compilations like *Forum*, complete this picture. These letters, which offer the wildest, most nonsensical of male reveries, do not celebrate rape, violence, or coercion. Rather, they are tales of male passivity and female assertiveness, stories of an ordinary guy minding his own business when a beautiful woman offers or, more typically, demands to have sex with him. The male burden of initiative and performance is lifted by these voracious, undiscriminating, approving women. The image that typifies pornography is not men raping women, but women seducing men.

Of course, all this ignores the *context* of women's social and economic powerlessness. Real life "seduction" is frequently rape or harassment. It is possible that these nonviolent images operate within men's psyches to contribute to actual violence. But the heart of the antiporn argument is that the violence lies *in the pornography itself.* If porn is violent only because society is violent, then every depiction of relations between women and men is violent.[5] If the roots of violence lie outside pornography, pruning its branches with censorship is a diversion from more vital work.

Violent Pornography: Core or Fringe?

Violent pornography is repellent. In the context of the real-world sexual violence that threatens every woman, pornographic melding of sex and violence is especially obscene. Antiporn activists suggest that nearly all porn is violent, that porn is everywhere, and therefore violent porn is everywhere, relentless, inescapable.

My own investigations, deliberate if inexhaustive, indicate that violent porn is not ubiquitous. I looked first at the corner grocery. They carried no porn at all. (I thanked the owner for that policy.) I went to the nearest 7-Eleven. They carried *Playboy, Penthouse, Cheri,* and the like behind the counter with only the titles showing. To study these and other porn magazines, I went to the biggest news dealer in town, where men linger furtively at the porn racks. Combining the scores of porn magazines on display—*Swank, Stag, Pub, Oui, Velvet, Partner*—I could find not one photograph depicting physical violence, bondage, or coercion.[6]

So I took the subway into the city, to Boston's Combat Zone. My roommate warned me to be careful. You don't go there unless you work there, you want something sexual, or you're lost. Cops stand around in clusters on the street, waiting for trouble.

My search ended at the Liberty Book Shop. They carried bondage and s/m magazines, maybe five to ten percent of their stock. The back cover of *Slave Auction* pictured a naked black woman bound and gagged. My stomach turned. Then I saw the cover of *Enslave,* which showed a leather-clad black woman yanking a bound and gagged white man on a chain leash. As I looked further, I discovered that the majority of these magazines showed woman as "dominatrixes" (Aggressive Women . . . Who Demand to Meet You!) over captive, humiliated men. Whoever was in charge, the scenes looked less realistic than professional wrestling. I saw no pictures of cutting, bleeding, mutilation, or death. I know these images exist, but I spent the better part of a day looking for them in a major urban center and could not find them.[7]

My modest research suggests, first, that explicitly violent pornography is not pervasive or predominant. It seems apparent that these magazines account for a small fraction of the porn market.[8] The Liberty Book Shop is not a place you'll walk into by mistake. With rare exception, the only way you'll encounter violent pornography is by seeking it out—or by living with someone who does.

Second, the frequency of male-submissive imagery in sadomasochistic magazines raises questions in my mind about assumptions that pornographic images translate directly into behavior. I don't pretend to know how these images operate in the lives of men and women, but the answer is not self-evident.

Finally, I was struck by the ferocity of images of male violence in magazines more readily available than pornographic magazines. Magazines glorifying guns and mercenary warfare are common at newsstands. Boxing and wrestling magazines carried at the corner grocery are filled with photographs of men brutally beating men, faces sometimes covered with blood, and men being subjected to severe pain and humiliation. Clearly, these images are propaganda for male violence against men. Horrible as is violence against women, male violence against men is more frequent. Men are three times more likely to be murdered than women and twice as likely to be assaulted.[9] Of course, we are trained from childhood to believe that men are appropriate victims of male violence while women are inappropriate (albeit frequent) victims. But the men's movement should know better. If we are outraged at images of male violence against women, where is our outrage at images of male violence against men?

The Road to a Just Society: No Shortcuts

If censorship is too blunt and dangerous an instrument to use against pornography, and if the role of pornography in real world violence is not clear cut, how do we fight sexual exploitation and violence?

The remedy to bad speech is not less speech, but more. The messages of pornography are insidious in part because they are virtually the only messages most men get about sex. In the absence of free and open discussion of sexuality, porn speaks to men without rebuttal. It is frequently the only sex "education" boys receive. It flourishes in the darkness. It thrives on taboo. In a society that encouraged inquisitive, guilt-free discussion of sex from childhood on, pornography would be an absurd irrelevancy. In the long term, the only effective strategy against porn and the values it represents is to build that society.

We need to bring sex out in the open, into the light. We need universal, relaxed, nonreproachful, nonhomophobic sex education. We need stories, drawings, photographs, poems, songs, street theater, movies, advertisements, and TV shows about the ways real sex with real people can be. We need to see each other naked, casually and nonsexually, at the beach and in our backyards, to know what real people look like, to preempt prurience. We need to think about and heal the hurts in our lives that have left us with sexual compulsions, addictions, and obsessions.

We need to continue the long struggle against sexism and violence. There are no shortcuts. We need more shelters for battered women and effective police response to domestic violence. We need to counsel men to stop abusing women and women not to tolerate it. We need a massive education campaign against rape—in schools, at workplaces, on the airwaves. We need boycotts of products advertised with sexist imagery. We need nonsexist textbooks and sports programs. We need to encourage children to feel proud and powerful. We need to elect feminist women and antisexist men to public office. We need to organize working women. We need gay rights. We need to involve men fully in raising and loving our children.

We must crack down on crime in the porn industry. Assault, battery, rape, and coercion occur in that industry like any other and should be prosecuted. The production of child pornography is virtually always child abuse and should be prosecuted. Publication and distribution of pornography that is made possible by unlawful coercion or violence against a "model" should be enjoined as a violation of her or his privacy rights. We can regulate the time, place, and manner of pornography sale and display so as not to offend the unwary. We can use picket lines to challenge the consumers of pornography to reexamine the way they think about women and about themselves.

A century ago, many feminists turned their energies away from women's rights toward moral purity. Alcohol became a scapegoat for innumerable social ills. It was widely believed that booze, by loosening men's inhibitions, brought out their inherently degraded nature. The result of this historic shift was the temperance movement, short-lived prohibition, and slowed gains for women. Let us not repeat this mistake with pornography out of frustration with the pace of our progress against the injustice that surrounds us.

Our society is misogynist and violent. Pornography is a sign of the times. Killing the messenger, however tempting, will not change the bad news. Sex and sexuality are complicated and poorly understood. The history of sexual legislation is frightening. It is the wrong course. We need more speech about sex, not less. Let us continue to talk in a way that cherishes the humanity in all of us.

Pornography and Its Discontents

by

RICHARD GOLDSTEIN

If my thoughts/dreams could be seen
They'd probably put my head in a guillotine
But it's all right, ma
It's life and life only.

—Bob Dylan

What light through yonder TV breaks? It is Little Kimmi Johnson, with her blue dress threatening to ascend and her schoolgirl pumps aflutter with anticipation as she coos, "I'm ready. I'm ready now."

An English teacher is "tutoring" Little Kimmi. Mother is eager to engage her in incest. Mother's boyfriend (despite a stern warning delivered in the bland tones of video erotica) teaches her to fellate him—and more. Little Kimmi goes through it all with blithe assurance, taking sex in as if it were a calliope. She never yearns for innocence or regrets her absence from what Nabokov called "the concord" of children's voices.

In reality, Little Kimmi would be a budding schizophrenic. In life, we would pity her and loathe her mentors. As testimony before a congressional subcommittee, her story would be stunning in its depravity. But in the video, Little Kimmi Johnson—played, I should point out, by a woman pushing 30—is hot.

Little Kimmi Johnson is an icon of heterosexual pornography; by which I mean, she turns me on. But how can I admit it? How can I acknowledge that, though this film arouses socially destructive passions, it also arouses me?

The personal is what's missing from critiques of pornography. D. H.

Lawrence doesn't say that, by propelling him toward masturbation, smut leaves him drained; instead, he informs us that it leaves the body "a corpse, after the act of self-abuse." Steven Marcus doesn't confess that pornography makes him feel things he identifies as infantile; he merely defines as pornographic "any discourse which presents sexual material, and is inconsistent with a mature adult sexual life."

In my reading, the closest anyone comes to acknowledging a personal response to pornography is Susan Sontag, who earnestly asserts that "works of pornography *can* belong to literature." They say "something worth listening to," she explains, but only in the context of a political critique. (Observers of Sontag's odyssey ought to go back to "The Pornographic Imagination" for the fervor she invests in blaming capitalism for our need to become involved with the stuff.) More typical is Andrea Dworkin, who never admits to being aroused by any of the pornography she so lavishly deconstructs. This mirror image of Norman Mailer would rather mimic the intensity of a film called *Whip Chick* than own up to a response. (". . . He rips her clothes and slaps her. He keeps hitting her. She screams. Then she says, 'Ooh, master. Hurt me. Punish me,'" Dworkin bristles, in a description and analysis that occupies six pages of her book, *Pornography.*) What's missing from Dworkin's posture of rage, and from Lawrence and Marcus's less threatened stance, is confession: Father, I have lusted. In my hand.

The evasion is understandable. Owning up to arousal by pornography shreds the purdah behind which our imaginations operate. It forces us to confront the implications of our fantasies. For pornography posits a world in which sexual impulse is at the heart of all action, in which the actions that spring from desire are inevitable, in which there is no escape from role except through another role; a world without consequences.

This is the realm of infancy, to which we may not, must not, return. Except symbolically. We don't want to live in a world where children are initiated into sex by their parents and teachers, but we may want to imagine it.

Men of the Midway opens with a Walker Evans landscape. Inside the faded clapboard house, Charley is awakened by his father, who announces between blasts from his cigar, "Things are gonna change around here." Now that "the old lady's not around anymore," Charley has to raise his share of cash by taking to the streets. And pop proceeds to teach Charley the tricks of that trade with a thick rubber dildo. "Talk to Daddy," he says when Charley begins to express his enjoyment, and, as the ordeal reaches its climax, "You're better than your mother."

Sick of the customers he's assigned and tired of having his legs tied to the ends of a broomstick for their convenience, Charley runs away from home and ends up at the carnival, where he's promptly impressed into sexual slavery by Randy. This surrogate turns Charley over to two black men, who greet his arrival with a hearty, "Good, the other one's spent."

Men of the Midway, as dreadful to behold as *Sister Carrie*, is also an anthology of conventions in gay pornography. It features a father/son dichotomy as well as polarities in race and physical prowess—all of them used as signatures of authority. The "old lady's" gone, leaving Charley at the mercy of men and their hierarchies, which must be navigated in a series of painful submissions until one's place in the order is secure. Charley does eventually find love, and reciprocal sex—with his boss!

If we manage to overlook the injustice of this paradigm, we can understand its logic. To dwell in the obvious, gay male films have no female object. They must either abandon sexual polarities altogether (hence, the preponderance of group action as well as solo performances in gay erotica) or reformulate them. From varieties of race, class, age, status and physical appearance, gay men eroticize the differences between them; and gay male porn reflects these castes. It adds the crowning touch of "attitude"—the sense of self we all project onto sex. Attitude hinges on a response to power (though it can involve aggression or submission). Charley begins as a wimp, whining in protest but too weak to resist; he's transformed by attitude into an eager bottom, and ultimately, into a clone (Everygayman).

Men of the Midway has more in common with *Little Kimmi Johnson* than most men might like to admit. These erotic *bildungsromans* share an age-old obsession with infantile helplessness and parental power. Charley is literally awakened by his father, while Kimmi is unveiled by the camera in a series of "candid" interviews. If she seems oblivious to sexual trauma —while Charley seems overwhelmed by it—that's because straight sex films, when not trafficking overtly in degradation and cruelty, disguise their intentions with elaborate displays of female ecstasy. From her yummy-yummy look at the sight of a man's penis to her squeals at the moment he plunges, poised in full muscular display, there must be no question about a woman's receptivity to the action on screen. But the men in gay films are often indifferent, if not downright hostile, to the acts they perform.

In place of consent, gay male porn romanticizes coercion. For a man to be brought to submission by another man, and thereby to "suffer" arousal—is that rape or football?

This subterfuge is hardly unique to pornography. You can spot the same response to aggression in most action/adventure films. What makes *Indiana Jones and the Temple of Doom* so shocking to good liberals (and so exhilarating to conservatives) is its unabashed embrace of traditional polarities. Race and sex are thinly disguised manifestations of a hierarchy of power in which the white male hero is the source of all strength and, ultimately, decency. He risks death to recover the stolen sacred object and then, rather than cashing in, turns it over to its rightful owners—people of color unable to recover it for themselves. As a fantasy of male omnipotence, it's right up there with the conversion of rape to love.

Steven Spielberg's secret weapon may not be his pilfering of bygone clichés, but his genius at priming the adrenal pump. Violence is to *The Temple of Doom* what sex is to pornography. It serves no "higher" purpose than to jolt us into arousal. Surges of shock, predictably paced, send us on a chemical roller coaster ride. We watch, not for meaning but for the impact of imagery. It is the pace of this movie we remember, not the plot.

Even the most ambitious porn films fail the way *Flashdance* does: they're only compelling once the dancing starts. The more sex is treated as a form of choreography, the more precisely it can be set to music; any similarity to rock video is not a coincidence. In *Men of the Midway*, the score sweeps from Prokofiev to Bach; *Romeo and Juliet* accompanies a rape, *The Passion According to St. Matthew* is appropriated for a homosexual love scene. That religious music can serve such a blasphemous master and still retain its core of meaning is incredibly arousing, almost as if the "passion" of submission and suffering were heightened by its association with pornography. The characters, too, are exalted by overcoming degradation. They are transformed by a desire that is ultimately beyond their control: the bottom doesn't want to have sex but comes to enjoy it; the top begins by demanding release but ends up expressing love.

For "good" Freudians—e.g., Robert Stoller—this conversion is always present in neurotic behavior; but it's also endemic to sexual fantasy. It recurs in so many guises in pornography that I've come to regard conversion as the mark of successful erotica, straight or gay. It's the ritual ground of porn, and partly explains its obsession with indignity, inequality, coercion, and rape.

If you're wondering whether Kimmi and Charley turn me on—poor waifs—they do. I am implicated in their transformation. I enact it as arousal and I come, signifying my triumph over trauma.

Even if there were no pornography, there would be pornography. The libido will not be denied its representations; though they may be covert, to the eye of the beholder, their intentions will be clear. Which is why the popular iconography of the '50s, when everything explicit was under-the-counter, seems comically intense to us today. The visual and written rhetoric of that decade is overwrought with pornographic implications we now relegate to "adult" films and magazines. I remember the Marilyn Monroe calendar my father brought home when I was a kid more vividly than any spread-beaver shot—and, I dare say, it had a greater impact on my hormones. The folds of red satin on which she lay are lodged so firmly in my imagination that I am still reminded of them at the sight of a red foulard protruding from the breast pocket of an ordinary business suit. To each his own *madeleine*.

Even if pornography were banned as a clear and present danger, we would still be left with the content of our fantasies, and our fantasies would still be laced with those images of "submission and display" by which anti-porn activists define pornography. The menu of insult and injury in the "adult" section of any home-video store is—and would remain—the stuff of dreams.

Readers of *The New York Times* were shocked (or perhaps consoled) to learn last year that men and women, straight and gay, frequently fantasize about forced sexual encounters. According to that study, coercion ranks with group sex and anonymity in the basic repertoire of sexual reverie. Among lesbians surveyed, rape was the most frequent sexual fantasy. But such variations are less significant than the similarities between homo- and heterosexuals, at least in the realm of imagination. Dreams of romantic interludes, the meat and potatoes of pulp fiction for women, ranked far behind fantasies of rape and promiscuity.

Porn, a free-market enterprise if there ever was one, reflects this hierarchy with brutal precision. Those who yearn for an erotic literature of full-blown characterization, where men and women exchange intimacies as in life, are at the wrong counter of the psychic emporium. What folks want in a stroke book (or film) is freedom from the trammels of personality. Those who long for realism in pornography—ordinary acts with plausible partners—ought to be condemned to dream that way. What we want, in those moments of escape from tangibility, is excess and extremity.

If there's no great porn film—not even *Last Tango in Paris*, for all its value as dramatic tour de force—that's because there's no unity in people's fantasies; some of us will always think a stick of butter is for bread. The result is that most pornography is an anthology of acts, only some of which arouse a given viewer. We wait out the rest, and sometimes we turn away. One man's ecstasy is another woman's boredom.

It's not only men who eroticize male power. That ought to be evident from a casual stroll through the world of Harlequin Romance. "Your passport to a dream" is how these hundred-million-selling bonbons are advertised; and the men in these books are as monumentally armored as any creation of gay pornography. "No trace of tenderness softened the harsh pressure of his mouth on hers," writes Elizabeth Graham in *Mason's Ridge*. "There was only a savagely punishing intentness of purpose that cut off her breath until her senses reeled and her body sagged against the granite hardness of his."

Though the penises are transmuted into "hard fingers brushing her arm . . . and bringing an urgent flutter of reaction from her pulse," there can be no mistaking the harsh polarities of gender in these books, or the roles men and women are bound to at the risk of offending each other's expectations. They are "permeated by phallic worship," writes critic Ann Snitow. "Cruelty, callousness, coldness, menace, are all equated with maleness and treated as part of the package." There's not a moan or metaphor in the Harlequin oeuvre than can be called sexually explicit, but in form and intention they're pure pornography. "The novels have no plot in the usual sense," Snitow continues. "There is no society, only surroundings." The women who anchor these books exist "in a constant state of potential sexuality." They "have no past, no context. They live only in the eternal present of sexual feelings, the absorbing interest in the erotic sex object."

This is surely what Steven Marcus had in mind when he described pornography as "a relentless circumscription of reality, with its tendency, on the one hand, to exclude from itself everything that is not sexual and, on the other, to include everything into itself by sexualizing all of reality." For Marcus, the neo-Freudian and lately neoconservative, this appropriation poses the terrible threat of regression into infantile sexuality—the bosom of omnipotence we all (reluctantly) leave behind. For Snitow, the radical feminist, the "boundlessness . . . of infant desire and its furious gusto" are something to be cherished; its persistence in fantasy is "a legitimate element in the human lexicon of feelings."

Pornography, Snitow reminds us, is "a memory"—not of events but of feelings: terror, rage, helplessness, and their transcendence through power, devotion, ecstasy. We use it to convert the raw material of degradation and depersonalization into erotic energy. It may be false to the spirit of everything we believe about men and women, love and even lust. But porn is true to fantasy. And fantasy is not fair.

But hold on! If pornography faithfully reflects fantasy, why aren't there homosexual acts in heterosexual films? Though "lesbian" sex is about as common as rape in straight pornography, sex between men virtually never occurs; if two guys so much as touch each other while working over the woman they are sharing, you know you're in for high kink. Indifference does not appear to be the reason for this lapse. The same survey that insists most of us are turned on by thoughts of sexual coercion also reports that homosexual fantasies are common among heterosexuals, and vice versa. Why doesn't pornography pander to that need?

The answer is evident: for straight men, there are grounds to fear arousal from gay pornography, even though, if truth be known, a hard-on does not a homosexual make. If our fantasies are mediated by our fears, so much so that we can't bear to look at how the other half lusts, why *can* we bear to look at the degradation of women? Why is there a market for that?

I've rented a film called *Bittersweet Revenge*. It's as different from *Little Kimmi Johnson* as the Marquis de Sade is from Uncle Remus. Two women —haughty and rejecting—are overpowered and bound, on the pretext that they're part of a drug ring and information must be wrung out of them. The women are whipped between the legs and across the breasts, prodded with clothespins, forced to drink semen from a jar, and left hanging by their hands in the dark. Their tall, dark inquisitioner— equally haughty and cool—never removes an article of *his* clothing, never shows an inkling of passion; he moves in a trance, like the killer in *Halloween*. And though he's finally shot dead by the women, there's no transformation of the victim or reconciliation with the victimizer.

If the other films I've described leave me with the option of insisting I've been watching erotic fairy tales, *Bittersweet Revenge* is all too plausible. Its aura of real destruction leaves me mortified, ashamed of the erection I'd sustained until the situation got to me. "I'll never think of straight sex films as innocent again," I remember telling my video dealer when I returned the tape. "It makes you feel real dirty," he smirked. "It makes you want to take a shower."

This, too, is pornography, available for home viewing by anyone who can muster up the two bucks and the gall. Though it has no explicit sex at all, its prurient intentions are inescapable; though it resembles *The Texas Chainsaw Massacre*, the unrelieved focus on a woman's pain at the hands of a man sets it apart from even the most brutal splatter film. Its mood is neither gothic nor fantastic; you can't laugh at its excess or take refuge in its special effects. *Bittersweet Revenge* is "acted," but in a style that's utterly, grimly verité.

To feel the threat a film like this must pose to women, I have to perform a transformation of my own. I have to imagine a film about a slave owner tormenting black women, or a Nazi and Jews. I have to imagine a whole genre of pornography in which straight men torture gay men. ("It makes you feel real dirty," says the dealer, and I run screaming from the store.) Or the whipping of a dog, and what it would mean if I could watch such a film for 90 minutes with an intermittent erection.

Why does the presence of a woman as victim give me permission to last through *Bittersweet Revenge*? The answer reveals the power relationships that inform our desires. In this culture, at this time, men see animals as innocent, blacks as underserving victims, gays as threatened—at least, some of us do; but we see women as powerful, desirable, implicated in their condition, and needing to be punished. Pornography is misogynist because the culture is misogynist, not the other way around. Sexual fantasies reflect—or, more precisely, refract—society. The libido is not a fixed and timeless entity; it is part of the dialectic between the world and our selves.

Anti-porn activists are right to regard pornography as, at best, a joke at their expense, and, at worst, a threat. They correctly read the hostility and contempt in its playfulness, the reality of rape in its rituals. They are right to fear its intentions. But need they fear its consequences?

The question is being thrust upon science with a bizarre urgency these days. Federally funded experiments are under way to measure the levels of androgen in the blood of boys exposed to *Playboy*; researchers are testing the effect of repeated exposure to images of sexual volence on the capacity of men to respond with horror to the real thing. The underlying assumption in these experiments is that pornography functions as an intoxicant, under whose influence men commit violence against women, as well as promiscuous and homosexual acts. Though the ambitions of individual scientists vary, those who are funding the research have been quite precise about what they hope to achieve: a Justice Department memo predicts "an action plan that will evolve from this process [with] the potential of linking theoretical research to clinical research to real world criminal justice intervention techniques on a national scale."

So the aim of those in government who seek to ban pornography is much broader: they want to use the criminal justice system to bolster the nuclear family; regulating fantasy is, for them, a prelude to intruding upon the most fundamental aspects of sexual choice. Many of the women spearheading the current drive against pornography would ultimately find the choices they have made subject to judicial review by their former allies. The revolution, too, will swallow its young.

Thirty years ago, when Alfred Kinsey demonstrated that sexual acts we weren't allowed to watch or read about were going on all around us anyway—that extramarital sex and homosexual experimentation were commonplace—"humanist" critics of that time were aghast. No less a personage than Lionel Trilling railed against Kinsey's "tendency to divorce sex from the other manifestations of life," and warned of a body of sexual knowledge so devastating that it could smother "the mystery and wildness of spirit." The "bland tyranny" Trilling saw coming down the pike is now upon us, although today it's not the liberal imagination or its libertarian fringe that is bent on setting science loose on sex. Trilling saw the authoritarian edge behind this process of materializing desire. "The act of understanding becomes an act of control," he warned. Regulating behavior through the manipulation of symbols and signs is what the New Pornology is all about.

We have been through this before. The Women's Christian Temperance Union was concerned with men leaving their homes, beating their wives and children, squandering their wages on drink. Alcohol was the *cause* of this behavior, Carrie Nation argued; ban the booze, and men would be proper husbands and fathers. The WCTU went so far as to urge a ban on tobacco as well, since men who smoked were likely to drink. They managed to convince Congress, not because their agenda was a kind of deformed feminism, but because it tapped a fundamentalist reaction to the modern era.

The anti-porn agenda is prohibitionism writ lib. It, too, depends for its success on an alliance with fundamentalists whose ultimate interests run counter to those of feminism. It, too, lays the blame for sexual violence on an "intoxicant." And it, too, imagines all men as the servants of their impulses, incapable of conscience or analysis. In the New Pornology, male sexual behavior is reduced to a sequence of responses to stimuli. There is no room for individual responsibility, not to mention environmental conditioning. Our lusts, our yearnings, our ambivalences, are merely the products of a hormonal cocktail. And we can curb desire by putting America on the wagon.

But even if sexually explicit imagery were contraband, popular entertainment would still be permeated with misogyny. Sexism would still be used to entice men into consuming products. Adolescent boys would still react to the sight of a woman in postures of "submission and display" with a rush of androgen. Even if a network of censors (masquerading as commissioners of civil rights) succeeded in scrubbing iconography off all offensive sexuality, the attitudes that make such imagery effective would remain. Those assumptions would continue to express themselves in real behavior. The danger would not pass.

Though it's no longer fashionable to insist, as Susan Sontag did in "The Pornographic Imagination," that "all art is dangerous," let's admit that *some* of it is. Among the works I'd include in that category are *Birth of a Nation* and T. S. Eliot's anti-Semitic poetry (". . . The rats are underneath the piles/The jew is underneath the lot"). These are compelling works of art which arouse socially destructive passions. Our critique of these passions diffuses the danger and makes it palatable as art.

Were racism not an active agent in our culture, we might be able to "read" *Amos and Andy* as a pornographic charade about black people, and enjoy its conversion of oppression into comic sensuality. Were homophobia not a clear and present danger, we might be able to grant Eddie Murphy's antigay routines the benefit of moral doubt. Is his comedy an attempt to overcome the trauma of black manhood by creating an inferior class of white males? Does his audience laugh to overcome its own terror of homosexuality?

But if I consider Eddie Murphy a pornographic comedian, how can I take *Bittersweet Revenge* less seriously? The answer is a revelation of my status as a man. I have nothing to fear from erotica; but in racist art (with its resonance of anti-Semitism) and in homophobic art, I feel the hot breath of retribution. As long as I am the object of such pornography, it makes me uneasy, and I look upon those who enjoy it as potential assailants. But when I become the subject, as a consumer of erotica, the threat abruptly melts away. If I lived in a world where straight men typically enjoyed films in which homosexuals are tortured, where magazines featured lavish spreads of gay men splayed across the hoods of cars like big game trophies, I might feel differently. (Indeed, I'd be afraid to walk down the street.) But since I don't live in such a world, I can afford to eroticize violence, even when it's directed against folks like me.

If I insist that pornography is not the cause of violence against women, mustn't I accept the same claim from all those people who line up to buy Eddie Murphy albums? Mustn't I grant those folks the right to engage in a ritual of personal transformation, and admit that it's not the root of my oppression?

I think I understand where the rage of anti-porn activists comes from. I, too, feel the weight of sexism. I, too, struggle against its definitions. I share a vulnerability to violence at the hands of men. And I know how tempting it is to wallow in helplessness before representations of that rage. But trying to destroy dangerous art is like shooting at a rainbow; you can never hit the source. No sooner do you succeed at banning one offensive work than others, more covert, arise. The intention remains intact and all the more dangerous for the illusion that, in attaining power over a text, we have managed to control the condition it describes.

Some day, Little Kimmi Johnson will rescue Charley from the midway, and together they'll ride off into the sunset (of polymorphous perversity?). When a film of that scenario is *hot*, we'll know the world has changed. We won't know that, if such a film cannot be made.

Forbidden Pleasures

by

PHILIP WEISS

The first unsettling thing about being a man in Minneapolis during the city's yearlong debate over antipornography legislation was the sense of having been preempted. The women were all so articulate. It wasn't that they were persuasive or even logical, but they had the words. They'd been thinking about these issues and talking about them for some time, and as soon as they struck they changed the language. Certain terms were used, and certain ideas. Other ideas had already been cashiered or were the subject of caricature. I felt that I was starting out at such a deficit, I had to keep my mouth shut. To say, I am a man who feels aroused by looking at and reading some of this stuff was no argument. It was like saying, I am a lizard.

I've always consumed pornography, in more or less passive ways, often guiltily. *Playboys* were a staple of my teenage years—I can still smell the dust of the barn loft to which my confederate, a giant friend with a straw thatch of hair, brought the magazines. Into adulthood I consumed porn on the sly, seldom buying "the slicks," as the mainstream publications are known, but finding ways to see them, say, at men friends' homes. There is always porn around.

Among most of my friends, the porn issue rarely came up. But then it never had to. Everyone knew porn wasn't right. Its double standard was too obvious; women didn't traffic in sexually explicit pictures of men.

In Minneapolis the antiporners brought these issues to the surface, and in the process disrupted my own pattern of covert consumption. To look at the proposed pornography law was to see elements of my lust pulled out like so many glistening fish guts, to have my unexamined guilt about the matter yanked from its shell. The ordinance defined as a viola-tion of a woman's civil rights the "graphic sexually explicit subordination of women, whether in pictures or in words." Any woman might claim that she had been discriminated against by material depicting women "as sexual objects for domination, conquest, violation, exploitation, possession or use, through postures or positions of submission or servility or display." Harsh, yes, but there, in part—once you have crowbarred off the manhole covers—I am.

Those words were point iv in the ordinance that the mayor ultimately vetoed. Point vi had to do with women shown bleeding, bruised, or hurt in a sexual context. I couldn't argue in favor of the male excesses, the stuff that seemed reptilian; I was happy to draw the line somewhere, probably through the use of obscenity laws. But I kept waiting for other men to stand up and defend at least the postures-of-display portion of point iv. No one did. There was the power of the feminist language—its newness, its passion about issues men did not generally discuss.

Often it seemed that the feminists were not really interested in what men had to say.

The city council had hired Catharine A. MacKinnon and Andrea Dworkin to draft the antiporn legislation at the same time the pair were teaching a course on pornography at the University of Minnesota Law School to sixty students, fifty-six of them women. The course analyzed, among other things, "the significance of penetration," and became a locus of the antiporn movement. Meanwhile, someone reported that MacKinnon had dismissed persistent questions about what material was and wasn't covered by the amendment as "a man's questions." MacKinnon, a respected constitutional scholar, argued convincingly that the report was a slur. But the gender issue was always there, and the feeling lingered that, in order to take part in the discussion, I had somehow to step out of my maleness, leave it like a husk, repudiate it.

No one induced this feeling as much as Andrea Dworkin. The author, visiting from New York, could be seen everywhere, armored in girthy overalls, roofed by tumultuous dark curls. She gave amazing performances. One night she read from her work in the basement of a church. I came late, held my ear to a half-inch crack in the door, and heard the husky Dworkin oratory. In a voice that seemed less a means of expression than an internal organ, something bloody, personal, and injured that she tore out of herself regularly in public, she invoked her hoarse vocabulary of cunts, assholes, blood, violation.

I shifted my head to peep at the audience. Attentive, calm, nearly churchly, they sat with shoulders squared.

Their faith in Dworkin, and the city's faith, amazed me. She was the one who had written eight years before that sexual relations between a man and a woman were politically acceptable only when the man had a "limp penis." It was a line I found myself repeating to women friends, each time studying the friend's face to capture even a flicker of agreement. How was it that this quotation had not been hung about Dworkin's neck like a bell when she came to town? How was it that the law the city had hired her to write was being discussed as though it involved snow emergencies or other quotidian civil processes, and not treated as an attempt to govern sexual politics, "the significance of penetration"?

Then something happened that pushed me toward Dworkin's side and made me wonder about my own role. It was a debate between Dworkin and Matthew Stark, the head of the Minnesota Civil Liberties Union. Stark stood up first. He spoke with a bullish eloquence about the difference between word and act, and about the First Amendment. He didn't talk about pornography really. Pornography, he seemed to agree in passing, was disgusting, but that was not the point. Then Dworkin got up and plunged headfirst into pornography. The audience was behind her. Her heavy left arm shook in the air, tears stained the spaces around her eyes into violet saucers. Unless the law were passed, Dworkin said, reducing matters to an attractively simple proposition, women would be regarded only as cunts. "We are to provide total access to every orifice, and allow forced sex as if there is nothing that can fill that aching void."

Two seats away from me in the front row, a middle-aged man in cowboy boots kept shaking his head. He had an unruly mustache and a somewhat gone-to-seed look. He turned to me—another man, a presumed ally—in disbelief. Then he began exclaiming aloud. At last he interrupted the speech with an obscene comment about Dworkin's thighs.

I hissed as loudly as anyone. Dworkin put him down, and he stood and walked out. One could sense a rush of satisfaction among the antiporners at having living proof. For he had provided, in corpus, Exhibit A: the scumball, the lizard, the consumer of pornography, the man for whom women were not human beings.

If you were a man who opposed the amendment, this was the choice you were left with: be like him and regard women as cunts, or be as aloof and granitey as the First Amendment, like Matt Stark, and say that porn was disgusting but that Nazis, too, must be able to express themselves. The qualities the women had brought to the table—sincerity, an emotional intensity about sexual issues—were somehow not available to men. You could be either a scumball or a constitutionalist, though in between there was a large and uncharted territory whose existence it would be easy to deny as long as no one opened his mouth.

But who would speak up? The public discourse had been narrowed; there was a sort of licensing of acceptable opinion at work. For a year the antiporn movement seemed to be the strongest voice in the city, and I now see that shame, the manipulation of traditional pruderies, was an important factor in its success. It specialized in demonstrations at which

male "secrets" were unveiled and linked with criminal behaviors. I especially remember the "porn drive," when antiporn groups, including the
Pornography Resource Center (or PRC, a think tank and mobilization
committee), issued a call for donations of pornography. Antiporners lit-
tered the marble floor of City Hall with the stuff, asserting that women
had smuggled it out of their homes at great risk.

The rhetoric hardly mattered; the antiporners' triumph was in confronting City Hall with men's closet items. Reporters—mostly men,
among them myself—buzzed around, uncertain where to focus the
Minicams. Crouched over a tangle of oro-genitally fastened bodies just a
few feet from the Father of Waters statue (naked himself, but judiciously
draped), I fought my prurience by taking indecipherable notes against
my knee.

And then, in a posture the public mind associates with a group of law
enforcement officials brandishing confiscated goods, three of the organ-
izers came to the microphone, one of them holding under her chin a
magazine opened to a randy bedroom scene. A woman in dishabille
straddled a man who appeared to be whacking her with a brush. Both of
them leered at the camera. I wanted to look at the pictures—in fact, the
PRC seemed to be daring us to—but I kept my face on the granite faces
of the antiporners, only occasionally stealing glances at what they'd
seized. Their point was that if you liked that stuff you liked to batter
women, and I walked out of City Hall a few minutes later trilling
vaguely with shame.

In responding to such assaults, I tended to be oblique. One thing I did
was telephone the PRC and, as a reporter, ask a series of what might
have been characterized as a man's questions.

"Five million people bought the Vanessa Williams issue of *Penthouse*.
Who are they?" I asked. "Wife batterers? Why did they want to see her?"

I might as well have been asking about the behavior of vermin. "I don't
know or care," said the PRC lady on the line.

Another time I called and asked her if she could give me the name of
one man who had reformed himself because of the antiporn movement,
one man who was formerly aroused by pornography and now sees that
he was wrong. She told me such men exist, that she would try and find
one for me. But she never called back.

Sometimes I wondered if I ought to reform myself. Partly this was the
effect of my girlfriend's house, which she shared with three other women
and where, upstairs by the bathroom door, someone had tacked a poem
about men not being able to dance. Sitting on the old couch downstairs
and listening to one of the roommates talk about patriarchal structure, I
would glance across the room into the pier glass, see myself nodding to
what was being said, and think, Who is that nodding? Someone who

was under construction, someone unmanned, lifted out of his male husk. Often I felt as if I'd wandered into a city of women.

The PRC's women were stone-faced, square-shouldered; in that city of women, they were the caryatids. I saw two of them at one of the cooperative restaurants where I ate; they were clearly gay, and my sense was heightened of living in a place where a culture that had little to do with my own appetites was establishing itself. The *Star and Tribune* raised the gay question as an aside in a news story but never addressed it head-on. There were things people didn't talk about. When a male writer in a gay newspaper wrote an article characterizing the porn amendment as a sort of radical-feminist-lesbian Trojan horse wheeled into City Hall by women in flannel shirts (male gays tended to oppose the bill), I quoted the line in a story and later opened the paper to find it had been cut. Time to keep your head down, I thought.

The other side had the floor. When anything happened, everyone waited to hear what the PRC had to say about it. After a disturbed, previously institutionalized woman set herself afire in a protest against porn inside a news shop that summer, all the media called the PRC. A spokeswoman likened the burn victim to Norman Morrison, a Quaker who had killed himself outside the Pentagon in 1965 after U.S. bombing raids had killed scores of Vietnamese civilians. Then a group of PRC women gathered on the sidewalk outside a porn theater on Lake Street to make an official statement. While lamenting the woman's decision, it acknowledged that burning "as an act of political protest" and noted that women live "under conditions of political and sexual terrorism." They dispersed without answering questions (though they did regroup and reread the statement for a late-arriving TV crew).

The conference had the urgency of a meeting with guerrillas in the mountains. I respected their power, and wanted to know what their agenda meant for me.

"A socially constructed sexuality": that was what one feminist had termed the goal of the antiporn amendment. This was what I'd wanted to see when I asked the PRC lady to show me one reformed man; it was the concept I was always struggling with.

A night last winter. My girlfriend and I have gone to see the film *Blade Runner*, about which the paper I work for had printed a listing written in the winking language of men. "Watch for the snake lady," it said. I understood from that, correctly, that the snake lady would be nude.

And now, on the way back, my girlfriend says she agrees with a friend's statement that the movie was violent toward women.

Irritated, I pause to calculate. "There were five people killed in that movie," I say. "Three of them were men."

"Yes, but the *way* the women were killed."

"The way they were killed?" I whack the steering wheel. "Those schmucks were killed horribly. They crushed that guy's skull on camera."

She's quiet. I've been yelling. I refocus on the road.

She says, "It was sexual, the way they were killed. The snake woman was naked through that clear raincoat. And Daryl Hannah looked like she was having an orgasm when she died."

"What do you mean?" I say.

"The leotard she had on. She might as well have been naked."

"That's ridiculous," I say. In fact, I am disappointed in Hannah; I had thought the movie was made early enough in her career that there would be a nude scene, but there hadn't been.

"You could practically see her nipples," my girlfriend says.

"You couldn't."

"You could."

"You couldn't," I say.

My voice, swelling with anger, fills the car. "I know," I say. "I was looking for them."

The sound reverberates. I haven't lost my temper like this in years, and there's a stunned silence. She and I pad into her house separately.

It's another hour before we speak to each other. I apologize. "You're right," I say. "I see now that the deaths of the women were sexualized in a way that the men's were not."

I hear myself speaking in an alien language. The words pile up, lodge in my throat like something friable and dry that others have formed with their hands.

Reconstruction started and stalled. Sexualized violence was abhorrent, yes. But mere objectification? I faltered.

The antiporners were emphatic. The very act of looking at a naked model was an artifact of male supremacy, the reduction of women to chattel. The women in the pictures had had no choice when they posed. In fact, the ordinance would have allowed participants in pornography to sue for its suppression on the grounds that they had been coerced. The ordinance defined coercion very broadly; it could include consensual agreements that the models later simply regretted.

The ordinance was saying that pornography is the inevitable condition of women in our society. Often I saw right-thinking men express similar views. Thus, *Washington Post* columnist Richard Cohen, who suggested that Vanessa Williams was a social victim; she had learned to value herself for the wrong things, both as beauty queen and porn subject.

What both Cohen and the antiporn legislation said was, in essence, just: people should be able to make of themselves what they want. And yet a universe of feeling was being flattened in the ethical rush. Vanessa Williams had a beautiful body. More, its display was plainly something she too had taken pleasure in. Sexual display is a way in which people feel valued, connect themselves without really connecting.

But there was still the sexism. Women were almost universally the subjects of porn (that endless line of $10-an-hour models), and though they might enjoy it, they were passive. It seemed always to be a man's eyes at work.

Of course, I could reply to myself, the roles were changing. Women also could be producers, like the women who were putting out porn focusing on male subjects for a women's home video market. I was like the urban liberal who hopes that a criminal suspect will turn out to be white—I wanted the blame spread equally. I got encouragement from *Elbowing the Seducer*, a fine and sexually explicit novel by T. Gertler, a woman, in which it was suggested that the protagonist, a writer, had taken the genderless byline D. Lietman so that she might appropriate a male privilege: the creation of prose with a pornographic component. Progress, I thought.

In the end, though, women's porn wasn't going to resolve my Minneapolis problem. As long as men's and women's roles in society were different, the porn would be, too. There would always be objections. This was the cul-de-sac the year kept driving me toward: men and women would always be at odds. I could never forget a scene at one of Matthew Stark's appearances when a woman friend of his, crouched and crying, her hands tensed like claws, renounced their friendship. My own women friends would always disagree with me. And there'd always be the women's reverence for their own fantasies, which they felt were inherently purer than the stuff of iv, v, vi, etc. Pornography *"is violence"* against women, Sheila Kitzinger, a respected anthropologist, baldly stated on one page of *Woman's Experience of Sex*, while elsewhere in the book, amid photographs of a woman pleasuring herself, women were told that "fantasy can be the poetry of sex."

Of course, we men didn't have Kitzingers. We had Gucciones, ethical Richard Cohens, and so on. But there was no corresponding male language of sexuality, no poets, intellectuals, advocates.

In retrospect, I see that we did have Tim Campbell. But Tim Campbell had been easy to ignore, and I didn't read him till months after the furor died down. Campbell was gay and ran the *GLC Voice*, a newspaper largely serving gays ("poofters," he called them). I'd avoided him for a bunch of reasons. He was given to ad hominem attacks (Dworkin suffered, he said, from a "lack of prettiness"). Also, he'd become a participant in the conflict. "I believe that the objectification of the sensual model is a healthy part of sexual experience," he'd said, and his home had been spray-painted, perhaps by the same people who decorated the sex shop a few blocks away with the slogan "Castrate Porn Users."

When I read Campbell's back issues in the library, I saw that he'd had my number. "I believe that men are going to have to do more than avoid the issues of content of pornography to satisfactorily deal with the 'radical feminists,'" he wrote. "Men are going to have to stand up and own their use of pornography. They are going to have to explain what goes on with them as they view pornography. And they are going to have to communicate a little better with straight women over their use of *Playboy*-like material . . . the Brownmillers of the world have got a lot of women convinced that dirty, rotten, awful things pass through straight men's minds when they look at pornography. There will be no peace over this issue until that lie is squashed. If it is not a lie, then maybe the 'radical feminists' should win."

His challenge still hangs there. I picture him: big and gourd-shaped, a redheaded satyrish figure in a tight brown suit at the back of the room during City Hall press conferences, "asking" his 50-second questions about porn. He wants an answer from me.

What I'd say is that porn's reductions, even its degradations, seem to go on in a feverish, removed zone. Because these thoughts are unspoken, because they violate norms, they've always seemed grotesque to me; they breed the conviction that I'm different and outrageous. Yet what relation do they bear to my actions? A study by two female researchers of women who read romance novels—a form of "mild pornography" generally entailing the rape of a young woman by an older man with whom she later falls in love—found that, despite savoring such Neanderthal fantasies, the readers expressed "liberal views" of a woman's place in society. Their porn is private, and I'm with them there. Porn, and the fantasies porn fosters, is like so many of the other dreams and movies that go on in one's head, that make life interesting. But I don't visualize emirs and pashas, nothing B.C. It's American, rock and roll era. What makes it male? Maybe that it's so gritty in detail, so aggressively superficial, nothing gossamer, nothing violent either. It's kaleidoscopic, with the frantic pacing and sudden absorption of an MTV video, and featuring the weird synecdoche of photographs, the reduction of a person to a close-up detail. As I say, often it seems grotesque. But I observe myself—living in Minneapolis has made me do that much—and I'm convinced that world is successfully private. It's about connecting without real connection: the flaring wants one has and does not act on, but which are still desires, that one turns in one's mind and does not seek to make into facts of life.

One Man's Pleasures: A Response to Weiss

by

DOUGLAS CAMPBELL

In his attempt to come to terms personally with what one feminist he quotes calls a "socially constructed sexuality," Philip Weiss does manage to speak to a conspicuous gap in the ongoing debate over pornography. But his perspective as a "passive," "often guilty" consumer of pornography reveals a limited appreciation of some of the key issues of that debate. Specifically, his assumptions about the nature of pornography and its social role are problematic.

Weiss claims that pornography is appealing, in general, because it is "gritty," "aggressively superficial," and "male." This characterization enables him to find entertainment in "the reduction of a person to a close-up detail," and to conclude that men relate to pornography in much the same way they relate to rock and roll. He suggests that there is a qualitative difference between the pornography that arouses him and that which seems "reptilian," the stuff of "male excesses." And he is content to allow traditional standards of obscenity to define that distinction.

Weiss's confidence that sexually explicit imagery can be judged solely on the basis of its subject matter reflects a shallow view of pornography. This is a relatively accessible approach, since if we focus only on visual content, pornography becomes easy to recognize and, in theory, easy to regulate. The depiction of certain activities—pedophilia or extreme sexual violence, for example—is so unambiguously objectionable that few among even the most vigilant guardians of free speech will openly justify it. Hence the task of establishing the lowest common denominator of acceptable morality is fairly uncomplicated. And pornography thus ceases to pose much of a problem.

The "problem" of pornography, however, has to do not only with what the specific images are and how they represent sex, but also with what they say, implicitly, about the nature of social-sexual relations between men and women. The ideological message in a given porn spread may not have been consciously engineered.

But the scenarios, postures, and facial expressions commonly represented in pornographic images speak for themselves. What they tell us is that the exercise of power, by men, within (and, by implication, beyond) the realm of sex is virtuous, desired, and fun. Therein lies the essence of pornographic fantasy.

Weiss argues reasonably that the fantasies *inspired* by pornography are harmless because they are private, contained, and have no bearing on actions: "Porn's reductions, even its degradations, seem to go on in a feverish, removed zone." While this may be true to some extent, it does not follow that sexual fantasies—and more general fantasies about male power—have no bearing on our attitudes toward social-sexual conduct.

Through its sheer prevalence and endurance, pornography has acquired a degree of social acceptance. We are, as noted, generally content to regulate the grossly obscene; the vast majority of porn is dismissed as little more than a curious aspect of contemporary culture. As a result, the social fantasy manifest through its images is quietly legitimized. Is it unreasonable to suggest that this fantasy of the pleasure of male power exerts a passive but nonetheless real influence on perceptions of social reality? The fine line of reason or instinct that separates fantasy and reality may well become obscured. In this context, pornography is properly understood not simply as a product, but as part of a social process.

The victims of this process are many. They include women who are compelled to participate in the business of pornography and who come to judge themselves as they are judged by men. They include all men who have been conditioned to objectify sex—to view it and value it in isolation from its essential personal or social context. (It is the absence of social context and the tendency to cater to a fixation on sexual anatomy which distinguishes traditional pornography from that which Weiss suggests is consumed by women in the form of romance novels and other pseudo-erotica.) Among the victims too are all men and women who find themselves falsely characterized as, respectively, sexual aggressors and sexual targets.

We must be actively concerned with more than the surface appearance of pornography. And we must not confine our critical analyses to the realm of traditional morality, where porn is judged according to a sense of "right and wrong." Rather, our attention should be directed to the social dimension of pornography. As such, porn should be judged in the context of social ethics: according to a reasoned assessment of the extent to which the interests of one group of individuals are being pursued at the expense of another's.

The challenge to men is not, as Weiss presents it, to venture into the fray of anti-pornographers, there to slay the myth that "dirty rotten, awful things pass through straight men's minds when they look at pornography." The real challenge is to recognize pornography's role as a pernicious socializing agent. Only then can we begin to appreciate its potential to inhibit the development of social-sexual relations between men and women that are not based on the exploitation of power. Only then can we undersand the extent to which it inhibits the realization of a socially constructed sexuality.

The Left and Porno

by

TODD GITLIN

Not so many years ago, pornographic films were flatly illegal, attractions for "private parties." Now, cities and towns fight to confine them to the outskirts of town. Once pornographers take root in a place, like Times Square, they turn it into outskirts. They make millions of dollars, but an actor (Harry Reems of *Deep Throat* and *The Devil in Miss Jones* fame) can be threatened with a long time in prison for his wham-bam performance. Porn occupies the shadow of legitimate culture, and extends the boundaries of it. The marginal moral enterprise, like all crime in capitalist society, becomes big business.

And it thrives because, like all business in capitalist society, it "gives people what they want"; that is, it meets the need of a large number of people. The need is both authentic and degraded. It is important to understand that the need *to have sex legitimate* is not wholly manufactured for the occasion, but, rather, it is a social need that is mobilized through the market. Pornography meets the need to see representations of sex, to make sex public, in order to make it legitimate. It meets the need in a perverse, dehumanized way, as the consumer society meets all social needs in a perverse, dehumanized way. By exploiting the exhibitionism of actors, and their hunger for fame, and probably their poverty, it shows an audience that sex is something larger than a personal fact, or a personal failure. It encourages the body to be more than an instrument of labor. It *certifies* sexuality.

At the same time, the dehumanization of sex in the very act of certifying it makes for a high order of sexual reflection: on the screen, a person is a sexual thing, period. A woman or a man is virtually identical to her or his organ and nothing else. The message is that sex, now certified, is an anonymous act, detachable from personal existence, especially detachable from feeling. This is the general theme, of course,

of the society of disposables: sex—or, for that matter, love or friendship—is a commodity to be turned in for next year's new, brand new
model. "I am I and you are you and if you don't like it, go fuck yourself,"
as the upper-middle-class version amounts to. A good deal of porno
confirms the image of the free-floater, the wham-bam wheeler-dealer
who knows too well not to get tied down. (In this it continues the
mainstream of American culture. Who was that masked man anyway?)
And like the Western, it often enough corrupts sex into violence. And
often enough it succeeds in being boring. Machines, after all, are mechanical: that is how they succeed in being good at what they are good
at. So, no sooner has pornography reminded one of one's native biological powers than it packages those powers in socially approved forms. It
quickens the blood and slows the mind.

And it does so for men more than for women, and thus against
women. The social situation of pornography—not the content of the
film—well-nigh guarantees its sexism. Not that the film necessarily objectifies women more than men; arguably the best, like *The Devil in Miss
Jones* and *Behind the Green Door*, are more devoted to women as sexual
initiators and enjoyers than to men. But in a society of female sex objects, men are the *voyeurs*, and women are drastically outnumbered in the
audiences. So, as an interaction *between* cultural object and audience—
and just as a culture critic should never stop at this dimension, neither
can one ever overlook it—pornography ends up sexist. Automatically, it
bolsters the patriarchal given.

In his essay on "Revolution and Sex," included in *Revolutionaries*, Eric
Hobsbawm has shown that "conventions about what sexual behaviour is
permissible in public have no specific connection with systems of political rule or social and economic exploitation." Hindu caste society built
temples devoted to the gorgeous depiction of voluptuousness, while
some egalitarian communities have been utterly restrictive. Neither sexual liberation nor puritanism necessarily lights any political flames in
particular. But Hobsbawm also points out that there is "a persistent affin-
ity between revolution and puritanism." The libertarian wings of revolutionary movements end up succumbing to the rigid. Why? It would be
too simple to say that revolutionary movements are genuinely threatened
by sexual liberation, since they need to collect sexual energy and to
focus it, to "sublimate" it, to "cathect" it to political activity. It would be
too simple to let the search for clarity end there; yet it would not be
wrong. Revolutionary movements are jealous lovers. And yet movements
that cannot allow to the body what the body demands are movements
that twist and corrupt the spirit, and build dungeons and H-bombs to
fight eternally necessary enemies. Movements predicated on renuncia-
tion end up extorting recompense, sadistically, from the Others in whose
name the revolution is pursued.

As for pornography, then, it has become not the alternative to puritanism, but its complement. To mechanical life, labor, work, and thought, it adds mechanical sex. In a society of great sexual repression, it proposes a mechanical release. As the current pop song tells it, and excitedly, "I'm just a love machine." But to blame the availability of techniques for the need makes no sense: when they are already pushed toward mechanical life in every other way, people will consent to be love machines too.

The alternative to pornography, then, stands or falls with the alternative to capitalist and patriarchal society as a whole. The alternative to pornography is not puritanism—not the suppression of sexual display, nor the constriction of body and spirit—but the liberation of sexuality from its oppressive social forms. One could imagine complete works of art that would incorporate (bring into the body) sexual naturalism, that would represent love and its frustration, that would reveal erotic love to be a resistance to social tyranny, and tyranny to be a stifling of life. Works would not be sexist, in other words, if they were attuned to the complexity of erotic experience; they could intimate the need for nonsexist erotic relations, in a decent society. It is hard to imagine such works in film under current conditions, though novels may approach them: perhaps John Berger's G. These works cannot strive toward the fully beautiful, though, until they are freed of explicit and implicit sadomasochistic themes; and those themes originate in the actual sexual relations of patriarchy. To dispose of the whip is an enormous task; which is not to say it cannot be done. It is exactly what needs to be done.

Pornography as Ideology and Other Ways to Get Off

by

ROBERT CHRISTGAU

In the preface to her remarkable *Woman and Nature: The Roaring Inside Her,* Susan Griffin offers the following proviso: "One of the loudest complaints this book makes about patriarchal thought (or the thought of civilized man) is that it claims to be objective, and separated from emotion, and so it is appropriate that the style of this book does not make the separation." Surprisingly, Griffin is right—it is precisely "by going underneath logic, that is by writing associatively," that she has her way with us. A long, skillfully woven prose poem which consists largely of male voices asserting "truths"—truisms that are almost always partial, often absurd, and sometimes hideously cruel—about women and the rest of the ultimately indomitable world outside, *Woman and Nature* serves as an overview for which I have little regard and less use, Adrienne Rich–style eco-matrifocalism. Yet like any thoughtful polemic it forced me to think in response, and like a poem it made me feel—feel why certain feminists choose to renounce so many of the delights of the world as we know it, the penis not least among them.

The first sentence of Griffin's new book, *Pornography and Silence: Culture's Revenge Against Nature,* takes a different tone. "One is used to thinking of pornography as a part of a larger movement toward sexual liberation," this emotionalist begins, signaling a turf by flashing the "one" construction, whose function is to obscure the position of the subject in the field of discourse. Coming from a writer who deplores Susan Sontag's failure to describe "her own experience" in re *Story of* O—and properly so, I think, having always wondered myself whether Sontag was actually turned on by the thing—such indirectness is confusing. It's clear that Griffin doesn't regard pornography as liberating now, but did she used to? One suspects not.

I can only adduce that Griffin, a poet by vocation, takes this more conventional, polemical, "objective" approach because once again she finds it "appropriate"—not to her critique this time, but to her intention. I'm pleased to report that she declines, however tersely, to "argue for the censorship of pornography." But if *Woman and Nature* was designed to move the spirit, *Pornography and Silence* means to change the world, by taking aim at the status of pornography in our male-dominated culture. And this target requires every bit of ammunition she can muster, because as far as Griffin is concerned pornography is everywhere. It's the model —the source?—of all racism, all chauvinism. All the tools of rational analysis—abstraction, categorization, objectification, perhaps even deduction itself—are associated by Griffin with "the pornographic mind," a phrase she uses almost interchangeably with "pornography" (she never just says "sexist mind," by the way). In fact, ours is a "culture which has fashioned itself after the pornographic mind." So assume authority, claim objectivity, bring on the rhetorical howitzers—this is war.

Underlying these vast generalizations is a thesis that bears repeating even if it's not as surprising or profound as Griffin thinks—at least to someone who knows pornography, which as Griffin grudgingly acknowledges "is not entirely ignorant of itself." Griffin believes that pornography serves a pathology in which men identify their need for sex and therefore women with a nature they cannot control, and ultimately with mortality itself. Sexual objectification, that old bugbear, thus becomes a symbolic means of dominating nature. And pornographic women in all their stock duality—the whore (I'd make that nympho) and the virgin who turns whore the first time she gets a taste—embody men's own schizophrenic relation to sexuality/nature, their desire (fine in its "natural" form, says Griffin) and their fear of desire. So that when a pornographic woman is brutalized, when pleasure is intermingled with violence, what's really going on is that men are striking out at their own capacity to feel—and to die.

As one theory of pornography, this is fairly insightful, but it's only one theory, partial at best. First of all, it doesn't apply to all pornography, although since Griffin never defines the term (syllogism, schmyllogism), it's hard to pin her down. I read along with equanimity, gleefully thinking of exceptions, until on page 104 I encountered a casual distinction between "pornographic images" and "simple, explicit depictions of sexuality" that was never referred to again. Then I realized that of course Griffin shared Women Against Pornography's position, still denied by the male chauvinist lexicographical establishment, that pornography isn't merely art whose function is sexual arousal—that it always involves violence. But since she never defines violence either, this doesn't get us very far. Clearly, it's no accident that she devotes many pages to de Sade (who as Angela Carter has written "is uncommon amongst pornographers in that he rarely, if ever, makes sexual activity seem immediately attractive as such") yet never mentions *Fanny Hill*. But what about the centerfold in which a woman pulls "apart the lips of her vagina, the same way a man might pull up the lips of a horse at an auction"? Just how exactly is that violent?

There are lots of ways for Griffin to answer that question. She might (and does) say that the intrusion of the camera (and the implied viewer) constitutes a kind of violence, or argue, tendentiously but not irrationally, that in the end it's the threat of physical harm that induces a woman to make such a display of herself. For even though the original meaning of violence (which still prevails in law) refers only to physical force, the word has been used metaphorically for centuries. But no matter how loose you like your metaphors, there's the inevitable logical flimflam— the move from the claim that pornography is *about* violence to fictional personages to the claim that it *does* violence to real people. Griffin doesn't just mean that it advocates and inspires violence, either, although that's certainly one of her concerns. Nor does she stop at the basically aesthetic sense in which a bank of garish skinmag covers is violent, or the propensity of pornography to (in her tellingly prim phrase) "offend sensibility." No—it goes a lot deeper than that. In Griffin's mind, pornography's most atrocious violence is ideological in the strictest sense— not its support of sex-role stereotyping or its unrealistic presentation of erotic possibility, the usual (quite justified) criticisms, but its propagation of more general habits of thought in which sex is divorced from feeling, matter from spirit.

As with many of Griffin's ideas, there are chicken-and-egg problems here. She doesn't maintain that pornography preceded mind-body dualism historically, but at times she seems to believe that without *Hustler* and X-rated movies the fallacy would wither away. And, in fact, it's Griffin's hostility to mind-body dualism that induces her to stretch the idea of violence so far—if you believe in the interpenetration of matter and spirit, you're not going to find much use for a discrete notion of "physical" force. Now, although you'd never know it from Griffin, mind-body dualism isn't in very high metaphysical repute these days, and I actually found myself cheering her on as she dispatched the smut peddlers' ridiculous claim that the magic of "catharsis" relieves pornography of any causal responsibility for nasty real-life incidents resembling the ones it depicts. As Griffin points out, all images "reach into the lives of the audience," and moreover, pornography's are designed to—the test of their aesthetic merit is whether they engorge genitalia. It's repulsive nonsense to hold that the effects always stop there (except perhaps when followed by tender acts of love)—that pornography always intervenes between the imagined rape and the real one. But Griffin's refusal to countenance any gap at all between image and reality, mind and body, feeling and sexuality is just as nonsensical. It may even be dangerous.

Like most late modernists, I prefer Blake to Pope, Heraclitus to Plato, organisms to machines, ecosystems to parking lots, and yin-and-yang to body-and-spirit. And as someone who has never shown much talent for the one-night stand, it so happens that I share many of Griffin's values about the uses of sexual pleasure. But unlike Griffin, who by her own testimony ought to know better, I'm not convinced of the objective truth value of my prejudices. And I'm certain they're not practical for every individual in every circumstance. I mean, the world really is inhospitable or unmanageable at times, and it's an irrelevant evasion to pass off its contradictions as manmade. To mistake these contradictions for purposeful hostility, an attitude which underlies all too much practical science, is a superstition with suicidal consequences. But the opposite superstition, in which people overcome through struggle and good will, has its own disadvantages, especially in the short run. Those who disagree should stop using umbrellas.

"He only fears who sees duality," Griffin warns, reverently quoting an Upanishad that takes the same all-purpose view of fear that she does of violence. Ignore duality as a construct, I warn, and you may not fear, but that won't mean something isn't out to get you. As Griffin must know but never comes out and says in this book, deduction, empirical method, and self-objectification are essential to a healthy life, and not only that —in the context of a healthy life, they can even be fun. Which brings us back (at long last) to sex. As I've indicated, I'm into what's called meaningful sex, maybe too meaningful for Griffin, whose "own experience" does remain vague. I've fucked the same woman exclusively for nine years and expect to keep it up until death or some other tragedy intervenes. Despite what the free-love lobby would have you believe, this doesn't mean that sex is off in a safe corner of our lives somewhere —we're moderately obsessed with it. And present in our sexual relationship—not in any central way, but definitely present—has been pornography, including stuff I have no doubt Griffin would manage to characterize as violent.

This is a second reason I find Griffin's thesis partial—not only does it leave some works out altogether, but it describes many others incompletely. In my life, the detachment of porn has not only been enjoyable in itself but has intensified my erotic-emotional involvement. Lots of books (from one-hand specials like Malcom Nesbit's *Chariot of Flesh* and Harry Street's *The Gilded Lily* to the high-middlebrow output of Alexander Trocchi, Marco Vassi, Frank/Odette Newman, and Tor Kung, and fuck all that arty French shit) and a few movies (*Behind the Green Door* and *Wet Rainbow* especially) have taught me tricks, put me in touch with lost lust, sensitized me to the grandeur and intricacy of flesh. And though she rarely touches the stuff, about which she's a lot more ambivalent than I am, my wife believes that porn's attitude toward sheer appetite has been, well, liberating for her. Which is to say that for us its uses extend beyond titillation and technique, delightful though both can be, into vision. After a life-couple's drama of mutual discovery lets up a little, after they get to know each other's masks and learn to accommodate each other's inconsistencies, after the fantasy of the double fantasy is accepted for the tantalizing reach-but-don't-grasp ideal it is, they are ready (on occasion) to confront sex itself—at a level more eloquent and raunchy (and unencumbered) than any zipless fuck is likely to provide. As model and inspiration, in its form (which Griffin ignores altogether) as well as its content, pornography helps us think about the shifting syntheses of intimacy and performance a deep sexual commitment involves.

Griffin might well consider this talk of "sex itself" more platonic fiddle-faddle and our marriage the obverse of the pornographic so-forth-and-so-on. But unless she has it in for the missionary position, a preference we didn't learn from dirty books, I can't see how she'd find our lovemaking violent. It's hard to be sure, though. She does stick a few sensual prose poems about roses and such into her argument, but "tongue into mouth" is as hot as they get, so I don't know how she'd feel about biting, say. And given her avowal that "the ability for a woman to be free is connected with her ability to love another woman," I wouldn't be surprised to learn that Griffin, who never declares herself a lesbian in this book, thinks heterosexual monogamy is sadistic by definition.

If such inferences seem arbitrary or fanciful, well, Griffin let herself in for them the moment she started in with the "truths"; her ambivalences (or bad faith) regarding partriarchal thought only makes her more self-righteous. First she's partial, then before you know it she's absurd or even cruel. For absurdity, try the flimsy associative grounds on which she tries to establish that the Nazis equated the Jews with nature (a classic case of a thinker enslaved by her own theoretical imperatives), or watch her get wrapped up in metaphor and rhetoric as she explains the "sense in which all women are motherless." And for cruelty, there is her inflexibly judgmental attitude toward how people get off. Antiporn activists always seem to assume that sexual "health" is every right-thinking citizen's first political duty. But even if women who crave cock really are brainwashed (stupid word), even if a taste for porn is nothing more than a patriarchal dysfunction, it's mean-spirited, arrogant, and moralistic to demand that each individual undergo the brutal psychological labor of deprogramming—people have a right to examine their schedules and decide that it's less trouble to continue to masturbate on Mom's high heels. And while I've found most of the committed libertines I've met appallingly shallow if not creepy, I'm convinced that they have access to information about sex than those of us who prefer a less extruded range of experience can put to good use.

Information—that's the key. It's one of those inescapable clichés: sex is a powerful mystery. Pornography—good pornography, an increasingly rare commodity—is another way to get at its secrets. I've made my difficult peace with it, and Griffin has made hers, but we'd be ill-advised to impose our solutions on others. Griffin devotes enough attention to the ideology of the genre to make clear that the battle she's joined has as its goal not merely the elimination of violence but the disappearance (if not outright repression) of ideas even more far-reaching than male dominance. Self-transcendence through ecstasy, the ultimate pornographic theme, has never seemed like much of a life-option to me. But sex itself is a turn-on. I await with interest new reports from explorers in the field.

Blacks and Pornography: A Different Response

by

ROBERT STAPLES

Although we represent 35 million American citizens or one in nine inhabitants of this country, the attorney general did not see fit to include one black person among his carefully selected commission. This is hardly surprising considering that Ed Meese is a known adversary of the black community. Perhaps he thought blacks were too perverse to ever agree that porn debased women, destroyed the family and caused violent rapes and sexual promiscuity. More likely he realized that it would be difficult to find a black representative of his/her community who viewed porn as a major issue. In one sense, we were relieved that Meese's attention was diverted from restoring us to our nineteenth-century status and that instead he had decided to concentrate on regulating what all Americans can do in the privacy of their own homes. To that extent, he has become an equal-opportunity enforcer of the denial of human rights to all members of this society.

Most blacks would agree with Dr. Morris Lipton, one of the experts on the 1970 presidential report on pornography, that "given the major issues of the day, pornography is a trivial issue." Blacks would add to that analysis the caveat that porn is a white man's problem—a particular kind of white man's problem. The presidential commission Dr. Lipton served on found that the typical consumer of porn was a white male and that blacks were underrepresented among the purveyors of erotica. However, blacks were not total abstainers from porn consumerism. Nor did they harbor any particular antipathy toward it. Indeed, many today do buy sex videocassettes, purchase *Penthouse* and enjoy risqué jokes, cartoons, etc. But as a group that earns only 56 percent of the income whites do, they often do not have the discretionary income with which to purchase erotica.

As for the black position on porn, it would certainly differ from that arrived at by the Meese Commission. Meese and his minions reflect a particular white worldview that there is something inherently damaging and sinful about sexual activity and interest outside the marital bedroom, and that any participation in other kinds of sexual behavior should pro- duce enormous amounts of guilt in the errant individual. Blacks have traditionally had a more naturalistic attitude toward human sexuality, seeing it as the normal expression of sexual attraction between men and women. Even in African societies, sexual conduct was not the result of some divine guidance by God or other deities. It was secularly regulated and encompassed the tolerance of a wide range of sexual attitudes and behaviors. Sexual deviance, where so defined, was not an act against God's will but a violation of community standards.

Rather than seeing the depiction of heterosexual intercourse or nudity as an inherent debasement of women, as a fringe group of feminists claims, the black community would see women as having equal rights to the enjoyment of sexual stimuli. It is nothing more than a continuation of the white male's traditional double standard and paternalism to regard erotica as existing only for male pleasure and women only as sexual objects. Since that double standard has never attracted many American blacks, the claim that women are exploited by exhibiting their nude bodies or engaging in heterosexual intercourse lacks credibility. After all, it was the white missionaries in fourteenth-century Africa who forced African women to regard their quasi-nude bodies as sinful and placed them in clothes. This probably accounts for the rather conspicuous ab- sence of black women in the feminist fight against porn. Certainly black men were unlikely to join with the likes of lunatic feminists such as Catharine MacKinnon and Andrea Dworkin, who treat pornography as discrimination against women. They belong to the same genre of femi- nists as Susan Brownmiller, whose book *Against Our Will* implied that black men deserve some kind of punishment for even thinking about the sexual possession of white women. She even suggests that Emmett Till, the murdered victim of white men in Mississippi, was engaging in more than innocent flirtation when he whistled at a white woman. In her view, lust in a male's heart translates into the mental rape of women.

The black community represents organic evidence against some of the assumptions of the Meese Commission on pornography. If porn is al- leged to lead to male sexual aggression, that is, rape, why are the lowest consumers of porn (blacks) so overrepresented among those arrested for and convicted of rape? A porn commission without a political axe to grind might have concluded that when other expressions of manhood such as gainful employment and economic success are blocked, those men will express their frustration and masculinity against women. In other words, it is the denial of economic rights, not porn, that is in large part responsible for rape in this country. Such a conclusion would not go down well with the Reagan administration, whose policies have led to the burgeoning number of unemployed black males.

As for the Meese Commission view that porn is related to sexual promiscuity, it is almost a laughable finding in the black community. One man's sexual promiscuity is another man's definition of sexual freedom. In most cases it refers to keeping women in their sexual strait-jackets so that sexual pleasure remains a male domain. The black community has exhibited a lusty sexual appetite while obeying certain rules of common sense and propriety in its sexual conduct. The kinds of kinky sex favored by a small minority of whites is almost unknown among the black population. Group sex, and sexual crimes other than rape, were and are rare among us. And a recent survey commissioned by the National Institutes of Health found that sexually active black women were more likely to be involved in long-term "serious" relationships than were sexually active white women, and that their serious relationships lasted longer than the relationships of white women.

Still, it is one of the ironies of American life that the one racial group in the U.S. whose image is so strongly linked to sexuality in the public mind should be excluded from a commission dealing with the sexual aspects of human behavior. Ranging from the thousands of lynchings of black men for the dubious sin of lusting after white women to the segregation of races in the South to prevent interracial sexual contact, we now have the more recent variation on the theme of black immorality.

While there may be cause for concern over the high rate of out-of-wedlock births occurring among black women in their teenage years, the Meese Commission refused to endorse the best weapon against teenage pregnancy—sex education. The same National Institutes of Health survey discovered that twice as many single black women as white women are having sex through their 20s without contraceptives. Nationally, a majority of all out-of-wedlock births occur among black women. Ultimately, blacks suffer more and are the chief victims of white sexual guilt. They are denied sex education in the public schools because a white-controlled bureaucracy either denies it to the school system or forces it to contain a largely moral content. However, in those few public schools that have decided to provide contraceptive services to their students, only schools with a predominantly black student body have chosen to do so. Using black high-school students as the first guinea pigs in these experiments is akin to the same kind of white colonialism that tested birth-control products on Puerto Rican women to see if they would be safe for white women.

Teenage pregnancy is a problem in the black community because the unwed mothers keep their children and many become dependent on public assistance. The N.I.H. survey found that half of the white women surveyed and only one-tenth of the black women aborted their first pregnancies. Young black women seldom resort to shotgun weddings, because their pool of potential husbands largely consists of young and unemployed black males. Were they to be provided a sound sex education or safe contraceptives, many would never face this dilemma.

The kinds of morals that Ed Meese and Ronald Reagan understand are related to nineteenth-century notions of sin. Blacks would prefer to see their morality expressed in the provision of jobs for the unemployed, shelter for the homeless and food for the hungry.

Finally, a most important reason why pornography is not a burning issue in the black community is that the morals of Ronald Reagan, Ed Meese and Jerry Falwell are not the morals of the kinds of people with whom blacks desire to be associated. Their past record is one of supporting racial segregation and black deprivation. Therefore blacks can only hope they will cease to interfere with the private lives of American citizens and adopt a real moral posture toward the conditions of poverty, nuclear disarmament and the conduct of government. Permitting poverty to exist and escalating the nuclear-arms race are the real sins and major issues of today.

How Pornography Shackles Men and Oppresses Women

by

MICHAEL BETZOLD

Pornography is booming. What was once found only in a few sleazy blocks in big cities is now available almost everywhere. Even small towns have their massage parlors, "dirty" bookstores, and skin flicks. In the cities entire blocks have been ravaged by the pornmongers. Why isn't pornography an issue for men? After all, men produce and consume the stuff and by doing so exploit women and promote their own worst fantasies.

Skin flicks and porn reading matter market women as commodities, denying physical uniqueness; women are presented as "tits and ass" with bulging breasts and painted-on smiles. This caricature of the female body and its reduction to a few sexual essentials is presented undisguised in the "hard-core" material and covered up with sophisticated packaging in *Playboy, Penthouse,* and "soft-core" porn films like *Emmanuelle.* Whether explicit or implied, the underlying message is the same: women are to be treated by the consumer (the male reader) as pieces of ass.

Besides this overt equation of "women as cunts," pornography contains hidden messages. For example, the recent surfacing of sadomasochistic material in more respectable publications like *Penthouse* illustrates how reactionary sexism gets mingled in with the turn-on photos. The material suggests that women should not only be fucked, but beaten, tortured, and enslaved—triumphed over in any way. *Penthouse* gets away with this murderous message by casting two women in the S/M roles, but it's no problem for a man to identify with the torturer—the victim is provided.

Pornography is loaded with attacks on feminism. Men are told to reassert their mastery over women. Perhaps this explains why porn is booming. Even if the consumer grows tired of the "wide-open beavers," he may continue buying for the ego-bolstering message that men are still on top, and that's where they should be.

While pornography promotes a male fantasy of continued societal power, its effect is to render men more powerless to meet their emotional needs. Besides reinforcing destructive fantasies toward women, porn promotes self-destructive attitudes in men. By providing substitute gratification, it provides an excuse for men to avoid relating to women as people. It encourages unrealistic expectations: that all women will look and act like Playboy bunnies, that "good sex" can be obtained anywhere, quickly, easily, and without the hassle of expending energy on a relationship. When men view women as sex objects, they are also objectifying themselves, a point not often appreciated.

Pornography contains an implied image of men. The porn reader imagines himself to be either a "Playboy"—with all the status that implies—a "Hustler" (a working-class version of the Playboy), a "Dude," a "Scamp," a "Stud," etc. Commercial messages about clothing, food, appearance, and behavior accompany these projected images.

Crucial to all these variations of the macho image is the demand for sexual performance. Pornography promotes our insecurities by picturing sex as a field of combat and conquest. Sex is portrayed as man's finest sporting event. The pressure is on for the man to perform flawlessly— how else could he possibly satisfy the voracious sexual appetites of the women presented to him?

Emotions get in the way of performance, so they must be controlled. Emotions are messy, so pornography attempts to render them superfluous. If casual sex is as available as porn implies, and all those women out there are just waiting to be taken, it's merely a matter of the male demonstrating his technical expertise in manipulating sexual response.

The obvious result is that the male consumer of pornography becomes deadened to his feelings. Emotional needs are denied altogether or telescoped mercilessly into the search to obtain exclusively genital satisfaction. Although what most men want is physical affection from another human being, what they end up thinking they want is to be laid by a Playboy bunny.

Coming to rely on pornographic materials to service sexual/emotional needs, men become ripe objects for manipulation. Powerful, suggestive advertising can exploit basic needs by inserting a commercial image between feelings and their resolution. So that more products can be sold and more profits made, superfluous artificial needs are created. Thus we are trained to consume TV dinners and other synthetic nonfoods which subvert our need for genuine nourishment. In a similar way porn sellers give us a need for artificial sex that diminishes our capacities to enjoy genuine sexual interaction. The sex of pornography is unreal, featuring ridiculously oversized sexual organs, a complete absence of emotional involvement, little kissing and no hugging, limitless capacities for orgasm, and superhuman erotic calisthenics. Porn presents sexual Olympics where the goal is to set new records of size, frequency, and capacity.

Substituting a supervised, manipulated, pseudo-sexual experience for the real enjoyment of sex is porn's way of coopting sexual liberation. The unbinding of Puritanical morality in the '60s unleashed potentially disruptive forces and uncovered the whole interlocking network of repressions that keep business going as usual. A freed sexuality directly threatens the system because people begin to realize how grossly the workplace and established social relationships distort their needs for sensual enjoyment and playful activity. Sensing this, the commercial entrepreneurs were one step ahead of the game. While "revolutionary" became a Madison Avenue catchword, sexual liberation was channeled into marketable sex.

Porn does not eroticize work or social relationships. On the contrary, it provides a cheap and non–time-consuming method of "servicing" freed sexual energies so that the worker can return contentedly to a job that is anything but satisfying.

Completing its subversion of sexual liberation, porn eventually compels a return to Puritanism. By its unlimited excesses, it provokes a reaction from the forces of repression. Because most porn is degrading, it justifies the Puritan's disgust with all sexuality. In its consumers, porn promotes a hatred for sex. By limiting sexuality through its standardization, sex becomes greatly narrowed and ultimately boring. By reducing sensuality to genital orgasm, porn contracts a large, varied and hard-to-control human need into a small, quick, controlled jerk-off. By unlimited exposure of breasts and cunts detached from real people, over-saturation eventually reduces to near-nothing the porn consumers' capacities to be genuinely stimulated by human beings.

Ultimately, pornography is anti-sex. While exploiting them, it maintains all the Puritan taboos. Special sections of bookstores are hidden from public view, require an admission price, and enforce an age requirement; advertisements for skin flicks leave out letters (S–X) or sport suggestive titles (*Behind the Green Door*) to emphasize the once-forbidden nature of the subject material. Sex is sold as dirty and evil to attract those who are fascinated by the forbidden. What is presented is generally so mindless and impersonal that any but the most hardened are soon turned off. The lesson is that turn-ons are really turn-offs, so why bother with sex? This sort of "liberation" is a deadend for everyone except those who profit from our inadequacies and powerlessness.

There may be several reasons why opponents of sexism have not acted more openly against pornography. We may fear being accused of harboring vestiges of Puritanism, of being anti-sex or "unliberated." We may fear being aligned with right-wingers. Probably we are most immobilized by a libertarian confusion.

The rallying cry of porn dealers is freedom of speech and the press, that the state has no right to interfere in the private sexual tastes of consenting adults. Censorship of any sort, we all agree, is reprehensible.

Yet we would be appalled if movies showed blacks being lynched or castrated, Chicanos being systematically beaten and tortured, and we would quickly protest. If whole blocks of a city were given over to the sale of material directly oppressing black people, we would run the merchants out of town with little thought about their First Amendment rights. But we say nothing when the same activity goes on with women as the victims.

The solution is certainly not to call upon the government to impose censorship. But anti-sexist men should be staging protests against the sale of pornography and trying to raise the consciousness of their brothers who consume it. The goal should be to put Hugh Hefner and all his imitators permanently out of business, to make the marketing of women as sex objects as impossible as the selling of blacks as slaves.

Porn as Therapy ?:
The Psychology
of Pornography

Porn as Therapy

by

BERNIE ZILBERGELD

Pornography has one great value that is often overlooked—its use in enhancing marital sex. Pornography can help to strengthen not only individual marriages, but perhaps the very institution of marriage itself. The importance of satisfaction in a good marriage is supported by scientific research and is recognized by many Christian ministers. Millions of ordinary married Americans benefit from erotica and will suffer if it is taken away from them.

Why do so many people refuse to admit that keeping sex interesting, exciting and satisfying in a long relationship is not easy? Couples have to work at it, using whatever aids they can find. Vacations without children, sharing fantasies and open communication are reliable ways to rejuvenate a marriage. Equally valuable is the sharing of erotic materials. It would be tragic if this loving opportunity were denied them.

Dr. June Reinisch, director of the Kinsey Institute, frequently gets letters like this: "My wife and I belong to the church, have three children and do everything right. But once a week we like to spice up our private lives with an erotic video. Why are people trying to take them away from us?" I hear similar things all the time from clients and others who talk to me about sex.

Many people in traditional marriages have turned to erotic films, books and magazines to enhance their sex lives. These people recognize that it is no easy matter to keep ennui at bay over a long period. Before turning to erotica, these spouses made love infrequently, found it either boring or unexciting and realized that much of their sexual desire was directed at people other than their partner. But they did not want affairs. Rather they preferred to rekindle passion for their own spouse.

Such couples often report that watching an erotic film, usually on a VCR in their own bedrooms, or reading sexual letters and articles in magazines like *Penthouse* or *Playboy*, leads to more frequent and more intense sex.

Obviously, erotic materials are not for everybody. Some people are turned off by them rather than on. I simply want to emphasize the popularity of erotica among many traditional couples.

Other benefits of pornography include learning specific sexual techniques and getting ideas about how and where to have sex with their partners.

Exposure to sexually explicit materials also leads to more open communication about sex. "I've always wanted to try that," or "Have you ever fantasized anything like this?" are common reactions to viewing pornography. Such honest conversations usually lead to increased closeness and better sex. I have found that exposure to erotica is one of the best ways to improve sexual communication between a man and a woman. Even if a person's initial reaction is "I could never imagine doing that," a useful dialogue often results. It's a scientifically proven fact that talking about sex plays an important part in a good sex life.

Most of what I have learned about the benefits of erotica comes from middle-aged churchgoers who believe strongly in monogamy and family. Some acknowledge that they would be tempted to have affairs if they failed to put some zest into their marital sex. Contrary to what the critics of erotica maintain, these people are using pornography to strengthen their marriages. But all the negative publicity about pornography causes them to be apologetic or embarrassed about discussing it. Even though they know its value in their own lives, they still feel that perhaps it indicates a defect in their personalities or in their love for one another.

Therapists who work with couples' sex problems are also familiar with the benefits of erotica. It's probable that more than half of all sex therapists recommend explicit sexual materials to their clients. A fair amount of research indicates that exposure to sexual materials increases both a couple's tolerance of the sexual behavior of others and desire for one another.

Many people in the media have a strange attitude toward pornography. A television executive planning a documentary on the subject became upset when I mentioned how married couples use it to enhance their sex lives. "You don't have to say any more about that," she said. "I get it from my married friends all the time.

"A few weeks ago I visited a couple in their late fifties, good friends of mine for many years, and they started in on this. They even showed me their collection of films, books and pictures. They claim it has done great things for them, but I think it's disgusting. I don't want a man to want me because he got turned on by somebody else on the VCR. I don't want him thinking about her when he's having sex with me. I want him to think only of me."

I replied that the kind of purity she desired is hard to come by in couples who have been together more than two months. Her response: "I know, but that means the relationship is over."

It's frightening to me that someone with such a rigid and unrealistic point of view should be in charge of making documentaries on the subject of erotica.

Maybe this executive's attitude explains why the media gives its attention primarily to pornography's alleged negative effects. I have yet to hear any media discussion of the positive and marriage-affirming benefits described above.

Personally I find the vast bulk of erotica to be poorly presented and boring. But I cannot deny the rewards it has brought to many American couples. It is sad to think that this gift may be taken away.

A Male Grief:
Notes on Pornography and Addiction

by

DAVID MURA

I. Premises

1

Start with the premise that a person—generally a male—may be addicted to pornography, and that this addiction may be part of a larger addiction to any number of other sexual "highs"—affairs, visits to prostitutes, anonymous sex, exhibitionism, voyeurism, etc. See where this premise leads.

2

A man wishes to believe there is a beautiful body with no soul attached. Because of this wish he takes the surface for truth. There are no depths. Because of this wish, he begins to worship an image. But when this image enters the future, it loses what the man has given it—momentary devotion. The man wishes for another body, another face, another moment. He discards the image like a painting. It is no longer to his taste. Only the surface can be known and loved, and this is why the image is so easily exhausted, why there must be another.

What is this danger that lies beneath the surface? How can it hurt him? *It* reminds him of the depths he has lost in himself.

3

At the essence of pornography is the image of flesh used as a drug, a way of numbing psychic pain. But this drug lasts only as long as the man stares at the image. Then his pain reasserts itself, reveals the promised power as an illusion.

What is it to worship an image? It is to pray for a gift you will never receive.

4

There are certain states of mind that the closer one understands them, the closer one comes to experiencing evil. This is certainly true with the world of pornography. The experience of those who view a pornographic work dispassionately, without a strong sexual response, is not pornographic, though they may capture some flickerings of that world. For in pornographic perception, each gesture, each word, each image, is read first and foremost through sexuality. Love or tenderness, pity or compassion, become subsumed by, and are made subservient to, a "greater" deity, a more powerful force. In short, the world is reduced to a single common denominator.

5

Such a simplistic world, of course, does not exist. But the addict to pornography desires to be blinded, to live in a dream. Any element which questions the illusion that sexuality is all encompassing, the very basis of human activity, must be denied. The addict can become enraged by any evidence, such as an inadvertent microphone, that the people on the screen are actors or less than perfectly tuned sexual beings. On a wider scale, those in the thrall of pornography try to eliminate from their consciousness the world outside pornography, and this includes everything from their family and friends to their business deals or last Sunday's sermon to the political situation in the Middle East. In engaging in such elimination the viewer or reader reduces himself. He becomes stupid.

6

Although the pornographic viewpoint attempts to numb any psychic urge but sexuality, such numbing can never be complete. We might envision those who engage in it as attempting to attack a Hydra, constantly cutting off what will appear again, only doubled.

7

Those who are addicted to pornography attempt to erase the distinction between art and life. On the one hand the addict knows, at some level of consciousness, that the world of pornography is unreal. To block out this knowledge, the addict tries to convince himself that all the world is pornographic, and that other people are too timid to see this truth. Thus the addict does not view or read pornography in the same way a scholar might read a poem about shepherds. While the latter acknowledges the fictional nature of the bucolic, the addict wants to deny pornography's fictional nature. In refusing the symbolic nature of art, the addict wishes to destroy the indestructible gulf between the sign and its referent.

8

Like all addicts, the addict to pornography dreams then of ultimate power and control. When reality invades this dream and causes doubts, the addict thinks: I have nothing else. I have, all my life, done my best to deny and destroy through my addiction whatever would replace this.

Thus, the addict returns to the inertia of the dream.

9

The addiction to pornography is not fun. Underneath all the assertions of liberty and "healthy fun" lie the desperation and anxiety, the shame and fear, the loneliness and sadness, that fuel the endless consumption of magazines and strip shows, x-rated films, visits to prostitutes. If addicts portray themselves as hedonists or carefree, this portrayal is belied in those moments and feelings they do not let anyone else see. Like all actors, they mistake their life on stage as being truest and most real. What happens offstage cannot possibly have a bearing on who they are.

10

In pornographic perception, the addict experiences a type of vertigo, a fearful exhilaration, a moment when all the addict's ties to the outside world do indeed seem to be cut or numbed. That sense of endless falling, that rush, is what the addict seeks again and again. Its power comes from a wild forgetting, a surrender to entropy, to what he knows is evil.

Those who stand back from the world of pornography cannot experience this falling, this rush. They cannot understand the attraction it holds. But for the addict the rush is more than an attraction. He is helpless before it. Completely out of control.

II. The Etiology of Addiction

1

One defense of pornography is that it defies repression and therefore represents an act of freedom. Such a defense ignores the repression that takes place within the world of pornography, for the pornographic world is so limited that to list what it leaves out would require an endless encyclopedia.

The libertarian defense of pornography also misconstrues the nature of freedom. The defense argues that freedom is the liberty to do anything to anybody. But this defense ignores the fact that nowhere in this world can such liberty exist for everyone. In particular, certain acts require an abuser and a victim, and in such acts, to possess the liberty to play the abuser, one must deny another the freedom to be anything but a victim. A hierarchy is set up which denies freedom. Sade's prisoners do not have a choice.

But is pornography an act which requires an abuser and a victim? And what if, of one's own free will, one chooses to be the victim? In examining these questions, feminist writers have, I think, convincingly argued that women are abused in pornography and are coerced into the victim role, and I will not go over their arguments here. Instead, what I want to show is that the person engaged in viewing the world pornographically is abusing himself, as well as women. In doing so, he becomes his own victim.

2

To start with, addiction is a learned behavior. Usually this behavior is learned as a child, and is reinforced and supported by a set of beliefs or ideology which is also learned by the child. The method of instruction is what is commonly called abuse, and this abuse can be sexual, physical or emotional, or any combination of these three.

But to decide precisely what constitutes abuse is problematic. We can say that it is obvious that a father who has intercourse with his seven-year-old, or a mother who whips her infant with a hanger, has abused the child. But this argument is merely tautological and does not answer the defense offered by many abusers: the child wanted it, or the child needed it for its own good. If such arguments seem outrageous, it should be remembered that these same arguments are used by pornographers to defend themselves against the charge of victimizing women. The women in pornography, say the pornographers, choose to be in it, the women make money, perhaps more money than they could in "straight" jobs.

To answer such arguments and to understand what constitutes abuse, we must, I believe, understand how people learn abusive behavior. I will examine this process in detail shortly. What I will argue is that abusive behavior is *not natural*. That is, it does not appear spontaneously without contact or instruction from others. This means, of course, that the person involved with abuse could have been taught other behavior, that there are options which have been denied to that person. And because of the narrowness and one-dimensional quality of the world of abuse, I will

argue that abuse represents a loss of knowledge about oneself and the
world, and, therefore, a loss of freedom.

3

A boy is sitting on the steps with his uncle. It is August, fireflies
sparking in and out of the dark, a few mosquitoes. The night films their
bodies with sweat, they are not talking. The boy is eight. Slowly the
uncle takes the boy's hand, rubs it against his groin. Soon the boy has
grabbed the uncle's penis, is kneading and stroking it through the khaki
pants. The uncle says they should go inside.

What does this boy feel? He scarcely knows himself. Perhaps he
knows he should not talk about what they are doing. Surely he feels
fear: at the size of his uncle's penis, at their mutual silence, at the sense,
vague yet strong, that what they are doing is wrong. The boy does not
protest. He fears his uncle's anger. The boy fears that the uncle will
blame him for what they are doing, will say that the boy made the uncle
do this. The boy fears the uncle will tell his parents, fears the excitement
the act incites in him, his sexual feelings. Since no oe has talked to him
about such feelings, he does not know what they are. And yet he is
drawn to them, to the dream-like quality of doing something he has
never done before, yet knowing, somehow, how to do it. The boy wants
to know what is happening, but fears asking questions. He knows questions are not what his uncle wants. The boy fears the attraction this act
has for him, how it brings his uncle's attention, how it brings caressing,
how it makes him feel that his uncle must love him. The boy feels
important. He fears being caught, going home afterwards, facing his
mother and father, his brother.

Most of all the boy learns this: to love his fears.

4

But there are other lessons in this one act, lessons even more difficult
for the boy to articulate. These lessons have to do with power and what
do with feelings. The uncle has used his power over the boy. This power
consists partly in the uncle's size, his physical superiority over the boy.
In turn, the boy knows the uncle is stronger, could take what he wants
by physical force; even if that threat is never exercised, both the boy
and the uncle know it is there. But more than physical superiority, what
gives the uncle power is knowledge. An adult might repel the uncle's
advances, would know he or she has the right to say stop. The boy does
not know he has this right. He does not know whether others would

believe him if he told them about this act. He does not know what they would do, or whose fault they would say it is. All the boy senses is that he knows less than the uncle, and he looks to the uncle, the adult, to guide him. In turn, the uncle knows the boy will accept his authority on what is right and wrong. The uncle knows the boy will believe his warnings against telling anyone, his threat that the boy will be punished. The uncle exploits the boy's ignorance, the boy's unawareness of choice. The uncle exerts power, control.

There is, in the boy, something that resists this power, this control. This resistance is, in part, the boy's semi-conscious knowledge that what he and the uncle are doing is wrong. Part of this knowledge comes from society, but part, I would posit, does not. We might say there is something in each of us that cries out against an injustice, and we might call the source of this cry the soul or spirit, but we cannot prove the existence of this source. We can only witness or, at times, dig for its cry. What the boy's cry says is that he is being used as an object, a source of energy for the uncle. As such the boy is not valued for anything but his sexuality and his weakness, which allows that sexuality to be exploited. The uncle does not wish to apprehend, to know who the boy is. He does not wish to know how the boy feels, his fears, his rage and sadness at not knowing what is happening, his vague sense that what is happening is wrong. The uncle does not care what effects his actions will have on the boy in the future, nor does he want to acknowledge that the boy is a child, though some part of the uncle, which he represses, knows this. In short the uncle does not truly love the boy. Perhaps later, if confronted, the uncle may maintain he did love the boy, but at the moment the uncle commits the act of abuse, this love is banished, destroyed. The cry of the boy says, "I want to be loved, to be known and cared for, to have my whole being acknowledged. In committing this act you are telling me I am nothing, a tool, that I am not allowed to express my feelings, that I have no feelings."

Once the cry is suppressed, and given the circumstances, it must be, the boy may then take this act for love. Whether verbally or silently, this is what his uncle has told him.

5

In taking the act of abuse for love, for the standard of sexuality, the boy carries this message: sex is the exertion of power by the stronger over the weaker, sex is the denial of feelings, sex is fear and secrecy, sex is shame (shame keeps us from speaking what we know, tells us we are unworthy), sex uses the other as an object, sex is not a means of knowing the other, sex is a devaluing of the self, sex is the maintenance of distance, of control over one's feelings, sex is how I can make others pay attention to me.

How deeply these messages are imprinted depends, in part, on whether or not they are congruent with the boy's family system. A boy from a healthy family system will be able to recover from such abuse, but a boy whose parents have given him the same messages as the uncle will have no other choice. The latter boy lives in a system where the ideology of abuse is the only available way of knowing the world. He grows up thinking power, secrecy, shame, fear, distrust, lack of feelings, and distance are the bases of human relationships.

Is it any wonder, then, that such a boy comes to crave pornography?

6

Although the boy I have described above is a victim of sexual abuse, it should be mentioned that physical and emotional abuse both have similar effects on a child. Also, therapists have argued that there may be "covert" forms of incest. In covert incest, while no sexual act occurs between the child and adult, the relationship between the two carries with it strong sexual overtones. For instance, many addicts of pornography grew up in families where they served as a surrogate husband for their mother and took care of her emotional needs. Such men grow up with an enormous amount of rage at how they became a target of their mother's misdirected rage and sadness, her lack of fulfillment. Pornography functions as an outlet for rage the boy could never express.

7

Of course the development of the child's addiction, its etiology, is never made clear to the child. Most of this remains buried beneath consciousness. Confronted with abuse, the child is confronted with his own powerlessness to stop it. Such powerlessness is terrifying, too terrifying for the child to contemplate. So the child invents an alternative reason for the presence of abuse in his world: he, the child, wanted it. In this way the child attempts to gain control, to stop his terror. After years of living with this alternative reasoning, the child can scarcely remember ever not wanting to experience abuse. All he knows is that he wants it; he cannot explain why. It is simply part of his nature. And his nature is bad.

8

What is the family system like where the seed of abuse grows into addiction? It is one where the abuse is denied. The child knows that if he or she tells about the abuse, no one will believe it. Or the parents will tell the child not to tell anyone else, to forget it ever happened. The feelings the child has concerning the abuse will not be acknowledged. The child will be told, verbally or non-verbally, that feelings are to be repressed.

The rules of such a system do not have to be stated out loud. Facial expression or body posture can tell the child what not to express. Or the child discerns tabooed areas of speech by observing what the family fails to talk about and how the family acts as if what is not talked about does not exist. The silence is a common occurrence in alcoholic families. Since no one admits the existence of alcoholism, no one can express his or her feelings over the damage done by the alcoholic.

9

Because the parents can enforce these zones of silence without verbalization, they can feign surprise when the child confronts them years later in therapy. "We never told you you couldn't express your feelings," say the parents. They refuse to see that by not providing their children with the tools to express those feelings, they were dooming their children to silence almost as effectively as if they had ordered them to be silent. In essence, what they have done is denied their children a right to recognize a part of the self. Their children, like them, live in alienation.

Of course the parents were taught by their parents and were raised in a similar system. And because of the silence, no new knowledge may enter.

10

In abused children, one often finds a troubling self-assurance, an adult-like manner that seems to deny any suffering or turmoil. This act of self-assurance protects the child from what would happen if the child were to feel the terror, rage, sadness and shame of abuse. It is a tool of survival.

As the child grows to adulthood, so much of what has happened, so much of what the child felt while being abused, is banished from consciousness. If the adult talks at all about acts of abuse, the acts are recounted without feeling, with a numbness that leaves each detail dull and grey, devoid of resonance or color. Or perhaps a story is substituted which focuses only on those elements which can portray a picture of happiness, postcards from a childhood the adult wishes had occurred. In such stories, the defeated child identifies with the parents and their official version of the past. (History, as Walter Benjamin has remarked, is the tale of the victors.) There is simply no record of any crime. The victim has disappeared in a conspiracy of silence.

We must admit the possibility of alternative histories.

11

So much of Kafka's world seems uncanny, as if we've dreamed it all before. In this world, the terror is that one will be punished, one does not know when or why. One is punished, and the reasons given do not make sense, or else no reasons at all are given. Afterwards, one knows punishment will come again, yet between the first and second punishment, one has been unable to learn anything to prevent the second punishment. Oftentimes, reading a work such as *The Trial* or *In the Penal Colony* as a political allegory, we probably repress the true horror of what Kafka presents. Sufferings like those K. undergoes are not limited to adults. In fact, for some, much of childhood is exactly like the world of Kafka. To undergo such experiences without the psychic defenses and skills of an adult, that truly is too horrible to contemplate. We know this world intimately and that is its uncanniness. We cannot bear our knowledge.

III. Evil and Ignorance/Knowledge and Intimacy

1

When a child repeats a self-destructive action he or she has learned, we generally do not accept the child's explanation that he or she genuinely desires to commit such an action. But when adults repeat such actions, we often listen to their reasons and may even become convinced that the self-destructive action is something the adult freely chooses. There are, of course, sound reasons for this difference. Children depend upon adults for the requirements of life, and do not have the option of leaving an abusive family system. But what if the only choice the adult knows is self-abuse and addictive behavior?

To adults, abuse seems natural, the only way to live. They lack sufficient knowledge of another way of acting, and this lack of knowledge denies them a choice. Viewed in this way, abuse is the very opposite of freedom. To speak of its victims as free to choose their victimization is a lie.

2

In imposing abuse, the abuser attempts to keep the victim from any knowledge of how to resist the abuse. In this way, abuse represents a closed system; any information which implies the abuse is wrong or which even implies the existence of a world beyond the system must be repressed.

This repression explains why children are so easy to abuse. They learn of the world mainly through adults, and what adults keep from them is nearly impossible for children to know, much less act upon. Moreover, once the system is in place within the child, he or she will automatically filter out or disregard any evidence which contradicts the system. This filtering out includes the child's own feelings.

3

Why does a child feel pain, sadness, rage and anger, rather than joy, at being abused? One explanation is that since abuse seeks to cut off knowledge, to impose a closed system, it is only sensible that our being would revolt against it. More, rather than less, knowledge would increase the chances of our survival as individuals as well as a species.

4

Feelings are a way of knowing the world: they tell us how the world moves beyond our control, beyond whatever boundaries or categories are set up by our intellect. In a sense, then, feelings are prior to language, closer to our animal being. Though they are expressed in language, they are much less erasable than other forms of knowledge and much less dependent upon learning. Abuse may be a learned behavior, but a child's emotional reactions to abuse are not.

This is true despite the fact that the child may quickly learn to suppress or circumvent the expression of these emotions. How, then, are we able to recognize them? To start with, the denial which the abuser forces on the child takes place through language, and the net of language is never without its loopholes, the spaces between the netting. It is through these spaces that alternative messages flow. As post-structuralists like Jacques Lacan have pointed out, the very structure of language is multivalent; each word in a sentence can be read as an endless chord whose composition constantly changes as the speaker or writer continues. Poets have known this for years, and the resonance of poems relies on and implies the inability of language to contain just one meaning, to communicate only the "official" message. In contrast, the parent who wishes to hear from the abused child a message of pure acceptance or obedience, a message with no other meaning, denies this quality of language. Such a parent strives for a control or power which does not exist.

Thus, with a child or the child grown into an adult, a therapist listens to the pain behind the words, behind the official or accepted version of the past, the white-wash of a happy or "normal" childhood. In this listening or reading, the therapist also acknowledges the language of the body, which communicates neither ideas nor facts, but the feeling self.

5

To link sexuality and intimacy is to link sexuality with knowledge, with an opening up of possibility rather than a closing down. In the choice between addictive sexuality and intimate sexuality, one trades a finite set of possibilities against an infinite set of possibilities. Addictive sexuality wishes to deny itself knowledge of the lover, of the lover's emotions, history, human fallible self and the possibilities of that self. Such sexuality views the other only in one dimension, for that is all it believes sexuality can contain. In contrast, intimate sexuality believes that sexuality can contain not only the other, but also one's own emotions, history, fallibilities and possibilities. Such an acknowledgment, though, is extremely frightening. It is an affirmation of all we do not control, a letting go of our defenses. It admits the knowledge of the pain we bear.

IV. The Bookstore

He keeps them in the closet. In piles. In years.
There are some with slick glossy pages, the faces of cheerleaders
or debutantes, his students at the college. Sometimes the
paper is cheaper, the color awry, and the women
have the look of someone who's been used, who's escaped from
Fargo or Farmington, her make-up too thick and pointed, bearing her class.
(He meets her in the saunas on Lake Street, the stage of the Faust.)
Their poses are improbable and promising, no flesh is hidden.
It is late afternoon, sounds of the freeway drift through the room.
His wife is working, she will not see him.
He is tired. He may or may not know he is depressed.
He goes to the closet. He rummages through the piles,
looking for one that will spark him, that will let him go.
Through the hundreds of magazines, not one can satisfy him . . .

He drives through stoplights, his mouth clamped on a joint.
Into a parking lot. Pulls in beside the spray-painted scrawl—
"Porn Hurts Women." Rushing past, he enters
a room with peeling green paint cracks, fluorescent lights,
cracked linoleum tiles, rubbed deep with dirt. Plywood racks
of *Oui, Playboy, Penthouse, Swedish Erotica, The Angel Series,*
anonymous issues of leather and bondage. He does not look
at the clerk, a young boy with bowl-cut hair and pimples, a dragon
tattoo exposed by his sleeveless t-shirt. Picking up the magazines
wrapped in plastic, the man tries to guess by the covers
what lies inside. Never quite sure, stoned, he takes

nearly an hour to make his choice. He takes one up to the counter.
   Then brings it back. It isn't right.
He asks for quarters. Heads back to the video booths.

The booths are painted black, also made of plywood.
On each door is a display with stills from the movies inside.
He goes from door to door, eyeing each one, trying
not to look at the gays, who lean in the corners, key chains
clinking, a cigarette or toothpick dangling from their mouths.
He is looking for the perfect film, the blonde that will stun
him with her moans, the whimpering that sets off a trembling inside him,
released by a cock of monstrous proportions, which dwarfs
his own with envy, with the certainty that only here,
here in this booth, its damp sticky floor, its private dark,
can he possess this image, let it consume his life.
He unzips his pants and slips in the quarter.
The reel rolls, music and moaning, ending abruptly.
Five minutes. Another quarter. Five minutes. Another quarter.
Again, again, from booth to booth, the hour slips by.
He does not want to come. He wants to hold it, the tension,
as long as he can. He leaves the store with three magazines
which he cannot help but begin unwrapping in the car.
He stops himself. He knows he needs to nurse their charge.
One time through and he will need another. He drives home
with one hand on himself.

                              Up in his bedroom, he undresses, spreads
the magazines on the bed, lies beside them.
He studies each image, noting each position, the expression
on each face. He reads the captions, how the women tell
the men how they want it, how they can't get enough.
He is still trying hard not to come.

                              An hour later
he hears his wife drive up. He picks up the magazines,
his pants, runs to the washroom, worried she will find
him, angered by her arrival, disrupting his peace.
He will rush his orgasm. He will not feel satisfied.
He will feel the hours he has wasted, the shame emerging.
He will say he needs to take a shower.
The magazines are in the bathroom. Already

they are not enough.

V. Economics and Pornography

1

In contemporary capitalism, pornography has become primarily visual rather than written. There is a distressing inevitability about this fact. As Susan Sontag has pointed out in *On Photography*:

> A capitalist society requires a culture based on images. It needs to furnish vast amounts of entertainment in order to stimulate and anesthetize the injuries of class, race and sex. And it needs to gather unlimited amounts of information, the better to exploit natural resources, increase productivity, keep order, make war, give jobs to bureaucrats. The camera's twin capacities to subjectivize reality and to objectify it ideally serve these needs and strengthen them.

Pornography effectively combines both the objective and subjective elements exploited by the camera. Clearly pornography involves the objectification of other people, since it limits their humanity to their use to the observer: they are, for that person, simply tools of sexual gratification.

Moreover, in the need for more and more images, all drained of emotional depth or a sense of personal history, the endless consumption of pornographic images derives from the mistaken assumption that one can feed a spiritual hunger through a desire for control, distance, and eventual destruction. Such a desire is not a desire of the flesh. As so many have pointed out, pornography is not primarily a sensual experience. Instead, the consumption of pornography is, in its profoundest sense, an intellectual and emotional perception which is based on repression and false premises. Since one's spiritual hunger can never be satisfied by such means, the addict can either keep consuming pornography in greater amounts, hoping that somehow quantity will change its quality, or else he can give up pornography and seek a different sustenance.

How can one complain of salt when there is this vast sea to drink? The anesthetizing qualities of pornography make it conveniently efficient in blinding one both to "the injuries of class, race, and sex" and to the injuries one is inflicting on oneself. As long as the addict receives his drugs, he is not likely to ask society to change.

2

In *On Photography* Sontag argues that what this endless consumption of images ultimately does is restrict our freedom: "The production of images also furnishes a ruling ideology. Social change is replaced by a change in images. The freedom to consume a plurality of images and goods is equated with freedom itself. The narrowing of free political choice to free economic consumption requires the unlimited production and consumption of images." Sontag's point here illuminates how fuzzy the debate on pornography and censorship often is. People from the ACLU ignore the fact that freedom, as defined by our society, is not actually freedom at all. Or, to put it another way, we are provided an unlimited freedom to consume images, but it is that very freedom and the overabundance it provides that denies us the freedom to choose what would ultimately nourish us: the freedom to stop consuming images. To argue that one can simply not look is to deny that one lives in a society where everyone is looking; the norms of the society constantly fight against our choice not to look. The energy required to overcome those norms constitutes our invisible bars.

One begins to see why the debates on pornography are so intense, and why, in such debates, proponents of pornography often seem to be wearing blinders. For the analysis of the harm of pornography points to the harm of our endless consumption of images. This consumption both tells us what to desire and who we are, and, in the same process, denies our spiritual and emotional needs. Pornography is just one extreme of capitalist consumption and the production of false desires. To follow this argument to its logical conclusion: not only does the harm of pornography put into question our notions of sexuality, it also questions the way our whole economy works. You cannot lop off pornography as a mere aberration. Pornography is instead the ultimate example of capitalism. No wonder people want to ignore the whole issue, no wonder they continue to assert that pornography does not create or inspire sexual desires but merely fulfills them. No wonder they argue that any sexual pathology or compulsion must be looked at separately from the images that feed such pathologies or compulsions. More than pornography is at stake here. It is the whole fabric of our society, the very structures of our lives.

3

There are those who assert that the proliferation of pornography in contemporary society does nothing to spur on the demand for pornogra-

phy or the addict's addiction to it. But such people refuse to acknowledge the symbiotic relationship between society and the individuals who
make up society. To say that suddenly more people wanted pornography
and that is why it is so abundant, begs the question. In order to answer
the question of why more people want pornography, one must inevitably
seek connections between pornography and the rest of society. Sontag's
view that capitalism relies on a consumption of images provides one
basis for examining why there has been an increase in the consumption
of pornography.

On a more mundane level, attributing pornography's growth to demand by individuals ignores what we know by experience: if one walks
down the street and sees ten images of women as sexual objects, one
may certainly be able to reject these images; yet it is also true that one
will have to expend a greater amount of energy rejecting these images
than if one saw only five or two or none at all. Assuming that human
beings have only a limited amount of energy, it is obvious that the more
images there are, the harder it will be for the individual to resist them;
one must, after all, expend energy on other activities too. The point at
which any one person forgoes his resistance to pornographic images or
images of objectification may vary, but there is, within each person,
such a limit. The greater the frequency of such images, the greater the
likelihood that they will overwhelm people's resistance. This fact is
known, of course, by all those involved in advertising and the media,
and is readily accepted by most consumers—except when it comes to
pornography.

4

Often, inside the addict is a boy who did not learn the word pleasure.
It lay like a stone on his tongue, hard, without taste, impossible to
swallow. He was told by his father, work till evening, till the sun disappears and you pull the blinds, till the silence invades you, the silence
which says the others have quit, have gone off to another life, are sleeping like animals, without conscience or law, without knowledge of the
work to be done. And there will always be work to be done.

When sex entered the boy's life there was no word of pleasure to name
it. It was sin, it was work. It was what kept him awake, deep into
darkness, when the others were asleep. It was the secret that kept him
ahead, outracing time. It knew no diversions, no wondering or wander-
ing, no waywardness or waiting. It was a weight to be lifted, a grimness
endured, a shield from the day, from the talk of others, their jokes, their
meals, their music, their mundane lies. It used anxiety as fuel, a fuel

always there and so to be trusted. It marked and measured, it drew from anger, it counted and counted. The list grew longer, it would never end, the tasks would keep coming. At last, when he was exhausted it let him sleep.

I do not know what he would have done had he known the word pleasure. It was where feeling might have flowed. It was kept a secret. It was kept for last.

VI. The End of Addiction

1

Why is it so difficult for the addict to give up his addiction to pornography? Why is the pull of pornography so powerful? Doesn't this indicate there is, in men's attraction to pornography, some natural urge?

The idea of what is "natural" has been debunked so often, one tires of going after it again (see, for instance, Roland Barthes' *Mythologies*). Except when the term enters debates among Marxists, "natural" is invariably used to preclude any investigation of whether or not people in other societies or in other times may have behaved differently. In addition, it discourages any examination of whether or not a certain behavior is learned. In such instances "natural" is not a step-by-step reasoned argument, it is an ideology. It is used to justify whatever is customary in a given society, to blind critical discourse.

In this particular case, the argument that pornography is "natural" ignores the fact that there are men who have given up their obsession with pornography and who have not died. Though these men may suffer withdrawal symptoms similar to those undergone by an alcoholic or drug addict, we have only begun to examine what is on the other side of this withdrawal. The mere evidence of such recovery combats the argument that pornography is "natural."

Throughout history there have been countless human activities, both just and unjust, which at one time were thought to be natural and which eventually disappeared. Or, if they have not disappeared, have come to be recognized as changeable rather than inevitable (the physical abuse of children, for example). Given the mutability of human culture and society, calling something "natural" is a buzz word: a command is being given not to think.

2

Even if men's desire for pornography is natural (i.e., genetically determined), this does not mean we must recognize it as good or inevitable.

We do not turn to the diabetic and say, there is nothing you can do, you must enjoy your disease.

3

When the addict commits an act of abuse, when he is sexual with a child or with a prostitute or a student or an employee, when he has sex with his wife while fantasizing of another woman, the addict believes that using another person as an object will relieve his unhappiness. And for a second that unhappiness is numbed and forgotten, and a rush of excitement does occur. But afterwards the unhappiness returns, the drug has worn off. And the addict becomes angry at the person he has used because that person has not done what he thinks that person should do — take away his unhappiness. He carries that anger to the next act of abuse, to the next person he abuses.

In this process some of the anger spills over to the addict himself and increases his self-hatred. But this anger is quickly repressed because the addict cannot bear the thought that he, and not the person he abuses, is responsible for his unhappiness. The result of this repression is deadness, numbness, depression. The cycle is fueled to start again.

4

Often, the last people the addict looks towards to express his anger are those who taught him this abuse (frequently, his parents). Of course the adult addict must be held responsible for what he does, for his acts of abuse and the hurt they cause. And part of his anger towards himself is justified; he is responsible for his actions. But in another sense, the addict is out of control, is controlled by a process and by laws which were written inside him as a child and which he has had no power to resist.

Only when the addict acknowledges this writing and the abuse that caused it, can he begin to redistribute within his consciousness the anger he feels. In this process he also learns to express his sadness at his child-hood victimization and all the loneliness and pain his addiction has caused. This redistribution of anger to its rightful sources is a delicate operation. At its initial stages it may be better for the addict to express his anger at the expense of acknowledging his own responsibility. The parental taboos against such expression are too well instituted to be dislodged in any other way. But eventually the addict must realize how abusive his expression of anger has been, that no one else but him is responsible for his own unhappiness.

When such a realization comes, the feelings of remorse and shame are shattering; the addict's facade of self-worth crumbles. What is revealed is a scared child, afraid he will be punished and banished for all he has done wrong, afraid he is unworthy of ever being forgiven or even granted the right of human contact (the addict is grandiose, even in his self-chastizing). At first, such feelings can be borne only briefly and are then repressed. Gradually, though, the addict learns to accept responsibility without denying the worth of his self. In this learning, a separation is made between the actions one commits and one's soul. Obviously this process, at least on earth, can never be completed. The addict's history has written itself upon him and cannot be erased. The addict cannot unlearn his compulsions; he merely learns new forms of behavior to cope with the compulsions. The ghosts and words of the past remain.

VII. Coda: Spirituality

1

Is the vertigo of the addict, that rush or high, merely a false substitute for the letting go of the self that comes with the spiritual? At the center of the addict lives the fear and knowledge that the self he presents to the world, the social self, is a lie: the addict wishes to destroy that self, yet fears that when that self is destroyed there will be nothing left. Similarly, at the center of spirituality there also lives the knowledge that the social self, the world of societal values, is a lie. But in the realm of the spiritual, to give up this social self does not leave one empty forever: into that void comes the calm of a greater knowledge. That greater knowledge creates rather than destroys.

2

Initially each addict was victim, was degraded by an act of abuse. This abuse was a message: it told the addict to devalue those things within himself which would protest the abuse—his will to resist, his feelings which told him the act was wrong, his soul. That this abuse was not recognized by the abuser or those around the victim, meant that the world for the child was divided in two: in one world the abuse existed and was not talked about; in the other the abuse did not exist and was not talked about. The latter was the world the addict as a child experienced in public, in society; the former is the addict's secret world, the world of shame. Only in the public world could the child-victim have told about the abuse without further abuse. But the child had no guarantee of this, was told instead that telling would bring further abuse.

If only the child could have escaped. But he could not. The world of his abuse was the world of his family. Its reality mocked the world's strictures against abuse. The child's inability to pull away from the world of abuse was not merely caused by the presence of physical force or the ignorance of choice; he could not defend himself because he could not name the abuse, could not place it in language. It remained an unacknowledged reality. Thus, as the child grew up and began compulsively to abuse himself, perhaps he found that glorifying his acting out was a mark of freedom. It brought things out in the open, combatted repression (thus, the philosophy of *Playboy* and "free love"). But the child, and the adult as an addict, do not see that what will end the craving for language to identify the abuse cannot be found in any description which glorifies the abuse, which does not name it correctly. Only a description of the abuse which names the harm it does, both to the abuser and the victim, can do this. This description must recognize abuse is an act of degradation, of devaluation, an act where power is used to steal from another what can only be given freely. Such a description tells the victim his true value. It acknowledges his soul.

3

What is the soul? The soul is what recognizes that we are being degraded in an act of abuse. It is the sum of what cries out in us. It includes our feelings and our conscious knowledge, and it is more than that. It cannot be pinned down or defined in any ultimate sense through language. It includes speech and it includes silence. It remembers the past, it admits the future. It keeps the pain we try to repress. It is the goodness inside us that resists evil.

Incest Pornography and the Problem of Fantasy [1]

by

JEFFREY MASSON

In 1970, while teaching Sanskrit at the University of Toronto, I began training to become a psychoanalyst. I had no particular awareness about violence against women at that time, but I was troubled by what I perceived to be a tendency on the part of psychoanalysts to discount or trivialize the effects of real traumas (for example, beatings and sexual abuse) or to regard the reality of what took place as insignificant next to what appeared to be going on in the patient's psyche.

I grew gradually to dislike most psychoanalysts, but my respect—even awe—for Freud remained high. In 1980 I was made projects director of the Sigmund Freud Archives and given privileged access to Freud's private papers. In time I began to question my respect for Freud, not as a thinker of genius, but as a person. I uncovered evidence that Freud had, after stumbling upon and recognizing the massive reality of the sexual abuse of children, engaged in a cover-up motivated by professional convenience and a loss of moral courage. When I began to present this evidence to colleagues I naively expected to be judged on the intellectual legitimacy of my scholarship and the historical evidence. Instead I was personally attacked for "betraying" Freud and psychoanalysis. The evidence was engaged only by feminists who had long known and written about men's massive denial of the reality of violence against women. I realized more clearly that psychoanalysis and psychiatry were very much part of the problem. To give but one salient example: A psychiatry text still in use in 1975 proclaimed that one girl in a million was likely to be the victim of incest. The truth is closer to one in four. Psychiatrists—the men most entrusted with the task of understanding and healing psychic suffering—were clearly out of touch with reality and wished to remain so.

I began to read more and more feminist literature and gained a deeper understanding of the violence against women and came to see pornography, with its degrading and mean-spirited view of women, as part of the problem. Incest pornography deserves our scrutiny as an egregious manifestation of wider sexism.

In any store that sells pornography, a section is reserved for short paperback books on themes of incest. There are literally hundreds of such books. I bought and read five of them. They are:

> Alice Briggs. *Daddy's Little Mouth Girl.* Hollywood, Calif.: Publisher's Consultants (American Art Enterprises), 1976; fourth printing, 1988.

> David Crane. *Hot Dogs for Daughter.* Los Angeles: Oakmore Enterprises, 1986.

> L. Kullinger. *Incest: The Secret Passion.* Hollywood, Calif.: Barclay House (American Art Enterprises), 1973; fourth printing, 1988.

> Cynthia Marshall. *Sex as a Family Affair.* Hollywood, Calif.: Barclay House, 1972; fourth printing, 1988.

> Lydia Wilkinson. *Slaves to Incest.* Hollywood, Calif.: Barclay House, 1975; second printing, 1988.

There can be no question of the purpose of these books: sexual arousal. There is also little question to whom these books are addressed: men.[2] There can be little doubt that these books, most of which are presented as "real," are entirely invented. They are not, as they claim, taken from psychiatric testimony or from a tape recorder. I also do not doubt that the "authors" are not the names given on the covers (some of whom are women). I believe that the books were all written by men, hack writers who use a formula over and over again, one designed to arouse the reader without really engaging his imagination. Like pornographic films, there are minimal plots, no characterization, and very elaborate descriptions of vaginal, oral, and anal intercourse, using the same obscene words over and over.

But when I say the books are addressed to men, the further question can be asked: What kind of men? The publishers would no doubt answer: men who enjoy the *fantasy* of incest. The very unreality of the case histories will be used to buttress this argument: "Nobody," the argument would run, "could mistake these inventions for real case histories." But this is not what the authors say. Thus Cynthia Marshall (should she exist) said in *Sex as a Family Affair:* "This study is a compilation of five case histories taken verbatim from people who had incestuous relationships." In other words, the reader is encouraged to believe that these are "real" cases, not inventions.

Then she explains why she has written the book: "This book has been written in the hope that its contents may lead the reader to a broader understanding of human nature and people's sex drives. The writer has set out to discover the rationale behind the overt act of incestuous intercourse and, in so doing, hopefully to contribute significantly to society as a whole."

Both statements about the cases being "verbatim" and the reason she wrote the book are proven false immediately. The first case history in this book is called "Wandella's Father" (for some reason, many of the girls in these books are called variants of "Wanda"), and is supposedly given in the words of Wandella herself. It begins: "I wanted to be my father's wife more than anything else in the world! Ever since I could remember, I always pictured him and me in bed . . . fuckin'." Of course, she achieves her objective:

> Leroy [her father] was almost as gone as I was. He was mutterin' and groanin' like he was in another world. "Shit, oh shit! Fuck it all to hell. Christ, it's good . . . oh, my God, it's good!" He was somewhere up my pussy—all of him—almost drownin' in the pleasure of it all. And I was a part of him, a real part of him, attached to him by his prick. I felt like I was never gonna want to leave him go again. All I wanted was to stay right where I was for the rest of my fuckin' life, hooked onto him by his beautiful prick, danglin' there on the edge of the world . . . fuckin' forever.

Nowhere, in any genuine account I have ever read of incest, is there any such language used. The "account" is interrupted periodically by the author. At one point (page 43), for example, she writes: "Wandella was the aggressor, the seducer. She waited until her father was somewhat over his initial grief [at the death of his wife] and then she set her incestuous plan into action, gaining the results she had hoped for. Her father was no match for Wandella, especially since he was in a bereaved and weakened emotional condition."

What is this, if not the age-old "fantasy" that the child seduces the adult, and where else does this derive except from the imagination of the adult who is burdened with a guilt he will not accept? Of course I am using the words "fantasy" and "imagination" as synonyms of "lies," which is what they are. The entire narrative is "positive," that is, Wandella expresses nothing but pleasure and happiness. She ends by telling her father:

"I love you, Leroy. Ma gave you to me, and now you're really mine—and I'm really yours. Finally!" You see, I really am Leroy's wife, now . . . and to prove it, I got his baby inside me. You can't take that away from me! And you can't really take Leroy away from me, either. You may separate us, but I've lived with him as his wife for enough years now that no one can take him away from me. He's inside me . . . in more ways than one!

But the author ends on a darker note, presumably to show the hypocrisy of society:

Wandella's case was not that unique, but her "marriage" was short-lived; she and Leroy were separated by law. Since Wandella was underage when she gave birth to her child, the authorities had her put it up for adoption. Since they lived in a state where incest was a felony, Leroy was sent to prison, where he died only a few years later. Wandella is still under psychiatric care.

Clearly the author "believes" (I use the word in quotation marks, since it is not clear that these "authors" believe anything at all) that what is harmful in incest is the response of society, as if to say that had Wandella and Leroy lived somewhere where it was acceptable, they would have lived happily into old age.

In another "case history" in the volume, a twelve-year-old girl, like Wandella, seduces her father: "The more I turned him on, the better a chance I'd have of getting a fucking out of him, and that was what I wanted more than anything else in the whole world right at that moment."

"Trudie" achieves her goal and says: "Fuck it, could my old man fuck! His cock was like a telephone pole up inside my juicy twat and I was creaming all over the place. . . . Then I started hollering at him 'cause I was coming so fucking hard: 'Do it, you mother-fucking bastard! Do it! Fuck the living hell outta me, you cocksucking, motherfucking son of a bitch!'"

She then explains:

Well, after that first day of fucking with the old man, whenever he came home from a day's prowling or working—or from the cooler —the first thing he would do was to haul me off to his bedroom and fuck me good. And I always looked forward to it. He was a good fucker. But what the fuck was I supposed to do when he wasn't around at home nowhere? I mean, when I need a cock up the old twat—*somebody's*—*anybody's?*

Clearly this is an alien, male voice (the pornographer's) indulging in one more violent cliché about women, that they are insatiable. But lest anybody think this is meant to be enjoyed, or to titillate, the author ends (page 163) with this moral: "Unless the members of the family are taught that incest is morally wrong and illegal, they will surely continue their sexual pattern as they grow into maturity and make their own families." Is this the means the publishers find of protecting themselves against obscenity, by claiming that their writing is a warning of the dangers of incest?

In *Incest: The Secret Passion*, sadism and anal sex are presented as playful and harmless:

> "How many cocks have been up you?"
> "Oh my god, Dad, you're hurting me!"
> "You lying cunt," he squeezed my cunt lips.
> "How the hell many," he asked.
> "Only two, just two times!" He slipped four fingers up my cunt and began stirring up the warm juices. I moaned. . . . Now he had my buttocks in both of his hands. I saw him place his thumbs beside the cheeks of my ass, then pull them open. . . . "I am now going to give you something that you'll never forget, even if you get fucked by a thousand studs. I'm going to fuck you like you ain't never been fucked before! When I get through with you, you won't be able to say *fuck* for a month. You are a cunt right up to your eye-balls, that's what you are! . . ." He stayed buried up my asshole. Nine inches of cock, like having an arm up my butt, were inside me. I felt the top of it displacing the inner organs of my body. Everything hurt. My sphincter muscles were benumbed. I was bleeding and raw inside.

But this, contrary to the description, produces nothing but ecstasy: "My arousal was beyond all belief." Once again, it is a male "fantasy" that violent anal intercourse of this kind is enjoyable, and harmless, even when the evidence is unmistakably present that it is dangerous and disabling.

In the same book, a case of mother-son incest is related. It begins:

> Eliot's arching cock pounded a hole in the smooth and cool satin sheet. . . . He felt the warm and sticky liquid oozing out of his mother's gaping opening, dribbling stickily and randomly across his still-smooth peach-fuzzed chin. . . . Her pudgy, bejeweled hand slid down the massive body. They traveled quickly, gently, forgetting to notice that fifty-odd pounds of excess, and spread the lips of her fleshy, cleanshaven cunt open wider for the attentive youth. . . .

"Feel all my love juices pouring out of my cunt . . . my hole, my cave, . . . my pussy! It's just for you, baby . . . just for you!"

The fathers in all these books are always perfect physical specimens; the mothers, by contrast, are repulsive to all but their sons. Once again, we are told this is a genuine case history: "The foregoing has been reconstructed from a psychiatrist's tapes regarding Eliot. What follows are Eliot's exact words describing the playing out of this incestuous relationship." What follows then are essentially identical descriptions of the ecstasy of Eliot. Like the other case histories, it ends (page 128) badly: "The mailman, mouth agape, forgot to ring twice. As a matter of fact, he didn't ring once until it was to the authorities downtown." The moral: You will be reported for indulging in a natural, instinctual, harmless activity.

In the book *Slaves to Incest*, by "Lydia Wilkinson" (so that men reading the book can say, "Well, this is not a man's point of view, it was written by a woman"—in fact I am quite certain the author is a man), we again see a twelve-year-old girl begging her father for sex (the main point of all these stories):

> I could feel his body next to mine, and it got me all hot. Daddy was going to fuck me! Daddy, my very own father, he himself was going to take my cherry! The thought of it thrilled me more than anything I've ever known—then or since . . . this was my birthday present. The most wonderful present anyone had ever received. And it made me wonder if all fathers fucked their daughters. At least, it should be a rule that only a father could take a daughter's cherry—only a father could be gentle and loving enough to do it right, to wait with his own passions that he didn't hurt a young girl or frighten her.

The father is equally philosophical: "'I'm fucking my little girl, oh my god! Thank You for this holy privilege of fucking my little girl. . . .' Somehow the words he was saying really turned me on and I began to join him. 'Daddy! Daddy!' I cried. 'Fuck Emily; fuck me real good. I want Daddy to come inside of me, to fill me up with all his wonderful come so I can make Daddy happy.'"

What does the author say of this "case history"? "The most obvious factor in this case history is, of course, that Emily is completely insane. Whether this insanity is a result of her incestuous affair with her father has not yet been fully determined by the doctors handling her case" (page 33). Why is Emily insane, when, according to the logic of the story, the book—indeed, all these books—such daughters and fathers are the only sane people there are?

The case ends (page 56) with the following comment: "It is with deep regret that we are forced to report that the doctors in charge of her case have marked her off as helpless, beyond even the point where she might possibly be helped by electroshock treatment." Why this commentary? Because of the wide publicity given to the damage created by incest, the author or publishers felt that they could best be protected by adding this warning note. But the whole point of this story, as well as every other one I read, is to glorify incest.

The two other books are presented as fiction. *Hot Dogs for Daughter* is about a family in which the mother and son have sex with each other and a pack of dogs in a tent ("'Wanna watch me fuck a dog?'—'Ooooh —yeah' he gasped") while the daughter and father do the same in the forest ("'You gonna beat me with that, Daddy?' Debby asked timidly, fluttering her eyelashes and looking as innocent and demure as a girl possibly could when she had doggy jism all over her mouth and chin").

The last book, *Daddy's Little Mouth Girl*, also ends with the obligatory insanity, when the police confront the father: "But Wanda saved the day. 'No, daddy and I have sex,' she said as her mind began unhinging. 'He calls me daddy's little mouth girl.' The officers looked at her vaguely. 'She needs help,' one of them said. 'I don't need help,' Wanda giggled, 'I need to get laid.'

For books that purport to be from different, real people, the language is identical, the plots are similar, the positions, the point of view, and so forth are all the same. That is because there is, of course, nothing real about any of these books in terms of the material they write about. To read any genuine book about incest (for example, Florence Rush's *The Best Kept Secret* or Diana Russell's *The Secret Trauma*) or accounts of genuine survivors (for example, Louise Armstrong's *Kiss Daddy Goodnight*) is to enter a totally different world, where the sorrow, the sense of betrayal, the pain and confusion are palpable. In the pornography books, oral intercourse is a mild, pleasant activity for the child. But here is an account by a survivor of her first body-memory of such an event:

> Spasms pass through me, powerful, involuntary—my pelvis contracts leaving my legs limp. My shoulders scrunch up to my ears, my arms press against my sides with the wrists flung out like chicken wings, my head bends back so far I fear my neck will snap, my jaws open wider than possible and I start to gag and sob, unable to close my mouth—lockjaw in reverse. These spasms do not feel random. They are the convulsions of a child being raped through the mouth. [3]

Let me quote from a letter I received from a victim of incest:

> I have been preoccupied with understanding the act of sexual assault on children for thirty-five years, since the moment I was my-

self assaulted. I liken this experience to being dropped (at five years old) from an airplane over the middle of the Pacific; whereupon I spent thirty years of my life swimming from one piece of debris to another, alone and vulnerable to attack. All the while I kept myself alive mentally by sheer determination to discover how this could have happened. . . . I recall my attacks vividly. My father had divorced and remarried, taking custody of me. My new stepmother's father came to visit and proceeded to attack me, twice. He would wait until I was asleep and then I would be awakened by a hand clamped over my mouth . . . and then he proceeded. The violation was as if an atomic bomb had gone off in my head. All I could think about was trying to ascertain whether or not I was dead or alive. I was actually fighting death face to face. I have no trouble understanding how some children actually die during such an attack. . . .

Compare this account with the lies told in incest pornography. The contrast is both startling and chilling. But, someone might argue, if these so-called case histories from pornography are mere fantasy, where's the harm? There is a confusion at play here. The novelized accounts of incest are fantasy, but the promotion of lies about women and incest, the propaganda, is no fantasy, but a form of action that serves to justify incest and insensitivity to survivors of incest. And, of course, incest itself is not fantasy. All the fallacies held by the public at large about incest are given legitimacy by these accounts:

1. Incest is harmless.
2. Incest is instigated by daughters, fathers simply respond; that is, daughters seduce their fathers.
3. Daughters who are willing victims are insane.[4]
4. Coercion plays no role in incest.
5. Any physical harm is so temporary that it is like a fantasy.
6. Fathers have incest with their daughters out of love.
7. Incest is a natural act.

These fallacies/fantasies (lies) have a distinguished lineage. For when Freud decided that the accounts of incest (which he first believed) were in fact nothing but the overheated fantasies of adolescent girls, he shifted the onus of responsibility from adults to children. Incest then became a question of wishes, fantasies, and impulses on the part of children toward their parent, not *acts* engaged in by adults.

These considerations allow us some insight into the all-important question of whether these books are read by men as fantasies and are confined to fantasies, or whether they act as legitimators of action. Clearly there is at least one action that the books are meant to initiate, and that is masturbation. In this they function exactly like a *Penthouse* centerfold. No, not exactly, because the centerfold does not have a context. These books do. The message is extremely clear: Twelve-year-old girls constantly think about fucking their fathers. They desire it and benefit from it (leaving aside for the moment the contradictions in its mysterious link to insanity). Men do *not* read these so-called case histories and think: "These are made-up fantasies, fun to think about, but corresponding to nothing in the real world." Why, then, should they confine themselves to "fantasizing" about an act that they are clearly told is real, harmless, and in fact beneficial? These books are part of a pro-incest lobby, a way of justifying and legitimating an activity that is engaged in. I cannot agree with the argument that a person who had not engaged in some form of molestation would not be "harmed" by reading these books. For one thing it seems to me far more likely that among the men who read these books are child molesters who are searching for evidence that they have done nothing wrong, that they have merely done the right thing in a hypocritical world.[5] These books would certainly act to assuage their conscience. And I have no doubt that the child molester will believe in the genuineness of the case material presented in these books. But these books also harm in a more general way by presenting the public with a deeply false picture of the world of incest, which may well have a slow and subtle desensitizing effect. Moreover, it would be naive to believe that men interested in incest are concerned only with fantasy. The fantasy theory is reserved for a defence: When accused, these men can say that it's all in the girl's head, a fantasy, as Freud demonstrated eighty years ago.

Do my arguments lead to the conclusion that we should censor such books? I am not sure about the best way to tackle the underlying problem, but I am completely convinced that it is a problem of serious dimensions, and one that has ramifications and repercussions far beyond the question of a few magazines and book shops. The numbers, as I indicated above, are not large (though, in fact, nobody knows how many of these books are sold, and the numbers may well be much higher than the information I was given). But far more serious is the fact that we are talking about people's real lives. We are talking about one in four women who before the age of eighteen have been victims of unwanted sexual assault. We are talking, then, about an enormous number of men who abuse children, especially girls, sexually. These men may not read or need for validation the incest pornography I have reviewed in this article, but they certainly subscribe to the same set of beliefs that are found in those publications. Unpleasant as it is, reading incest pornography allows us some insight into the kinds of rationalizations in which child molesters engage.[6]

The most hopeful sign to me for dealing with this very real problem at a practical level is the civil-rights ordinance by Catharine MacKinnon and Andrea Dworkin, which I fully support.[7] They define pornography as "the graphic, sexually explicit subordination of women whether in pictures or in words" and correctly see this as a violation of women's civil rights, for which they ought, legally and logically speaking, to be able to seek redress. The concern is with the victim, which means all women who suffer from the images and ideas purveyed in pornography. Which means all women. I am dismayed that so many men interested in issues of civil liberties have taken issue with this proposal, in an effort to defend the rights of pornographers, claiming that the pornographers will become the victims if this proposal is put into law. But as Dworkin has forcefully argued in her "Against the Male Flood: Censorship, Pornography and Equality," pornographers "are the instruments of terror, not its victims. . . . What pornographers do to women is more like what police do to political prisoners than it is like anything else: except for the fact that it is watched with so much pleasure by so many."[8] Equally hopeful is the quality of writing by women on these issues. Diana Russell, Gloria Steinem, Susan Griffin, Catharine MacKinnon, Andrea Dworkin, have all written profoundly engaging works that have made a large number of people aware of the deeper issues involved. We are at last becoming aware of the problem that lies behind pornography in a way that has not been true until the last few years.[9]

On the negative side, I am concerned at the public response to the Meese Commission's report on pornography.[10] The report, which I obtained only with great difficulty, was filled with excellent and authentic reports. It was lambasted everywhere. The public never had access to it, since no publisher would issue it in an accessible form, whereas the earlier presidential commission (the *Report of the Commission on Obscenity and Pornography*) published by the U.S. Government Printing Office in 1970, which did *not* condemn pornography, was immediately snapped up by a commercial press and became a best seller, available in every drugstore. And while the 1986 Meese report was almost completely unavailable, a completely silly and harmful book published by a propornography lobby was offered for a small price at every newsstand.[11]

Some months ago somebody sent me a copy of *Penthouse* magazine, which published a "sexy" photograph in which Asian women, evidently dead or dying, were hanging from trees. Every woman I know and even quite a number of men who saw this found it repugnant. It sent a chill down my spine: Is this the world that pornography has made, where men take sexual pleasure in seeing a woman close to death? I was deeply ashamed for my sex when my thirteen-year-old daughter saw it and looked at me, puzzled. What explanation could I give her? Well, at least I could quote to her the extraordinarily moving words by Andrea Dworkin on this same photograph, in her testimony to the Meese Commission, where she tells them: "I am asking you as individuals to have the courage, because I think it's what you will need, to actually be willing yourselves to go and cut that woman down and untie her hands and take the gag out of her mouth, and to do something for her freedom." Men would do well to heed Dworkin's eloquent exhortation.

Pornography is not about fantasy. At best, it is the dim echo of what was originally an act, and an act directed against the body of another person. Incest and rape and wife-battering are real activities, not fantasies. Pornography is an integral part of that world. Many feminists influenced by psychoanalysis have tried to argue that fantasy is harmless, since it is merely the symbol of desire. But let us be clear: Pornography may well be an expression of desire, but the desire is to subordinate and do harm to another person. Pornography is of a piece: To the extent that it harms the child (incest pornography) it also harms the adult woman, which means that ultimately we are all, men and women alike, harmed in our deepest humanity. The insult of pornography cannot be confined, for it touches us all. It is time that men stood up to insult and demanded an end.

The Antidialectic of Pornography

by

JOEL KOVEL

A Visit to a Porn Parlor

Dostoevsky held that the character of a civilization could be determined by a look at its prisons. We could say the same for sex shops. For the sex shop is a kind of prison, albeit of desire. Its topography both manifests and reinforces this fact: three rows of cubicles, like so many stalls in a public bathroom, or cells of solitary confinement. At the end of each row is a poster announcing fifteen or so video programs, thereby providing as many as forty-five options for the sufficiently zealous and patient man. Each cubicle is furnished with a chair, a Panasonic twelve-inch video monitor, a slot for tokens, an electronic display announcing the number of quarters deposited and the time remaining, a button to change from one show to another, and a waste receptacle for wet tissues. A quarter entitles the spectator to ninety seconds of an unrestricted view of genitals, mouth, and anus in more or less nonstop motion. The machine accepts ninety-nine of these metal tickets to paradise. Thus for a mere $24.75 a man can stay in his cell for almost two and a half hours. The sex machine consumes wealth, then, at roughly the same rate as the average worker gains it.

Penal servitude is exceedingly onerous. No matter how "humane" the prison, to lose freedom of movement is a ghastly punishment. In jail, desire points outward, beyond prison walls, while the violence of the State holds the prison in. In the porn parlor, on the other hand, the compulsion to stay is internal. Desire holds the spectator like a fly to flypaper, as he passively beholds the machinery of sex, piston into cylinder, the locomotive that goes nowhere. The writing bodies are as fixed

Presented at the 1987 symposium "Psychoanalysis/Pornography/Representation," sponsored by the Center for the Psychological Study of the Arts, State University of New York at Buffalo, and reprinted by permission of the author.

as the frieze above the Parthenon. The more they move, the less they move, while dissociated motion is reproduced between the spectator and his desire: he remaining fixed, while desire pulls and tugs, translocating the self from its moorings. There is nothing to be done in the chamber but look and/or masturbate, thus nowhere to go but back, to the image of prick into cunt; and this leads desire onward again. It is exhausting, like a day spent stopping and starting before the paintings of a museum. I do not want to foreclose the debate concerning the degree to which pornography induces men to violence, sexual or otherwise. No doubt, there are individuals for whom this could take place, men whose dispositions and circumstances are such that the pornographic experience releases them into violence (although it must be added that I cannot imagine proving this relationship in a scientifically satisfactory way). Nevertheless, the immediate experience of the sex machine, with its stimulation, frustration, and moral nihilism, points in the vast majority of instances toward a paralytic standoff. Indeed, it could just as well be argued (and as little proved) that pornography can drain a man of his violent tendencies.

There is more to the sex shop than can be suggested in the metaphor of prison. Pornography cannot be divorced from the means of its representation—or indeed from the entire mass of social relations of which it forms a part. Thus pornography is not conceivable in a primitive society, or in peasantries, while it is on the way out in places like Sandinist Nicaragua, where laws have been passed forbidding the use of images of the female body for purposes of advertising. This is not said to extol the sexuality of such societies, but only to indicate that although pornography certainly has a long and interesting history, it cannot be said to have come into its own until the present. As pornography is the marketing of sex, it needs an advanced commercial society, with highly developed technology and marketing, if it is to flourish. It is under monopoly capital, where the consumer society is most developed, where we will find the most developed pornography. There would be no "pornography crisis" if there were no cheap reproduction of images, or means of subjecting these images to the strictest commodity exchange, or decline of genuinely productive work, or masses in a state of restless sexual unfulfillment, or a permissiveness which has to be induced in order to keep commodities rolling, or an imperative to cancel out serious political struggle in favor of self-indulgence, and so forth. All these elements signify our time, and they all combine to expand the pornographic product.

Pornography is an essential part of our economy, and a highly efficient and realizable part at that. The economies are indeed impressive: 3.6 seconds per penny of watching a stud at work is a bargain within reach of the poorest worker, even many on the public dole. This has been made possible by the genius of Japanese electronics and the rationalization of money into time as announced on the electronic display. So, too, are the paraphernalia displayed on the walls electronically packaged and for sale. Each magazine—there are scores, manifesting virtually every logical permutation of human sexuality—is hermetically sealed in perfectly transparent plastic, with an explicit photo on the cover. Thus everything is shown, and everything is hidden, and all at once: an impressive example of merchandising skill. Many a supermarket could learn a thing or two from the sex shop.

And yet the sex shop is also a zone of shame. This is interesting, since a great deal is made nowadays of the emancipation of sexuality from "Victorian" constraints. Moreover, one might have thought that pornography's clinical style and thorough commodification would have eliminated all traces of shame from its consumption. And it is true that much has become normalized. During a visit to the sex shop, for example, police were seen outside the door. This led to a moment's alarm: Had they come to raid the premises? No, not at all; they were merely frisking somebody for drugs. The sex shop itself was neutral territory, as routine as a grocery store, and had only drawn the attention of the law because of its serviceable parking lot. Yet acceptance and rationalization do not succeed in neutralizing what goes on inside. The depersonalized supermarket succeeds in making sexual commodities widely available but not in lifting the burden of shame from their consumption. One can see this in the furtive looks of the customers, the averted eyes, the monadic relations between the men. I find it hard to believe that a man would feel better about himself after a visit to the porn parlor.

On the Shamefulness of Pornography

One of the essential features of pornography is the Commandment: Thou shalt not be ashamed. Either the conquest of shame forms part of the plotline of the pornographic product (as in the classical porn film, *Behind the Green Door*), or else it is simply announced de facto, by the conventions of the work. And yet sexuality contains an eternal dialectic of shame. I mean by this that shame is part of sexuality, and not simply that we are ashamed about sexuality. This may not be a good thing, but it is essential. What we call sexuality has a dynamic that includes the dialectic of shame. Sexuality is not sex, is never encompassed by biology; sexuality is the human expression of sex, the sexual dimension of being human. It is our humanity, the expressive life of the self, as it encounters its sexual dimension. Because this dimension is very special (and indeed the self would not exist without its sexuality), the self differentiates at the zone of its sexuality: There is a sexual self, and an everyday self. The existence of this distinction is a condition for the specialness of sexuality, and its rapture, or ecstasy. But the presence of the divide also dictates a tension between the two phases of the self— and this tension is broadly experienced as shame, the judgment of the everyday self on the sexual self. To be more precise, shame is the subjective element of the sexual differentiation of the self. There is an objective side, too, composed of the immense and intricate web of codes and taboos institutionalized to express the given stage of sexual differentiation at any particular historical and social place. These codes comprise what is right and proper to sexuality, from practices of gratification, to distinctions between the genders, to how the body should be covered, and, indeed, to the very discourses which take place about sexuality (including, needless to say, this discourse itself). When the codes are breached the sexual self comes to life—and also comes into some degree of conflict with the everyday self. Thus the presence—and the breaking —of taboo are as essential to sexuality on the objective side as shame is on the subjective side. The subjective effect of shame is a manifestation that the codes have been broken—and an impetus to do something about it. Finally we must add that the dialectic of shame includes the denial of shame, which is the terrain occupied by pornography.

It goes without saying that this state of affairs is restless and in a constant state of flux on an individual as well as a social level. In particular, late capitalist society, with its cult of postmodernity, ensures that the coding of sexuality is in an accelerated state of renegotiation, with a broad assault on traditional restraints. In this sense it is true that much has loosened and that people today can do a great deal more sexually without shame than was the case a generation ago. Within my lifetime, there has been an amazing shift in the degree of sexual representation considered acceptable.[1] But this is a redeployment of boundaries, not an elimination. Sexuality will always be accompanied by lines to cross, and on the other side will lie the possibility of shame. That is the human condition, and it applies to the pornography of contemporary urban America as much as to the courtly love of the Middle Ages or the erotic life of Melanesians.

The dualism of sexuality means that we are both more and less of ourselves when we are sexual. We are lessened insofar as sexuality involves a rupture with the world of work and decency established to sustain the everyday self. Whether we take off our clothes or withdraw attention to an erotic fantasy, we are that much less encoded with the ordinary being of selfhood. But this diminution can be overcome by its opposite, which is also a matter of nakedness. For the emergence of the sexual self is a baring. It is an exposure of certain essentials: a nakedness of bodily fact, but much more besides, including nakedness before the other, which is to say, potentially the universe. The opening creates a

potentiality for the radical enhancement by the other. We must under-
score the notion of potentiality here. The opening of self to other is no
more than a possibility within sexuality. It is also quite possible, and
taken all in all, rather more probable, to be fully unclothed and hide
everything, as pornography demonstrates. But even in the instance of
pornography, even in the most degraded and pathetic sexual spectacles,
the players—performers and viewers alike—remain fully human, which
is to say, they are never things, never identical to their physical substance—even if this be part of the illusion they seek to create. If, therefore, pornography succeeds in making its actors into locomotives of
fucking, then its meaning is to be read not as the *equivalence* [human being
= locomotive], but as the *difference* [(human being = locomotive) −
human being].

Now, if sexuality engages humanness, we must also say that humanness engages sexuality. The farthest point to which this theme has been
taken is that of Georges Bataille, who wrote, "As often as not it seems to
be assumed that man has his being independently of his passions. I affirm, on the other hand, that we must never imagine existence except in
terms of these passions."[2] In his *Erotism*, the extraordinary work from
which this quotation is drawn, Bataille adopts the perspective of Freud,
without, however, subjugating the erotic, or sexual self to the productive, or everyday self defined by the given social reality.[3] He recognizes,
with Freud, that our inner being is sexual, but he refuses to adopt Freud's
bourgeois hostility to instinct. For Bataille, rather, eroticism is the mode
of self-realization, traversing death and dissolution, but opening onto
the spirit. "Human eroticism differs from animal sexuality precisely in
this, that it calls inner life into play. In human consciousness eroticism is
that within man which calls his being into question" (page 29). In his
work, "flights of Christian religious experience and bursts of erotic impulses are seen to be part and parcel of the same movement" (page 9).
The chief difference between Freud and Bataille, then, is not simply the
latter's sympathy for the instinctual, but also the fact that he takes spiritual experience seriously instead of explaining this away as an infantile
residue. Bataille can therefore regard the dissolution of the everyday self
which is intrinsic to sexuality as a spiritual rather than a clinical problem.
Sexuality is not simply, then, the deepest part of human nature: it also
has transcendent possibilities.

Bataille sharply distinguishes human eroticism from animal sex—although he is equally clear that not all "really existing" human sexual
activity is erotic. From this standpoint we might say that the mechanical
copulation displayed in the standard porn parlor is far from any notion of
the erotic. And the reason, more than any other, is its manifest *shameless-
ness*—the characteristic insistence that everything be permitted. That

the men in the porn parlor react with a vestige of shame to the spectacle of shame conquered is a sign that their eroticism is not dead, which is to say, their humanity is not dead.

It is among the beauties of human sexuality to resist and eventually dissolve all attempts to be comprehended in discursive language, or *logos*. Thus there is something farcical about *sexology*. Similarly, the distinction between "sexual self" and "everyday self," while useful for calling attention to the omnipresence of shame in sexuality, is not very helpful at all when it comes to a deeper understanding of sexuality itself. We would be betrayed if we assumed that the term "self" repre-sented the same kind of thing in the two categories. For the "sexual self" is not an alternate self, another card to be played or hat to be pulled out of the closet. It is, rather, a dissolving of the everyday self. Nor is the sexual self a higher spiritual *Aufhebung*, or realization of the everyday self. It is, rather, a derealization. There is no progress in sexuality, as Freud and Bataille recognized, even if they differed on whether transcendence lay at the other end of the erotic. The tension inherent to eroticism is between being and nonbeing. In this respect Bataille develops an extreme tendency of Freud's later years. As ex-pressed in *Beyond the Pleasure Principle*, Freud's most far-reaching theoreti-cal work and, predictably, the one most rejected by the psychotherapeutic industries, the erotic occupies the ground between individual existence, with its separateness, and fusion with the ground of being. In other words, sexuality is intrinsic to the dialectic of life and death. This is the deeper meaning of the necessity for taboo— and the transgression of taboo, which is inherent to taboo and is the sine qua non of the erotic. The erotic can by no means simply be identified with a "life force." It is life and death together, differen-tiated by a historically unstable codification of taboo.

The dynamic of taboo and transgression is present in all primitive societies.[4] No matter how little they may wear or how exuberant their sexual life, primitives set very definite restrictions upon sexuality. In-deed, it is a safe generalization to claim that sexuality is part of the realm of the sacred in the primitive world view. In any case, it is never shame-less—except in the dialectic sense of shame denied under highly codi-fied and ritualized conditions. The centuries of development culminating in postmodern society have drastically altered the nature of the codifica-tion without changing the necessity of taboo and transgression. As we have seen, the fact that pornographic representation includes the mes-sages "everything is permitted" and "do not be ashamed" does not dis-prove this in the least. It only shifts the ground of opposition to that between the taboo of everyday life and the licentious spectacles of the sex shop. These, then, become our rituals of transgression, sharply dif-ferent from those of traditional preindustrial society in that they serve no socially cohesive purpose (except that of the ruling class, insofar as they contribute to a politically burnt-out population). But they are evidence of taboo. If there were no taboo to transgress, there would be no interest at all in pornography.

The Repressiveness of Sexual Politics

The view of sexuality afforded by Bataille, the later Freud, and psychoanalytic radicals such as Sandor Ferenczi[5] is profoundly different from prevailing opinion. More, this difference is not a function of manifest politics, inasmuch as the three authors noted above belong to no coherent political category, while the views of those who differ span the known political spectrum. Thus we have, in the prevailing camp, a range from the frank repressiveness of the traditional Right along with antipornography feminists, to the hygenic sex-therapeutic culture so central to late-capitalist society, to groups on the Left espousing the ideology of sexual liberation drawn from the sixties and seventies (and ultimately from the sexual politics of Wilhem Reich[6]). At first glance nothing would seem common to such widely disparate attitudes except an interest in sex. Closer inspection reveals, however, that a common assumption lies behind this interest, and that this assumption—which may be necessary to assert a particular political stance about sexuality—is distinctly different from that of Bataille, Freud, and Ferenczi. For, in each of the instances, whether of Right, Center, or Left, sexuality is regarded as one, single, determinable thing to which a coherent moral valence adheres. From another perspective, sexual politics demands that sexuality be mapped onto its behavioral manifestations, that it be practically identical to its objectification. About this the whole spectrum of sexual politics agrees. What they differ on is the moral valence attached to sexual behavior.

For the Right, the free expression of sexuality is bad because it belongs to a carnal realm condemned by fundamentalist religion and the Roman Catholic Church. "Better to marry than burn," said Paul, and repressive civilization has continued to press the theme forward despite its dubious claim to spirituality. As far as repressive feminism is concerned, sexuality is bad insofar as it can be positively correlated with male dominance over and violence against women.

For the hygienists—who comprise the main group and ideal type of late capitalist society—sexuality is either healthy or sick, two categories which mutually exclude one another. If healthy, it is good—both fun in itself and good for one's "organism." If sick, sex is bad, and contaminated with the prudery of the Victorian era and the repressiveness of the church (though still good to do, in hopes of overcoming one's "hangups"). In any case, it is a matter-of-fact phenomenon, which can be placed into a calculable scheme of relations according to the pleasure or, to be more exact, stimulation it affords. In the words of a famous sex therapist, sexuality is nothing but "friction plus fantasies," the key word here being the arithmetical operator, which places the fantasy on the same ontological plane as the friction and makes them both objectifiable. By objectifying sexuality and transvaluing it onto the dimension of health ethics, the hygienic culture achieves a status far beyond its own modest practices: It enables sexuality to become commodified and a spoke in the great wheel of capitalist accumulation.

The sexual Left, among whose numbers would be included large segments of the feminist and gay movements, is both opposed to the Right and bound by similar assumptions about sexuality, even if this is viewed positively instead of negatively. The reason is understandable, inasmuch as the Left must rebel against assumptions about sexuality which have been defined by the Right. In a sense, the gay movement has no choice, besides knuckling under to the repression of traditional society, other than to affirm the univalent goodness of its sexuality. Sexuality is a basic need—if not for physical life then for human existence.[7] Those who have been denied their rights of sexual expression might be expected to value what they are missing as unequivocally as a hungry person would value food. However, sex and hunger are not the same drive, and a single-minded view of the former is not a true one, no matter how just it may be.

Pornography is no problem for the sexual Right, which simply sees it as the work of the devil, or for the hygienic center, for whom it functions as a stimulant. However, it poses an acute dilemma for sexual liberationists, since it constitutes an assault on right-wing sexual morality, on the one hand, while being manifestly sleazy and oppressive on the other. If the purpose of pornography is to stimulate sexual arousal, and if objective sexual activity is deemed both good and necessary, then it is hard to avoid endorsing pornography, no matter how dreadful it may be.

To circumvent the dilemma, the category of the erotic is often differentiated from that of the pornographic. In this way, rescue is attempted of what is valued in sexuality from the commodification and violence of capitalist relations. This is an understandable and even laudable project. Unhappily, it is impossible within the framework of a linear and objectivistic view of sexuality, for the simple reason that such sexuality must become identified with objective performance and conscious stimulation. Once this link is established as primary, all negativity is expelled and sexuality collapses into its behavioral manifestations. One is forced into a univocal evaluation: either good or bad. Such a sexuality cannot be considered erotic. Within the terms of sexual politics, it would be more honest, as Alan Soble has pointed out,[8] to oppose "acceptable" to "unacceptable" pornography than to talk of the erotic alternative to pornography. An honest solution, but a depressing one, since there is no way of avoiding the sense that an encounter with pornography, acceptable or not, is a descent into barbarism.

The Erotic and the Pornographic

Sexuality cannot take place without representation. The final pathway of representation is subjective, in what psychoanalysis calls "mental representation," this being the way in which objects of desire are constituted. Subjective representation is not, however, simply the labor of an isolated mind but also the internalization of culture. Pornography is the mass-cultural mode of sexual representation, which channels, directs, and codifies the taboos and boundaries according to which desire is deployed. To talk of erotic as well as pornographic representation means, then, talking of erotic as well as pornographic sexuality. The erotic is also a mode of cultural representation, although for reasons we shall soon discuss, it is not mass cultural.

If we are to adequately distinguish between the erotic and the pornographic—and I believe we should, as there is something worth rejecting in pornography and worth saving in erotica—then we have to break with "single vision"[9] and achieve a dialectical view of sexuality. For erotic representation is dialectical, while pornographic representation is single visioned. Pornography is distinguished from the erotic by its inability to grasp the negative moment in sexuality. Hence its literal-mindedness and humorlessness, despite crude attempts in this direction.

There is no tension internal to pornography. The tension is external, between the single-visioned pornographic work and the internally conflicted spectator. This boundary, which feeds off the very literalness and stupidity of the pornographic work, generates a powerful, indeed, virtually limitless appeal. The source of the appeal derives from the negation of the dialectic of sexuality, with the painfulness of its desire. And for this negation to succeed, all dialectical elements have to be abolished from pornography. Thus pornography is more than undialectical; it is *antidialectical* sexuality. Its denial of the tension and dissolution inherent to the erotic is precisely what arouses erotic interest, since it is in the nature of the erotic to refuse the limitations inherent to separate being. The erotic needs to believe in the impossible—and what is impossible includes pornography's promise that it will offer a sexuality free of all restraint, boundedness, and taboo. "At all times as well as in all places," claims Bataille, ". . . man is defined by having his sexual behavior subject to rules and precise restrictions" (page 50). What better taboo to transgress than the law of taboo itself?

In pornographic sexuality, taboos become mechanical, fixed, and easily crossed. There is taboo on one side, and "free" pleasure on the other, in a tabooless zone. As we have observed, this generates the endless appeal of the "everything is permitted," but it also fails to engage the spirit at any depth. As a result, pornographic consumption is marked by rapid boredom, along with the search for new means of gratification. This is perhaps the readiest way of telling whether a given work is pornographic. For erotic sexuality, by contrast, the taboo and the moment of gratification are not to be extricated one from the other. The relationship is dialectical rather than mechanical, which is to say, it can never be subsumed in logos, can never be objectified or subjectified. Sexuality and the taboo against sexuality are always present. There is no flattening in the erotic, no point of rest even at the moments of greatest rapture and fulfillment. This forces desire, which seeks the overcoming of taboo, deeper, eternally seeking to escape itself and the burdens of existence. The omega point of erotic sexuality is summed up and realized in the passage from being to nonbeing, for which reason it engages the spirit at the point where spirit emerges from desire. This profound mystery was represented by Freud as the tension between Eros and Thanatos, by Bataille in his linkage between sensuality and death, by Ferenczi in his regressive view of copulation (in which coitus is regarded as a return to the phylogenetic origins of life from the sea)—and by the progenitor of the modern erotic tradition, Sade, in his phantasmagoric vision of a totally unbounded sexual power. Erotic sexuality is sexuality as madness.

However, the erotic is also constituted in everyday life itself through the representation of an eternally recurring opposition—one of those irruptions of unreason which give the lie to our self-characterization as the rational animal. One common example is the coding of female genitalia relative to the rest of the body. The female organs are not specially charged so far as a gynecologist is concerned, and they lose erotic characteristics when the time arrives for them to function as a birth canal. In these non-erotic moments, the woman's genital is an organ, nothing more—a wondrous part of nature, no doubt, yet no more so than any other organ. When, however, the genital is erotized,[10] it is defined as absolute negativity and radical mystery. This is turned about again and rerepresented in the traditional "civilized" notions of feminine beauty. The coding of woman's beauty ensures the maximum degree of contrast between the fair, hairless delicacy of the idealized face and the gross, smelly hairiness of the genital.[11] To be sure, fairness and grossness are in the eyes of the beholder—and a very historically determined beholder at that. Note in this regard the grace note established in certain European traditions of having a little dark mole painted on the woman's fair face. But in whatever case, the qualities subjected to opposition are placed for the benefit of the erotic as it strives for realization within a given historical context. And in that context, the erotic serves the function of overcoming history itself: of dedifferentiating the socially constructed self, of turning the human away from itself and so revealing its actual, soiled humanity. This quality, of being perpetually at the margins of existence, provides the erotic with subversive potential—a potential seized upon by Sade at the beginning of the modern era, and since furthered by waves of sexual radicals.

It is scarcely an original observation that the configurations of desire which are given the name of erotic are traditionally defined by males for the enjoyment of males. Or that in this configuration, the female is the generic object to the male subject, violently torn into her antithetical representations—of mother and whore, saint and animal, the delicate lady and the coarse cunt. There is much more that could be said of the ramifications of this pattern. Here let us merely assert the obvious, and brutally elemental: that injustice and domination are sealed into the category of the erotic no less than they are into the pornographic. While the oppression of women is based in economic subjugation, it is lived out in terms of erotic debasement. The dialectical presence within the erotic does not in any sense confer virtue or morality upon it, and its superiority to pornography is not to be thought of in terms of justice. In fact, one could argue the reverse: The erotic, grounded as it is in an eternally recurring escape from individuated existence, poses a greater danger than dim-witted pornography to the moral order. One can understand the option for Agape over Eros, even if the loss might be too great to bear. In the erotic fusion with the other, the other loses her/his individual being. No one who is an object of the erotic can be thought of as an end in her/himself; the other is rather drawn into the being—and the power—of the self. This was the singular insight of Sade, developed in obsessive detail throughout his work and lived out in his life. We should not forget that the great apostle of sexual liberation was arrested for the whipping of a young woman and the pouring of wax into her wounds. And Bataille, arguably the greatest exponent of the erotic in our time, was rejected by André Breton as being too extreme for the surrealists, a verdict one may share after reading *The Story of the Eye*, which will make the flesh of the most jaded reader crawl, in its wanton expression of evil. Bataille's greatness lies in his going to the limit, not in any consolatory message. As he wrote in *Erotism*, "the greater the anguish . . . the stronger the realization of exceeding the bounds and the greater the accompanying rush of joy." And, "beauty has a cardinal importance, for ugliness cannot be despoiled, and to despoil is the essence of erotism" (page 145). What is despoiled goes beyond physical beauty, to include the whole moral order and even economic rationality itself:

But once we have ventured along the path of sensuous disorder it takes a good deal to satisfy us. Destruction and betrayal will sometimes go hand in hand with the rising tide of genetic excess. Besides nudity there is the strangeness of half-clothed bodies; what garments there are serve to emphasise the disorder of the body and show it to be all the more naked, all the more disordered. Brutality and murder are further steps in the same direction. Similarly prostitution, coarse language and everything to do with eroticism and infamy play their part in turning the world of sensual pleasure into one of ruin and degradation. Our only real pleasure is to squander our resources to no purpose, just as if a wound were bleeding away inside us; we always want to be sure of the uselessness or the ruinousness of our extravagance. We want to feel as remote from the world where thrift is the rule as we can. As remote as we can—that is hardly strong enough; we want a world turned upside down and inside out. The truth of eroticism is treason. (Pages 170–171).

Compared to this vision, pornography is tame, not because of the subject of its representation, which can mime any of the stages on Bataille's anti-*viacrucis*, including murder,[12] but because the mode of its representation denies the dialectic according to which the viewer can become swept away into a serious confrontation with nonbeing. That is why no pornographic work as such can enter the domain opened by Bataille's notion of the erotic—a realm in which the economic process itself is demolished. To the contrary, pornography is lashed to economic reproduction, both as a commodity-in-itself and a mode of ensuring loyalty to the order signified by the commodity. It does so by a bimodal motion: forcing the spectator to remain within the bounds of desire, while bringing desire itself under control, submitting it to *logos* and therefore the ordination of capitalist rationalization. Thus the spectator of pornography is being herded into the system tethered to desire. For there should be no mistake: The men—and increasingly, women—who consume pornographic commodities are kept very much in line by doing so. Can one imagine any genuine resistance, any critical capacity whatsoever, germinating in the sex shops? Pornography is good for business, just like health clubs and corporate sponsorship of tennis matches or the Olympics. Because it remains trapped by desire, it permits desire to wear down the capacity for critical resistance. A nation of pornography consumers is no different, politically speaking, than a nation of heroin junkies. It is not hard to envision the video-display terminals of the office of the future being programmed to show pornography—soft-core, no doubt—during lunch breaks, and perhaps after-hours, as a way of sweetening the separation of home and workplace.

Indeed, this is the main point of distinction between the erotic and the pornographic: that the latter represents sexuality firmly under the control of capital while the former dissolves capital—not in the interest of any alternative, but simply as part of its universal corrosion, because it dissoles, or to use Bataille's metaphor, squanders everything else—including desire itself. For desire seeks an object. Once opened onto nonbeing, with its objectlessness, desire can no longer evade a spiritual confrontation. It is for this reason that the erotic can move outside of mass culture, while the pornographic belongs to mass culture—not in mass culture's middle ground, which must remain with the virtues of home and hearth, but on the boundary at which mass culture assimilates desire. Pornography will never replace the Disney family film; it will, however, shadow it, and its mode of production will shadow the mode of production of the mainstream forms of bourgeois representation, a mangy camp-follower employing the canons, the techniques, and the rising or falling surplus actors of the industry.

From another angle, pornography is the captivity of the erotic within mass culture. It is the erotic less its negativity, less its ambivalence, its association of sexuality with death, and, finally, its truthfulness. For truthfulness is the one property of erotic representation which redeems the whole and gives to it the possibility of aesthetic realization. The *r*epresentation of the erotic moment of dissolution requires fidelity to the tragic character of existence, requires the capacity to look into the abyss beyond desire and give it signification. Truthfulness stands forth as the ultimate value of the erotic, and truthfulness inheres in the internal relation of the elements of the work and not in its manifest subject. For this reason great erotic art need not be at all explicit in its depiction of sexuality. A poem by Emily Dickinson is no less erotic than a work by Bataille, even if the latter confronts the problem of the erotic directly. Similarly, no more erotic novel has ever been written than *Anna Karenina*, even if it lacks any direct representation of sexuality. By contrast, the attempt to make pornography more "erotic" by improving production values, introducing more or less credible kinds of characters, and cutting out the ranker forms of exploitation, succeeds only in softening the pornography and expanding its market further into the normal zone of mass culture, where it now abuts upon the domain of the soap opera. Softer pornography is more acceptable, especially to women (who now comprise, I have heard, forty percent of the pornographic videotape market), but it remains fully pornographic, indeed, signifies the assimilation of sex-hygiene into pornography.

The erotic necessarily (and in contrast to the pornographic) points beyond itself. Since the question of nonbeing—as Thanatos or death—is contained in the erotic, erotic questions are, as we have seen with Bataille, also spiritual questions, and questions about ultimates. If there is evil sedimented into the erotic, it is the evil which happens to be in the world, and which the erotic can expose. The spiritual scale of the erotic enables us to achieve a critical perspective on this evil and to explode the myth of evil's naturality. Of course, this perspective must be actively grasped, through an effort of the critical will—the very critical will which is under assault in the pornographization of the erotic.

In any case, if erotic representation signifies the social relations of fascism, it is because fascism is in the world. Pornography can never overcome fascism, while the erotic contains a possibility of doing so. A hard pornography of fascism will directly increase the world's fascist quotient, so to speak, while a soft pornography of pseudotenderness will increase it indirectly, through its erosion of the critical will. Erotic representation of fascist sexuality, on the other hand, rubs our face in reality and forces a response. This was the original, prefigurative project of Sade, whose depiction of pure power relations drew the Hobbesian limits of an emerging capitalism and foresaw by more than a century the fascist breakdown of bourgeois society. His intuition was developed in hideous erotic detail by Pasolini in his film *Salo*, based on the *120 Days of Sodom* and intended to reveal the actuality of Italian Fascism. *Salo* may be the most gruesome film ever made, but it remains one of the few adequate representations of fascism in the history of cinema,[13] precisely because its representations of sexuality are formally linked both to Sade's original text and to the concrete historical situation in Italy. How else can such a reality be brought home? And yet *Salo's* manifestly unbounded sexuality is in fact constantly bounded—and thereby negated—by the unseen framework of critique. Compare this, for example, with the work of Brian DePalma. DePalma's representations of "sadism" are linked, it is true, to an ongoing set of allusions to the history of cinema. But this history itself is organized entirely about the value of the "sensational." More, within the frame of the works themselves, DePalma proceeds according to the rule of pure effect, or display; the question we are repeatedly faced with is whether he can top his previous outrage. This is an inherently addictive schema, without reference to any critical, much less transcendent, possibility; consequently, there is no internal negation of the violence, which appears, as many have noted, gratuitously. DePalma's work belongs therefore to the pornographic—as does the great mass of gratuitous violence characterizing late-capitalist cinema.

A few points by way of conclusion. It should be clear that the categories of the erotic and the pornographic should not be regarded as neat boxes into which one work or another can be thrown, or according to which a seal of approval or disapproval can be given. They are, rather, kinds of questions to be put to various forms of cultural representation, questions to which we need not expect positive nor univalent answers. After all, pornography can range from the harmlessly silly to the actively fascistic, while the erotic can contain ecstasy as well as critique. More, just as erotic representation need not engage manifest sexuality, so may pornography range far beyond the sex shop. Indeed, given the key relation to a ubiquitous mass culture, I think we are obliged to disclose the track of pornography wherever desire is untruthfully manipulated within the framework and means of this mass culture. Thus it makes perfect sense to talk of pornographic politicians, or a pornography of the Holocaust. What is intended by this goes beyond the meaning of the words, sentimental or insincere. It refers also to a definite political project, of assimilation into the consumerist and one-dimensional order of late capitalism through the use of desire to blunt critique.

Given the unchained nature of desire and the fundamentally corrupt structures promoted by society, pornography will often break out of the containment afforded by the canons of mass culture and become frankly criminal. This would include the fascistic edge alluded to above. One thinks here, for example, of the pornographic exploitation of children. In such instances I think we have no choice but to press for legal measures; the situation is simply too immediately threatening. On the other hand, an attempt to bring all of pornography under control through censorship would be both disastrous and futile. It would be disastrous because it would add to the repressiveness which creates the need for pornography in the first place. And it would be futile because pornography is not some wart on the surface of capitalist culture but part of the heart of capitalist culture. A society that would twice elect the pornographic President Ronald Reagan cannot control pornography through legislation or the courts. We should, it seems to me, take the same attitude toward pornography as Marx did toward religion, regarding it as a symptom of a corrupt society and the embodiment of an emancipatory force suppressed and distorted by that society, a force will not be freed until society itself is transformed. In the meantime, the only adequate response to pornography is to build the critical imagination—and remain open to the erotic.

Intrusive Images and Subjectified Bodies: Notes on Visual Heterosexual Porn

by

TIMOTHY BENEKE

1. Introduction

In recent pornography debates, feminist struggles against sexism and violence against women, liberal (and sometimes feminist) aspirations toward sexual openness, freedom, and tolerance, and reactionary fears of sex mingle and collide like bits of mercury forced together. We are asked to be *outraged* at the sexism in men's minds and its ubiquitous dissemination in porn and inexorable expression in violence toward women, *grateful* that we can *finally* honestly acknowledge, and freely explore and express, our sexuality, and *appalled* the the presence of such filth in our community. I take the first perspective very seriously, the second somewhat less so, and the third not at all, though I think the third nudges and constrains me in visceral, semiconscious ways.

Pornography (which for the purposes of this essay I denote the varieties of heterosexual visual porn found in most American porn stores) offers some of the most vivid, sensational, and widely accessible manifestations of sexism and misogyny to be found in American culture. This is not to say that all men who use, or could be excited by porn are necessarily misogynist or sexist in their actions; it would also be outrageous to argue that women who are excited by sadomasochistic porn want to be treated in a sexist or misogynist fashion. I wonder whether, in a culture with little or no violence against women, porn might exist without protest against its sexism. Given that men can be antisexist yet excited by sexist porn, a world where men were antisexist yet enjoyed porn seems psychologically conceivable. In contemporary American cul-

Many people discussed the ideas in this essay with me. I especially want to thank Allan Creighton, Chuck Stephen, Barbara Dixson, Arlie Hochschild, George Lakoff, Michael Kimmel, Marcel Hausmann, George Marx, Maeve Neuman, Blair Sandler, and, most of all, Kathy Anolick. Copyright © 1988 by Tim Beneke. All rights reserved. Used by permission of Tim Beneke.

ture, where violence against women is widespread and where men have yet to seriously acknowledge, much less stop, sexist violence, identifying and objecting to sexism in all forms is necessary.

In what follows I attempt to shed light on heterosexual men and their visual experience of women, their sexual distress, their difficulty identifying with women's experience, and their use of porn. Since I seek to understand certain forms of male suffering that I take to be real and that men use to justify sexism and rape, I want to be clear: To understand or even empathize with someone's distress is not to legitimate what it is used to justify or what may appear to issue from it. Any such attempts to understand male sexual distress must be undertaken with an eye to gaining insight as to how men might finally stop doing the many horrible things they do—to women, to each other, and to themselves. The ultimate "solution" to the "problem" of pornography is to stop sexism and violence against women and thereby render porn irrelevant. Sex could then be a domain free to express itself without being perceived through the oppression of gender. There is little evidence that men are as yet willing to do the work necessary to make this possible.

A final note. When I refer to men here I mean heterosexual men; I elide distinctions of class and ethnicity in the hope that what I say will, with appropriate emendations, have broad application. I am writing about heterosexual visual porn—magazines mostly. (I have seen few porn films.) My biases are white, middle-class, and no doubt unconsciously inform the picture of men I present.

2. Intrusive Images

Pornography cannot be fully understood apart from men's daily social experience of looking at women. I want to distinguish four kinds of men's visual experience of women and women's bodies: authorized images, stolen images, intrusive images, and authorized stolen images.[1]

Authorized images include that which one is socially authorized to look at; a man is socially authorized to look at a painting of a nude woman in a museum, a nude statue, or a woman's face in a personal interaction. Judges judging bathing beauties, gynecologists doing an examination, male art students painting a nude model, are all authorized to look in certain predefined, more or less explicity prescribed ways.

But if a man stares at the crotch of a nude statue or painting, or at the breasts of a woman in a social interaction; or, if the gynecologist, judge, or art student looks lustfully at what he is authorized to see, the image becomes stolen. Notice that stolen images come in two forms: looking at something one is not authorized to look at and looking lustfully at what one *is* authorized to look at. And there are images men are authorized, indeed expected, to notice, but not authorized to stare at: the visible crease of a woman's breasts in a low-cut dress, the legs of a woman in a miniskirt. And, as I have suggested, there are images one is authorized neither to notice nor look at: the faintly visible underwear of a woman sitting wearing a short skirt. Stealing images of women's bodies is a troubled activity that pervades many heterosexual men's adolescent and postadolescent social experience. A fifteen-year-old boy sitting bored in a classroom notices the inner thigh of a girl sitting across the room; he is titillated and wants to look but feels socially prohibited from staring. So he may present what Erving Goffman calls a "body gloss." Through bodily signification, a body gloss helps free him from the undesirable charactero- logical implications of what he finds himself doing. Sample body glosses: a man standing on a suburban sidewalk late at night waiting for a ride casts exaggerated glances down the street to signify his reason for being there; a man lifting a heavy object around others exaggerates his grunts and groans to mask his actual difficulty and vulnerability at lifting the object. And our fifteen-year-old boy scans his eyes in the direction of the girl's thighs, avoiding staring, allowing himself to catch an occasional glance; or he solemnly stares in the vicinity of the image as if lost in thought while keeping the image in the barely accessible periphery of his visual field. It's an art many boys learn. (Nude beaches and restaurants with topless wait- resses are places where people, authorized to notice but not to stare, selectively disattend erotic images and use glosses to mask staring. As Goffman puts it, "When bodies are naked, glances are clothed."[2]) Stealing images and glossing one's activity are deeply humiliating and isolating for men, not in the way that striking out with the bases loaded or dropping a pass in the end zone are consciously, acutely humiliating, but rather as a chronic, fearful, humiliated stance toward women that often pervades men's daily social experience of sexual longing. This activity is humiliating because it is desperate and outcast, because one works so hard for so little, and, perhaps above all, because it shuts one out from social mutuality.

Part of the social prohibition of sexual looking is both reflected and perpetuated by a central metaphor for seeing in English: Seeing is touching. We say that a woman could "feel a man's eyes on her"; a couple makes "eye contact"; a man can't "take his eyes off of her"; his eyes were "glued to her"; he "ran his eyes all over her body."[3] Marshall McLuhan is reported by Tom Wolfe to have cleverly invoked this meta- phor while having dinner at a topless restaurant: "These women aren't nude," said McLuhan. "They're wearing *us*."

Intrusive images is a category more personal than social; variations in personality will cause images to feel intrusive to some but not others. I distinguish: ordinary intrusive images (intrusive to most "normal" people, i.e., sighted, able to hear); arousing intrusive images that require a prior condition of need to arouse; and arousing, intrusive, erotic images.

Some ordinary intrusive images: an alarm clock going off; the bright lights of a passing car hurting one's eyes; a twenty-dollar bill seen on the sidewalk; flashing neon signs; tiny hairs scratching and stinging one's skin after a haircut; sudden physical pain.

Arousing intrusive images: The smell of pizza wafting from a restaurant is smelled by a hungry person on the sidewalk; a man trying to quit smoking smells the smoke of his favorite cigarette; a person trying to quit caffeine smells coffee; an eighteen-year-old eager to buy his first car is distracted by a TV commercial for cars.

I will only discuss arousing intrusive erotic images that are felt by heterosexual men. Advertising is full of images of women likely to catch men unawares, either by providing a sexy image of a woman to favorably associate a product with sex or by putting forth such an image to help sell a product to a woman so that she might more easily seek to emulate it. I counted nine potentially intrusive erotic images in this morning's paper, most of them associated with advertising. Sexually attractive women in and of themselves can clearly be felt by men to be intrusive; what begins as an intrusive image may become a stolen one. Images can be simultaneously stolen and intrusive; one feels them intruding in one's field of vision and is authorized to notice but not stare, so one steals. Talking to a woman wearing a sexy low-cut dress, one may find her breasts intrusive and cast stolen glances at them. A kind of power struggle may go on as the man attempts to dominate and "defuse" the intrusive image. It is extraordinary the degree to which whole industries exist to make women's presence feel potentially intrusive and arousing to men; women's makeup, perfume, jewelry, and clothes are all in varying degrees attempts at this.

In the last fifty years we have seen a massive dissemination of erotic images in advertising, contrived with increasing skill and designed to distract, arouse, and awaken male sexual feeling. While psychoanalysis has sought to integrate and demystify disowned fragments of the self through making explicit the meaning of sexual (and other) dreams, images, and fantasies, consumer culture generally, and advertising in particular, has done the reverse. Erotic images in advertising exploit half-conscious unintegrated feelings and needs through subliminal or semiconscious arousal. In television advertising, this is sometimes done with extraordinary rapidity and subtlety. The result is a vague, amorphously directed sexual resentment of women and resentment of sexual desire itself. Men feel sexually stimulated against their will, hence powerless, distracted, and resentful.

In interviewing men on the subject of rape, in one form or another I often heard men say: "I have been injured by women. By the way they look, move, smell, and behave, they have forced me to have sexual sensation I didn't want to have. If a man rapes a sexy woman, he is forcing her to have sexual sensation she doesn't want. It is just revenge."

The view of a woman's appearance as a weapon, or at least a powerful physical force, is metaphorically structured in English. A sexy woman is *a bombshell, a knockout, dressed to kill, a femme fatale, devastating, ravishing, striking,* or *stunning*. (While in "seeing is touching," seeing is understood as an active intervention, seeing is understood here as being passively acted upon.) Consider the overwhelming intrusiveness implicit in those words and the disruptiveness suggested by three men's comments:

> Growing up, I definitely felt teased by women. I think for the most part women knew I was attracted to them so women would sit a certain way or give a three-quarter beaver shot or give you a little bit of tit and maybe not give much more, or lift their skirts a certain way... I definitely felt played with, used, manipulated, like women were testing their power over me. I hated it with a passion! With a *fucking* passion![4]

> When you see a girl walking around wearing real skimpy clothes, she's offending you...
> When you have a steady girlfriend or if you're married, girls will flirt with you to give you that enraged temptation. They know you're not going to do anything to them, so they're going to push real hard to make you real mad.[5]

> Where I work it's probably no different from any other major city in the U.S. The women dress up in high heels and they wear a lot of makeup, and they just look really hot and really sexy and how can somebody who has a healthy sex drive not feel lust for them?
> ...I feel that they have power over me just by their presence. Just the fact that they can come up to me and just melt me and make me feel like a dummy makes me want revenge.[6]

Such feelings are not uncommon in men. The magazine *Men's Health* surveyed 444 readers, ninety-seven percent of whom were men, on women's sexual harassment of men in the workplace.[7] Forty-nine percent said there were women in their offices whose dress was "pointedly provocative"; thirty-three percent of the respondents believe men should report such women for sexual harassment. Consider: A third of these men believe a man is being seriously, legally harassed by a woman on the job if she simply looks sexy and dresses sexily!

There is a deep feeling of injustice in men about the relation between stolen and intrusive images that I have never heard explicitly expressed. It goes like this: "Women not only have the right, but often work hard to make themselves look sexy and to distract, disrupt, and intrude upon me just by their presence; yet if I notice something sexy about a woman, I have to mask my need to look, and furtively steal glances. Either way I'm humiliated. If they have the right to intrude, I should have the right to look. But I don't."

When men as a group harass a passing woman they are, among other things, seeking revenge against women for the humiliation they have suffered; they are unconsciously attempting to remedy a perceived injustice about their right to look.

Intrusive erotic images help create unwanted (or ambivalently wanted) erections in adolescent and other men; the experience of having, hiding, and getting rid of such erections is humiliating and sometimes shaming. One may attempt to hide one's arousal physically or mask it through appearing solemn or overly vigilant in doing what one is supposed to be doing. (High-school classrooms are the most common domains where all this occurs.) But when a male adolescent attempts to think and feel his way out of an erection, he engages in a process much deeper than body glossing, a process sociologist Arlie Hochschild calls "emotion work."[8] Emotion work is the work of making oneself feel (or not feel) particular emotional states in order to satisfy the demands of a social or personal circumstance. It is deeper, more basic work than the work of simply signifying or presenting an outward appearance. Hochschild distinguishes emotional *labor* that has exchange value as part of a service offered in one's job (for example, a stewardess who makes herself feel pleasant and nurturant) from emotion *work* or *management* where the same acts are done outside of a work context. Sample acts of emotion work: making oneself feel more aggrieved than one is at a funeral; talking oneself out of feeling in love; giving oneself a pep talk before a football game.

The emotion work of getting rid of an erection is difficult to describe. The simplest description: One relaxes, disattends sexual stimulation, goes about one's business, and lets the erection go away by itself. Actively positive, that is, autosuggestive, thinking may or may not help. The emotion work of getting rid of erections is something most boys learn, or try to learn. Consider this progression: A boy is "struck" by an intrusive erotic image, say, the sight of a girl's thighs and underwear across a classroom; he casts masked stolen glances at the image; he finds himself becoming erect and enjoys the erection until he starts to feel self-conscious; he engages in the emotion work of getting rid of the erection; that night he calls upon the image in fantasy while masturbating; the image becomes part of his "image repertoire," visual property to be called upon for arousal and gratification at another time. He has suffered humiliation by the image and, in a sense, conquered it by gaining control over it and perhaps in the process gained some control over the relation between images, erections, and orgasms. One of the functions of masturbation is to get training in the emotion work of controlling erections and controlling the relation between image and arousal.

This relation is intensified by the disruptive experience of wet dreams, where one controls neither the image nor the orgasm.

Intrusive erotic images can be more or less simply pleasurable and incur no resentment in men. But their effect on many male psyches is to create stress, distress, and a longing for relief and control. And that is clearly one role for pornography. Pornographic images are both authorized and stolen but generally not intrusive; one is authorized to pull out a centerfold in one's bedroom, but not, at least not quite yet, in a restaurant or on the bus. "Society at large" in some sense defines pornographic images as in varying degrees stolen; the framing of pornographic images and the content of the images themselves attempt to authorize men to look, fantasize, and masturbate. Consider *Playboy*: Hugh Hefner produced a whole industry replete with a "philosophy," special clubs, emblems, books, a magazine, a grant-giving foundation, a palace, and a TV show, all more or less to authorize men to look at nude women. (One doesn't know whether to laugh or cry.) And by being really three magazines—one for intellectuals, one for consumers, and one for masturbators—*Playboy* sought to cushion men's humiliation about looking at women's bodies. And the facial expressions and body postures of the women posed were meant to make men feel proud in looking. The essence of porn is to seek arousal and gratification without vulnerability, without risk to the self. For male adolescents, looking at women is full of risk in the form of humiliation, desperation, and sexual distress. Since masturbation itself is often experienced as risky, ambiguously approved by the world, and a sign of failure, porn must cushion its implicit risk.

I suspect that the more men feel victimized by intrusive images, the more they will need pornographic images; and that intrusive images, because they are experienced as nonconsensual by so many men, are more likely to encourage men to justify violence against women than is pornography, which, although often sexist, is at least felt as consensual. Much pornography strikes me as a kind of revenge against women's putative capacity to arouse through appearing sexy, revenge against the pain caused by intrusive and stolen images, revenge against women's sexiness itself. (Male lust is often felt as revenge.) Pornography is a kind of prop that attempts to offer training in the emotion work of attaining sexual arousal and gratification while feeling proud, and feeling little identification with women.

Radical feminists have argued that pornography, more than being the mere depiction of the degradation or subordination of women, *actually* degrades and subordinates women. Many people find this formulation problematic. How can pictures do more than depict? How can they actually degrade or subordinate? The answer lies in seeing that in our social practices we have many symbolic methods of degrading and celebrating people and classes of people.[9] I think the formulation is correct for much (but not all) of porn. I would amend it to say: Much porn degrades and subordinates "sexy" women or "sexiness" in women and by implication all women. Some porn seems ambiguous in this regard, complex and difficult to classify in terms of social grading.

A brief comparison of pornography with the male sports media may be instructive. Within the context of our social practices the male sports media, that is, the sports page, sports magazines, televised and radio broadcasts of male sports, serve not merely to report or make accessible sporting events. Rather, they also serve to celebrate, honor and *superordinate* the class of athletically skilled men. They help male consumers of sports feel more manly, proud, and, in certain respects, superior to women through helping them vicariously identify with men of extraordinary physical skill.

Much pornography attempts to help men feel manly and proud through feeling aroused by, and superior to, sexy women. Thus, much pornography subordinates and degrades sexy women, not, as I will argue, through treating women as objects without consciousness, but through treating them as bodies given stereotyped subjectivities that encourage men to feel superior.

3. Subjectified Bodies

"Objectification" may be the central concept in the feminist critique of pornography. Porn is often decried for presenting women as mere objects or things, and for encouraging men to so regard them. As Susan Griffin puts it:

> At the very core of the pornographic mise-en-scène is the concept of woman as object. A woman's body forms the center of a magazine. She spreads apart her thighs and stares into the camera. Her tongue licks her lips. *Her eyes reflect back nothing:* she *is not human.* . . . She wears white sheer stockings . . . white pearls. . . . She is decorated in whiteness. In her image all the meanings of absence are realized. Her "whiteness" opens out to a *blank space in the mind.*
>
> . . . For the pornographic camera performs a miracle in reverse. Looking on a living being, a person with a soul, it produces an *image of a thing.* (Italics mine.)[10]

And Diana Russell and Laura Lederer attack nonviolent porn on similar grounds:

> Not all pornography is violent but even the most banal pornography objectifies women's bodies. An essential ingredient of much rape and other forms of violence to women is the objectification of

the woman. This is not just rhetoric. It means that women are not *seen* as human beings but as *things*. (Italics mine.)[11]

These views strike me as misbegotten and in need of demystification. The notion that pornography teaches men to view women as objects or things has, roughly speaking, at least two disparate, sometimes conflicting, meanings. An object or thing differs from a person in two relevant ways: (1) an object lacks autonomy and is treated as such, that is, it is meant to be *used* for one's purposes; (2) an object lacks subjectivity or consciousness and is so experienced (and is thus to be "used" in the first sense). The "use" sense of objectification differs significantly from the "lacks subjectivity" sense. Griffin, Russell, and Lederer seem to believe that through denying women's subjectivity in the depiction of women and encouragement of fantasy, porn encourages men to use women sexually without respecting their autonomy.

But notice some ways men use women sexually and the wide range of acknowledgment of subjectivity that can accompany them:

1. A rapist projects false subjectivity onto a woman and scares her into "consent," rapes her, then asks for a date. A not uncommon phenomenon.
2. A rapist with exaggerated vigilance accurately attends a woman's subjectivity, perceptively identifying her moods, and maneuvers as she seeks emotional and physical survival.
3. A rapist minimally notices a woman's subjectivity and physically overpowers her.
4. An intelligent, articulate, perceptive, sexist, "classically bastard" man scrupulously attends a woman's subjective states, listening well, commenting perceptively, signifying a nonexistent concern, making her feel "understood" in order to gain consent. After the conquest, he envinces little interest in her.

Readers can make up their own examples. Using a woman sexually can and does involve a wide range of acknowledgment of the woman's subjectivity. Treating people as if they had no feelings ("using them like a Styrofoam cup and discarding them") is not the same as *experiencing* them as if they had no feelings. A man can objectify a woman while remaining attentive to her subjectivity. In using porn, as in masturbating using one's own fantasies and images, men certainly *use* images of women, and the images of women themselves will "contain" varying degrees and kinds of subjectivity; I don't know if, when, how, or why such processes lead men to exploit (use) women sexually.

But what of the stronger claim that pornographers depict, and men view, women in pornography as things or objects, that is, as lacking subjectivity or consciousness? This view strikes me as wrong for two reasons. First, it is extremely difficult for a person in Western culture to look upon the human body—especially the face—without investing it with subjectivity. (Eye doctors work hard to cultivate a posture in which they can filter out the eye's signification as a subjective gaze, and examine the eye clinically.) Just as it is difficult to experience the food we eat as possessing subjectivity (gingerbread men and animal crackers aside), it is a part of our preintentional acculturated stance toward live human bodies, or images of such, to experience them as subjects. Such a stance is "sedimented" in our nervous system; it is how bodies "show up" for us, temporally and phenomenologically prior to our particular thoughts and beliefs about women and their bodies.

My second objection to the view that porn empties women of subjectivity is that a central ingredient in the sexual charge of most porn, and in the work and motivation of the pornographer, is to present women's bodies that signify subjectivities either sexually exciting to men or that make men comfortable looking at or masturbating to the image, or both. Porn does not so much turn women into objects or things; rather, it turns them into narrowly *subjectified bodies*. In a porn store one is inundated with images of women's bodies conveying stereotyped subjectivities: women as lusty, fearful, alluring, childlike, coy, trusting, hardy, compliant, mean, resistant, and so forth. But, above all, *subjectivities*: unclad women unambiguously signifying certain stereotyped psychic states to fit men's fantasies or cushion men's egos. And the subjectivity signified is inseparable from the body, its posture and, most of all, facial expression. Part of fantasizing (or actualizing) using a woman's body for pleasure involves using the body's subjectivity, that is, the woman's imagined experience of pleasure (or whatever). It is my impression that when focusing on a woman's body in masturbation, whether porn-aided or not, the commonest subjectivity projected is strong sexual heat, and that men's own sexual excitement fuses with that imagined for the woman's body; indeed the particular image of the body is chosen because it can signify sexual heat.

It may well be asked: What of men who have sex with blow-up dolls, mannequins, or dead bodies? Do they project subjectivity onto their "partners" during sex? My hunch is that they seek the tactile and visual simulacra of sex with none of the hassle and anxiety of dealing with an actual person; they are free to project any subjectivity they wish within the constraints of the inexorable preexistent significations of their "partners."

John Berger, writing about the history of painting, makes a useful distinction between the naked and the nude:

> To be naked is to be oneself.
> To be nude is to be seen naked by others and yet not recognized

for oneself. . . . Nakedness reveals itself. Nudity is placed on display.
  To be naked is to be without disguise.
  To be on display is to have the surface of one's own skin, the
hairs of one's own body, turned into a disguise. . . . Nudity is a form
of dress.[12]

And for Berger the point of the nude "form of dress" is to project a
certain stereotyped subjectivity that flatters the painting's probable male
viewers. In my terms the nude is a form of sophisticated, stylized subjectification of women's bodies. The "naked," the woman painted or photographed as herself, also occurs in pornography; for example, in porn
films where a couple is enjoying each other sexually despite lights and
camera, the woman (and man) may be honestly reflecting her subjective
states. (Men may still project a distorted subjectivity onto the woman.)
  In *Playboy's Women of the World*,[13] I count 149 pictures of unclad women;
148 are subjectified bodies; one (mysteriously included) is a picture of a
woman who happens to be without clothes, being herself. What distinguishes her from the other 148? In the 148 subjectified bodies, the two
main signifiers of subjectivity, facial expression and body posture, both
refer to the fact that their bodies are being viewed by men; their subjectivity is a complement to their viewability as bodies. It must be seen to
be understood. (Compare a picture from a nudist magazine with a *Playboy* centerfold.) It isn't that the subjectified body lacks subjectivity and
the woman being herself possesses it; rather, the fact of her nude body
defines the subjectivity of the subjectified body; the felt mood of the
woman being herself defines her subjectivity.
  It is this overdefining of subjectivity that constitutes the most egregious sexism of pornography. Nothing sexist inheres in the visual presentation of unclad women. (Although some men can only relate to such an
image in a sexist way.) It is porn's encouraging of men to possess a
distorted knowledge of women as subjects that is sexist. For most heterosexual men, being sexually attracted to a woman, in part, means being
excited by her body; what is sexist is the inability to simultaneously feel
that excitement and accord women the respect and acknowledgment
they deserve.
  Two motives for the particular subjectification of women's bodies are
to excite and, in varying degrees, to flatter and comfort and give pride
to men. These two motives meld together in porn and may be only
conceptually distinct. But clearly a part of the woman's subjectivity is
presented to turn masturbation and looking at women's bodies into a
proud experience. Male masturbation to porn is fraught with shame for
several reasons: It suggests one's failure as a man for not having a real
woman; it involves looking at an image of a sexy nude woman, an activ-

ity fraught with humiliation in actual experience when stealing, or feeling intruded upon by, sexy images; it involves an absence of mutuality; it
evokes a lingering folk heritage of degradation—it can give one warts,
insanity, or blindness—connected to puritanical impulses; it has for fifteen years been decried as sexist by women. Given this context of
shame, one task of the visual pornographer is to make the male viewer
feel superior, to authorize men to look.

4. Pornography and the Fear of Identification with Women

A third motive in the subjectification of women's bodies is to offer
men arousal and gratification while minimizing men's risk of identifying
with women. I have suggested that porn seeks to offer men sexual
arousal and gratification without risk to the self, and that men's social
perception of women's bodies—whether authorized, stolen, or
intrusive—involves risk. In the partial service of reducing risk we find in
porn not images of whole, erotic, autonomous women, but rather, subjectified bodies of women, that is, bodies whose putative consciousness
and subjectivity, as manifest through facial expression and body posture,
refer, and are a mere complement to, their viewability as bodies to be
fantasized about by men. I want to try to comprehend men's fear of
women and men's need for dominative sex through a look at certain
features of the experience of sexual arousal and sexual relating itself. To
do this I will draw upon the psychoanalytic feminist works of Dorothy
Dinnerstein and especially Nancy Chodorow.[14]

The experience of sexual arousal and "having sex with another" necessarily involves a loosening of one's identity boundaries. Predominantly
mother-raised men get their often tenuously held identity as masculine
by slowly separating from a mother with whom they were nearly psychically inseparable in early infancy, and identifying with a remote father
and rather grandiose cultural stereotypes of masculinity. This shift in
identification leaves some men perpetually uncertain of their masculinity
and in possession of an insatiable need to prove it. Having sex with a
woman threatens men's masculinity by unconsciously signaling a desire
to regress and experience a certain infantile safety and union that was felt
in the arms of mother. Hence, men defend themselves against this desire
by relating to sex as an occasion for domination. Pornography can be
seen as a kind of training in the emotion work of achieving arousal and
gratification with minimal identification with women.

How does this process work? First, a look at arousal and sexual relating: Generally speaking, sexual arousal involves a diminution of self-
consciousness and ego control and regressively allowing biological
processes to run their course. Sexual arousal loosens identity boundaries
for several reasons: It causes one to focus on spontaneous, somewhat

involuntary, physical sensations and excitations rather than identifying with one's thoughts, (the more one focuses on physical sensations instead of thoughts, the looser one's ego boundaries); sexual arousal relaxes muscular tensings and holdings that give one a felt sense of control over body image and one's ongoing background sense of identity; one's facial expression is more fluid and out of control—altering one's facial expression actively alters self-image.

If sexual arousal itself loosens ego boundaries, having sex with another person further intensifies the process. Mutual sexual arousal usually involves instantaneous patterns of recognition of desire: I am aroused at my recognition of your arousal at your recognition of my arousal at my recognition of your arousal. And so on. My desire and your desire respond to and feed each other with such instantaneous automaticity that they may seem to fuse. Part of the meaning of one's own desire is to seek recognition of itself through arousing the other's desire by recognizing the self's desire.

Whatever the sources of such structural fusings in sex, they are intensified by the simple experience of being held. The more two lovers are focused and attuned to physical sensations of comfort and pleasure, and the less identified with thoughts, the greater the likelihood that they will feel fused and part of some larger, autonomous biological process. And the melting sensation of orgasm can further loosen one's boundaries.

I will now shift to the psychoanalytic; I want to pursue some intuitions as to why the experience of having sex with women might threaten some men's sense of themselves as masculine and would cause them to defend against this by viewing sex as an occasion for domination. My view follows that of Nancy Chodorow. Chodorow accounts for certain differences in men and women through an analysis of certain psychic patterns that result from being parented in early childhood predominantly by a woman. In early infancy both boys and girls experience a psychological oneness, or "primary identification," with the mother, in which the baby's identity is fused with the mother's. For my purposes, it doesn't matter whether such an absolute psychological oneness exists; a strong feeling of identification and safety will do. As boys and girls separate from the mother, they have two radically different developmental tasks. The little boy must realize that he will grow up to be a man and so must shift his identification to his father—a difficult, wrenching trial. But in shifting identification he may also shift some erotic attachment; this he may learn is unacceptable and must be defended against. The girl must shift her erotic attachment to her father while retaining her maternal identification. The father in this traditional model is a distant, remote, often absent figure. The boy is likely to distort and glorify his remote father and identify with his distorted perception of his father's role, and with grandiose cultural stereotypes of masculinity. The boy's understanding of his father—and masculinity—is insufficiently constrained by his father's presence. The boy comes to define his masculinity negatively— as that which is not feminine; he attempts to repress his internalized primary identification and dependence on his mother. He represses what he regards as feminine within himself and devalues what he perceives as feminine in the external world. As a result, masculinity becomes a life-long problem that is never completely resolved. The boy becomes accomplished at separation and the denial of relationship; his ego boundaries are rigid and less essentially relational than those of a girl. The young girl, by contrast, identifies with a mother who is present; her sense of herself as feminine is less likely to be problematic.

The all-too-familiar man who is (1) deeply insecure about his masculinity and possesses an insatiable need to prove it, (2) homophobic and defends himself against homosexual desire, and (3) has difficulty identifying with women and puts them at a distance, relating to them in a sexist fashion as either "Madonnas" or whores, can be better understood in terms of Chodorow's model. Male homophobia and sexism have in common the inability to identify with someone sexually attracted to men.

To Chodorow's account I want to add the following. Because emotional and physical distress causes a mother-raised infant boy to need and identify with the mother, as the boy grows older, creating and conquering emotional and physical distress becomes a way of proving masculinity and separating from the mother. Virtually any form of physical or emotional distress can be converted into an occasion for "taking it like a man" and proving one's manhood: physical pain, fear, sorrow, alcohol, unpleasant smells, "grossness" generally, psychological pressure of any kind, are examples. Male sports and the meaning of male competence generally cannot be separated from the dynamic of creating and conquering distress to prove masculinity. Those who cannot succeed at this are castigated as feminine: sissies and momma's boys. And to repeat: It is precisely because emotional and physical distress for so many years caused the boy to burrow into his mother's arms for safety that such experiences are threatening to boys and men and must be ritually or nonritually created and conquered without regression (crying or weakness or incompetence) in order to prove masculinity. This dynamic informs and motivates social form.

But the greatest threat of all to men's sense of masculinity is *women*. Being held by a woman carries with it for many men the threat that they will give in to a deeply repressed desire to return to the safety of their mother's arms. Such a desire is felt as threatening because it might entail a loss of the sense of the self as masculine and possibly an appearance of homoerotic desires. (If I am identified with mother, I may become attracted to father.) It should be easy to see how sex becomes an occasion for men to prove masculinity through "dominative fucking." Sex becomes something a man *does to* a woman. Our most fundamental conception of sex, as manifest through language, views it as an act of aggressive degradation done by a man to a woman: "I want to fuck her."

Men's need to be in control of sexual feeling may in part be a need to control a repressed desire to identify with women. Pornography can thus be seen, in light of all the above, as a means of achieving arousal and gratification without risking identification with women. Being aroused by looking at what one can control—an image held in the hand—is safe for men. Looking distances men from women; the stereotyped images of porn further distance and defamiliarize women from men. Women become the "other."

And there is a way men have sex with women as if their partner's body is a pornographic image: They fuck the image of the body more than the body itself. The visual supercedes the tactile. The tactile, with its greater threat of identification, is diminished. And the use of sexually exciting images during sex can offer a man a kind of safety against the threat of identification.

What might porn look like if men felt freer to meld and identify with women during sex? If women and sex were not so often for men an occasion to prove masculinity through a dominating phallic athleticism? It is impossible to describe what does not yet exist. I will only say that porn would be less pathetically worshipful of the penis, more respectful of women, perhaps even evocative of a certain love.

Heterosexual men may deeply fear identification with women because they unconsciously desire it. But they also badly need nurturance and sex from women. And, for many men, to have both at the same time is too threatening. So women are divided into Madonnas and whores; the Madonna offers nurturance and the whore offers sex—but only at a safe psychic distance. Both views of women are important to consider in struggling to think politically about porn.

5. Madonna Sexists and Whore Sexists, Sex as Pleasure and Sex as Relating

The attempt to arrive at a politics of pornography has divided the world of feminist women. It divides me as well. Porn is like a prism attracting and diffracting the light generated by competing, often implicit, models of sex and forms of sexism: The spectrum of light it reflects is a function of the part of the light it receives. What one sees when one looks at porn tends to be a function of the light generated by implicit, sometimes unconscious assumptions about sex and sexism. A situation exists where sexual conservatives decry porn because it's wildly sexual, feminists attack it because it's perniciously sexist, advocates of sexual freedom celebrate it because it's sexual, and still other feminists acknowledge its sexism but seek to honor its potential to help liberate women's sexuality. In what follows I aspire not so much to offer a finely polished coherent position (a "foolish consistency") as to present some of my own struggles to think about porn and, in so doing, to offer a few useful insights along the way.

I want to roughly distinguish two conceptions of sex and two kinds of sexism. The two conceptions of sex: the human relating model and the intensity of pleasure model. Two kinds of sexism: whore sexism and Madonna sexism. These distinctions are meant as fluid, provisional aids to thought, identifiable methods by which porn can be, in fact is, understood. I want to first explain these models, show something about how they "interact," and then apply them more concretely to pornography.

The human relating model views sex as a form of communication, an expression of affection and love, and (in its traditional form) preferably as heterosexual and sanctified by matrimony. Sex is sacred, beautiful, dignified, pure, clean, tender, and gentle. Sexual pleasure is an intimate gift offered to the beloved. The relating model represents the proper view of sex associated with the mainstream America of the 1950s and advocated by many sexual conservatives today.

The intensity of pleasure model legitimates sheer pleasure as a motivation for sex. Varieties of partners, the absence of required intimacy, the exploration of technique, the presentation of self and perception of others as potential sources of sexual pleasure, and tolerance of diverse desire are all part of the pleasure model. The pleasure model has most purely manifested itself of late in parts of the pre–AIDS gay subculture. The pleasure model has evolved among heterosexuals in the last thirty years as a response to the putative hypocrisy, repressiveness, and intolerance of the relating model. The increased availability and effectiveness of birth control has freed women to explore pleasure sex. The advent of AIDS has encouraged everyone toward relating sex. Pleasure sex and relating sex exist as historical and psychological complements. Generally speaking, proponents and practitioners of pleasure sex tolerate proponents of relating sex far better than the reverse. Pleasure sex is sometimes presented as a supplement to relating sex; conservative Christians like Marabel Morgan have encouraged wives to learn to give their husbands intense pleasure in the service of God and Marriage.

Whore and Madonna sexism reflect tendencies to relate to women either as degraded objects of lust or as nurturant, "pure" mothers and wives. Whore sexism expresses male lust as a kind of revenge against women's capacity to arouse. Whore-sexist men may have great difficulty honoring women's subjectivity and autonomy. Rape is the most egregious expression of whore sexism. Whore sexism is always denigrating but not always lusting; a man or woman might engage in whore sexism by denigrating a sexually expressive woman without lusting after her.

Madonna sexism exalts women's domestic role as nurturers and sentimentalizes the soft, gentle, and fragile feminine. Madonna sexism tends to view women as too soft to engage with the harsh, unsentimental realities of life; hence women function best in the safety of the home. Madonna sexism denies and would repress the reality, complexity, and earthiness of women's lust. Whore sexism and Madonna sexism coexist strongly in many men, who would be glad to see "that bitch wiggling her ass in a miniskirt get raped" (whore sexism) while feeling ready to kill anybody who touched their wives or sisters (Madonna sexism). Men or women may be more overtly whore or Madonna sexist, but it is impossible to be one without supporting the other. Whore sexism and Madonna sexism uphold and imply each other. They both define women in terms of the same categories, sexuality and nurturance, only the Madonna is up and the whore is down. The whore has wildly sexual things done to her and can experience sexual pleasure; she is not nurturant. Men are not allowed to touch the Madonna; she is the essence of nurturance. Both conceptions view women as primarily passive and victimized; both distance and defamiliarize women from men. Both view women in terms of men's power over them. Any conception of women that distances women from men and makes it difficult for men to relate to women's experience is sexist and oppressive to women (and men). Whore sexism and Madonna sexism both seek to destroy women's sexuality: whore sexism by making sexual freedom and expression unsafe for women through sexual abuse and denigration; Madonna sexism by denying the varieties of possible sexual expression in women. Words such as "slut," "cunt," and "piece of ass" are whore sexist; words like "womanhood," "femininity," and "virtuous woman," when used prescriptively, are Madonna sexist.

The pleasure model of sex tends to encourage whore sexism in men because many men cannot find a woman sexy without wanting to degrade her sexiness. The relating model of sex tends to encourage, and be associated with, Madonna sexism, and vice versa. Both minimize the association of woman and pleasure. Pleasure sex is only morally defensible if people possess the willingness and ability to acknowledge and respect each other's "humanity." Given men's historical difficulty at respecting women, pleasure sex is morally problematic.

On the other hand, a woman experimenting with pleasure sex may well be striking a blow against Madonna sexism. The threat of whore sexism (sexual abuse or denigration for being sexual) can move a woman away from pleasure sex toward relating sex.

Men and women actively opposing whore sexism, for example,

through anti-rape work or through opposing the whore sexism of pornography, run the risk of supporting Madonna sexism. In opposing sexual domination and objectification and rape, in struggling to be respectful of women, it is easy to fall into traditional Madonna sexist modes of respectfulness and sentimentality: Since women aren't really whores and sex objects to be fucked, they must really be Madonnas who want sex to be nurturant, loving, and communicative. It is a mistake to allow rapists and whore sexists to define what sex ought or ought not to be between consenting, antisexist men and women; to do so gives them far more power than they deserve. There is nothing *inherently* sexist about a man wanting to do things with or to a woman's body as long as such desires are balanced with a strongly enacted respect for, and acknowledgment of, women.

To apply the above-discussed models of sex and sexism to pornography, I have chosen an example that is probably somewhat atypical but that helps bring out some of the ambiguities of porn. A *Penthouse* centerfold spoke with pride of her work as a stripper, describing herself as slowly, artfully arousing her mostly male audience and herself, taking them "as far as they could go" and herself "as far as she could go." When they could "stand it no longer," she walked off the stage.

Consider seven views of this pornographic performance:

1. A man or woman involved in pleasure sex might like it because it's sexually hot.
2. A sexual conservative who views sex as relating might disapprove because it misvalues sex and its appropriate place in human life.
3. An antiporn feminist might oppose it because it encourages men in whore sexism and is thus whore sexist itself.
4. A whore-sexist man might like it because it makes him feel superior to and sexual toward women. He might regard the stripper as "a nice piece of ass."
5. An antiporn Madonna sexist might oppose it because it assaults the honor and dignity of womanhood, that is, it threatens his or her Madonna sexism.
6. A feminist woman might like it because it exemplifies a woman being sexual and powerful and thus strikes a blow against Madonna sexism.
7. A primarily Madonna-sexist man, resisting his sexual attraction to the stripper through whore sexism that is denigrating but not lusting, might regard her as a despicable slut.

The example is atypical in that most strippers probably do not feel much pride and power in their work; it would probably be difficult for most feminists to see many strippers as striking a blow against Madonna sexism. But it is useful in revealing the range of responses to porn and its potential. For most of us, competing models of sex and sexism live in our psyches and compete for attention as emotional responses when we contemplate porn. Emotional responses always involve and presuppose, in fact *are* in part, evaluations of the world. It is both useful and necessary to identify the cognitive sources of such evaluations. Otherwise much confusion can ensue.

For example, the religious right has opposed porn, in part because it threatens Madonna sexism, that is, because it degrades *femininity* or *womanhood*, two Madonna-sexist notions of women. Feminists have opposed pornography for its whore sexism, because it degrades *women*. There is a world of difference between being against pornography because *it is* whore sexist and being against it because it affronts *one's own Madonna sexism*. Feminist sympathies with the Meese Commission seem to rest on the shaky ground of common opposition rooted in different principles.

One of the reasons I find pornography difficult to assess is because it is genuinely possible for a pornographic image, film, or performance to encourage, or at least be an occasion for, whore sexism and militate against Madonna sexism *at one and the same time*. The stripper described above is encouraging men to view her as an object of lust; to encourage lust is to encourage whore sexism in some men. Yet in being erotically wild and proud and powerful she is legitimating a part of women's sexuality that Madonna sexism would repress. Porn can be a force against Madonna sexism (and by implication whore sexism) when the woman appears to be proud, erotically powerful, and authentically human.

Any "sexy" image of a woman, even if the content of the image is not whore sexist, will be related to by many men in a whore-sexist manner. And any image of sexy women that is sold, no matter what the content, will encourage men to view women and sexual pleasure as commodities to be bought, sold, gotten for free, or stolen—that is, raped. But the fact that many men don't respect women ought not to keep other men and women from exploring their sexuality through nonsexist images.

Another source of confusion. To say that the dissemination of an image is sexist or objectionable is not to say that the practice depicted is sexist or objectionable. For example, in a society where men massively disrespect women, we do not need images disseminated of women bound and gagged, because such images are likely to legitimate such disrespect. On the other hand, a woman exploring her sexuality, playing with being tied up, may well be doing something anti–Madonna sexist. We ought to discourage disrespect for women in images, yet free women and men in consensual sexual practices.

It is a mistake to view all of sexuality as a manifestation of gender and men's oppression of women. Gender does not "own" sexuality, sexuality is a child that, to a degree, can talk, walk, indeed strut, by itself. It has a life, history, hierarchies, and modes of legitimation all its own. People, independent of gender, are oppressed by the fact of their sexual practices. Men's oppression of women can cause us to perceive sexuality as an unattractive stepchild of gender. A man on top of a woman, powerfully thrusting into her vagina, is not necessarily reproducing men's domination of women. A woman getting excited by feigning resistance with her lover and being overcome is not necessarily reflecting some "internalized oppression" as a woman. It is (to repeat) a mistake to allow rapists and other oppressive men to define the appropriateness of our sexual pleasures for us. Sexual pleasure, like the pleasures of eating, may just be various, shifting, idiosyncratic, eccentric, and not necessarily psychologically or sociologically motivated. Because the "content" and "effect" of sexual pleasure will always in part be psychological does not mean the *motivation* for what *gives* pleasure must be.

Having stated all of the above, I want to close by reiterating a point made earlier. Most of what I see in the magazines in porn stores strikes me as whore sexist, that is, disrespectful of women and rather vengeful toward women's capacity to arouse. Whatever porn's potential to help free us, it is not being realized.

6. Conclusion

After milling around porn stores, inspecting my sexuality and sexism, questing after insight, appropriating concepts, finding myself in states of reaction and vacillation, posturing and rejecting postures, what stands out is the humiliation that surrounds pornography: the presumption of the pornographic image that men's prior condition is one of humiliation, the humiliation of men sheepishly eyeing images, the humiliation of desperate women in ridiculous poses, of men hiding their humiliation under a false bravado—and so few men able or willing to acknowledge or talk about it. It bears repeating that America is a place where women are brutalized and few men seem to care enough to take action. The challenge of the few is to find a way to break through the straitjacket of men's pain and ambivalence, gain a new kind of clarity and courage, and stop violence against women.

Enter the Academics:

Social Science Research

on Pornography

Eros Thanatized:
Pornography and Male Sexuality

by

HARRY BROD

Feminist critiques of pornography have inveighed against it as that lesser evil which leads to greater sins. Pornography is the relatively milder (and sometimes not so mild) expression of the same masculine mindset that leads in its more extreme forms to rape, battery, and other misogynist crimes of violence men commit against women. But if this analysis is correct, as I believe it is, in order for pornography to play its role as incitement for more extreme behavior, it must at the same time be rooted in more subtle aspects of male domination. Its appeal and efficaciousness cannot be sui generis, unconnected to other aspects of the male psyche. It is this latter link, the connection between pornography and so-called "normal" male sexuality, that is the subject of this essay.

It may surprise some to hear that an analysis claiming to be feminist focuses on the drawbacks to men of present forms of male sexuality. Feminist theory is often considered to be that theory which demonstrates the benefits men derive from their mistreatment and exploitation of women. An analysis that bemoans the sufferings of men is usually assumed to be at best non-feminist and suspected of being at least implicitly anti-feminist.

Nonetheless, I shall attempt in this essay to construct a male feminist analysis of pornography. Feminist critiques of pornography have claimed that in women's opposition to pornography morality and self-interest coincide. That is to say, the image of women in pornography presents both an immoral degradation and exploitation of women, and an image of women's sexuality that has been damaging to women's interests. Arguments used to enlist men in crusading against pornography have usually been based solely on moral appeals, asking men to give up the satisfaction they receive from pornography for essentially altruistic reasons. Such appeals assume that men do receive real pleasure from pornography, and that a stance against pornography requires men to give up on moral grounds inherently desirable aspects of male privilege. This essay argues against these assumptions. I shall argue that when the real effects of pornography on men are understood, one can see that in being asked to give up pornography men are being asked to give up disadvantages, not advantages, of their position.[1]

I shall begin by situating pornography in the social context of its production and distribution, and move from there to a discussion of the negative effects of pornography on male sexuality, invoking as I go along such theoretical models as will elucidate the issues involved. I shall conclude by assessing the possibilities for mobilizing men against pornography. It should be noted that I am here concerned with sexuality and pornography as general social forces and trends. The extent to which any particular individual has internalized the pornographic image of male sexuality discussed here will of course vary from case to case. While I believe that no man can be entirely unaffected by the sexual dynamics analyzed here, the extent to which, for example, heterosexual pornographic standards also enter into homosexual relationships remains outside the scope of this essay.

Pornography is a form of commerce—intrinsically, not coincidentally. The commercial aspect of pornography lies at its very roots. The word itself comes from the ancient Greek words "porne" and "graphein," combined to mean "writing about prostitutes/female captives." Thus pornography has never been merely an image of sex. It has always been an image of the commercialized sexuality of a victim. No matter how subterranean the pornographic market, it is intrinsically tied to that market. It is not simply the case that pornography is first produced for some other purpose, like an erotic work of art designed to express some aesthetic/erotic impulse, and then put on the market. Rather, pornography is produced for the market. Consequently, those who see pornography as fundamentally a free-speech issue misconceptualize it, as do those who see it as an expression of personal sexual freedom. The proper framework for discussion about the manufacture and distribution of pornography is neither sexual ethics nor civil liberties, but business ethics. Anti-pornography campaigns should be conceptualized not as attempts at literary censorship, but as consumer boycotts for product safety. We shall see later some of the deeper reasons for this common misconceptualization.

It follows, then, that there is no such thing as private, personal pornography. No matter how explicit or erotic it may be, a canvas, photograph, work of prose or poetry, etc., created solely to express and thereby enhance an individual's truly personal erotic pleasures cannot be

pornographic. Unless, of course, socially defined stereotypes of eroticism have been so deeply internalized by the individual that one's own
erotic taste is viewed solely as a personalized exemplar of the tableau of
public pornography. In this case, one's pleasure is vicarious, and again
mediated through the public marketplace. It is an open question to what
extent, if any, completely personal erotic experience remains a possibility in today's commercialized society, or whether the ingression of mass
media into the human psyche has become so pervasive that all sexual
experience has become to some extent pornographized, i.e., stamped by
commercial imagery. (This is not to deny the social construction of sexuality in earlier periods as well, but to take note of the unparalleled degree
and sophistication of today's mass manipulation of the human mind and
body.)

For men at least, the latter possibility seems to most accurately reflect
the realities of male sexuality today, and to provide graphic illustration
of how the pornographic industry, usually conceived of as working to
the advantage of men and the detriment solely of women, deprives men
of personal satisfaction as well. To the extent that men are dominated by
public images of what constitutes beauty, they are deprived of develop-
ing their own interpersonal relationships and experiences. Consider the
common "1–10" rating scale by which male banter judges women. The
scale is taken to measure objective features about the woman herself, not
subjective factors of the individual male's response. The difference between the statements "She's a 10" vs. "I'm attracted to her," the latter
being self-referential while the former is not, demonstrates the pseudo-
objectivity men try to reach by evading their own subjectivity in their
pursuit of public sanction for their sexual desires. The latter is more
intimate, and hence more threatening, to the traditional masculine
psyche. The attempt to turn feelings into facts, and the accompanying
self-alienation and stress, are important factors in the emotional straitjacket men are forced into, and for which they pay the price in many
ways: lack of real friendship with either gender, tension-related health
problems, etc.

The vicarious possession of the female in pornography clearly goes
hand in hand with a more general possessiveness men feel towards
women, all part of the same general public appropriation of women's
bodies. The extreme case of "woman as trophy" is of course rape, as
Susan Brownmiller, among others, documents in her tales of conquering
armies appropriating the women of the conquered.[2] But this mentality
also enters into sexual relationships in much more subtle ways. A nice
illustration of how this backfires against men is given in an old cartoon
by Jules Feiffer. We see two men talking over drinks, with one announcing to the other that he's "quit going out." Perplexed and disturbed, the
other asks why. The first proceeds to tell a tale of "the loveliest, purest

experience I ever hope to have—a fantasy come true—me with the most beautiful, delightful girl in the world—and she *loves* me! She loves *me!*" The story includes superb food, conversation, lovemaking, etc. The punch line has the lucky fellow telling his companion, "And all that time do you know what I was thinking? . . . Wait till I tell the fellas."[3] Now, if part of one's consciousness is not in the present situation but is already occupied with the victory tale one is going to tell one's male companions, obviously a part of oneself is not in touch with the present and able to enjoy the experience. The activity of mentally putting "notches on your cock,"[4] as one man put it, clearly limits male sexual satisfaction at the same time that it exploits women. This is the dimension of male sexuality Susan Griffin can be understood to be referring to when she writes: "This detachment at the core of experience is another aspect of the creation of pornography which reflects the essence of the pornographic sensibility."[5]

In order for the body to be used as a trophy, as it is in pornography, the type of conquest and the shape of the body conquered must be of a form validated by the society as a whole. Pornographic and more general standards of beauty, such as those used in advertising, accordingly shift in tandem. Two trends can illustrate this connection. As the women's movement popularized a more assertive image of women, a pornographic backlash emerged in which child pornography became more prevalent in an attempt to infantilize women again, and in which pornography became more explicitly sadomasochistic. The former was reflected in the general culture as the image of the sex goddess became progressively younger, until some of the highest-paid models were in their early teens. Brooke Shields was the most famous figure in this trend: the same mass culture industry that feigned shock at her portrayal of a child prostitute in the film *Pretty Baby* later apotheosized her desirability as a sex object. Increased sadomasochism is reflected in today's "post-assault look" in fashions. In any previous era, a civic-minded person finding a woman walking the streets with her clothing torn in the manner of today's styles would have rushed her to a medical facility and asked if she knew the identity of her assailant. Today, the perpetrator's name is likely to be prominently emblazoned on the garment in a designer label. Both trends mirror pornographic developments.

Commercialized sex requires dependably replicable standards of beauty. Hence, personal idiosyncratic tastes must be obliterated and sexual desire forced into a single mold, with minor variations whose function is to obscure the fundamentally monolithic nature of the image. If taste were left free to develop, one would expect a great deal of variety in the objects of desire, if indeed in a truly free society there would even be anything approaching what we today think of as "standards" of beauty. Perhaps individuals in such a society would be free to appreciate the natural beauty of all. In any case, the ease with which consensus is reached today on what makes someone "attractive" reveals the degree of coercive manipulation imposed on all of our sexual desires. The supposed freedom all men then enjoy to participate in joint evaluations and grading of women's bodies, whether in pornographic literature, in the streets, or in organized beauty pageants, is in reality a sign of how completely men have internalized the standards of the commercial industries that dominate them. The same system that sells women's bodies also uses them to sell some men's products to other men, and requires the same standardization and levelling of differences for both purposes. A freedom that amounts simply to discretionary application of the standards used by others to control one's own desires is a freedom hardly worth the name.

Pornography, then, obliterates specific differences among people in order to achieve a standard uniformity in the objects of desire sought in the culture. Hence its fixation on lone interchangeable body parts in isolation from the unique totalities of the bodies of which they are parts. In so far as Aristotle was correct to maintain that a human hand detached from a human body is no longer really a human hand, pornography, then, does not really deal with living bodies. Reducing the diversity of desire and the humanity of the object of desire tends to correspondingly reduce the intensity of desire. As one analyst of the effects of pornography on men puts it:

> By limiting sexuality through its standardization, sex becomes greatly narrowed and ultimately boring. By reducing sensuality to genital orgasm, porn contracts a large, varied and hard-to-control human need into a small, quick, controlled jerk-off. By unlimited exposure of breasts and cunts detached from real people, over-saturation eventually reduces to near-nothing the porn consumers' capacities to be genuinely stimulated by human beings.[6]

In so far as pornography lessens desire, it may therefore be said to be anti-erotic. Indeed, in many ways pornography seems more closely allied to what some, following Freud, have referred to as the death instinct, Thanatos, than to what is referred to as the life forces, Eros. A closer examination of these concepts will help elucidate other dimensions of pornographic sexuality.

The death instinct (which is Freud's usual term, "Thanatos" becoming the favored term for followers in the Freudian tradition) represents a desire for stasis and equilibrium. In such a state, there is no felt want or tension. Thanatos represents the cessation of desire. In contrast, the life instinct, Eros, is not a state of repose but a state of creative tension. Erotic pleasure generated by an object of desire presupposes some distance in which the desired object is differentiated from the desiring subject. Erotic arousal arises from the union achieved in the overcoming of this differentiation. (Speaking of an "object" of desire here does not preclude the possibility that this "object" is itself recognized as the repository of its own subjective desires. Indeed, as I shall argue shortly, erotica, as opposed to pornography, requires such recognition.) As Freud puts it:

> It is easy to show that the value the mind sets on erotic needs instantly sinks as soon as satisfaction becomes readily obtainable. Some obstacle is necessary to swell the tide of the libido to its height.[7]

Eros is an integrative force, as opposed to the entropic dissolving force of Thanatos. It seeks not the cessation or satiation of desire, but its prolongation. Rollo May contrasts sex with eros in these terms:

> The pleasure in sex is described by Freud and others as the reduction of tension; in eros, on the contrary, we wish not to be released from the excitement but rather to hang on to it, to bask in it, and even to increase it. The end toward which sex points is gratification and relaxation, whereas eros is a desiring, longing, a forever reaching out, seeking to expand. . . . eros seeks union with the other person in delight and passion, and the procreating of new dimensions of experience which broaden and deepen the being of both persons.[8]

In contrast, and in relation to the death instinct, Freud notes "the likeness of the condition that follows complete sexual satisfaction to dying,"[9] and Herbert Marcuse writes:

> The death instinct operates under the Nirvana principle: it tends toward that state of "constant gratification" where no tension is felt—a state without want.[10]

It is in this sense that pornography is thanatic, or anti-erotic. Its presentation of the immediate availability of the female body, ignoring the independent will of the female, precludes any erotic state of desire. Since the female in pornography is one already possessed by the male, it does not grant the requisite autonomy to its object which would allow desire to arise. The fear of women expressed by pornography's images of domination over women also bespeaks a lessening of desire since, as Susan Griffin notes, "the feeling of fear acts to prevent feeling, especially desire."[11] In this regard, pornographic sex can be spoken of as not really pleasurable. To quote Marcuse again:

> What distinguishes pleasure from the blind satisfaction of want is
> the instinct's refusal to exhaust itself in immediate satisfaction, its
> ability to build up and use barriers for intensifying fulfillment. [12]

In its most general terms, the difference between erotica and pornography can be understood as the difference between the sexual subject
and the sex object. Even the noun vs. adjectival forms of "sex" vs. "sexual" in these locutions reflects the difference between dynamic process
and reified product. In pornography the body is reduced to an object,
and no personality shows through. In erotica, the personality is expressed through the body as the subjective agent behind the sexual self.
We shall return to this matter of the relation between the person and the
body shortly. For the moment, it suffices to contrast the popular image
of the centerfold model with the erotic nude. In the former, all other
aspects of the portrait are there simply to call attention to the body
merely as sexual object, from the positioning of the body and the facial
expression to accouterments like bedding and drapery. An erotic portrayal, however, presents interaction between the person and the environment, an interaction not solely between the viewer and the body in
the work but one testifying to the personality inside that body. In fact,
the centerfold is rarely fully nude, fully interactive with her environment. Some article of clothing remains: jewelry, drapery fallen over a
limb, undergarments, etc. These point to the fact that the most conspicuous presence in the pornographic image is the absence of the woman's
clothing. Symbolically, this is a woman who has been denuded, a
woman whose clothes have been removed by her audience. In contrast,
the body in erotica represents the body before its encounter with society, in its purity before the social self is donned in clothing, not the
body that has been more or less forcibly removed from its social setting.
The pornographic nude demonstrates the power imbalance between the
object portrayed and the male audience; the erotic nude portrays reciprocity between the unadorned self and its environment. Whereas erotica unites and expands relations between the self and others and aspects
of the self, pornography isolates and constricts these elements.

Attempts to understand the connections between violence and pornography must therefore begin at this fundamental level of pornography's depersonalization and objectification of its subjects, which are
symptomatic of the early stages of inculcating predispositions towards
violence, and not merely consider the degree of violence explicitly depicted in the image. It should be stressed that those who cite a supposed
failure of empirical laboratory research to demonstrate that increased
exposure to pornography increases propensities towards accepting or
committing violent acts are guilty of a non sequitur in using this to argue
against the claim that there are causal relationships between pornogra-

phy and violence. Such studies, of which a significant and growing number do in fact affirm a link between violence and pornography, can only measure whether *increased* levels of exposure to pornography lead to *increased* levels of pro-violent attitudes or behaviors above what is considered a societal norm. They do not and cannot measure the effect of the general circulation of pornography in establishing a norm of dominating and exploitative sexuality throughout the culture, thus raising the general level of acceptability of violence in the ethos of the culture. While cross-cultural comparisons might be relevant to the latter question, much of the evidence often cited in this debate is decidedly not.

In the pornographic image, the necessary corollary to the presence or the absence of the woman's clothing is the absence of any real presence of the woman herself: she, as a living individual presence, is not there at all. What is there is an indealized other, an ideal of a female body. At the heart of pornography, then, lies a great void, to be filled by the male imagination. The pornographic image, in contrast to the erotic image, or indeed to any aesthetic image, which presents a unified whole, is radically incomplete. It depends on the male imagination to complete it. To fulfill this task, the male imagination must be suitably prepared. This entails that pornography is dependent on its social environment to fill in its missing gaps in a particular way, and is thus parasitic upon the social conditioning operative in the society in which it appears.

The male imagination can fulfill its part in the manufacture of the pornographic image because it already performs the same mental operation with other women in the society. It abstracts their sexuality from other aspects of their individuality, and fixates on bodily parts or attributes which one woman has in common with others. Male sexuality, in contrast to female sexuality, is radically discontinuous, isolated from other aspects of human life. Whereas women's sexuality is usually more integrated with their emotional and intellectual lives, men tend to compartmentalize and separate sexual from other feelings. Here the greater compartmentalization of men's lives into disparate spheres of work, home, and play enters into men's sexual lives as well. And here too this discontinuity has negative consequences for men, alienating them from a more humanly fulfilling sexuality. Again, the same forces that objectify women work to restrict and limit male sexuality as well. Male sexuality, under pornographic influence, has restricted male sensuality. Excessive emphasis on the genitals as the sole source of sexual satisfaction and on the orgasm as the goal of sexual activity has narrowed the range of male sexual satisfaction. The male performance principle has herein moved from the workplace to the bedroom, making the male exclusively focused on the end result of sex, its product, seen as the male orgasm, rather than on the entire sensual process.

The model that sees the goal of sex as the release of tension is, as we have seen, anti-erotic. Despite the widespread belief that pornography serves as a release for male sexual tension, those who peddle pornography are aware that it actually serves to increase male sexual tension and discomfort, not the positive sort of creative, interactive tension alluded to earlier as erotic, but a debilitating, isolating nervousness. The following report from a man who worked on an offshore oil rig tells well the effect of

> the porno mags and skin flicks provided by the companies, suppos-
> edly to release sexual tension. . . . Its real purpose is to keep our
> appetites directed at suitable female objects in a situation where
> any *personal* expression of sexuality would get one in trouble. The
> shared hunting-pack horniness of a group of men jeering at a skin
> flick lets everyone feel quite normally male. The relief function is a
> sham: these sessions are meant to *keep* us tense, to keep our hetero-
> sexual identity in shape. [13]

The reshaping of the male body into a tool of aggression comes through in the way the male body is referred to in pornographic writing. It becomes a hard machine, with the penis its primary weapon. In this context, one can begin to understand how the same slang term "hot rod" can undergo historical transformations which enable the same term to refer to an automobile, gun, or penis. To bring themselves into relationship with an objectified female body, males must objectify their own bodies as well. The necessary corollary to pornography's myth of female instant availability is its myth of male perpetual readiness. Just as the former is an important source of misogyny, creating anger as real women fail to live up to the expectations of pornographic fantasies, so is the latter an important source of male insecurity, as men fail to live up to pornographic standards of sexual acrobatics performed by oversized organs. As Bernie Zilbergeld writes of what he calls "The Fantasy Model of Sex":

> Not only are fantasyland penises much larger than life, they also
> behave peculiarly. They are forever "pulsating," "throbbing," and
> leaping about. The mere sight or touch of a woman is sufficient to
> set the penis jumping, and whenever a man's fly is unzipped, his
> penis leaps out. . . . Nowhere does a penis merely mosey out for a
> look at what's happening. . . . The names given to these penises re-
> flect their inhuman nature—tools, weapons, rods, ramrods, batter-
> ing rams, shafts, and formidable machines. Somehow the humanity
> of the penis has been lost. [14]

The mechanization of sex appears in some unexpected, nonpornographic quarters as well. Some sex self-help manuals for men which claim to solve problems of male sexual dysfunction can end up reinforcing the problem by perpetuating this kind of dehumanizing technologization of the male body to the extent that they remove sexuality from its interpersonal context and treat it solely as a question of techniques through which the male can learn to manipulate his or his partner's body to achieve the desired orgasmic result on demand. Male sexual dysfunctional problems ranging from adolescent embarrassment at inopportune tumescence to impotence of various sorts can be traced at least in part to pornographically induced obsessions with penile performance. These obsessions directly contradict biological facts. Despite all the mythological overtones which have accrued to the functioning of the penis, making it a symbol of strength, virility, and musculature, the fact remains that the penis contains no muscle tissue. Its rigidity when aroused results simply from the engorgement of its spongy tissue by the increased blood flow to the area which occurs during sexual arousal. The male erection is nothing more than localized high blood pressure. Its glorification is simply social myth and biological nonsense. The inevitable consequence of all this is male self-deprecation and the loss of fuller sexual satisfaction. As Michael Betzold sums up pornographic distortions of men's self-images:

> When men view women as sex objects, they are also objectifying themselves, a point not often appreciated. . . . Pornography promotes our insecurities by picturing sex as a field of combat and conquest. . . . Emotional needs are denied altogether or telescoped mercilessly into the search to obtain exclusively genital satisfaction. Although what most men want is physical affection from another human being, what they end up thinking they want is to be laid by a Playboy bunny. [15]

Since, as Betzold notes, for men the nonsexual expression of emotional and physical intimacy is so severely inhibited by the traditional male sex role, all of these relational needs become channeled into sexual (i.e., genital) activity, which is then required to bear more than its possible share of human need fulfillment. This accounts for much of the sense of urgency, of being overwhelmed by need, of feeling bodily desires as an external force acting on them, with which many men uncomfortably experience sexual attraction. With various emotional needs experienced but unexpressed as such, and hence unmet, in the sexual situation, sex then becomes disappointing. Furthermore, communication with a female sex partner often moves at cross-purposes over this dynamic. While women tend to experience relational affection as part of sexual activity, men tend to experience it as extraneous prelude or as "just foreplay," prefatory to the real thing. While women then tend to seek the inclusion of more non-orgasmic centered sensuality into lovemaking as an *expansion* of sexuality, men tend to see it as an *intrusion* into sexuality.

Man's alienation from his own body is not simply an incidental feature of male experience. It has had a major impact on the shape of the Western intellectual tradition, going to the core of conceptions of the self, morality, and sexual ethics. At issue here is what philosophers refer to as the mind/body dualism and its relation to the basic framework in which sexual morality is conceived. At this level of generality, pornography is more manifestation than causal agent of this phenomenon, but the connections are nonetheless important.

One's sexual conduct has traditionally in many people's minds been the crux or crucible for one's moral code. When one hears of someone having "loose" or "questionable" morals, sexual connotations predominate. But why should this be so? What is the intrinsic connection between sexuality and morality that makes sexuality of such paramount moral concern? Two opposing answers emerge from the Western intellectual tradition.[16] The dominant perspective reflects the mind/body dualism alluded to above. Here, morality is conceived of as the province of an essentially disembodied, universalized moral self. The desires of the body and the flesh are here thought of as limitations or temptations for this moral self, whose duty it is to resist merely natural inclinations. These desires are events which happen to the self, conceived as moral agent. In contrast, there is another perspective to be found in the philosophical tradition, in which desires and emotions do not *happen to* the self, but they are rather seen as *actions* which the self *takes*, and through which it expresses itself. This is a more integrated vision of mind/body unity. Here, rather than appearing as a limitation of the self, the body is seen as the most intimate and immediate embodiment and expression of the self. The two perspectives do not so much provide opposing answers to a given set of questions defining the problems of sexual ethics as they provide different frameworks in which to pose questions of sexual ethics. For the former, the question of sexual ethics is the question of to what degree bodily desires can or should be limited or restrained so as to allow the self to function as a free agent. For the latter, the question of sexual ethics is the question of constructing sexuality so as to allow for the most liberating, authentic self-expression through sexual modes.

From this perspective, one can see that the classic civil libertarian position on pornography, which sees pornography solely as an issue of the right of self-expression vs. restrictive censorship, still operates within the male-oriented mind/body dualism framework, though within that framework it takes the extreme position of advocating no restriction of sexual expression. Still, because its concern is only with the quantitative question of *whether* sexuality is expressed or repressed, and not with the qualitative *content* of that sexual expression, it remains entirely within that framework. In contrast, feminist perspectives on pornography have been more coincident with the more integrated, holistic vision of mind/body unity, in that they have questioned whether an authentic self is portrayed in pornography. A male feminist approach to sexual ethics would concern itself not with the release of desire as presently constituted, but with the construction of liberating erotic relationships.

The present social construction and restriction of sexuality has a great deal to do with why it is so easy for males to slip into seeing pornography as sexually liberating. Given the sexually repressive nature of our society, any expression of sexuality, even of a distorted kind, can easily appear as liberating. What is missing in such an attitude, however, is an awareness of how pornography feeds on and reinforces the repressive attitudes towards sexuality it is ostensibly in rebellion against, at least if one listens to the self-justifying rhetoric of magazines like *Playboy*. To the extent that pornography's dehumanizing version of sexuality is accepted as valid, it lends credence to an antisexual morality. Furthermore, much of pornography's appeal, especially to adolescent males in their formative years, lies in its "forbidden fruit" content. Pornography flourishes in and is parasitic upon a repressive, not a liberated, sexual atmosphere, the Victorian case being a clear example. While earlier in this essay increasing violence in pornography was attributed to a backlash against the success of feminism in increasing women's social status, this increase can also be attributed in part to a failure to achieve a truly liberating sexual ethic, and the attendant return, in the same period, to more repressive standards of sexual behavior (repressive in terms of the quality of eros, not the quantity of sex, in people's lives). In this sense, pornography represents the underside of repressive standards of "propriety," the return of the repressed in a still repressed form, one which indeed validates the context that reprises it. The antidote to salaciousness (a term with connotations of morbidity, which shares with the term "assault" a common etymology relating to the Latin "salax," the leap of the male animal) is the cultivation, not the suppression, of eros.

At this point, an objection to this litany of male woes must be considered. While this analysis has emphasized pornography's constriction of male sexuality, little has been said of its expansion of male power. Pornography does express and enhance men's power over women. Might not the enjoyment of this power more than compensate for the losses described above? Might the former not be sufficient to motivate the latter? If this were true, it would falsify the claim made at the outset of this essay that in being asked to give up the use of pornography men were being asked to give up disadvantages, rather than advantages, of their position. I believe, however, that my claim can survive an examination of men's pornographic power over women. [17] Just as earlier reference to the Freudian psychological tradition helped elucidate dimensions of disadvantages for men in the pornographic model of male sexuality by providing a suitable conceptual model for the analysis of distorted desire, so can reference to the Hegelian-Marxist philosophical tradition help elucidate other dimensions of this question by providing a model for the analysis of distorted social reciprocity. I have in mind specifically the analysis Hegel offers of the consciousness of mastery and bondage in his *Phenomenology*, and analogous analyses other theorists have made by drawing on Hegel's argument, whether implicitly or explicitly. There are, for example, relevant echoes of Hegel in Sartre's *Anti-Semite and Jew*, where he shows how anti-Semitism fundamentally distorts the entire personality structure of the anti-Semite, and in Susan Griffin's analysis of the distortions projected onto others by what she calls "The Chauvinist Mind." What follows is not intended as a systematic interpretation of Hegel's master-servant dialectic and its influence, but rather a selective appropriation of salient points of Hegel's depiction of the limitations of the consciousness of the lord, him who dominates the servant and to whose will the servant is subservient.

Based on his prior analysis of the nature of human life and desire, Hegel postulates an innate need for self-consciousness to have its subjective autonomy objectively validated through recognition by another self-consciousness. While the lord assumed his dominant position in order to force this peer recognition upon the other, the fundamental contradiction and inadequacy of his position, according to Hegel, is that his superior position makes such recognition impossible. His dominance precludes the establishment of the requisite peer relationship. The analogy to men's power over women is obvious. How can a sexual relationship with someone over whom one's will is dominant fill the need for authentic validation with which men come to the relationship?

The corrupting influences of such power have of course been discussed in other idioms as well. To give one example, in an insufficiently noted passage of Mill's *The Subjection of Women*, Mill gives the elimination of the following effects of unmerited authority on the male mind as the first benefit which would follow the establishment of full equality for women:

> Think what it is to be a boy, to grow up to manhood in the belief that without any merit or exertion of his own, though he may be the most frivolous and empty or the most ignorant and stolid of mankind, by the mere fact of being born a male he is by right the superior of all and every one of an entire half of the human race. . . . Is it imagined that all this does not pervert the whole manner of existence of the man, both as an individual and as a social being?[18]

To continue with Hegel's analysis, Hegel discusses the lord's alienation from the productive activity of the servant in ways similar at several points to the Freudian analysis presented earlier. The lord's role is simply to consume and enjoy what the servant has done the labor of preparing. Having one's needs met by another in such immediate fashion means that one never experiences the full range of one's own capabilities. Hence, in Hegel's presentation, the lord's consciousness remains ensconced at this relatively primitive level, while it is the servant who eventually experiences his own transformative power, whose consciousness is transformed and provides the impetus for progress.

Here, several parallels can be drawn with male pornographic consciousness. Men become alienated from their own sensual bodily processes in their focus on the supposed end product of sexuality, orgasmic satisfaction. This leads not only to lessened sensuality, but to many other aspects of estranged bodily awareness men disproportionately suffer from: heart attacks, ulcers, hypertension, etc. Furthermore, as a Hegelian analysis intimates, it is women, the oppressed, who have taken the lead in challenging modes of experience detrimental to both women and men. In terms of applying Hegel's analysis to such social and political liberation movements, the obvious model is Marx's application of it to the relationship between bourgeoisie and proletariat under capitalism. In the primary text in which Marx elaborates his appropriation of Hegel's concept of alienated consciousness, the *Economic and Philosophic Manuscripts* of 1844, Marx alludes to the alienation of the capitalist under capitalism. His remarks there are relevant to the discussion here.

Marx sees the capitalist's consciousness as stagnant, the worker's as dynamic. Just as to the pornographic mind bodies become interchangeable, so too the capitalist is concerned only with the abstract exchange value of commodities, not with their intrinsic function and particularity. "*All* the physical and intellectual senses have been replaced by the simple alienation of *all* these senses, the sense of *having.*"[19] While capitalists as a group control workers, they are in turn controlled as individuals by the market. It is in reference to the alienation of people from their bodily, natural selves that Marx comments that from the character of the relation between men and women, humanity's "whole level of development can be assessed."[20] While this comment is valuable, it has been overemphasized as a sign of Marx's feminist predilections, overemphasized because it retains a romanticized metaphor of woman as nature which much feminist theory rejects. Nonetheless, in that part of the analysis relevant to our discussion here, Marx goes on to contrast the capitalist conception of wealth as minimizing needs through possession with a truly liberated conception of wealth under full communism in which "the wealthy man is at the same time one who *needs* a complex of human manifestations of life, and whose own self-realization exists as an inner necessity, a need."[21] Here we find united in Marx's concept of alienation many of the themes enunciated earlier in the analysis of the drawbacks to men of the thanatic pornographic model of sexuality: the numbing effects on one's sensibilities of the loss of particularity in the pursuit of abstract possession, the loss of one's natural, bodily self, and the reduction of the wealth of needs through which one can develop and express oneself.

If the analysis of male pornographic sexuality has been analytically strengthened by appropriating an analogy from Hegelian-Marxist philosophy, it also stands to have been politically weakened by that appropriation. For, central to both the Hegelian and Marxist analyses is the conclusion that lords or capitalists are inescapably bound to their mode of consciousness, and that liberation can only come from the activities of the underclass. While the use of this analogy may have strengthened the case for the necessity and desirability of a *men's* anti-pornography movement to parallel the women's movement, if this conclusion is transposed to anti-pornographic politics, it augurs poorly for the likelihood of its emergence. It should be noted that Marx's demonstration that capitalists too are alienated under capitalism strengthens his claim that capitalism is an all-encompassing system which consequently needs to be overthrown in its entirety, and not simply reformed. Similarly, the analysis presented here of the ways in which the same pornographic forces that oppress women also harm men should strengthen feminist analyses of the systematic nature of patriarchy and the necessity for its overthrow. Nonetheless, though Marx was willing to include the capitalist's alienation as part of his indictment of capitalism, and even to venture the prediction that as class antagonisms intensified, select individuals from the capitalist class could be expected to change their class allegiance and enlist in the proletarian cause, he would have thought it a waste of strategic resources to attempt to organize capitalists as a group against capitalism. To analytically demonstrate the disadvantages to men in pornography is one thing. To claim that these disadvantages are demonstrable enough to men to motivate significant numbers of them to take action against pornography is quite another. Are there, then, any reasons to believe that one can realistically hope for the emergence of a viable male anti-pornography movement?

To return to the analysis above, the reasons for Hegel's and Marx's pessimism about any change of consciousness among the privileged were the immediacy of their gratification, which provides neither motivation nor opportunity for critical reflection on that gratification, and their passive relationship to the actual productive process, which denies access to the necessary means of inquiry. While the critique of gratification holds when applied to male sexuality, the critique of passivity does not, at least not to the requisite degree. Males are more actively and directly involved in building the social system responsible for their own repression than are Hegel's lords or Marx's capitalists. We must recall that for both Hegel and Marx the purpose for showing that alienation results from the self-alienating activity of the subservient group is not to "blame the victim," in modern parlance, but to allow for the possibility of liberating self-transformation. Not only is this kind of self-liberating emancipatory consciousness possible for men, but there are currently signs of its emergence.

There is in this country a growing anti-sexist men's movement. Its current organizational embodiment on the national level, the National Organization for Changing Men, has an active Anti-Pornography Task Group, and the movement's major journal, M.: Gentle Men for Gender Justice, has carried numerous articles attempting to construct male feminist theory and action along the lines of the perspective presented here. Moreover, in addition to individual men who have joined many feminist actions, anti-sexist men's groups around the country, such as Men Against Rape groups in Santa Cruz and other cities, Boston's EMERGE: A Men's Counseling Service on Domestic Violence, St. Louis's RAVEN (Rape and Violence End Now), and the Men's Alternatives to Violence Task Group of the California Anti-Sexist Men's Political Caucus, have made work against pornography part of their agenda.

The dominant male response to the critique of gender roles mounted by the women's liberation movement has been to see it solely as a movement aimed at liberation *from* men, and certainly not *for* men as well. The most widely publicized male response to women's new sexual freedoms and demands is for men to feel threatened by them. Women's liberation is seen as having been achieved at the expense of men. Rising reports of male impotence, for example, are widely attributed to hostility towards men seen in the women's movement. Women's assertiveness is seen as threatening to the fragile male ego. In contrast, the anti-sexist men's movement has seen in the liberation of women's sexuality the promise of the liberation of men's sexuality—not liberation from women, but liberation from repressive self-imposed sexual standards. Instead of women's sexual awakenings imposing new and additional performance pressures on men, they can actually aid in removing the old ones.

The men's movement's consciousness of the self-destructive effects of pornography has even begun to filter out into other movements. For example, a particular incident was reported in the men's jail during the Diablo Canyon anti-nuclear blockade. While most of the activities had a strong feminist consciousness, once 800 men were separated into the prison and prison authorities distributed pornographic literature along with other reading material, "that atmosphere began to disintegrate," as one of the participants put it. His account continues: "Some courageous and concerned men began to see what was happening and, within a few days, succeeded in changing the jail environment back to something very close to what it had been in the camp itself [prior to the blockade]." A statement was read which, in part, defined pornography as "a disastrous pattern in which gender and sexuality are formed as weapons of power and control—in which men are formed into nightsticks, in which we become terrorists of the flesh." He reports that the pornography subsequently either disappeared or went underground, and that men talked about the role of pornography in their lives, making connections to the other forms of exploitation and domination they were there to protest. [22]

Men do experience the drawbacks of the pornographic model of sexuality in their sexual dissatisfactions, in their fears and self-doubts about meeting up to pornographic performance principles, and in their lack of reciprocity in their relations with others. They can on that basis respond to a call to action against pornography on the grounds that if the love men feel for others is perverted by imposed pornographic sensibilities, then, in the words with which Marx concludes his analysis of alienation, "your love is impotent and a misfortune." [23]

Pornography, Sexual Callousness, and the Trivialization of Rape

by

DOLF ZILLMANN and JENNINGS BRYANT

Research on the behavioral effects of extensive exposure to sexually explicit writings, photographs, and motion pictures has been guided, if not controlled, by prevailing attitudes about human sexuality. Sex, according to the values manifest in these attitudes, is generally wholesome and good fun; the description or depiction of such behavior, regardless of how sexually stimulating and enticing it might be, must be free from censure (e.g., 15). Eysenck and Nias (9), for instance, promoted this type of moral stance. However, they hastened to point out that the portrayal of sex is occasionally neither wholesome nor good fun, and they went on to declare matters such as pederasty, rape, sadomasochism, and bestiality as socially undesirable and to advocate censorship for the pornographic exploitation of these sexual themes.

Sex that entails any form of coercion or the deliberate infliction of pain is often deemed undesirable. Feminist Gloria Steinem (24) arrived at a similar dichotomy of good and bad sex and at corresponding classes of uncensurable and intolerable portrayals of sex. She declared the depiction of "mutually pleasurable, sexual expression between people who have enough power to be there by positive choice" (p. 37) to constitute "erotica," and she endorsed the use of such sensuous stimuli, as they "give us a contagion of pleasure." On the other hand, Steinem condemned as "pornography" any erotic message that features "violence, dominance, and conquest." For erotica to be "erotica," she insisted, portrayals of sex may involve neither a conqueror nor a victim. And she was vehement in her rejection of any pornographic attempt to convince anybody that to women "pain and humiliation . . . are really the same as pleasure" (p. 37). Again, sexual materials that are victim-free are given "a clean bill of health," and those entailing any kind of victimization are not.

There is considerable ambiguity in such definitional approaches. In the portrayal of sadomasochistic behaviors, for example, the parties involved may be said to be there by "positive choice"; or in depictions of bestiality the animals may do what they do for morsels of food rather than in avoidance of the whip. Despite this ambiguity, the cited approaches appear to express a prevailing consensus among researchers.

Increasingly, investigators of the effects of pornography on aggression have turned away from "standard fare" and have concentrated on violent erotica (25), sadomasochistic themes (18, 30), bestiality (29), and portrayals of rape (6). And in accordance with the value premise that any effect of pornography on sexual behavior in all non-violent variations can only be wholesome, investigators have exhibited little interest in this relationship. As a result, it is virtually unknown how early access to standard or not-so-standard erotic fare might affect sexual development and sexual socialization. It is utterly unclear, for instance, how pornographic fare, with its common script of fellatio, cunnilingus, coition, anal penetration, and multiple partnership, influences and shapes the sexual expectations of young teens who are increasingly likely to be exposed to pornography prior to becoming sexually active.

In short, and perhaps still in the wake of the most controversial research-discouraging verdict of "all effects are trivial" by the 1970 U.S. Commission on Obscenity and Pornography (26, 27; see also 5, 7, 9), researchers have not exhibited a great concern for the consequences of exposure to standard pornographic fare. Additionally, the public at large has been surprisingly quiet—in part, perhaps, because any criticism of pornography places the critic in jeopardy of being accused of adhering to antiquated, non-progressive, obsolete sexual morality. The notable exception has been the women's movement in the United States.

Women have spoken out against pornography generally (1, 2, 4, 17), contending that female sexuality and women as such are being degraded. Pornography is viewed as a powerful force undermining liberal ideology, rather than as a celebration of sexual freedom. To Longino (17), for instance, "pornography is the vehicle for the dissemination of a deep and vicious lie about women. It is defamatory and libelous" (p. 48). And to Brownmiller (2) it "is the undiluted essence of anti-female propaganda" (p. 394). "We and our bodies," she writes, "are being stripped, exposed and contorted for the purpose of ridicule to bolster that 'masculine esteem' which gets its kick and a sense of power from viewing females as anonymous, panting playthings, adult toys, dehumanized objects to be used, abused, broken, and discarded. This, of course, is also the philosophy of rape" (p. 394). Some might disagree with the insinuation that in pornography all sex is rape-like and point to the apparent eagerness on the part of women to participate in that which promises pleasure. Likewise, many might take issue with the declaration of ridicule as a purpose and acknowledge a loving preoccupation with basal sexual lust instead. Few would object, however, to the charge of a preponderance of the characterizations of women in pornography as anonymous, panting playthings that men liberally exploit for sexual self-gratification and any self-enhancing concomitant thereof. Indeed, pornography appears to thrive on featuring social encounters in which women are eager to accommodate any and every imaginable sexual urge of any man in the vicinity. These socially non-discriminating females are typically shown, in fact, to encourage and actively solicit the specific sexual behaviors that are dear to men but not necessarily to women (e.g., fellatio, anal penetration; see, e.g., 22). Perhaps most importantly—and presumably a vital part of what has been referred to as *"male* sexual fantasy"—women are portrayed as hysterically euphoric in response to just about any sexual and pseudosexual stimulation they receive at the hands of the "male magicians."

Needless to say, sexual reality tends to fall short of such magic. Men, inspired by pornography, may well feel cheated and accuse perfectly sensitive women of frigidity. Lacking corrective information, women might actually come to doubt their own sexual sensitivities. Regarding untried activities, pornography again projects euphoria where it might not exist—at least, not for many. That pornography thus entices actions, and that the resultant experimentation leads to less than satisfactory results, can hardly be doubted. Russell (22) has documented that women take the brunt of this type of pornography-inspired experimentation. Men were found to have made women comply with their requests to try what had been seen. Activities ranged from oral sex to group sex, from being gagged to being beaten, and from urination into the mouth to having intercourse with pets at hand. Requests tended to be backed by brute force, and many women reported feelings of degradation and humiliation in addition to having been hurt physically.

It would seem naive, then, to believe that pornography entertains without affecting perceptions of sexuality and behavioral dispositions toward sex and gender. Interestingly, however, research has failed to deal with these potential effects.

Eighty male and eighty female undergraduates from a large eastern university were randomly assigned to four conditions. In three conditions, students participated in experimental sessions over a period of six weeks. Exposure to pornography was massive, intermediate, or nil during that period. In the first and second week after the exposure treatment, the students served in two experimental sessions in which habituation effects were assessed. [1] During the third week after the exposure treatment, students returned once more to the laboratory and were tested for perceptions of sexuality and dispositions concerning sex and gender. A fourth experimental group without any prior treatment was engaged at this time and subjected to the same tests.

Students in the three experimental groups met in six consecutive weekly sessions. They watched six films of about eight minutes' duration each and evaluated aesthetic aspects concerning the production of these films, this evaluation being the ostensible purpose of the research in which they were assisting. In the *massive exposure* condition, students saw six explicitly sexual films per session. This amounts to about 48 minutes of exposure. Over the six-week treatment period, then, they watched 36 erotic films, for a total exposure time of about 4 hours and 48 minutes. In the *intermediate exposure* condition, students saw three erotic films and three non-erotic ones. They consequently saw 18 erotic films in all, exposure time being about 2 hours and 24 minutes. In the *no exposure* condition, all 36 films were non-erotic. The exposure treatments were identical in all respects other than the described variation in erotic stimulation.

All erotic films depicted heterosexual activities, mainly fellatio, cunnilingus, coition, and anal intercourse. None of these activities entailed coercion or the deliberate infliction or reception of pain. The non-erotic films were educational and entertaining materials that had been judged to be interesting. None of these films depicted or made reference to sex-related behaviors. None of the erotic or non-erotic films was presented more than once to a group.

During the third week following the completion of the prior-exposure treatment, the students who had received one of the three treatments and those who had not received any prior treatment participated in a final session. They first estimated, as a percentage, the portion of U.S. adults performing particular sexual acts, common ones as well as uncommon ones. Among other things, they estimated the percentages of sexually active adults, adults employing oral-genital stimulation techniques, and adults practicing anal intercourse, group sex, sadomasochism, and bestiality.

Students were then introduced to a rape case, reading the newspaper coverage of a hitchhiking that resulted in the sexual offense. The rapist's conviction was reported, but a sentence was not stated. Students were asked to recommend a prison term for the particular offense. The length of the term was considered to indicate disapproval or condemnation of rape. Sexual callousness toward women was expected to find expression in minimal prison sentences. Students also indicated their support for the female liberation movement on a scale ranging from 0 (no support) to 100 (maximal support). This assessment was included to learn whether callousness, should it be created, generalizes from sex to gender.

Students were then exposed to a novel sexually explicit film and asked to (a) report their affective reactions (e.g., "it offends me," "it is pornographic") and (b) register the degree to which they objected to measures designed to curtail the distribution of pornography (e.g., restrictions for minors or for broadcasting). All ratings were made on 100-point scales. The second set of measures was employed to assess the general acceptance of pornography.

Finally, the male students filled in a questionnaire designed to measure men's sexual callousness toward women. This questionnaire, developed by Mosher (19), contained items such as: "Pickups should expect to put out," "A man should find them, fool them, fuck them, and forget them," "A woman doesn't mean 'no' unless she slaps you," and "If they are old enough to bleed, they are old enough to butcher."

Table 1, which summarizes perceptual changes, shows that students massively exposed to pornography perceived the use of particular sexual practices and endeavors to be more pronounced than did students who had viewed less pornography. Estimates of persons being sexually active followed the same pattern and were also significantly differentiated ($F(3, 152) = 8.77$, $p < .05$).[2] None of these effects was associated with gender differences or interactions between gender and exposure treatment, all F ratios being close to unity. All effects, then, were the same for men and women.

Table 1. Estimates of the percentage of adults practicing common and uncommon sexual behaviors as a function of exposure to pornography

	No exposure	Intermediate exposure	Massive exposure	No prior treatment	F(3, 152)
Fellatio/cunnilingus	34.0[a]	49.6[b]	67.2[c]	36.2[a]	29.88
Anal intercourse	12.1[a]	19.6[b]	28.5[c]	12.4[a]	11.43
Group sex	10.9[a]	18.2[b]	30.2[c]	11.8[a]	21.95
Sadomasochism	7.4[a]	8.4[b]	14.8[c]	8.6[a]	7.80
Bestiality	6.6[a]	7.9[b]	12.0[c]	8.0[a]	4.31

Note: Means having no letter in their superscripts in common differ at $p < .05$ by the Newman-Keuls test. All F ratios are associated with $< .05$.

Massive exposure to pornography apparently produced visions of people doing more of anything pertaining to sex. Compared to the two no-exposure control groups, visions of hypersexuality seem to be created. Such comparison does not necessarily imply, however, that exposure to pornography distorts assessments of sexuality in society. The determination of distortion rests, of course, on the comparison with reliable estimates of sexual practices in society. While truly reliable assessments do not exist (cf. 8), data on sex aggregated in non-representative surveys (e.g., 16) might be considered the most acceptable basis for comparison. Such comparison with survey data suggests that massive exposure to pornography does not distort the perception of usage of sexual practices that are very popular in society. Estimates of the use of oral-genital stimulation, for instance, more closely approximated estimates based on recent survey data the more students were exposed to pornography. Massive exposure thus could be said actually to correct distorted views of sexuality.

However, estimates of less popular and less accepted sexual practices —such as intercourse with more than one partner at a time, sadomasochistic actions, and animal contacts—approximated survey estimates less closely the more students were exposed to pornography. The popularity of unusual sexual practices was in fact grossly overestimated. Massive exposure to pornography consequently might be said to distort the perception of many aspects of sexuality by fostering the lasting impression that relatively uncommon sexual practices are more common than they actually are. Interestingly, this perceptual shift from uncommon to common is the result of massive exposure to erotica featuring rather common practices. It can only be speculated, at this point, that massive exposure to materials exhibiting sadomasochism and bestiality would have produced an even stronger distortion in the perception of the popularity of these behaviors.

Table 2. Evaluation of an explicit erotic film and recommendation concerning accessibility, as a function of exposure to pronography, on scale from 0 to 100

	No exposure	Intermediate exposure	Massive exposure	No prior treatment	$F(3, 152)$
Is offensive	75.2[c]	42.9[b]	26.3[a]	68.8[c]	18.91
Is pornographic	70.1[c]	47.3[b]	28.9[a]	68.2[c]	18.11
Need for restrictions on minors	83.5[c]	53.6[b]	36.8[a]	76.4[c]	17.69
Need for restrictions on broadcasting	80.8[c]	61.2[b]	43.6[a]	80.5[c]	15.33

Note: Means having no letter in their superscripts in common differ at $p < .05$ by the Newman-Keuls test. All F ratios are associated with $< .05$.

Table 2 summarizes the findings concerning the effect of exposure on dispositions toward pornography itself. As can be seen from the first two rows, pornography was considered less offensive and objectionable by those who had been most exposed to it. This effect applies to men and women alike, as interactions were of trivial magnitude ($F < 1$). Independent of the frequency of exposure, however, women found pornography significantly more objectionable than did men. The mean scores (out of a possible 100) on "is offensive" were 46.9 for males and 59.7 for females ($F(1, 152) = 5.95$, $p < .05$) and on "is pornographic" were 49.0 for males and 58.2 for females ($F(1, 152) = 4.00$, $p < .05$).

The bottom two rows of Table 2 report the perceived need to curtail access to pornography. Recommendations to curtail such access may be assumed to reflect the students' belief that exposure might produce undesirable effects in others and thus is harmful. Again, massive exposure to pornography produced strong and consistent effects, with any concern about potential ill effects apparently diminished by repeated exposure. The effects were again parallel for men and women, as interactions were trivial ($F < 1$). However, whereas females exhibited more concern than males about minors having access to pornography ($F(1, 152) = 4.58$, $p < .05$, mean scores $= 57.1$ for males and 68.0 for females), both genders were similarly concerned about unrestricted broadcast of pornography ($F(1, 152) = 1.71$).

Table 3. Number of months[a] of incarceration recommended for rape, as a function of massive exposure to pornography (by gender)

	No exposure	Intermediate exposure	Massive exposure	No prior treatment	Combined
Male	94.6	78.0	49.8	93.7	79.0[y]
Female	143.6	101.4	77.0	119.7	110.4[z]
Combined	119.1[b]	89.7[ab]	63.4[a]	106.7[b]	

[a] Recommendations are in months, but were made in years and months in response to a specific case.

Note: Means having no letter in their superscripts in common differ at $p < .05$ by the Newman-Keuls test.

Dispositions toward rape, as measured by the incarceration recommendations for rape, are presented in Table 3. As can be seen, massive exposure to pornography resulted in recommendations of significantly shorter terms of imprisonment ($F(3, 152) = 3.61$, $p < .05$). Such exposure, it seems, made rape appear a trivial offense. The frequency of recommendations of minor sentences (incarceration up to a maximum of one year) lends support to this interpretation. The number of students who recommended minimal sentences was markedly higher under conditions of massive exposure than in the other conditions. Surprisingly, this trivialization of rape was evident in women as well as in men. There was no indication of differential effects, F being less than unity for the treatment-gender interaction. However, and consistent with earlier observations (e.g., 10, 21, 23), females treated rape as a more serious offense and acted more punitively toward the rapist than did males ($F(1, 152 = 6.12$, $p < .05$).

Table 4. Support for the women's liberation movement as a function of massive exposure to pronography (by gender), on scale from 0 (no support) to 100 (maximal support)

	No exposure	Intermediate exposure	Massive exposure	No prior treatment	Combined
Male	71.0	48.7	25.0	66.8	52.8[y]
Female	82.0	59.2	52.2	76.2	67.4[z]
Combined	76.5[c]	54.0[b]	38.6[a]	71.5[c]	

Note: Means having no letter in their superscripts in common differ at $p < .05$ by the Newman-Keuls test.

The findings summarized in Table 4 suggest that the apparent loss of compassion for women as rape victims, occasioned by massive exposure to pornography, generalizes to a loss of compassion for women per se, thus undermining supportive dispositions for women's causes. The effect pattern concerning support for the women's liberation movement closely paralleled that reported for the punitive treatment of rapists. Support is lowest when exposure to pornography is greatest ($F(3, 152) = 12.34$, $p < .05$), the effect being of similar strength for men and women ($F < 1$ for the treatment-gender interaction). Women expressed more support than men overall, however ($F(1, 152) = 8.77$, $p < .05$).

Finally, massive exposure to pornography significantly increased men's sexual callousness toward women ($F(3, 76) = 14.79$, $p < .05$). The mean scores of sexual callousness for men were 10.5 in each of the two control conditions, 15.6 in the intermediate exposure condition, and 23.8 in the massive exposure condition. The latter score was reliably ($p < .05$ by the Newman-Keuls test) above all others. Thus, massive exposure to pornography clearly promoted sexual callousness toward women.

It is conceivable that these findings might be considered to be due to experimental demands. Specifically, it could be contended that students who were massively exposed to pornography may have inferred that such materials are harmless, because if they were not, the researchers would not have subjected them to these stimuli. Favorable evaluations of pornography, then, may have resulted from the fact that the researchers legitimized exposure. While this possibility cannot be ruled out, it should be noted that this form of legitimization closely parallels what happens outside the laboratory: pornography is culturally legitimized by the lack of censure. If the students inferred innocuousness from the researchers' tacit sanction, the so-called man in the street is likely to infer innocuousness from the fact that no one in any position of authority objects to people being liberally exposed to pornography in public movie theaters and elsewhere. The possible laboratory "demand" thus can be considered to simulate the actual process of cultural legitimization. Moreover, any suggestion of experimental demand as an explanation for the findings is limited to changes in the evaluation and acceptance of pornography. The findings concerning sexual callousness are unaffected by such suggestions, as it cannot possibly be argued that the experimenters were thought to condone or encourage hostility toward women and rape, in particular, merely because they presented erotic materials.

As with other media effects (e.g., 3, 11, 12, 20), the reality projected in pornographic imagery mingles with that deriving from immediate and socially mediated experience; and to the extent that the two "realities" differ, the projection is likely to modify experience-based assessments in a predictable way. If, for instance, the portrayal of violence on television misrepresents reality and thus can be expected to alter perceptions of crime in society and feelings of personal safety, pornography that misrepresents reality may likewise be expected to foster inappropriate perceptions and unwarranted dispositions. Just as Gerbner and Gross (11) found that heavy TV viewers give a "television answer" to questions about real-life incidences of violence, students in our study who viewed the most pornography can be said to have given a "pornography answer" to certain questions tapping perceptions of sexuality and dispositions toward sexual behaviors.

But if there seem to be similarities in the consequences of exposure to reality-distorting portrayals of violence and sexuality, critical differences are apparent, too. Unlike the public status of criminal violence, sexuality is cloaked by privacy. The citizen has ready access to comparatively reliable accounts of the crimes committed in his or her neighborhood, community, state, or nation and consequently can (in theory) correct grossly exaggerated impressions attained from exposure to fiction. The citizen is at a loss, however, in correcting impressions about sexuality. Primary experience is limited, and hearsay by friends and neighbors is unlikely to be devoid of self-enhancing distortions. Even the academic community has little to offer by way of corrective information. As indicated earlier, truly reliable assessments are not available; and patently partial accounts (e.g., 13, 14) that concentrate on persons eager to exhibit their sex lives have probably further misled those seeking trustworthy information about sexuality at large. It would seem, then, that when it comes to sex, citizens are immensely vulnerable and prone to adopt much of an uncontested "pornography answer."

Another factor contributing to the potentially powerful effect of audiovisual pornographic fare on perceptions of sexuality and on related dispositions may be the seemingly factual nature of the portrayal. Clearly, the usually contrived circumstances that bring the participants in sexual endeavors together are transparently fictional. But the remainder is live and real, giving the pornographic film the status of a documentary—i.e., the status of a form of representation that can be considered to provide the closest approximation to primary experience.

While our investigation focused on sexual callousness toward women, demonstrating that massive exposure to standard pornographic materials devoid of coercion and aggression seemed to promote such callousness (in particular, the trivialization of rape), the findings are suggestive of further anti-social consequences. It can be extrapolated from the data on perceptual changes, for instance, that those massively exposed to pornography will become distrusting of their partners in extended relationships. If women were thought to be as socially non-discriminating and as hysterical about any type of sexual stimulation as pornography makes them appear, men massively exposed to pornography might come to fear being cheated on and to invest less in a relationship than men who had viewed less pornography. Needless to say, as distrust grows and caring diminishes, it is the thing called "love" that is being undermined. Pornography thus might not only victimize women, but—through the erosion of love—harm men as well.

Another likely consequence of the perceptual changes occasioned by massive exposure to pornography is a growing dissatisfaction with sexual reality. Russell's (22) observations, cited earlier, give evidence that men readily succumb to the suggestion of hyper-euphoria that pornography connects with assorted sexual techniques. Who wants to miss out on manic sensations? The lure is bound to produce disappointment and dissatisfaction. Blame is likely to be placed, conflict is likely to result, and women are likely to take the brunt of the onslaught.

There are reasons, then, to anticipate some undesirable consequences of massive exposure to pornography of the "least objectionable" variety. But while this is meant to be a plea for further exploration of these consequences, it is not a call for censure. It is hoped that the reported effects might lead to a reassessment of the value of pornography.

Postscript

Since its original publication in 1982, our article about the trivialization of rape through prolonged exposure to common pornography has attracted considerable attention from both the media and academic circles. The media, counter to what one might expect on the basis of stereotypes, gave it astoundingly detached matter-of-fact coverage—the pornography press being the notable exception. But interestingly, many academicians felt compelled to comment, and they did so, again counter to stereotypes, in a strangely accusatory and value-laden manner. As the critiques in question have been published, along with our replies, we would like to alert the interested reader to them.

A first assault came from Christensen (1986, 1987), who accused us of trying to promote censorship, both by conducting our research in a biased fashion and by promoting it at antiporn rallies. We never promoted censorship, nor did we take part in antiporn rallies. And the only "partiality" we can be said to have shown lies in asking ourselves questions about the effects that our research brought to light.

Somewhat more rational criticism came from Brannigan (1987; see also Brannigan and Goldenberg, 1987). An attempt was made to explain our findings as the result of selective subject attrition. However, not only was there no selective attrition, there was no attrition.

Finally, a host of accusations came from Linz and Donnerstein (in press). These were, essentially, that we had used edited erotic material rather than intact films—although state-of-the-art, intact films had been used. More importantly, it was alleged that our findings have not been replicated. But replications and extensions exist (Zillmann, 1986; Check, 1985), and replication failures are the likely result of substantial changes in the research procedures.

We refer the reader to the detailed discussion of these issues in the indicated publications. We would like, however, to express our amazement at the apparent unwillingness to give credence to findings that, in many ways, only prove the obvious. Is it not more prudent to expect, in line with a multitude of demonstrations of specific media influences (Bryant and Zillmann, 1986), that presentations glorifying casual sex *can have some degree of influence* on sexual dispositions than to proclaim, categorically, that they are inconsequential? And should one not at least contemplate the possibility that prolonged consumption of pornography, in which the joys of casual sex are continually documented, might be capable of undermining the belief that sexually active, healthy women are traumatized and can be scarred for life by a few minutes of sex with a partner who is not exactly of their choosing?

In a survey conducted by the Rhode Island Rape Crisis Center (Banks, 1988) it was found, among other things, that about one-quarter of young men (grades six through nine) deemed rape justified if a girl had allowed ten to fifteen dollars to be spent on her, and two-thirds of these men thought the rape of a reluctant woman was called for after she dated someone for half a year. How do such callous attitudes evolve? We surely do not mean to propose that ready access to pornography is the only condition of consequence. In all probability, numerous forces are involved and operate in concert (Mosher and Anderson, 1986; Mosher and Sirkin, 1984). On the basis of our findings we would suggest, however, that pornography is one of these forces—no more, no less.

Mass Media,
Sexual Violence, and Male Viewers:
Current Theory and Research

by

EDWARD DONNERSTEIN and DANIEL LINZ

The influence of pornography on male viewers has been a topic of concern for behavioral scientists for many years, as well as a recent volatile political and legal question. Often research on pornography and its effects on behavior or attitudes is concerned with sexual explicitness. But it is not an issue of sexual explicitness; rather, it is an issue of violence against women and the role of women in "pornography" that is of concern to us here. Research over the last decade has demonstrated that sexual images per se do not facilitate aggressive behavior, change rape-related attitudes, or influence other forms of antisocial behaviors or perceptions. It is the violent images in pornography that account for the various research effects. This will become clearer as the research on the effects of sexual violence in the media is discussed. It is for these and other reasons that the terms *aggressive pornography* and *sexually violent mass media images* are preferred. We will occasionally use the term *pornography* in this article for communication and convenience.

In this essay we will examine both the research on aggressive pornography and the research that examines nonpornographic media images of violence against women—the major focus of recent research and the material that provokes negative reactions. Our final section will examine the research on nonviolent pornography. We will also refer to various ways in which this research has been applied to the current political debate on pornography and offer suggestions to mitigate the negative effects from exposure to certain forms of pornography and sexually violent mass media.

Reprinted from *American Behavioral Scientist* 29 (May/June 1986): 601–618. Reprinted by permission of Sage Publications. Copyright © 1987 by Sage Publications.

Research on the Effects of Aggressive Pornography

Aggressive pornography, as used here, refers to X-rated images of sexual coercion in which force is used or implied against a woman in order to obtain certain sexual acts, as in scenes of rape and other forms of sexual assault. One unique feature of these images is their reliance upon "positive victim outcomes," in which rape and other sexual assaults are depicted as pleasurable, sexually arousing, and beneficial to the female victim. In contrast to other forms of media violence in which victims suffer, die, and do not enjoy their victimization, aggressive pornography paints a rosy picture of aggression. The myths regarding violence against women are central to the various influences this material has upon the viewer. This does not imply that there are not images of suffering, mutilation, and death—there are. The large majority of images, however, show violence against women as justified, positive, and sexually liberating. Even these more "realistic" images, however, can influence certain viewers under specific conditions. We will address this research later.

There is some evidence that these images increased through the 1970s (Malamuth & Spinner, 1980). However, more recent content analysis suggests that the increase has abated in the 1980s (Scott, 1985). The President's Commission on Obscenity and Pornography of 1970 did not examine the influence of aggressive pornography, mainly because of its low frequency. This is important to note, as it highlights differences between the commission and the position outlined in this chapter. The major difference is not in the findings but in the type of material being examined. (The Commission on Obscenity and Pornography was interested only in sexually explicit media images.)

In many aggressive pornographic depictions, as noted, the victim is portrayed as secretly desiring the assault and as eventually deriving sexual pleasure from it (Donnerstein & Berkowitz, 1982; Malamuth, Heim, & Feshbach, 1980). From a cognitive perspective, such information may suggest to the viewer that even if a woman seems repelled by a pursuer, eventually she will respond favorably to forceful advances, aggression, and overpowering by a male assailant (Brownmiller, 1975). The victim's pleasure could further heighten the aggressor's. Viewers might then come to think, at least for a short while, that their own sexual aggression would also be profitable, thus reducing restraints or inhibitions against aggression (Bandura, 1977). These views diminish the moral reprehensibility of any witnessed assault on a woman and, indeed, suggest that the sexual attack may have a highly desirable outcome for both victim and aggressor. Men having such beliefs might therefore be more likely to attack a woman after they see a supposedly "pleasurable" rape. Furthermore, as there is a substantial aggressive component in the sexual assault, it could be argued that the favorable outcome lowers the observers' restraints against aggression toward women. Empirical research in the last few years, which is examined below, as well as such cases as the New Bedford rape, in which onlookers are reported to have cheered the rape of a woman by several men, suggests that the above concerns may be warranted.

Aggressive Pornography and Sexual Arousal

Although it was once believed that only rapists show sexual arousal to depictions of rape and other forms of aggression against women (Abel, Barlow, Blanchard, & Guild, 1977), research by Malamuth and his colleagues (Malamuth, 1981b, 1984; Malamuth & Check, 1983; Malamuth & Donnerstein, 1982; Malamuth, Haber, & Feshbach, 1980; Malamuth, Heim, & Feshbach, 1980) indicates that a nonrapist population will show evidence of increased sexual arousal to media-presented images of rape. This increased arousal primarily occurs when the female victim shows signs of pleasure and arousal, the theme most commonly presented in aggressive pornography. In addition, male subjects who indicate that there is some likelihood that they themselves would rape display increased sexual arousal to all forms of rape depictions, similar to the reactions of known rapists (Malamuth, 1981a, 1981b; Malamuth & Donnerstein, 1982). Researchers have suggested that this sexual arousal measure serves as an objective index of a proclivity to rape. Using this index, an individual whose sexual arousal to rape themes was found to be similar to or greater than his arousal to nonaggressive depictions would be considered to have an inclination to rape (Abe et al., 1977; Malamuth, 1981a; Malamuth & Donnerstein, 1982).

Aggressive Pornography and Attitudes Toward Rape

There are now considerable data indicating that exposure to aggressive pornography may alter the observer's perception of rape and the rape victim. For example, exposure to a sexually explicit rape scene in which the victim shows a "positive" reaction tends to produce a lessened sensitivity to rape (Malamuth & Check, 1983), increased acceptance of rape myths and interpersonal violence against women (Malamuth & Check, 1981), and increases in the self-reported possibility of raping (Malamuth, 1981a). This self-reported possibility of committing rape is highly correlated with (a) sexual arousal to rape stimuli, (b) aggressive behavior and a desire to hurt women, and (c) a belief that rape would be a sexually arousing experience for the rapist (see Malamuth, 1981a; Malamuth & Donnerstein, 1982). Exposure to aggressive pornography may also lead to self-generated rape fantasies (Malamuth, 1981b).

Aggressive Pornography and Aggression Against Women

Recent research (Donnerstein, 1980a, 1980b, 1983, 1984; Donner-stein & Berkowitz, 1982) has found that exposure to aggressive pornography increases aggression against women in a laboratory context. The same exposure does not seem to influence aggression against other men. This increased aggression is most pronounced when the aggression is seen as positive for the victim and occurs for both angered and nonangered individuals.

Although this research suggests that aggressive pornography can influence the male viewer, the relative contribution of the sexual and the aggressive components of the material remains unclear. Is it the sexual nature of the material or the messages about violence that are crucial? This is an extremely important question. In many discussions of this research the fact that the material is aggressive is forgotten and it is assumed that the effects occur owing to the sexual nature of the material. As we noted earlier, the sexual nature of the material is not the major issue. Recent empirical studies shed some light on this issue.

The Influence of Nonpornographic Depictions of Violence Against Women

It has been alleged that images of violence against women have increased not only in pornographic materials but also in more readily accessible mass media materials ("War Against Pornography," 1985). Scenes of rape and violence have appeared in daytime TV soap operas and R-rated movies shown on cable television. These images are sometimes accompanied by the theme, common in aggressive pornography, that women enjoy or benefit from sexual violence. For example, several episodes of the daytime drama "General Hospital" were devoted to a rape of one of the well-known female characters by an equally popular male character. At first the victim was humiliated; later the two characters were married. A similar theme was expressed in the popular film *The Getaway*. In this film, described by Malamuth and Check (1981):

> Violence against women is carried out both by the hero and the antagonist. The hero, played by Steve McQueen, is portrayed in a very "macho" image. At one point, he slaps his wife several times, causing her to cry from the pain. The wife, played by Ali McGraw, is portrayed as deserving this beating. As well, the antagonist in the movie kidnaps a woman (Sally Struthers) and her husband. He rapes the woman but the assault is portrayed in a manner such that the woman is depicted as a willing participant. She becomes the

antagonist's girlfriend and they both taunt her husband until he commits suicide. The woman then willingly continues with the assailant and at one point frantically searches for him. (p. 439)

In a field experiment, Malamuth and Check (1981) attempted to determine whether or not the depiction of sexual violence contained in *The Getaway* and in another film with similar content influenced the viewers' perceptions of attitudes toward women. A total of 271 male and female students participated in a study that they were led to believe focused on movie ratings. One group watched, on two different evenings, *The Getaway* and *Swept Away* (which also shows women as victims of aggression within erotic contexts). A group of control subjects watched neutral, feature-length movies. These movies were viewed in campus theaters as part of the Campus Film Program. The results of a "Sexual Attitudes Survey," conducted several days after the screenings, indicated that viewing the sexually aggressive films significantly increased male but not female acceptance of interpersonal violence and tended to increase rape myth acceptance. These effects occurred not with X-rated materials but with more "prime-time" materials.

A recent study by Donnerstein and Berkowitz (1985) sought to examine more systematically the relative contributions of aggressive and sexual components of aggressive pornography. In a series of studies, male subjects were shown one of four different films: (1) the standard aggressive pornography used in studies discussed earlier; (2) an X-rated film that contained no forms of aggression or coercion and was rated by subjects to be as sexual as the first; (3) a film that contained scenes of aggression against a woman but without any sexual content and was considered less sexual and also less arousing (physiologically) than were the previous two films; and (4) a neutral film. Although the aggressive pornographic film led to the highest aggression against women, the aggression-only film produced more aggressive behavior than did the sex-only film. In fact, the sex-only film produced no different results than did the neutral film. Subjects were also examined for their attitudes about rape and their willingness to say they might commit a rape. The most callous attitudes and the highest percentage indicating some likelihood to rape were found in the aggression-only conditions; the X-rated sex-only film was the lowest.

This research suggests that violence against women need not occur in a pornographic or sexually explicit context in order for the depictions to have an impact on both attitudes and behavior. Angered individuals became more aggressive toward a female target after exposure to films judged not to be sexually arousing but that depict a woman as a victim of aggression. This supports the claim by Malamuth and Check (1983) that sexual violence against women need not be portrayed in a pornographic fashion for greater acceptance of interpersonal violence and rape myths.

In the Malamuth and Check study the victim's reaction to sexual violence was always, in the end, a positive one. Presumably the individual viewer of nonsexually explicit rape depictions with a positive outcome comes to accept the view that aggression against women is permissible because women enjoy sexual violence. In the studies by Donnerstein and Berkowitz, however, several other processes may have been at work. Exposure to nonpornographic aggression against women resulted in the highest levels of aggressive behavior when subjects were first angered by a female confederate of the experimenter or when the victim of aggression in the film and the female confederate were linked by the same name. Presumably subjects did not come to perceive violence as acceptable because victims enjoy violence from this material. Instead, the cue value or association of women with the characters in the film (Berkowitz, 1974) and the possibility that the pain cues stimulated aggression in angry individuals might better account for the findings. When the individual is placed in a situation in which cues associated with aggressive responses are salient (for example, a situation involving a female victim) or one in which he is predisposed to aggression because he is angered, he will be more likely to respond aggressively both because of the stimulus-response connection previously built up through exposure to the films and/or because the pain and suffering of the victim reinforces already established aggressive tendencies.

An important element in the effects of exposure to aggressive pornography is violence against women. Because much commercially available media contain such images, researchers have begun to examine the impact of more popular film depictions of violence against women. Of particular interest have been R-rated "slasher" films, which combine graphic and brutal violence against women within a sexual context. These types of materials do not fit the general definition of pornography, but we believe their impact is stronger.

The Effects of Exposure to R-Rated Sexualized Violence

In a recent address before the International Conference on Film Classification and Regulation, Lord Harlech of the British Film Board noted the increase in R-rated sexually violent films and their "eroticizing" and "glorification" of rape and other forms of sexual violence. According to Harlech:

> Everyone knows that murder is wrong, but a strange myth has grown up, and been seized on by filmmakers, that rape is really not so bad, that it may even be a form of liberation for the victim, who may be acting out what she secretly desires—and perhaps needs— with no harm done. . . . Filmmakers in recent years have used rape

as an exciting and titillating spectacle in pornographic films, which are always designed to appeal to men.

As depictions of sex and violence become increasingly graphic, especially in feature-length movies shown in theaters, officials at the National Institute of Mental Health are becoming concerned:

> Films had to be made more and more powerful in their arousal effects. Initially, strong excitatory reactions [may grow] weak or vanish entirely with repeated exposure to stimuli of a certain kind. This is known as "habituation." The possibility of habituation to sex and violence has significant social consequences. For one, it makes pointless the search for stronger and stronger arousers. But more important is its potential impact on real life behavior. If people become inured to violence from seeing much of it, they may be less likely to respond to real violence.

This loss of sensitivity to real violence after repeated exposure to films with sex and violence, or "the dilemma of the detached bystander in the presence of violence," is currently a concern of our research program. Although initial exposure to a violent rape scene may act to create anxiety and inhibitions about such behavior, researchers have suggested that repeated exposure to such material could counter these effects. The effects of long-term exposure to R-rated sexually violent mass media portrayals is the major focus of our ongoing research program investigating how massive exposure to commercially released violent and sexually violent films influence (1) viewer perceptions of violence, (2) judgments about rape and rape victims, (3) general physiological desensitization to violence, and (4) aggressive behavior.

This research presents a new approach to the study of mass media violence. First, unlike many previous studies in which individuals may have seen only 10 to 30 minutes of material, the current studies examine 10 hours of exposure. Second, we are able to monitor the process of subjects' desensitization over a longer period of time than in previous experiments. Third, we examine perceptual and judgmental changes regarding violence, particularly violence against women.

In the program's first study, Linz, Donnerstein, and Penrod (1984) monitored desensitization of males to filmed violence against women to determine whether this desensitization "spilled over" into other kinds of decision making about victims. Male subjects watched nearly 10 hours (five commercially released feature-length films, one a day for five days) of R-rated or X-rated fare—either R-rated sexually violent films such as *Tool Box Murders, Vice Squad, I Spit on Your Grave, Texas Chainsaw Massacre, Maniac;* X-rated movies that depicted sexual assault; or X-rated movies that depicted only consensual sex (nonviolent). The R-rated films were much more explicit with regard to violence than they were with regard to sexual content. After each movie the men completed a mood questionnaire and evaluated the films on several dimensions. The films were counterbalanced so that comparisons could be made of the same films being shown on the first and last day of viewing. Before participation in the study, subjects were screened for levels of hostility, and only those with low hostility scores were included to help guard against the possibility of an overly hostile individual imitating the filmed violence during the week of the films. This is also theoretically important because it suggests that any effects we found would occur with a normal population. (It has been suggested by critics of media violence research that only those who are already predisposed toward violence are influenced by exposure to media violence. In this study, those individuals have been eliminated.) After the week of viewing, the men watched yet another film. This time, however, they saw a videotaped reenactment of an actual rape trial. After the trial they were asked to render judgments about how responsible the victim was for her own rape and how much injury she had suffered.

Most interesting were the results from the men who had watched the R-rated films such as *Texas Chainsaw Massacre* or *Maniac*. Initially, after the first day of viewing, the men rated themselves significantly above the norm for depression, anxiety, and annoyance on a mood adjective checklist. After each subsequent day of viewing, these scores dropped until, on the fourth day of viewing, the males' levels of anxiety, depression, and annoyance were indistinguishable from baseline norms.

What happened to the viewers as they watched more and more violence? We believe they were becoming desensitized to violence, particularly against women, which entailed more than a simple lowering of arousal to the movie violence. The men actually began to perceive the films differently as time went on. On Day 1, for example, on the average, the men estimated that they had seen four "offensive scenes." By the fifth day, however, subjects reported only half as many offensive scenes (even though exactly the same movies, but in reverse order, were shown). Likewise, their ratings of the violence within the films receded from Day 1 to Day 5. By the last day the men rated the movies less graphic and less gory and estimated fewer violent scenes than they did on the first day of viewing. Most startling, by the last day of viewing graphic violence against women, the men were rating the material as significantly less debasing and degrading to women, more humorous, and more enjoyable, and they claimed a greater willingness to see this type of film again. This change in perception due to repeated exposure was particularly evident in comparisons of reactions to two specific films —*I Spit on Your Grave* and *Vice Squad*. Both films contain sexual assault;

however, rape is portrayed more graphically in *I Spit on Your Grave* and more ambiguously in *Vice Squad*. Men who were exposed first to *Vice Squad* and then to *I Spit on Your Grave* gave nearly identical ratings of sexual violence. However, subjects who had seen the more graphic movie first saw much less sexual violence (rape) in the more ambiguous film.

The subjects' evaluations of a rape victim after viewing a reenacted rape trial were also affected by the constant exposure to brutality against women. The victim of rape was rated as more worthless and her injury as significantly less severe by those exposed to filmed violence when compared to a control group of men who saw only the rape trial and did not view films. Desensitization to filmed violence on the last day was also significantly correlated with assignment of greater blame to the victim for her own rape. (There types of effects were not observed for subjects who were exposed to sexually explicit but nonviolent films.)

Mitigating the Effects of Exposure to Sexual Violence

This research strongly suggests a potential harmful effect from exposure to certain forms of aggressive pornography and other forms of sexualized violence. There is now, however, some evidence that these negative changes in attitudes and perceptions regarding rape and violence against women not only can be eliminated but can be positively changed. Malamuth and Check (1983) found that if male subjects who had participated in such an experiment were later administered a carefully constructed debriefing, they actually would be less accepting of certain rape myths than were control subjects exposed to depictions of intercourse (without a debriefing). Donnerstein and Berkowitz (1982) showed that not only are the negative effects of previous exposure eliminated, but even up to four months later, debriefed subjects have more "sensitive" attitudes toward rape than do control subjects. These debriefings consisted of (1) cautioning subjects that the portrayal of the rape they had been exposed to is completely fictitious in nature, (2) educating subjects about the violent nature of rape, (3) pointing out to subjects that rape is illegal and punishable by imprisonment, and (4) dispelling the many rape myths that are perpetrated in the portrayal (e.g., in the majority of rapes, the victim is promiscuous or has a bad reputation, or that many women have an unconscious desire to be raped).

Surveys of the effectiveness of debriefings for male subjects with R-rated sexual violence have yielded similar positive results. Subjects who participated in the week-long film exposure study that was followed by a certain type of debriefing changed their attitudes in a positive direction. The debriefings emphasized the fallacious nature of movie portrayals that suggest that women deserve to be physically violated and emphasized that processes of desensitization may have occurred because of long-term exposure to violence. The results indicated an immediate effect for debriefing, with subjects scoring lower on rape myth acceptance after participation than they scored before participation in the film viewing sessions. These effects remained, for the most part, six weeks later. The effectiveness of the debriefing for the subjects who participated in two later experiments (one involving two weeks of exposure to R-rated violent films) indicated that even after seven months, subjects' attitudes about sexual violence showed significant positive change compared to the preparticipation levels.

This research suggests that if the callous attitudes about rape and violence presented in aggressive pornography and other media representations of violence against women are learned, they can likewise be "unlearned." Furthermore, if effective debriefings eliminate these negative effects, it would seem possible to develop effective "prebriefings" that would also counter the impact of such materials. Such programs could become part of sex education curricula for young males. Given the easy access and availability of many forms of sexual violence to young males today, such programs would go a long way toward countering the impact of such images.

The Impact of Nonaggressive Pornography

An examination of early research and reports in the area of nonaggressive pornography would have suggested that effects of exposure to erotica were, if anything, nonharmful. For instance:

> It is concluded that pornography is an innocuous stimulus which leads quickly to satiation and that the public concern over it is misplaced (Howard, Liptzin, & Reifler, 1973, p. 133).

> Results . . . fail to support the position that viewing erotic films produces harmful social consequences (Mann, Sidman, & Starr, 1971, p. 113).

> If a case is to be made against "pornography" in 1970, it will have to be made on grounds other than demonstrated effects of a damaging personal or social nature (President's Commission on Obscenity and Pornography, 1970, p. 139).

A number of criticisms of these findings, however (such as Cline, 1974; Dienstbier, 1977; Wills, 1977), led to a reexamination of the issue of exposure to pornography and subsequent aggressive behavior. Some —for example, Cline (1974)—saw major methodological and interpretive problems with the Pornography Commission report; others (for example, Liebert & Schwartzberg, 1977) believed that the observations were premature. Certainly the relationship between exposure to pornography and subsequent aggressive behavior was more complex than first believed. For the most part, recent research has shown that exposure to nonaggressive pornography can have one of two effects.

A number of studies in which individuals have been predisposed to aggression and were later exposed to nonaggressive pornography have revealed increases in aggressive behavior (such as Baron & Bell, 1977; Donnerstein, Donnerstein, & Evans, 1975; Malamuth, Feshbach, & Jaffe, 1977; Meyer, 1972; Zillmann, 1971, 1979). Such findings have been interpreted in terms of a general arousal model, which states that under conditions in which aggression is a dominant response, any source of emotional arousal will tend to increase aggressive behavior in disinhibited subjects (for example, Bandura, 1977; Donnerstein, 1983). A second group of studies (Baron, 1977; Baron & Bell, 1977; Donnerstein et al., 1975; Frodi, 1977; Zillmann & Sapolsky, 1977) reports the opposite —that exposure to pornography of a nonaggressive nature can actually reduce subsequent aggressive behavior.

These results appear contradictory, but recent research (Baron, 1977; Donnerstein, 1983; Donnerstein et al., 1975; Zillmann, 1979) has begun to reconcile seeming inconsistencies. It is now believed that as pornographic stimuli become more arousing, they give rise to increases in aggression. At a low level of arousal, however, the stimuli distract individuals, and attention is directed away from previous anger. Acting in an aggressive manner toward a target is incompatible with the pleasant feelings associated with low-level arousal (see Baron, 1977; Donnerstein, 1983). There is also evidence that individuals who find the materials "displeasing" or "pornographic" will also increase their aggression after exposure, whereas those who have more positive reactions to the material will not increase their aggression even to highly arousing materials (Zillmann, 1979).

The research noted above was primarily concerned with same-sex aggression. The influence of nonaggressive pornography on aggression against women tends to produce mixed effects. Donnerstein and Barrett (1978) and Donnerstein and Hallam (1978) found that nonaggressive pornography had no effect on subsequent aggression unless constraints against aggressing were reduced. This was accomplished by both angering male subjects by women and giving subjects multiple chances to aggress. Donnerstein (1983) tried to reduce aggressive inhibitions through the use of an aggressive model but found no increase in aggression after exposure to an X-rated nonviolent film. It seems, therefore, that nonaggressive sexual material does not lead to aggression against women except under specific conditions (for example, when inhibitions against aggression are lowered deliberately by the experimenter).

Almost without exception, studies reporting the effects on nonviolent pornography have relied on short-term exposure; most subjects have been exposed to only a few minutes of pornographic material. More recently, Zillman and Bryant (1982, 1984) demonstrated that long-term exposure (4 hours and 48 minutes over a six-week period) to pornography that does not contain overt aggressiveness may cause male and female subjects to (1) become more tolerant of bizarre and violent forms of pornography, (2) become less supportive of statements about sexual equality, and (3) become more lenient in assigning punishment to a rapist whose crime is described in a newspaper account. Furthermore, extensive exposure to the nonaggressive pornography significantly increased males' sexual callousness toward women. This latter finding was evidenced by increased acceptance of statements such as, "A man should find them, fool them, fuck them, and forget them," "A woman doesn't mean 'no' until she slaps you," and "If they are old enough to bleed, they are old enough to butcher." Zillmann and others (such as Berkowitz, 1984) have offered several possible explanations for this effect, suggesting that certain viewer attitudes are strengthened through long-term exposure to nonviolent pornographic material.

A common scenario of the material used in the Zillmann research is that women are sexually insatiable by nature. Even though the films shown do not feature the infliction of pain or suffering, women are portrayed as extremely permissive and promiscuous, willing to accommodate any male's sexual urge. Short-term exposure to this view of women (characteristic of early studies of nonviolent pornography) may not be sufficient to engender changes in viewers' attitudes congruent with these portrayals. However, attitudinal changes might be expected under conditions of long-term exposure. Continued exposure to the idea that women will do practically anything sexually may prime or encourage other thoughts regarding female promiscuity (Berkowitz, 1984). This increase in the availability of thoughts about female promiscuity or the ease with which viewers can imagine instances in which a female has been sexually insatiable may lead viewers to inflate their estimates of how willingly and frequently women engage in sexual behavior. The availability of thoughts about female insatiability may also affect judgments about sexual behavior such as rape, bestiality, and sadomasochistic sex. Further, these ideas may endure. Zillman and Bryant (1982), for example, found that male subjects still had a propensity to trivialize rape three weeks after exposure to nonviolent pornography. It is important to point out, however, that in these studies long-term exposure did not increase aggressive behavior but in fact decreased subsequent aggression.

Unfortunately, the role that images of female promiscuity and insatiability play in fostering callous perceptions of women can only be speculated upon at this point because no research has systematically manipulated film content in an experiment designed to facilitate or inhibit viewer congnitions. One cannot rule out the possibility, for example, that simple exposure to many sexually explicit depictions (regardless of their "insatiability" theme) accounts for the attitudinal changes found in their study. Sexual explicitness and themes of insatiability are experimentally confounded in this work.

Another emerging concern among political activists about pornography is its alleged tendency to degrade women (Dworkin, 1985; MacKinnon, 1985). This concern has been expressed recently in the form of municipal ordinances against pornography originally drafted by Catharine MacKinnon and Andrea Dworkin that have been introduced in a variety of communities, including Minneapolis and Indianapolis. One central feature of these ordinances is that pornography is the graphic "sexually explicit subordination of women" that also includes "women presented in scenarios of degradation, injury, abasement, torture, shown as filthy or inferior, bleeding, bruised, or hurt in a context that makes these conditions sexual" (City County general ordinance No. 35, City of Indianapolis, 1984). These ordinances have engendered a great deal of controversy, as some individuals have maintained that they are a broad form of censorship. A critique of these ordinances can be found in a number of publications (for example, Burstyn, 1985; Russ, 1985).

The framers of these ordinances suggest that after viewing such material, "a general pattern of discriminatory attitudes and behavior, both violent and non-violent, that has the capacity to stimulate various negative reactions against women will be found" (Defendants' memorandum, U.S. District Court for the Southern District of Indiana, Indianapolis Division, 1984, p. 8). Experimental evidence is clear with respect to the effects of pornography showing injury, torture, bleeding, bruised, or hurt women in sexual contexts. What has not been investigated is the effect of material showing women in scenarios of degradation, as inferior and abased.

No research has separated the effect of sexual explicitness from degradation, as was done with aggressive pornography, to determine whether the two interact to foster negative evaluations of women. Nearly all experiments conducted to date have confounded sexual explicitness with the presentation of women as a subordinate, objectified class. Only one investigation (Donnerstein, 1984) has attempted to disentangle sexual explicitness and violence. The results of this short-term exposure investigation, discussed above, revealed that although the combination of sexual explicitness and violence against a woman (the violent pornographic condition) resulted in the highest levels of subsequent aggression against a female target, the nonexplicit depiction that showed only violence resulted in aggression levels nearly as high and attitudes that were more callous than those that resulted from the combined exposure. The implication of this research is that long-term exposure to material that may not be explicitly sexual but that depicts women in scenes of degradation and subordination may have a negative impact on viewer attitudes. This is one area in which research is still needed.

Conclusions

Does pornography influence behaviors and attitudes toward women? The answer is difficult and centers on the definition of pornography. There is no evidence for any "harm"-related effects from sexually explicit materials. But research may support potential harmful effects from aggressive materials. Aggressive images are the issue, not sexual images. The message about violence and the sexualized nature of violence is crucial. Although these messages may be part of some forms of pornography, they are also pervasive media messages in general, from prime-time TV to popular films. Males in our society have callous attitudes about rape. But where do these attitudes come from? Are the media, and in particular pornography, the cause? We would be reluctant to place the blame on the media. If anything, the media act to reinforce already existing attitudes and values regarding women and violence. They do contribute, but are only part of the problem.

As social scientists we have devoted a great deal of time to searching for causes of violence against women. Perhaps it is time to look for ways to reduce this violence. This essay has noted several studies that report techniques to mitigate the influence of exposure to sexual violence in the media, which involves changing attitudes about violence. The issue of pornography and its relationship to violence will continue for years, perhaps without any definitive answers. We may never know if there is any real causal influence. We do know, however, that rape and other forms of violence against women are pervasive. How we change this situation is of crucial importance, and our efforts need to be directed to this end.

Legalized Pornography in Denmark

by

BERL KUTCHINSKY

Pornography is an example of a rather trifling issue, which—due to certain constellations of forces at a certain juncture in the cultural history of the Western world—has become a major issue of the day. Though of ephemeral importance, it has, in most countries, precipitated heated debate in public and in private, in the mass media and in literature, in parliaments and in the courts, in committees and in commissions.

The "porno wave"—a metaphor referring both to the period in which pornography has become easily available and widely distributed and to the period in which the topic of pornography has become "an issue"—varies in depth and intensity from one country to another. In Denmark it began around 1964 and had receded by 1970. In countries like Great Britain and the United States, the controversies and the porno wave have lingered on. One major reason is active opposition against pornography. The more active the opposition against pornography, the longer pornography remains an issue. Inevitably it will be longer before the point of general satisfaction and satiation is reached. *If* pornography is a vile monster—another metaphor sometimes used about this material by its most vehement opponents—it belongs to the special breed of science-fiction monsters which are nourished by the explosives being shot at it. This kind of monster—assuming it is one—starves and withers through lack of attention. After all, a monster only remains ominous as long as it is able to scare people.

Is pornography a monster? In Denmark it has been in abundant supply for a long time. Since 1969 it has even been free from the legal restraints that exist in most other countries. The Danish experience tells us that pornography is not a subject of which to be scared. In this essay I shall

Part of this article appeared earlier in *Censorship and Obscenity*, edited by Rajeev Dhavan and Christie Davies. London: Martin Robertson, 1978. Copyright © 1978, 1989. All rights reserved. Reprinted by permission of Berl Kutchinsky.

briefly review the Danish experience. What is pornography like? Who makes it? Who uses it? What do they use it for? Finally, what kind of psychological and social effects does it have?

The Danish Porno Wave

Explicit erotic descriptions in pictures as well as in words have existed since antiquity and have flourished at various periods in the cultural histories of Europe and Asia. In the eighteenth and nineteenth centuries, Europe experienced a porno wave which, as far as number of publications are concerned, far surpassed similar porno waves of the present time. It is no accident that the best-selling pornographic book in the Danish porno wave, *Fanny Hill*, was written during that period.

Nevertheless, there are at least two distinguishing and unique points about the present situation. First, pornography is becoming the property of the masses while earlier it was more or less restricted to the economic and intellectual upper class. Second, in many circles pornography has become morally and socially acceptable and in a few countries even legal, which has not been the case for as long as prints have been easily available.

An important factor in this development is that new technologies have made possible the mass production of color magazines, films, and videos of high technical quality at a very low cost. Another, and probably the most important factor, has been the emergence of a more liberalized view of sexual behavior, which has exonerated the naked body and the sexual act from certain indictments of sinfulness. This new sexual liberalism, the so-called sexual revolution, has been influential in several different ways. It has awakened and strengthened a latent need for erotica among many people. It has made possible the economic exploitation of this new attitude. And it has paved the way for a more lenient enforcement and eventual abolition of existing bans. This leniency emerged through an accelerated interaction among three groups: the producer, the consumer, and the authorities—with the mass media playing the hard-working and indispensable intermediary role.

In Denmark it is possible to distinguish two distinct phases of the contemporary pornography era. The "literary porno wave" first began around 1962. While in 1961 a total of 75,000 copies of erotic books were printed, the figures for 1962 alone reached almost 250,000 copies, to which should be added about 200,000 copies of sex-education books. During the subsequent years the production of erotic books increased steadily until 1965, when *Fanny Hill* was acquitted by the Supreme Court, creating an almost free market for pornographic literature while the laws were still unchanged. This resulted in a further steep increase, until the production reached its climax with 1.4 million copies in 1967.

This was the year in which the legal ban on pornographic literature was repealed. By 1969 the era of porno literature was completely over.

During the period 1962–1968, Danish publishers printed more than 5.3 million erotic books, which averages out at about 1.2 copies per inhabitant. It is therefore no wonder that most Danes acquainted themselves with porno literature during these years.

This was confirmed in a study in which a representative sample of the Copenhagen adult population, four hundred men and women aged eighteen to sixty years, were interviewed about their use of pornography. No less than eighty-seven percent of the men and seventy percent of the women had read at least one pornographic book. However, there were great differences as to how many books people had read. While twelve percent of the men interviewed had not read more than a single book, eight percent had read more than fifty books. The female subjects had read about half as much as the males. But here too there were great individual differences, and while twenty-seven percent had not read any porno books at all, twenty percent had read ten books or more.

Literary pornography dominated the scene in Denmark until the mid-1960s, while descriptions acceptable in words were not yet tolerated in pictures. Then followed an influx of the so-called porno magazines. Until 1965 there were numerous "girlie" or "nude" magazines depicting near-naked pinups or sun-bathers. However, later magazines began to depict pubic hair, and models were shown spreading their legs and showing their genitalia. A significant change in picture pornography occurred when the first so-called petting magazines showed two or more models together in erotic but noncoital situations. At the same time, pinup girls became overtly provocative. The sale of these magazines quickly reached millions, in spite of—or perhaps because of—numerous police crackdowns and seizures.

The "petting" magazines did not dare show active sexual organs. The first coital pictures existed only in the form of black-and-white photo series. But from 1967 the production of actual (illegal) porno magazines began. The first ones were black-and-white coital pictures with single couples. During the years 1968–1969 these developed into full-color magazines with group sex in all thinkable variations. Homosexual and sadomasochistic magazines were also produced during those years.

From 1970 a number of variations and specialties began to appear, although usually in small quantities: women having intercourse with animals (dogs, horses, hogs, etc.), pictures including children, and the so-called bizarre magazines, showing people urinating or defecating. In the late 1970s such magazines became increasingly scarcer, and in 1980 the reproduction and sale of child pornography was made illegal (the process of making such pictures, of course, was always illegal, inasmuch as sex with children is a crime). Since the market for such material was always very small, it immediately disappeared from the bookshelves, although private collections may still exist. Later allegations in the United States that child pornography is still being produced and exported from Denmark are based mainly on differences of definition of what constitutes child pornography (Kutchinsky, 1985). In Danish law child pornography depicts someone (appearing to be) under fifteen. (In the United States, people under eighteen are seen as children.)

The sale of pornographic magazines is more difficult to estimate than that of books. It is quite certain, however, that since 1965 more than one million copies of such magazines have been sold to the Danes per year. Sales increased steadily to two or three million magazines by 1969, but since then the consumption of pornography by the Danish reader has considerably decreased. This decrease was for some years compensated by an increasing export market, but as more and more countries began to repeal or mitigate legal restrictions during the 1970s, even the Danish export of pornography began to dwindle. Today most Western European countries, as well as the United States, are self-supplied with pornographic magazines, while films and videos are made mainly in the United States, Germany, Holland, and France. Only very short—originally 8 millimeter—hard-core movies, later combined into videos, have been made in Denmark.

It is important to note that even when the picture porno wave was at its climax, the sale of pornographic magazines made up only a very small part of the total volume of entertainment magazines sold—men's and women's weeklies, hobby journals, comics, and so forth; the total sale of pornographic magazines in 1969 amounted to about 130 million copies.

The study of adult Copenhageners mentioned earlier showed that in December 1969, eighty-eight percent of the men and seventy-three percent of the women had seen at least one pornographic picture magazine. No less than thirty-nine percent of the men and twenty-three percent of the women had read one during the previous month. On average, males had read approximately three times as many magazines as the women. Fifteen percent of the men had seen an average of 150 to 170 magazines altogether, while twelve percent had not seen any magazines, and twenty-seven percent had not seen any kind of erotic material at all.

Pornographic films account for a good part of the total turnover in the porno business. Nevertheless, only a few of the subjects in the Copenhagen investigation of 1969 had ever seen a pornographic film. Later this situation changed. During the 1970s pornographic movies (usually foreign) were shown in numerous small theaters, but in the 1980s the scene has changed once again: Pornographic movie theaters have become rare as more and more homes have become equipped with video recorders, suitable for showing videos for rent or sale in porno shops.

What Is Pornography Used For?

We have seen that a majority of Copenhageners—and no doubt other Danes as well—became acquainted with pornography during the years of the porno wave. This does not mean there was an "obsession" with pornography in Denmark. It merely reflected the fact that pornography became a commodity, almost as easy to get hold of as comic magazines or women's weeklies. The fact that production and sales reached considerable heights in the course of a very few years was wholly due to the fact that such sale had hitherto been forbidden. The interest in pornography during the second part of the sixties was an expression of curiosity. Everybody wanted to know what this much-debated matter was about.

So the answer to the question "What has the enormous amount of pornography sold during the porno wave been used for?" is that it was used to satisfy a temporary curiosity. Apart from this, however, our investigations show that pornography is mainly used for two purposes: for entertainment and to accompany masturbation or, more rarely, coitus.

The use of pornography as an aphrodisiac—a means of sexual arousal—emerges from the answers to some of the questions in the study mentioned earlier. It was found, first of all, that forty-eight percent of the men and twenty-nine percent of the women thought that either pornographic books, pictures, or films could be sexually arousing. Fourteen percent of both men and women found books exciting. Twice as many men as women, twenty-two percent as against eleven percent, found pictures arousing. Three times as many men as women, sixteen percent as against five percent, thought that pornographic films were sexually arousing.

Twenty percent of the men and five percent of the women in the study said that they sometimes use pornography when masturbating. Six percent of the men and ten percent of the women said that they used pornography once in a while in association with sexual intercourse. Although the sample was small, it is interesting to note that twice as many women used pornography in association with intercourse as with masturbation.

Who Are the Porno Users?

As already stated, the amount of pornography used, whether books or picture magazines, is considerably larger among men than among women. There are also more men than women who find pornography arousing and who use it for masturbation. Nevertheless, the difference between males and females in this respect is considerably less than was found in earlier studies of this type. About forty years ago, Kinsey (1953, p. 672) found that porno users in the United States were almost exclusively males. However, recent American studies have arrived at the same conclusions as we have. From this one can assume that in recent years there has been a considerable increase in women's interest in the use of pornography. This change no doubt has something to do with the increased acceptance, by both sexes, that women are interested in these matters. A parallel can perhaps be seen in a change in the "public" attitudes toward female masturbation.

The remaining difference between men's and women's interest in and use of pornography may be explained by the fact that the types of pornography produced so far cater mainly to the male appetite. It is arguable, as Kinsey thought, that there is also a biological component in the fact that males are more likely to be sexually stimulated by pornography (especially by pictorial pornography) than women. Whether this is true or not, there is hardly any doubt that the somewhat callous and unromantic, intense preoccupation with the sexual organs and sexual act is a masculine characteristic in our culture. It is possible that the feminine equivalent of the elaborate porno magazines of the males are the "true romance" magazines. Since that sort of popular literature is still very much alive, the increased interest of women in sexual matters that have hitherto been considered rather exclusively masculine can perhaps be understood as part of a general extension, rather than a change, in women's patterns of sexual attitudes and behavior.

Another important background variable is age. Young people are generally more interested in pornography than are older people; this is true of both men and women. Young men use pornography for masturbation more often than older men; among women there is a tendency in the opposite direction. A more permanent interest in and frequent use of pornography is found among males between the ages of twenty-five and forty. This coincides with the results of a study of Copenhagen pornoshop customers, who belong primarily to that age group.

As might be expected, therefore, gender and age are the most important background variables. It is surprising, however, that no particular connection could be established between the use of pornography and social or educational level. Kinsey's investigations, as well as the American studies from the late 1960s solicited by the Commission on Obscenity and Pornography, have shown that more pornography was consumed by the better-educated or higher social classes. The Danish experience suggests that this difference disappears when pornography becomes more available. In other words, people from the lower social strata, with a lower educational standard, are probably just as interested, or uninterested, in pornography as everybody else. But if pornography is difficult to obtain and therefore expensive, then it is obtained primarily by those with money and connections.

Equally surprising is the fact that religious convictions could not be closely correlated with the use of pornography, except that more religious people said they had *never* seen a pornographic magazine.

While gender and age are influential factors as to whether a particular person would be interested in pornography, the real determining elements are of course individual psychological and social factors. Analysis of the information available so far suggests that, providing pornography is easily available, the individual consumption of this material is primarily dependent on two factors: (1) the general strength of the sexual drive and (2) the degree to which this drive can be satisfied in a social context. With some modification, these criteria could probably also be applied to the frequency of masturbation. There is little doubt that masturbation and the use of pornography are closely related. It is evident too that the need for pornography is greater for those whose sexual satisfaction is exclusively dependent upon masturbation, the "sexually lonely" (sociosexually deprived) than for those whose masturbation is an addition to an active, social sex life.

A regular and extensive use of pornography is therefore found primarily among people who have a strong sexual drive and who, for some reason or another, suffer from a degree of "sociosexual deficit." Obviously, so-called sexual deviants are likely to be sexually lonely more often than nondeviants and are, all other things being equal, more likely to become regular and extensive users of pornography. The important point here is that sexual deviants become users of pornography not because they are sexually deviant but because their sexual deviance makes them sexually lonely. The use of pornography, even when extensive and frequent, is a normal reaction to what may sometimes be abnormal conditions of life.

Another group of relatively large-scale consumers of pornography have a strong sexual drive but do not appear to be sociosexually deprived—quite the opposite. To these people an interest in pornography is merely part of a strong and varied interest in sexual matters and activities. The total consumption of pornography in this category may be large, but the use does not have the regularity of the above-mentioned group of sociosexually deprived people.

Harmfulness—A Moral and Political Issue

Recently considerable interest has been expressed in the psychological and social effects of pornography. This interest is justified for many reasons. In the past hundreds of thousands of works of literature—valuable and valueless alike—have been destroyed, and publishers, printers, and booksellers have been punished severely for handling them, because it was thought that erotic books could have serious damaging effects on their readers. In most parts of the world today, both secular and religious authorities still believe that pornography attacks morality, produces sexual perversions and sexual offenses, and causes psychological and social imbalance and disruption.

Opinions about the harmfulness of pornography appear to be closely related to moral attitudes toward sexuality. People and organizations who consider the depiction of the naked body, sexual organs, and the sexual act abominable in itself usually consider pornography dangerous, both for the public and the individual. Not long ago, serious medical works would list virtually hundreds of diseases and other ill effects that could arise from masturbation. Medical scientific progress has helped to eliminate some of these myths but their influence should not be overestimated. The idea that masturbation is dangerous began to disappear when it ceased to be considered sinful—not the other way around. Similarly, the myths about the danger of pornography will persist—in spite of scientific evidence—for as long as this material is condemned on moral grounds.

The reception of the Danish and American "obscenity reports" by their respective governments and legislative bodies clearly illustrates my point. In 1966 the permanent Danish Penal Code Commission (consisting of four legal scholars) published a pornography report of 103 pages, including an appendix of opinions from various experts and bodies—the Pornography Report of the Penal Code Council ("The Danish Pornography Report," 1966). The U.S. Commission on Obscenity and Pornography had nineteen members, employed a full-time staff of eleven sociologists, psychologists, and lawyers, sponsored and financed scores of scientific investigations, and in 1970–1971 published a report ("The Obscenity Report") more than 3,000 printed pages long. The Danish report was based on a modest amount of scientific evidence available at the time of its writing. The U.S. report presented and utilized an overwhelming amount of scientific evidence. The two reports arrived at the very same conclusions, namely that there is "no evidence that exposure to or use of explicit sexual materials play a significant role in the causation of social or individual harms such as crime, delinquency, sexual or nonsexual deviancy or severe emotional disturbances" ("The Obscenity Report," 1970, p. 52).

The fates of these two reports in their homelands are well known: The Danish Pornography Report was favorably received and accepted—in fact, a majority of members of all political parties in Parliament voted for the bill recommended by the report. In the United States, The Obscenity Report was promptly rejected by the president, and in 1973 the U.S. Supreme Court overruled the conclusion of the report when deciding that the question of whether there is a direct causal connection between obscenity and antisocial conduct is "inherently unprovable."

A very similar fate overtook the report in 1979 by the British Committee on Obscenity and Pornography ("The Williams Report," 1979), which once again arrived at similar conclusions, this time based on even more evidence. Meanwhile, pornography had become increasingly condemned not only by its old enemies, various religious organizations, but also by feminists who considered pornography degrading to women and likely to cause rape (Lederer, 1980).

These groups, of course, applauded the recent report by the U.S. Attorney General's Commission (the Meese Commission)—the first officially appointed committee to conclude that pornography had clearly adverse effects. The Meese Report (1986), however, was rejected by social scientists for misrepresenting the studies on which it claimed to base its conclusions (e.g., Linz, Penrod, & Donnerstein, 1987). Among many gross distortions of research on pornography in the Meese Report, those in relation to the Danish studies probably take the prize (Kutchinsky, 1987).

What follows is a brief account of the results of a number of Danish investigations into the effects of pornography—sometimes supplemented by American studies. We look first at the immediate effects and then at the longer-term effects.

What Happens When People Use Pornography?

The immediate effects of pornography, that is, the way people react when they read or view pornography, can be illustrated by an experiment carried out in Copenhagen in 1970. The subjects, seventy-two students of both sexes, mainly married couples, were exposed for one hour to hard-core pornography in the form of films, magazines, and reading aloud. Before and after the exposure they filled in questionnaires about their backgrounds and attitudes in a number of ways. Afterward, they were asked in various ways to indicate what they felt, sexually and otherwise, during the stimulation period.

The results showed, among other things, that eighty-six percent of the men and sixty-one percent of the women said they had experienced "genital sensations" at some stage during the performance. However, only one-fifth of the men said they had had full erection. Although a majority had reacted sexually at one time or another, sexual feelings did not dominate. Only one-quarter of the experimental subjects (men and women alike) indicated that toward the end of the session they had felt "sexual arousal" and "urge for sexual activity." On the other hand, no less than two-thirds had felt bored and many had felt "oversatiated" and "disappointed." A similar overwhelming boredom was found in the vast majority of the visitors at the Sex Fair in Copenhagen in October 1969.

The conclusion, which is in close agreement with that of other similar investigations, is that when confronted with pornography, most people get certain vague sexual sensations, but most people also quickly tire of it. A minority are sexually aroused to a higher degree. Extremely few express strong feelings of disgust or embarrassment. The investigation also showed that people who are favorably disposed toward pornography from the outset are more likely to react positively, while people who are unfavorably disposed usually react negatively. The experiment summarized here used only students as subjects. Later Danish investigations using nonstudents as subjects suggest that the findings in the experiments could be generalized to include adult subjects of any educational level.

What Happens Afterward?

For good reasons, the short-term effects on "ordinary people" are the ones that have been most thoroughly investigated. In the Danish experiment it appeared that thirteen percent of the experimental subjects (both men and women) reported an increase in the frequency of their masturbation within twenty-four hours after the pornography performance. Almost twice as many (twenty-four percent) declared that they had increased the amount of their coital activity within the same period. Sexual behavior in the majority of subjects was unaffected by the pornographic performance.

Whether or not a person increased his or her sexual activity after the pornography performance seemed to be closely correlated with the immediate reactions of that person to the pornography. Those who disliked the pornography, who had quickly become bored by it or had otherwise reacted unfavorably to it, rarely responded sexually afterward. This connection was particularly close for women. With great accuracy, one could predict a female subject's sexual response within twenty-four hours on the basis of her immediate reaction to the pornography. Half of the men who had reacted positively to the pornography during the performance increased their sexual activity within twenty-four hours after. It was noticed also that the pornography had practically no sexual aftereffects on those men whose sexual life, according to their own estimate, was not very satisfactory. Among the men who indicated that their sexual life was highly satisfactory, coital activity increased in about half (among the women there was no such correlation).

Four days after the porno stimulation, very few experimental subjects thought that their sexual activity had increased, and two weeks afterward no effects could be traced. The pornography did not influence the sexual behavior of the participants in any other way (with the exception of one male subject, who mentioned that the experiment had inspired him to try a new coital position).

Attempts were also made to study the aftereffects of the pornography on the participants' attitudes toward various other matters. Among the results, it may be noted that the pornography had no effect on attitudes toward sexual offenses. Nor was there any indication that moral attitudes were influenced by the pornography. However, the experiment did indicate two clear aftereffects. The first was that a large number of participants had become "sick and tired of pornography." One hour wallowing in pornography seemed to have satiated their own interest in this material for a long time. Only one man said that the experiment had increased his interest in pornography.

The second strong aftereffect of the experiment came as a surprise. Part of the questionnaire, which was completed before the porn session and again four days and then two weeks after it, dealt with the participants' interest in trying a number of "advanced" or "special" forms of sexual behavior, such as group sex, the use of various sexual implements, sadomasochism, and so forth. It appeared in a majority of participants that they felt a decreasing interest in such activities—only a few had actually tried them.

The results of the Danish experiment on the short-term effects of pornography were remarkably similar to those of several contemporary American ones: There was no indication that pornography leads to "moral decay," "sexual excesses," or "pornomania."

Two American experiments, in which the effects of repeated pornography stimulation were studied over a somewhat longer period, yielded the same results. Mann, Sidman, and Starr (1973) used eighty-five middle-aged married couples as subjects in an experiment on the effects of a porn film show once a week for four weeks. Fifty-one married couples watched erotic films, seventeen couples watched nonerotic films, and the rest saw no films. All couples who saw films completed eighty-four consecutive daily checklists of sexual and marital behavior. After each erotic film show, the sexual activity of a minority of the experimental couples increased somewhat (the percentage was almost exactly the same as in the Danish experiment). Apart from that, no significant changes were found in the behavior of those who had seen the erotic films.

Even ninety minutes of porn stimulation repeated fifteen times in the course of five weeks had no long-term effect on experimental subjects (twenty-three male students) other than a considerable lowering of both their interest in and response to pornography (Howard, Liptzin, & Reifler, 1973).

Does Pornography Cause Rape?

More recent experimental research has suggested that subjects who have been angered before being shown *violent* pornography are more likely to respond aggressively immediately afterward (Malamuth & Donnerstein, 1983). Other studies have not been able to obtain this effect (Fisher, 1988). It is in any case more than doubtful whether such an increase in aggressiveness induced under extreme experimental conditions can be translated into increased readiness to commit rape in a real-life situation (Kutchinsky, 1988).

More interesting than laboratory studies of American college students are laboratory studies of the sexual reactions of convicted rapists who were shown either violent or nonviolent pornography. It was expected that rapists would respond more to violent pornography, especially when compared with nonrapists. These studies showed, however, that, on the whole, both rapists and nonrapists preferred nonviolent to violent pornography and there was no difference between the two groups in their reactions to these two types of pornography (Marshall & Barbaree, 1984).

Is it at all possible to obtain a clear answer to the question "Does pornography lead to rape?"

I believe it is. Or, to be more precise: It is possible to put the statement "Pornography leads to rape" to a crucial test. In Denmark and several other countries pornography has gone, within the last two decades, from a state of extreme scarcity to easy and abundant availability. If reading or watching pornography actually can lead to rape—even in a small proportion of cases—then there must have been an increase in cases of rape in these countries along with the appearance and growing availability of increasingly hard-core and even violent pornography.

The fact is that in Denmark rape did not increase for several years after pornography was legalized in the late 1960s, and only in the late 1970s did these crimes begin to increase somewhat. During the same period there was a strong increase of nearly all other crimes, including nonsexual violent crimes, while all other sexual crimes decreased. The same is true in Sweden, where pornography was also legalized and became abundantly available at the same time as in Denmark.

In West Germany, where pornography was legalized in 1973, the development is even more clearly indicative of the incapability of pornography to cause rape. During the entire period from the early 1960s (when no pornography was available) to date (when it is easily available in all varieties), rape not only did *not* increase, it in fact decreased somewhat. Moreover, it is conspicuous that the most serious forms of rape decreased more than the least serious forms. In West Germany, rape in the form of assault by strangers decreased by one-third, while gang rape has decreased by more than two-thirds since 1971. Since these forms of rape are practically always reported to the police and duly registered in the crime statistics, there can be no doubt that the decreases are real.

While no one claims it was pornography that led to the *decrease,* these developments, as well as the Danish and Swedish experience, leave hardly any doubt that pornography does *not* cause rape.

A Lesson to Be Learned?

The Danish experience shows that pornography quickly becomes a nonissue when bans are lifted. Not much of it is used and the users do not become morally corrupted and depraved; they do not change their sexual orientation or habits; they do not commit sex offenses because of this use.

Some people do not like to see pornography. Some people feel it is in itself immoral, humiliating, or degrading. They should not read or watch it—and nobody should force them to. In Denmark pornography must not be displayed in public or shown, given, or sent to people who have not asked for it.

But just as people who do not like pornography should not be forced to see it, people who like it should not be prevented from seeing it. In a free society, no one should dictate what others should be allowed to watch, read, or do, as long as they do not harm others. Since pornography and masturbation are so closely related, forbidding pornography would be like forbidding masturbation.

The Danish experience can easily be translated to other countries. All comparisons between the United States and Denmark suggest that people who use pornography react very similarly. About the same amounts of pornography are produced and used, by the same kinds of people and for the same reasons (Kutchinsky, 1985). The only major differences are found among those who dislike pornography. In Denmark, most people dislike pornography and therefore stay away from it. In the United States, many of those who dislike pornography want *others* to stay away from it. That is a blemish on one of the freest nations in the world.

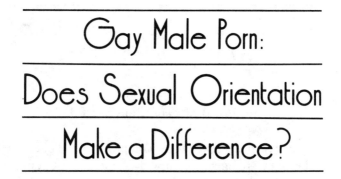

Gay Male Porn:
Does Sexual Orientation
Make a Difference?

Gays and the Propornography Movement: Having the Hots for Sex Discrimination

by

JOHN STOLTENBERG

The World of Gay Male Sex Films

The typical gay male sex film is comprised of explicit sex scenes, frequently between strangers, often with a sound track consisting solely of music and dubbed-in groans. During these sex scenes there is almost always an erect penis filling the screen. If the camera cuts away from the penis, the camera will be back within seconds. Scenes are set up so that closeups of penises and what they are doing and what is happening to them show off to best advantage. Most of the closeups of penises are of penises fucking in and out of asses and mouths, being blown, or being jacked off. A penis that is not erect, not being pumped up, not in action, just there feeling pretty good, is rarely to be seen: You wouldn't know it was feeling if it wasn't in action; and in the world of gay male sex films, penises do not otherwise feel anything.

Curiously, there is a great deal of repression of affect in gay male sex films—a studied impassivity that goes beyond amateur acting. The blankness of the faces in what is ostensibly the fever pitch of passion suggests an unrelatedness not only between partners but also within each partner's own body. This is sex labor that is alienated, these dead faces seem to say.

The film edits go by quickly. A few seconds at one angle. Then a few seconds over there. The camera on the cock. Almost always on the cock. The cock almost always hard and pumping. No moments in between anything. How did they get from that to this? Quick cut to the

Adapted from speeches delivered during the Tenth Annual Southeastern Conference for Lesbians and Gay Men, Chapel Hill, North Carolina, April 13, 1985, and "The Sexual Liberals and the Attack on Feminism" conference, New York City, April 4, 1987. A shortened version appeared in *Changing Men* 19 (Spring/Summer 1988). Copyright © 1985, 1989 by John Stoltenberg.

cock. Wait, in between there, wasn't there a moment between them when they just briefly—? Cut. Cut. The rhythms of the sex film are the staccatos of sexual disconnecting; they are not the rhythms of any credible sequence of sexual communion—those moments of changing pace, touching base, remembering who you're with, expressing, responding. All of that is cut out. All of that doesn't show. All that shows is "the action": the progress of the cock, the status of the cock.

Most of the sex acts are acts of detaching. They give the illusion of forging a connection, in the sense of hooking up plumbing; but they seem to be experienced as acts of abstracting apart, of getting off by going away someplace, of not *being there* with anybody. Sucking shots are classics of this sort: There the two men are, a blow job going on between them, and they might as well be at a glory hole.

The sex that is had in gay male sex films is the sex that is showable. And what is shown about it is the fetishized penis. When the obligatory cum shot comes, you see it in slow motion, perhaps photographed from several angles simultaneously, the penis pulled out of its orifice just for the occasion, being pumped away at, squirting, maybe someone trying to catch it in his mouth. There's no way to show how orgasm feels, and the difference between the reality and the representation is nowhere more striking than in the cum shot—a disembodied spurt of fluid to certify the sex is "real." Even leaving aside the rough stuff of gay male pornography—the scenes of forced fellatio, assault and molestation, humiliation and exploitation, chaining and bondage, the violence interlarded among the allegedly noncoercive sucking and fucking, as if to tip us off that in all this sex there is an undercurrent of force and domination—even leaving aside all of that, what exactly is there in the merely explicit sex scenes that recommends itself as good sex? What are we being told that sex can mean *between* people, if anything? What are we being told about what men must become in order to have what looks like blockbuster sex? What are we being told to do with the rest of ourselves?—what are we being told to lop off from ourselves and the history of our relationships with one another and our responsibilities to one another in order to feel at liberty to have sex at all?

The values in the sex that is depicted in gay male sex films are very much the values in the sex that gay men tend to have. They are also, not incidentally, very much the values in the sex that straight men tend to have—because they are very much the values that male supremacists tend to have: taking, using, estranging, dominating—essentially, sexual power-mongering.

I wonder sometimes: Has the saturation of the gay male subculture by these values created a population completely numb to the consequences of pornography for women? Can gay men who are sexually hooked on these values ever perceive the harm that pornography does to women?

Or has the world of the gay male sex film become the only world they want to know?

Homophobia and Woman-Hating

Like a lot of activists in the radical-feminist antipornography movement, I've been trying to figure out the hysteria that for several years now has come at us from the gay community. There has been no dearth of explanations available in the gay press—ranging from innuendos about feminists' prudery to outright misogynist malice, with the specter of a crackdown by right-wing homophobes thrown in for good measure. But I don't *buy* all those explanations. They don't quite wash. I believe there's something else—something deep and unnamed—going on.

I begin with a very simple question: Why is our queerness despised? And the most basic answer I know is that men who have sex with men are believed to be treated like a woman in sex. The Bible, in the book of Leviticus, calls it an abomination: to lie with a man as with a woman.[1] This text was the basis for English common law against male-male homosexual acts, and its euphemism provided the language of many early sodomy laws in this country. A typical one, passed in New Hampshire in 1791, declared "that if any man shall carnally lie with a man, as a man carnally lieth with a woman, . . . the offender . . . shall suffer death."[2] The "infamous crime against nature" is in effect a crime against the presumed nature of people with penises: *They do not get fucked.* That is masculinity's line of defense against gender blending—its bottom line, so to speak— and therein lies the nub of social prejudice that we know as cultural homophobia.

Some of us who are queer *have* been treated like a woman in sex, of course; in fact, some of us know viscerally what it feels like to be put down through sex when someone is doing it directly to our flesh. That, we understand, is what it really means to be treated like a woman. Male supremacy says it's okay to put someone down through sex if they were born without a penis, but it's not okay if they were born with one.

Homophobia is totally rooted in the woman-hating that male supremacy thrives on. The male-supremacist social hierarchy necessarily derogates both those who are female and those who are queer—namely, those who are male anatomically *but not male enough sociosexually.* Some of our gay male contemporaries seek safety and escape through macho, hypermasculine costumes and posturing, but the fact remains that cultural homophobia is a by-product of cultural misogyny: The faggot is stigmatized because he is perceived to participate in the degraded status of the female—and it doesn't matter one whit whether that's how he perceives himself. The dyke is held in contempt already as a woman and even more so for having the gall not to flatter the phallic ego—and it doesn't matter one whit whether she tries to emulate the sexual sadism of men.

I use the words "male supremacy" on purpose, because they imply an angry point of view about the existence of a sex-class hierarchy, a political system of discrimination based on sex. Sex discrimination means, in my view, being put down or treated in a second-class or subhuman way on account of the social meaning of one's anatomy. It's what happens to people without penises—in rape and battery and sexual harassment, for instance. It's what people with penises do to those without, as a matter of course, out of a sense of a entitlement, a birthright to power that derives from other people's powerlessness.

Those of us who are queer have a fairly obvious special interest in ending sex discrimination, because homophobia is both a consequence of sex discrimination and an enforcer of sex discrimination. The system of male supremacy requires gender polarity—with real men as different from real women as they can be, and with men's social superiority to women expressed in public and in private in every way imaginable. Homophobia is, in part, how the system punishes those who deviate and seem to dissent from it. The threat of homophobic insult or attack not only keeps real men aimed at women as their appropriate sexual prey; it also keeps men real men. Homophobia is central to the maintenance of sex discrimination.

Homophobia is not just in the social system, it's not just in the structure, it's not just in the laws. You can feel it in the muscle power of cops when they're cracking gay heads, and you can feel it in the taunts of teenage boys who are on a rampage of gay-baiting and queer-bashing. It's a kind of sexualized contempt for someone whose mere existence—because he is smeared with female status—threatens to melt down the code of armor by which men protect themselves from other men.

And you can also feel homophobia inside yourself. When you're living in an erotic hierarchy, where to be demeaned in sex is to be feminized, and to have power over someone else is to be male—when that's the sexual structure you're supposed to fit into—it leaves you hanging, as if clinging by your fingernails to a cliff, scrambling for the top, terrified to fall. It leaves you eroticizing masculinity as power over other people. And it leaves you enamored of male supremacy as an erotic ideal.

To have internalized homophobia as a gay man means you too dread the degraded status of anything feminine about yourself; it means you too dread that anything about your body might remind you of females in general, or perhaps your mother in particular; it means that in your own queer way, you're in a constant quest "to be the man there." One of the commonest ways to do that is by seizing on the masculinity of someone else whom you perceive as more of a real man than you—because you want to be like him, you want to acquire and assimilate his maleness in order to recharge your gender batteries, which seem to keep running down; because you need the jolt of some juice from a positive pole— and so you try things to interest him or you ingest him or you submit to his aggression sexually or you let him leave some violence on you, on your body, so you'll feel it in the morning. And it works; you get a heavy load of his manhood and it makes you feel as if it's in you too, purging your body of those soft and awful feelings you get from having had one of your parents be female. The patterns of subordination that go on between men help resolve internalized homophobia, momentarily, while you're having sex. Power-game, dominance-and-submission sex works because it lets someone "be the man there"; in fact it can let *two* males be the man there if they're courteous about it, if they follow the rules. The trouble is, this kind of sexuality can escalate; and often as not it must, completely crossing the line of what is physically and emotionally safe for one partner or the other. Thoroughgoing subordination in sex is not victimless; there *must* be victims, and there are—nobody really knows how many. Coroners know when someone gets killed from something that looks a lot like extreme S/M; there are boys who have been molested, gay men who have been battered and raped in sexual relationships. Nevertheless, there is a sexiness in subordination, and its sexiness for gay men in particular has a lot to do with the fact that subordination in sex helps resolve a misogynist struggle to cling to male supremacy. For a gay man who wants to have that kind of identity—a femiphobic sexual connection with other men—subordinating someone helps reinforce during the time of sex his tenuous connection to an idea of manhood that only exists because it exists over and against women. It works— until it doesn't work. It tends to leave you rather addicted to forms of passion that exclude compassion, and it can lead very easily to forms of restraint and bondage, control-and-power head trips, and physical abuse that can leave someone in the relationship feeling very much unsafe, very unwhole, very unequal, and very ripped off.

Consider in this context the current political strategy to achieve social acceptability for queers loving queers. We cannot chip away at this thing called homophobia—through laws and litigation and luncheons and so on—without going to the root of the sex-class system, without dismantling the power structure of men over women, which is an *eroticized* power structure. So long as that structure stays in place, homophobia will stay put too, because homophobia is necessary to the maintenance of men's power over women. The system of male supremacy can't tolerate queerness; it will never tolerate queerness. It needs the hatred of women and of queerness in order to prevail, in order to keep men doing to women what men are supposed to do to women.

The system of gender polarity requires that people with penises treat people without as objects, as things, as empty gaping vessels waiting to be filled with turgid maleness, if necessary by force. Homophobia is, in part, how the system punishes those whose object choice is deviant. Homophobia keeps women the targets. Homophobia assures a level of safety, selfhood, self-respect, and social power to men who sexually objectify correctly. Those of us who are queer cannot fully appreciate our precarious situation without understanding precisely where we stand in male supremacy. And our situation will not change until the system of male supremacy ends. A political movement trying to erode homophobia while leaving male supremacy and misogyny in place won't work. Gay liberation without sexual justice can't possibly happen. Gay rights without women's rights is a male-supremacist reform.

The Eroticization of Sex Discrimination

Sex discrimination has been culturally eroticized—made sexy—and those of us who are stigmatized for being queer are not immune.

It may be difficult to realize how completely sex discrimination has constructed the homosexuality that many of us feel. Though some of us perhaps think we know something about how male supremacy constructs the heterosexuality we have observed, or participated in, we're probably less aware of how sex discrimination has affected the way our personal homoeroticism has taken shape in our lives. But try to imagine, if you can, the difference between making love with someone when gender is not important, when gender is totally irrelevant, and having some kind of sexual release with a partner when what is paramount is your urgency to feel your or your partner's sexedness. If I were to put into words something that would help jog your memory of these two different experiences (assuming you've had at least one of each), I would say it's the difference between, on the one hand, a kind of overwhelming blending or a deeply mutual and vigorous erotic melding, and on the other hand a kind of tactile combat or tension in which various hierarchy dramas have an erotic impact. The difference is the difference between eroticized empathy and eroticized power disparity—or between eroticized equality and eroticized subordination.

Being a male supremacist in relation to another body is a quite commonplace mode of sexual behaving. Sometimes, though not always, the urgency to "be the man there" gets expressed in ass-fucking—while one guy is fucking, for instance, he slaps the other guy's butt around and calls him contemptuous names, swats and insults that are sexually stimulating, which may progress to physically very brutal and estranging domination. Many gay men seem to think that there is no woman-hating in the sex that they have. Sexualized woman-hating, they believe, is the straight man's burden. So why do gay men sometimes find themselves all bent out of shape after a relationship between two lovers goes on the rocks—and it was a relationship in which one man was always objectified, or always pressured into sex, or forced, or battered, or perhaps always dominatingly ass-fucked, and in his growing unease over this arrangement of power and submission he found himself feeling "feminized" and resenting it, meanwhile his partner just kept fucking him over, both in and out of bed? No woman-hating in gay sex? Clap your hands if you believe. Sexualized woman-hating does not have a race or a class or a sexual orientation.[3] It does not even have a gender, as lesbian devotees of sadomasochism have shown.[4] Gay men play at treating each other "like a woman" all the time. Sometimes in jest. Sometimes in grim earnest.

The personal classified ads in certain gay periodicals bear concise witness to the way in which the male-supremacist sex-class system has constructed many men's homoeroticism:

> Hot blond model 30's hot buns & face loves to be degraded by sexy kinky guys . . .

> Submissive WM [white male] 40 sks strict dad 35–50 for discipline sessions. Can be spanked with strap or whip. Can be tied up . . .

> Wanted: Yng hot jocks to play pussy! Scene: I drop by your apt. U greet me in black lace panties, stockings, and bra. In my sweats is a 9" red hot tool. The fun begins . . .

> Very dominant/aggressive master 29, 6'2", 170 lbs. hung 8" seeks slaves for verbal abuse, slapping, & handcuffing. You must be 6' in height, weigh over 180 lbs. and work out. Hairy chest and beard a plus . . .

> White master & son need houseboy for lifetime ownership . . .

> I am looking for slaves to fill an opening in my selective stable . . .

> I'm seeking a dominant master in full leather who is willing to train a real novice. Age and looks are unimportant, but you must be a masculine, serious, demanding, health-conscious top . . .

> [Gay white male] slave 35 6' 170 clnshvn broad shoulders big chest gdlkng wishes to serve tall slim master 28–42. Training may include [verbal abuse, bondage, bootlicking, discipline] . . .

And finally, here's one headlined simply "Punishment":

> Ass strapping, bend over paddling, abrasion, [deep fist-fucking, cock-and-ball torture, tit torture, bondage and discipline, humiliation] . . .[5]

The political reality of the gender hierarchy in male supremacy requires that we make it resonate through our nerves, flesh, and vascular system just as often as we can. We are *supposed* to respond orgasmically to power and powerlessness, to violence and violation; our sexuality is *supposed* to be inhabited by a reverence for supremacy, for unjust power over and against other human life. We are not supposed to experience any other erotic possibility; we are not supposed to glimpse eroticized justice. Our bodies are not supposed to abandon their sensory imprint of what male dominance and female subordination are supposed to be to each other—even if we are the same sex. Perhaps *especially* if we are the same sex. Because if you and your sex partners are not genitally different but you are emotionally and erotically attached to gender hierarchy, then you come to the point where you have to impose hierarchy on every sex act you attempt—otherwise it doesn't feel like sex.

Erotically and politically, those of us who are queer live inside a bizarre double bind. Sex discrimination and sex inequality require homophobia in order to continue. The homophobia that results is what stigmatizes our eroticism, makes us hateful for how we would love. Yet living inside this system of sex discrimination and sex inequality, we too have sexualized it, we have become sexually addicted to gender polarity, we have learned how hate and hostility can become sexual stimulants, we have learned sexualized antagonism toward the other in order to seem to be able to stand ourselves—and in order to get off. Sex discrimination has ritualized a homosexuality that dares not deviate from allegiance to gender polarity and gender hierarchy; sex discrimination has constructed a homosexuality that must stay erotically attached to the very male-supremacist social structures that produce homophobia. It's a little like having a crush on one's own worst enemy—and then moving in for life.

If indeed male supremacy simultaneously produces both a homophobia that is erotically committed to the hatred of homosexuality *and* a homosexuality that is erotically committed to sex discrimination, then it becomes easier to understand why the gay community, taken as a whole, has become almost hysterically hostile to radical-feminist antipornography activism. One might have thought that gay people—who are harassed, stigmatized, and jeopardized on account of prejudice against their preference for same-sex sex—would want to make common cause with any radical challenge to systematized sex discrimination. One might have thought that gay people, realizing that their self-interest lies in the obliteration of homophobia, would be among the first to endorse a political movement attempting to root out sex inequality. One might have thought that gay people would be among the first to recognize that so long as society tolerates and actually celebrates the "pornographizing" of women—so long as there is an enormous economic incentive to traffic in the sexualized subordination of women—then the same terrorism that enforces the sex-class system will surely continue to bludgeon faggots as well. One might have thought, for that matter, that gay men would not require the sexualized inequality of women in order to get a charge out of sex—or that a gay man walking through a porn store, perhaps on his way to a private booth in a back room, would stop and take a look at the racks and racks of pictures of women gagged and splayed and trussed up and ask himself exactly why this particular context of woman-hate is so damned important to his blow job.

Gays and the Propornography Movement

Once sexual sensation becomes enmeshed in sex discrimination, then how can there be sexual freedom? Once all the sexualized violence required to shore up male supremacy becomes institutionalized in culture and internalized in human personalities, then how can there be sexual justice?

Sex discrimination: being put down or treated in a second-class or subhuman way on account of the social meaning of one's anatomy. That is what the bulk of pornography is *for*, and that is what the radical-feminist antipornography movement is *against*.

The radical-feminist antipornography movement is now more than a decade old, and over the years its analysis has become more and more sharply focused on pornography's role in maintaining sex discrimination. What began as a recognition of pornography as sexist, degrading, demeaning, and woman-hating propaganda has grown into a politically astute legal theory that pornography, because it subordinates women to men, is a form of sex discrimination and that therefore pornography violates the civil rights of women. In late 1983, in Minneapolis, radical feminists Catharine A. MacKinnon and Andrea Dworkin drafted a statute that became widely known as the Dworkin/MacKinnon civil-rights antipornography ordinance. Their new law was designed to give individuals who claim that they have been injured in or through pornography a right to bring certain civil lawsuits against pornographers. The law made actionable pornography in which women are presented graphically, by sexually explicit pictures or words, as dehumanized sexual objects to be raped, mutilated, hurt, humiliated, or degraded. A plaintiff could sue if she was coerced into the production of that material, *or* had that material forced on her, *or* was attacked by someone in a way that was directly related to someone's use of that material, *or* was injured by belonging to a particular class of people who are all put down through the sale or exhibition of that material. This civil-rights antipornography ordinance became a lightning rod for the storm of outrage that had been accumulating in the gay community around the issue of pornography since the radical-feminist antipornography movement began.

In many ways over the past decade, the gay community—at least as it is reflected through most gay and lesbian publications, commercial and

advocacy organizations, leaders, and spokespeople—has been rather
obviously committed to a course of defending the rights of pornographers. Despite the presence of many lesbians and some gay men in
the radical-feminist antipornography movement, most gay people believe—some cynically but some very sincerely—that if our nation does
not impede its thriving pornography industry, it will someday recognize
the civil rights of gay people; but if in any way the rights of pornographers are encroached upon, then surely gay liberation will be jeopardized. People frame this point of view in many different ways, but it
basically comes down to an equation between the future of gay civil
rights—and sexual freedom for gays—and the free-enterprise rights of
pornographers.

This is not merely a philosophical meeting of minds between gay-
rights advocates and pornographers; there have been countless actual
coalitions and political convergences—substantial money contributions
to gay-rights organizations from pornographers, lawsuits brought jointly
by gay activists and pornographers, campaign support from pornographers for pro–gay-rights politicians, pages upon pages in pornography magazines offered to gay writers to trash the radical-feminist
antipornography movement, and so on. I don't think anyone needs convincing that the gay community, taken as a whole, tends to view its
naked political self-interest as lying somewhere in bed with the likes of
Al Goldstein, Hugh and Christie Hefner, Bob Guccione, and Larry
Flynt. *Hustler* publisher Flynt, for instance, also owns the Flynt Distribut-
ing Company, which distributes a lucrative mélange of straight and gay
pornography, including *Chic, Exposé, Harvey, Hooker, Honcho, Honcho Hunks,
Honcho Presents Men of Zeus, Hustler, Hustler Beaver Hunt, Hustler Fantasies,
Hustler Mag Presents Honey, Hustler Rejects, Hustler's Kinky Sex Guide, Inches, Jock,
Juggs, Juggs All Stars, Juggs Presents Milkmaid Parade, Male Review, Mandate,
Playguy, Torso,* and *Turn-on.* (But just so you don't get the wrong idea,
Flynt also distributes the *New York Review of Books* and *Knitting Elegance.*)[6]

A cozy ideological huddle between gay-rights activists and the propornography movement has also been at the very center of game plans
for getting homosexual sex acts decriminalized. In the 1985 Supreme
Court *Hardwick* case,[7] for instance, arguments put forth from the gay-
rights camp turned primarily on the so-called right of privacy—a dim
legal doctrine that exists only through constitutional inference. Justice
William O. Douglas first spelled out this privacy right in *Griswold* v.
Connecticut in 1965, where it was applied to "the sacred precincts of marital bedrooms."[8] But the privacy principle really blazed into the libertarian limelight with a case called *Stanley* v. *Georgia* in 1969, where the
Supreme Court ruled that a man may legally possess obscenity in his
home, even though the stuff is criminally banned everywhere else. Basically, the Supreme Court declared,[9] "a man's home is his castle," at least

where obscenity is concerned; and this was the narrow crack through which gay-rights advocates hoped the esteemed justices would also want to slip when it came to consensual sodomy. The prosodomy legal argument in *Hardwick* was mostly written and choreographed by Laurence H. Tribe, of Harvard, and he made quite explicit that gay sex in private should be defended on the same grounds as the private possession of obscenity:

> It would be ironic indeed if government were constitutionally barred, whatever its justification, from entering a man's home to stop him from obtaining sexual gratification by viewing an obscene film—but were free, without any burden of special justification, to enter the same dwelling to interrupt his sexual acts with a willing adult partner. The home surely protects more than our fantasies alone.[10]

Thus, before the highest court in the land, the besieged gay-rights position had its honor defended and its flanks protected through a defense of homey corn-holing that pivoted, ever so gingerly, on a man's right to his personal whack-off stash. In case you can't tell, this ignoble equation of same-sex sex acts with obscenity was the "liberal" position.

A single-minded privacy tactic might have seemed expedient and pragmatic, given the Supreme Court's historic hostility to homosexuality.[11] Legally, however, the tactic was sheer sophistry, claiming a shield for criminal sodomy only "in the most private of enclaves," the home (motel rooms, presumably, did not qualify), but completely conceding the state's power to delegitimatize homosexuality however and anywhere else it pleases: "There is thus no cause for worry," argued Tribe, that a favorable ruling from the Supreme Court "would cast doubt on any administrative programs that states might fashion to encourage traditional heterosexual unions."[12] That could only be reassuring if one is a heterosexual man—to whom women are invisible. And in the age of AIDS, what exactly did he mean by "any administrative programs"?

Politically, the argument gets even worse. Consider, for instance, the fact that for women in heterosexual unions, the home is the most dangerous place on earth—it's where women get raped most, assaulted most, and killed most. Moreover, the privacy-based argument embarked on a slippery slope that could seriously erode the state's ability to protect individuals from injury such as incest. Essentially, by appealing narrowly to the privacy right, Tribe's line of argument paid tribute to some linchpin precepts of male supremacy (among them, men's right to sexual release, in fantasy and in fact, no matter at what cost to anyone else) and opened not a single area of jurisprudential discourse that might conceivably defy the forces which keep homophobia alive and well.

One does not need a great legal mind to grasp that if one's claim to legal entitlement rests on a self-interested sellout of others who are powerless, one has a craven and shabby case. If the Supreme Court had struck down all state antisodomy laws because it had *accepted* the privacy argument as put forth by Tribe et al., it would have done so for wretchedly wrongheaded reasons. More honorable arguments exist. For instance, to argue that laws against sodomy deny homosexuals Fourteenth Amendment equal-protection rights would be to say something that is self-evidently true and also something that would strengthen the body of sex-discrimination law—rather than undermining it by appealing to the right of privacy.

The *Hardwick* case demonstrates the reactionary ideological alliance between gays and the propornography movement. So long as the gay-rights movement is committed to dissociating itself from the radical-feminist project to uproot sex discrimination completely and to create sex equality, gay liberation is headed in a suicidal direction. So long as the gay community defends the rights of pornographers to exploit and eroticize sex discrimination, we who are queer do not stand a chance. So long as the pornographers get to own not only the Constitution but also our most intimate sexual connections with one another, we will have lost all hope. Sex discrimination is what we must oppose, even if it turns us on. It's what puts queers down because it's what puts women down, and ultimately it's what does us all in. You can't fight sex discrimination and protect the pornographers at the same time.

Why Pornography Matters

The political function of pornography is analogous to the centrality of segregation in creating and maintaining race discrimination. Segregation was speech in the sense that it expressed the idea that blacks are different and inferior. But it was speech embodied in action—wherever there was segregation, there was something done to a class of victims: There was discrimination created, perpetuated, and institutionalized; there was damage to hearts and minds. Similarly, pornography contains and expresses many ideas about the "natural" servility and sluttishness of women, about how much women want to be ravished and abused, but in the real world, pornography functions as speech embodied in a practice —a thing actually done to an individual victim, the woman in it, and a thing actually done to women as a class.

Mere sexual explicitness does not create sex discrimination. And no damage to anyone's civil rights is done by so-called erotica, which may be defined as sexually explicit materials premised on equality, mutuality, reciprocity, and so forth. Pornography is something else. Pornography, which creates and maintains sex discrimination, is that sexually explicit material which actively *subordinates* people on account of their sexual anatomy; it puts them down, makes them inferior. Subordination is something that is done *to* someone; and it is often invisible, because the values in pornography link it to what many people think of as sex: a social hierarchy between men and women; objectification, which robs a person of his or her human status; submission, as if it's a person's "nature" to be a slave, to be servile; and violence, viewed as "normal" when it comes to sex. Pornography is what does that; pornography is that which produces sex discrimination by making subordination sexy.

Most pornography subordinates women, and women as a class are most imperiled by what pornography does. But it can happen to other people as well. The Dworkin/MacKinnon civil-rights antipornography ordinance is drafted to be both sex-specific and sex-inclusive at the same time. Its statutory definition and four causes of action—coercion, force, assault, and trafficking—are written to describe injuries to women, but the ordinance also plainly says, in effect, if something happens to any person in the same way and that person is a child, a man, or a transsexual, that person too can sue.

As lesbians and gay men ought to know better than anyone else, subordination does not have a sexual orientation. There are lesbians and gays who could use this ordinance. Not a few of the people who have been coerced into performing for pornography are lesbians and gays. Film documents of their abuse are still on the market. Some of these people have already come forward in public hearings to testify about what has been done to them; some have only spoken privately; some are still silent—terrified, ashamed, alone, utterly powerless. Imagine what it feels like to those people to hear the gay community unanimously defend the rights of their exploiters—and the profit motive for their abuse.

There also exists a mass of pornography that targets gay men for homophobic violence because it contemptuously presents them as faggots, and a mass of pornography that targets black men for racist violence because it presents them as rapists. Dworkin, a coauthor of the ordinance, has said that, in her opinion, the law is written so that gay men and black men in particular could use the trafficking provision of the ordinance by making the argument that pornography has had a devastatingly negative impact on their civil status.

And what about those gay men and lesbians on whom pornography is used in assaults by their partners? What will it mean if the gay community declares that the rights of the abuser supersede the rights of the abused? What will it mean if the gay community tries to protect people's freedoms by expanding the rights of exploiters instead of by giving rights to the people who are being exploited?

And what does it mean personally for gay men who are standing in the way of empowerment for women by forging an alliance with the power of pornographers? The price women pay for this alliance is enormous, but what is its psychic cost to those gay men? How much has homophobia already cost them and how much more hatred do they self-inflict by clinging to it, by saying the rights of women don't mean shit? So long as we are hating women in that way, we are hating something in ourselves—and that hate stands dead in the way of feeling freely with anyone. If we do not stand with victims of pornography in courage and solidarity and collective compassion, we have not yet tested our capacity for any empathy with anyone. If we cannot recognize women's rights, if we cannot identify with the reality of women's lives, how can we ever connect with anyone? Any time we blockade compassion, it is a rehearsal for alienation.

I first became active in the radical-feminist antipornography movement in 1976. That was when a movie called *Snuff* opened in Times Square, and hundreds of women and dozens of men picketed it because it purported to show the actual murder of a woman for sexual entertainment. What it showed was a man disemboweling a woman, cutting out her uterus, holding it up, and seeming to have an orgasm. It turned out not to be a real murder, although today real snuff films exist, movies in which a real murder is filmed; and women who have seen them report there are now movies in which there is something called skull-fucking— after the woman is murdered, a man fucks her skull through the dead eye sockets.

I remember that back in 1976 the gay community was already fairly antipathetic to the growing feminist antipornography movement. During the *Snuff* protests, I remember, I called on an official of the National Gay Task Force and asked for the group's participation or endorsement because the film could incite sexual violence against women. No, she said, it's not a lesbian issue. And I remember just a year or two later, all the gay men in New York City who hadn't supported the *Snuff* protest were now filling the streets to demonstrate against the movie *Cruising*, because, they said—probably not remembering the feminist origins of their argument—its portrayal of the S/M subculture could incite violence against gays.

Basically, over the past decade, there hasn't been any cogent political analysis about why gay people as gay people should be concerned about what is happening to women in pornography. I've laid out what I mean to be a serious effort in that direction. But the truth is, I'd like to believe that an analysis should not be necessary. We are, after all, human. We have feelings. We bleed. We weep. Our hearts need not always have theories in order to have real reasons. We might simply out of our own frail humanity feel grief and pain when another human being is degraded, put down, sexually abused, sexually violated, not cared for. We might simply out of our own experience of what it means to be vilified feel rage against anyone who peddles sexualized hate. We might simply out of a passion for justice—the queerest passion of all—want sex to be about equality instead of hostility. Why indeed should we need an analysis of our political self-interest when it is so obviously in the interest of our own best selves simply to do right by other human beings?

Radical Feminism and Gay Male Porn

by

SCOTT TUCKER

While I was writing this essay, I took a break from my work to engage in an activity which John Stoltenberg and many radical feminists find ethically suspect: I jerked off while looking at some of my favorite porn, in this case photographs of Roy Stagg from Colt Studios. Roy Stagg may not be his real name and I know him only as a square-jawed blond with a laborious physique. Maybe he's a plumber or a poet, but in certain pictures he is costumed as The Leatherman and The Cowboy. I have no idea to what degree these impersonations express or constrain his identity, or whether his identity simply includes the fact that he's an impersonator. An actor who plays Hamlet might provoke similar speculations.

One reason we are discussing gay male pornography tonight is precisely because radical feminist ideology has directed so much of our activism, and has dominated so much of our discourse on sexuality, both within the women's movement and within the lesbian and gay movement. Rather than challenging radical feminists directly when we had good reason to think they were wrong in their analysis and actions, we have responded too often with guilt and defensiveness. Radical feminism is one current among many within feminism; radical feminists are known to disagree among themselves; and radical feminism is a misnomer when it becomes neither radical nor feminist. Radical feminism has, unfortunately, become increasingly identified with the antipornography movement—and, indeed, with reactionary populism directed against a whole range of polymorphous "perversions." Ellen Willis, a radical feminist herself, is no partisan of porn, sadomasochism, or cross-generational

A somewhat different version of this piece was presented at a forum on gay male pornography held at the Gay and Lesbian Community Center of Philadelphia, with John Stoltenberg and I speaking. Reprinted from *The Native*, July 18, 1983. Copyright © 1983 by Thomas Scott Tucker. All rights reserved. Used by permission of Thomas Scott Tucker.

sex. Yet she and other dissenting women have come under sharp attack from radical feminists for pursuing an *open* debate on sexuality. "It is the antipornography movement," wrote Willis in *The Village Voice* last December, "that, almost unchallenged, came to dictate the terms of feminist discussion of sex, despite the fact that it has *never* spoken for all feminists." It is time to challenge the antipornography movement directly, and to criticize certain dogmas and slogans of radical feminism.

I'm not willing to dismiss radical feminists for their so-called "extremism," the usual charge levelled against *any* form of radicalism. No, what I find best and truest in radical feminism is precisely extremist, extremist in the sense of aiming to take nothing for granted, and challenging common sense. Extremist in the sense that radical feminism would require the ultimate dismantling of every terrorist government on this planet, which accords with my own anarchism. Extremist in the sense that radical feminism means reintegrating nature and culture. Extremist, finally, in the sense that there are extreme falsehoods which stunt and enslave us, and the truths which are dawning on us also come to us in extremity. Black schoolchildren leading a revolt in South Africa, prostitutes occupying a church in Paris, women defying the mullahs in Iran, queers smashing up City Hall in San Francisco, workers telling Communist bureaucrats to drop dead in Poland—this extremism of the oppressed keeps breaking through the old crust of common sense whenever it is becoming common nonsense. This is the extremism, for example, of Lucy Stone, who addressed a Woman's Rights Convention in Cincinnati in 1855, saying, "In education, in marriage, in religion, in everything, disappointment is the lot of women. It shall be the business of my life to deepen this disappointment in every woman's heart until she bows down to it no longer."

I understand why many radical feminists have one eye staring in grief and rage at all the messages of degradation and danger which pornography carries; I only wish they would open the other eye and take a look at the desires for freedom and pleasure it also expresses, in however commodified a form. One freedom and pleasure I have when I look at those photos of Roy Stagg is to fantasize having that shape and mass as my own, but in everyday life I am quite content to spend much more time at my desk than at my gym. I am quite content with this particular division of labor between Roy Stagg and Scott Tucker: he must devote as much care to his calves and biceps as I devote to my sentences and paragraphs, and I assume he loves his work as much as I love mine. It's true we objectify persons whom we know only as bodies in two-dimensional pictures, and it's true we objectify persons who are strangers, who have lives and desires unknown to us, when we pass them in the street and wish to kiss them, embrace them, have sex with them. It's equally true we objectify persons who are doctors, artists, factory workers, and farmers, relating to each other in an economic realm where the erotic is both suppressed and advertised, where love and work both suffer from a structural antagonism. Every division of labor is a division of human potential and a division of human beings. These divisions have taken destructive and irrational forms throughout society, but without some way of dividing labor there is no society at all, no individual identity, and no human freedom.

The alternative to a despotic division of labor is the democratic division and sharing of labor. Fourier, the French utopian, imagined a society based on gardening and small-scale industry, a society in which individual passion and talent would be encouraged to find its own best form, and in which the most specialized erotic manias would be as cherished as the rarest rose. Fourier had no patience with either reactionary or "revolutionary" notions of Universal Humanity; he recognized that people are particular persons with particular passions. In this respect his utopianism was an extension of his realism, in contrast to a certain tendency which might be dubbed Bambi-Among-the-Buttercups-Utopianism. This tendency is rampant among radical feminists (and many anarchists); it's the sentimental flip-side to mechanical forms of Marxism. According to this utopian school, power is just a form of violence and must be utterly dissolved. Since power is regarded as purely oppressive, these utopians offer new practical proposals to empower the oppressed.

In their utopia of homogenized humanity, every person will always deal with every other person at all times and places as "a whole person" —not just as a doctor, an artist, a factory worker, or a farmer, and certainly not as a sex-object. But isn't it possible and even probable that even in utopia you and I might not care how beautifully a bricklayer can lay bricks, if only that bricklayer happens to be beautiful and what we need most is sex, not shelter? And what if what we need most is shelter, not sex, and we don't care how beautiful that bricklayer is if only she or he can lay bricks beautifully? If I happen to have a fetish for beautiful bricklayers who lay bricks beautifully, do I come closer to dealing with "the whole person" than does someone else who may be interested *either* in laying the bricklayer, *or* in the bricklayer laying bricks? Which one of us, in this case, objectifies the beautiful bricklayer to a greater or lesser degree?

To answer these questions, we can guess that in such a sentimental and sublimated utopia all people will be equally beautiful to all people; perhaps there will be no such gross concept as beauty, and perhaps no such gross activity as sex. In this utopia there will be no fetishes or fixations of any kind, because we shall all be polymorphous (though not perverse, thank Goddess, not pederastic, and certainly not incestuous). Without Madison Avenue dictating our needs and desires, perhaps we shall be subject to supervision by "the Eupsychian police academy," an institution invented by the humanistic psychologist Abraham Maslow, and mentioned in his published journals. Out with Coca-Cola and the cop's club, in with touchy-feely persuasion and Cosmic Consciousness. In this utopia there will not even be any bricklayers, because each and every one of us will lay bricks, grow food, perform brain surgery, program computers, and write erotic (though not pornographic) poetry. Does someone object that this is a parody? True, and what now often passes for radical feminism is also a parody of what once began as *radical* feminism. To take one striking example: Once upon a time, Shulamith Firestone was able to imagine a society in which the taboos on adult/child sex and on incest had been dissolved, but radical feminists today are largely hostile to such utopianism. Instead, radical feminists now imagine a society in which division of labor has magically ceased to be an issue, and in which the mantra of *eroticism* has finally subdued *sex*. Radical feminists are thus capable of being fiercely confrontational and fiercely escapist.

As a utopian myself, my assumption is that even in utopia human beings will have only one life to live and only one skin to live in, though perhaps our science-fiction writers are true prophets of cosmically conscious clones. My assumption is that even in utopia life will have a tragic dimension, if only because one person can't be in all places at all times, nor be all things to all people. Choice means both transcendence and tragedy. Any choice we make, no matter how freely, means a circumscription of what we can do and be. But no matter what forms of freedom may arise in the future, the antipornography movement is by no means the best way to get from here to there, from the world as it exists to utopia. On the contrary, pornography itself has a utopian dimension.

The orgiastic scenes drawn on Greek pottery, the Tantric sculptures of India, the explicitly erotic Japanese prints, the photographs of Baron von Gloeden, a gay porn film like *Boys in the Sand*, and a *Playboy* centerfold —are all these simply drugs and weapons, are these purely and equally products of patriarchy and repression? To complicate matters, consider much feminist art today: for example, Tee Corinne's *Cunt Coloring Book* (reissued as *Labiaflowers*), or Judy Chicago's *Dinner Party* (with plates painted with vaginas), or various posters and calendars in which orchids and irises are very suggestive. Since a vagina does not express personhood more essentially than a woman's hands, can we doubt that feminist artists use sexual objectification in their work? Instead of the "pornographic" close-up cunt shot, we get the "erotic" close-up metaphor of sex and flower. Fine, but feminists should be the first to recognize that vaginas (and women) are not, in fact, flowers, and that this kind of romanticism is not strictly feminist. Woman as Flower has often been simply a reversal of Woman as Meat: think of the *Hustler* magazine cover in which a woman's legs stuck out of a meatgrinder, then think of centuries of male art and poetry. Suze Randall, a porn photographer we observe at work in the anti-porn film *Not a Love Story,* goes to great trouble to make a porn model's cunt "look like a flower." I doubt this poetry will be appreciated by the audience, mostly male, that will view Randall's final product, but her erotic imagination would be no more feminist even if it were. Nor is it apparent that a cunt that looks like a cunt is *anti*-feminist, whether seen in a porn parlor or in a women's photography exhibit. Metaphors can, of course, be signals of certain truths, they can enhance both sex and art; and it's a good thing *women* are gaining more power to make and break metaphors, to choose new words and images.

Making sexually explicit and arousing images seems to be as basically human as making and singing songs: in both cases there is behavior which is playful even when most serious, charged with passion and meaning. And like any human passion or product, pornography can take forms which are more or less malignant or benign. Pornography often exhibits what Freud called "the return of the repressed." In pornography we often find that every valley has been exalted, every mountain and hill made low. What is despised in everyday life is either glorified or further reduced to abjection; what is glorified in everyday life is also either despised or further magnified. In pornography, erotic tension is often built by playing upon sexual and social dualism: Man/Woman; Black/White; Straight/Gay; Professional/Blue Collar; Younger/Older; Weaker/Stronger. Pornographic dualism does not require that men dominate women, or that whites dominate blacks, or that straights dominate gays. Indeed, a *reversal* of social reality often distinguishes porn scenarios. Pornographic dualism requires difference and mystery, not necessarily domination and mastery. Feminists argue that even when pornography *reverses* social roles, this reversal is merely a fantasy which the man controls. In this view, women are always at the dead-end of sexual dualism, with no real power either to keep or to give.

If women were, in fact, so utterly powerless today, then sisterhood would *never* be powerful even in utopia. You must have *some* strength to gain *more* strength, and women are not so weak as radical feminists sometimes argue. Anytime anyone reverses social and sexual roles—even in play, even in art, even in pornography—there is always the possibility that the world will be turned upside down. The more reversible such roles become, the more playfully we approach them. If there is no freedom to imagine ourselves and the world differently, then there is no freedom to act and be different. To play is one way to gain power. Pornography is one form of play, a form of play which both replicates sexual and social roles and which also subverts them. If pornography purely and simply replicated sexual dualism, then perhaps the Moral Majority would turn theological somersaults and find *some* way to bless porn as the gospel truth.

I assume most of you are familiar with the various genres of erotica and porn, and with current gay male iconography. If ballet dancers turn you on, you might buy an issue of *After Dark;* if your preference is construction workers, you may find your fantasy in *Mandate*. In a recent issue of *Torso* a body-builder poses in a jock and football jersey next to a photo of Michelangelo's David. (Does lust desecrate High Art, or does High Art sacralize lust?) Here, in brief, are the plots of some gay male porn flicks I've seen: a father leaves his family in the car to blow and get blown in the gas station toilet; a young executive is seduced by a delivery boy at his office; a teacher tutors a student; a painter puts aside his brush and pallet and kneels before his model and male muse to suck him off; prisoners on a chain-gang escape to have sex in the wilderness; a straight construction worker finds out he's not so straight and that gays aren't so strange; and so forth. Pornographic plots tend to be simple mechanisms designed to produce erotic friction between desire and reality, not to reveal character in-depth. Pornography—not just gay male porn—gives us a glimpse of a world in which the erotic erupts into everyday life, in which people break out of family, work, school, and prison; in which forbidden territory is trespassed.

Ideas and images have consequences: they do not merely reflect reality, they also help to shape it. Rape is *one* way in which the erotic erupts into everyday life, and radical feminists pay particular attention to porn in which there are simulations of rape and sexual violence. They then translate all other pornographic scenarios into rapist propaganda. Given a culture charged with sexism at every level, it's not surprising that pornography also carries sexist messages, nor is it surprising that some men who use porn also rape. It's not necessary to establish a direct cause-and-effect connection between *all* porn and rape in order to conclude that *some* porn is particularly sexist, particularly likely to make us insensitive to the abuse of women, and therefore particularly worthy of protest. Anti-porn feminists face a strategic problem when they picket a porn arcade which has twenty booths with twenty different films, some sexist, some simply sexual. They save themselves the trouble of making distinctions by chanting slogans such as "Pornography is violence against women," as is documented, for example, in the anti-porn film *Not a Love Story*.

Lisa Orlando has written in *The Village Voice* ("Bad Girls and 'Good' Politics," December 1982) that "the pornographic image is itself contradictory," which is one way of saying porn has more than one meaning. "As a feminist," Orlando wrote, "I'm of course aware that the genre isn't a model of enlightenment. But what pornography gave me years ago was a set of models antithetical to those offered by the Catholic Church, romantic fiction, and my mother. The 'bad girls' it portrayed *liked* sex, even sex with women. Fearless and sensual, they scoffed at respectability, and were often as independent and aggressive as men. The images not only affirmed my budding desire but also gave me a first glimpse of freedom." By affirming her own experience of pornography, Orlando is not denying the experience of women who react to pornography with outrage and pain. It makes no sense, however, to assume that all women are exposed to the same kind of pornography or that they will respond to it with one mind and heart. Furthermore, as Ellen Willis wrote in the same issue of *The Village Voice* ("Who Is a Feminist?"), "We must also take into account that many women enjoy pornography, and that doing so is not only an accommodation to sexism, but also a form of resistance to a culture that would allow women no sexual pleasure at all."

My own experience was that gay male pornography gave me more trust in my own lust. My family was liberal and secular, my parents had read Dr. Spock. But neither my parents nor Dr. Spock prepared me for my passionate crushes on older men and boys of my own age. Instead, I read Cocteau and Gide; during my teens I had an affair with an older man and got involved with gay liberation, marching up Fifth Avenue in gay parades. When I finally went to see gay porn flicks at the 55th Street Playhouse in New York City, it was a further validation of my desires. I knew I had more chances in life than many of the furtive figures in that dark theater. For many of those men that theater was merely a more commodious closet, but for me it was one more step out into the world as a gay person. What I once wrote for *Gay Community News* I should repeat here: "The pornography industry is owned and run mostly by men; lesbianism is often portrayed only as a kinky adjunct to a man's pleasure. Women are fighting to be viewed as more than a collection of chicken parts, and so pornography becomes a burden or assault for many women. For gay men the case is different. Whereas 'real' men learn early that 'real' women are to be judged *essentially* according to sexual tributes and services, the same men may never, ever look upon other men as potential sexual partners. Gay male pornography is a capitalistic industry like any other, but it has served to affirm the sexuality of many gay men. To that extent it is a real and positive part of gay male culture."

In an article called "Sexual Objectification and Male Supremacy" published in the *New York Native* (May 24, 1982), John Stoltenberg wrote, "Not all sexual objectifying necessarily precedes sexual violence, but there is a perceptible sense in which every act of sexual objectifying occurs on a continuum of dehumanization that promises male sexual violence at its far end." Why not say that not all hunger necessarily precedes cannibalism? The continuum Stoltenberg speaks of does exist, but I maintain that matters of degree matter greatly, sexually and politically. Everything *can* be connected to everything, but then you may have trouble distinguishing anything from anything. Susan Griffin, for example, trivializes both Nazism and feminism when she writes, in her book *Pornography and Silence,* "that the pornographic mind is identical both in form and in ultimate content to the Nazi mind." Neither "the" pornographic mind, nor "the" Nazi mind, nor "the" feminist mind is so monolithic: pornography, Nazism, and feminism were and are products of many minds, *and this matters politically.* Some radical feminists have come to use Nazism as a general form of abuse (thus "the" sadomasochistic mind is also akin to "the" Nazi mind, etc., etc.). Men, according to radical feminists, are hooked on power, particularly sexual power over women, and porn is a weapon which strips a woman of her self and will, which strips her down to her sex so that her sex itself can be commodified, consumed, or trashed. The radical feminist critique of pornography has been focused most sharply on heterosexual porn; it has been applied with less accuracy to gay male porn as well. It makes no sense to assume, for example, that whenever two men fuck each other they are necessarily trading "male" and "female" roles.

John Stoltenberg uses a radical feminist critique of sexuality to insist that an act is not "outside the pale of ethical examination if at any point along the course of it there is an erection, an orgasm, or an ejaculation." I would not mind the positively Presbyterian earnestness of John Stoltenberg if only he chose to let us know precisely what an ethical erection or ejaculation *would* be. What means or process of erotic arousal *would* be acceptable to Stoltenberg and his colleagues? Radical feminists often answer that question by rhapsodizing about an eroticism of the whole person—in which the genitals are strangely taboo. Thus they also make a drastic and quite arbitrary distinction between erotica and pornography. Who defines kissing as erotica, who defines fucking as porn, and why? Does kissing lead to fucking and does erotica lead to pornography the way marijuana leads to heroin? Ellen Willis, writing in *The Village Voice,* affirms that she and other feminists have "declined to glorify diffuse, romantic, non-genitally-oriented sensuality as the sole criterion that sex is 'erotic,' female and good, or to stigmatize powerful, assertive desires for genital gratification as 'pornographic,' male, and bad." What Willis is responding to is a strong streak of sentimental and quite sexist idealism among radical feminists themselves. It is the same sexist idealism which has raised some women on pedestals as virgins, wives, and muses—and which has thrust other women into the gutter as whores, bitches, cunts.

From a radical feminist perspective, John Stoltenberg insists that men do not simply *react* to pornography: sexual objectification is an act in itself, and consumers of pornography are responsible for their choices and behavior. Men who make the bad choice to enjoy porn are merely exercising male power. Women who choose to enjoy porn must be explained some other way: they become robots programmed by patriarchy. Pat Califia is a lesbian feminist who writes on such topics as porn and S/M for *The Advocate*, a paper whose readership is overwhelmingly gay and male. She has been accused of being a female token and a gay male clone. But what, then, are we to make of the fact that John Stoltenberg is the only male contributor to a radical feminist anthology just published called *Against Sadomasochism*? Shall we say that John Stoltenberg has become a male token and a radical-feminist clone? I tend to think tokenism exists to some degree in both cases, but this does not mean that either Califia or Stoltenberg have become robots. No, both have made political and sexual choices.

Stoltenberg claims in his contribution to *Against Sadomasochism* that any woman who chooses to enjoy sadomasochism has not, in fact, been free to choose. She is a victim of patriarchy, not a seeker of pleasure. "The woman's compliance or acquiescence," Stoltenberg writes, "is therefore entirely delusional and meaningless. In no sense does she share in the man's privileged capacity to act. Moreover, there is no reason to presume that a masochistic woman is exercising more freedom of choice or acting more autonomously if her constrained will and body are subjected to the sadism of another woman." For ages men have told women what their true strengths and weaknesses *should* be, what their true needs and desires *must* be. Women calling themselves radical feminists have now taken on this role, and now, for a real double whammy, John Stoltenberg has been welcomed into their ranks. Once again, a man who knows better is telling women that they are capable of choosing.

At this point, we might well ask if pornography and sexuality is worth such debate and uproar. Isn't fighting against racism and for economic justice more important than pornography, isn't preventing nuclear war far more important than pornography? To think along such lines is merely to rank sex, race, and class according to some obsolete leftist game plan for revolution. Sexual and cultural struggle are as crucial as any other kind, and feminists are correct to claim that some forms of pornography may damage us as ethical, perceiving, and acting organisms. But I feel the same way about editorials in *The New York Times*, Presidential speeches, Papal sermons, etc.

Why indeed have some radical feminists made anti-pornography protests a primary strategy for women's liberation, leaving the whole system of wage slavery, for example, to be dealt with by the dinosaur left? When a mainstream major motion picture appears which is sexist but soft-core, anti-porn feminists do complain but rarely mobilize their forces in protest. Apparently they have made a strategic decision that they can rouse more populist moralism against Times Square than they can against Hollywood, and they are right. Also, when fighting porn you can win symbolically satisfying victories: it is so much easier to close down a single porn shop in an urban area destined for redevelopment than it is to close down a single advertising agency on Madison Avenue. This strategy, however, marks a troubling convergence between fundamentalists and radical feminists; both have been known to advocate government censorship. In the political space of democracy which feminists thus abandon, the less astute civil libertarians and the more sexist "liberals" move in and declare that *any* protest or boycott of print and film may encourage censorship. These folks forget there is no democracy without protest; if the First Amendment can be sold to the highest bidder, then of course millionaire politicians, Hollywood directors, and pornographers can buy more "free" speech than the rest of us. "The men," as radical feminist Andrea Dworkin has written, "have counseled us to be silent so that 'freedom of speech' will survive." I agree with Dworkin that "if the First Amendment does not work for women, it does not work."

A few years ago a coalition between gay men and radical feminists was possible when protests and boycotts were directed against the anti-gay and anti-lesbian Hollywood films *Cruising* and *Windows*. These films are not pornographic—they are violent, soft-core, tourist guides to "the lower depths"—and in my estimation the messages in these films are more explicitly reactionary and brutalizing than most porn, precisely because plots in pornographic films are so rudimentary. At one meeting held to organize protests, a radical feminist said she was willing to protest against *Cruising* as long as gay men were willing to condemn the S/M sexuality which the film exploited. I responded that if this condemnation was a condition for organizing a coalition, then gay men would protest alone. That coalition survived then, though I doubt a similar coalition in a similar situation would survive today.

It's a sign of the times that the Canadian anti-porn film *Not a Love Story* does not fail to credit the Toronto vice-squad for their cooperation (the same cops who raided gay baths and terrorized gay men). Perhaps Bonnie Klein, the feminist director of that film, favors the social and legal climate of Canada—a country in which the leading gay liberation journal is repeatedly charged with obscenity and repeatedly dragged through expensive fights in court. In any case, Klein states explicitly in an interview in *The Guardian* (Jan. 19, 1983) that "there are some forms of censorship that should be considered, such as drawing a parallel between pornography and hate literature, as well as nuisance laws." If government hacks, vice squads, and right-wing groups are considered tactical allies by "radical" feminists, then gay men and feminist radicals had better prepare now for a political realignment. In moments of raw rebellion, an oppressed person may strike out at some target which is symbolically loaded, or perhaps draw the line of resistance at some other place than we might choose ourselves. But feminists like Bonnie Klein tread dangerous ground when they leave open the possibility that the government and the cops will intercede by censorship on behalf of feminism.

Just as pornography means more things than one, so patriarchy and capitalism are not one system of oppression but many. Does patriarchy make all men brothers? In some cases, in some contexts, yes. But the high-bidding gamblers in the pornography industry and the real-estate market are quite pleased to cut each other's throats. In October of 1979 six lesbian women wrote an open letter in response to a demonstration called by Women Against Pornography in Times Square. These women pointed out that WAP was receiving funding from The League of New York Theatre Owners and Producers, as well as New York Off-Track Betting. At that time, the 42nd Street Redevelopment Corporation, at the request of the Midtown Enforcement Agency (itself a part of the New York Police Department), was providing free office space for WAP. They also pointed out the anti-sexual ideological convergence between WAP and Morality in Media, a right-wing group which solicited support from feminists. Finally, these women argued that feminists should show solidarity with prostitutes rather then participating in a police clean-up of Times Square. "Focusing on Times Square," they wrote, "may also contribute to the oppression of Third World people. Because many women and men of color work in the Times Square area, along with other poor people, a march on Times Square perpetuates racist stereotypes which see all women of color as greater sexual threats than white men. In this way, attention is deflected from rich white men who are the primary perpetrators of violence against women. Feminists should be aware that some of the enthusiasm generated by their campaign against pornography may draw upon racist and classist stereotypes."

This remains true now as well. Even the distinctions which feminists draw between erotica and pornography often reveal a striking class bias. Robin Morgan, for example, defines *The Tale of Genji* as a piece of *real* erotica, as opposed to unerotic porn. *The Tale of Genji* happens to be a very long, very subtle, and indeed sometimes erotic novel written by a Japanese aristocrat, Lady Murasaki, almost 1,000 years ago. Another feminist, writing a letter to *The Village Voice*, puts the erotic seal of approval on Brantome's *Lives of Fair and Gallant Women in the Court of Henri II*. Nothing is too good for the working class, and I look forward to the day when all working people have the leisure and education to enjoy Brantome and Lady Murasaki—if they so choose. If there is *any* legitimate distinction between erotica and pornography, then it cannot be that porn is hard-core and in Bad Taste, whereas erotica is soft-core and in Good Taste. If a distinction must be made, then I'd say that erotica ideally succeeds better than porn does on its own terms: that is, erotica should be more passionate, more comic, more tragic, more utopian, more complex and exuberant in every way than porn, including sexually. "Our moods do not believe in each other," as William James wrote, and even in utopia I and others may prefer erotica on Monday, pornography on Tuesday, and perhaps algebra on Wednesday.

"Pornography is the theory, and rape is the practice": so Robin Morgan declared in 1974, and her words have become the animating slogan of the anti-pornography movement up to this day. In the course of insisting that rapists practice what pornographers preach, radical feminists have often confused fantasy with reality, and have done so with great conviction and consistency. And since any form or degree of sexual objectification *may* lead down the slippery slope to rape and murder, these same feminists have found it useful to take the sex out of erotica, and to equate sexually stimulating material with sexually violent material.

Another slogan of radical feminism is "The personal is political." This slogan has many sound uses, but what began as feminist integrity has sometimes become a feminist Inquisition. Since the political is also personal, one feminist is fond of signing off a radio program in Philadelphia with the slogan "Feminism is the theory, and lesbianism is the practice." Pity the poor heterosexual feminist who does not practice what she preaches! Some radical feminists claim that no woman can truly consent to sex with a man; all heterosexual fucking is a form of rape. The fact that heterosexuality has become an oppressive institution does not mean that all women are utterly powerless to make sexual choices—including between heterosexuality and lesbianism.

John Stoltenberg expresses one line of feminist thinking very consistently when he insists that consent "is a concept that only has meaning between two persons who are equally enfranchised by culture to act willfully and without constraint—people, that is, who are genital males." By such logic *all* gay men are freer to be "consenting adults" than *any* woman, no matter how rich, white, and straight she may be. This trivializes the real oppression gay men suffer for being gay. By the same logic, lesbians cannot truly consent to lesbianism—only genital males can truly consent. To consent to sadomasochism and cross-generational sex is, of course, impossible as well. If patriarchy and pornographic propaganda have so deeply and thoroughly perverted us all, then our wills and spirits must be broken beyond hope. In this case, can *any* person alive today consent to *any* form of relationship? Sex and love become guilty until proven innocent.

Once we've pondered certain radical feminist slogans, we still have not faced the central dogma of radical feminism. "Women," wrote Robin Morgan in 1970, "were the first property when the Primary Contradiction occurred: when one-half of the human species decided to subjugate the other half, because it was 'different,' alien, the Other. From there it was an easy enough step to extend the Other to someone of different skin shade, different height or weight or language—or strength to resist." Primary Contradiction! Where have we heard this phrase before? From the "scientific socialists," of course, who claim class rather than sex is now the Primary Contradiction from which all others proceed. Marxists and feminists alike often claim that once we overcome the Primary Contradiction, then it is also "an easy enough step" to overcome all other forms of oppression.

Workers of the world may unite, but will women still do the housework, as well as build roads and bridges? Sisterhood may be powerful, but will a woman president of General Motors give power to women workers? Radical feminists are sometimes expert at red-baiting, yet they have inherited some of the shabbiest conceptual baggage of the old left. Robin Morgan called one collection of her work *Going Too Far* and in her essay on "Metaphysical Feminism" she thinks she goes very far indeed by claiming that women are "the essential proletariat." Tell that to Jeane Kirkpatrick and Margaret Thatcher: they won't respond with metaphysical solidarity.

Marxism and radical feminism fail to go far enough. There is not one magic key which will unlock the gates of heaven, especially heaven on earth. Systems of oppression based on sex, race, and class are interlocked but also distinct, and each form of oppression requires a shift in theory and practice. Radical feminism has made it almost impossible to discuss pornography without also discussing society and sexuality as a whole, and this has been a useful challenge to all of us, even if some of us reach conclusions which may be directly opposed to those of some radical feminists. The dissenting idealism of radical feminists can still be a great force for change, but how do we find paths towards utopia if we cannot take the first steps here and now? Here and now we may be capable of less than perfect consent; our choices may be few and not ideal; but most of us are not subject to absolute constraint. Here and now gay men and heretic women should insist on the validity and integrity of our own experience. Here and now we should tell our own story and demand our share of power and pleasure.

Postscript

Since writing this essay, I've experienced a more personal exposure to the various sex industries, including the performance and production of pornography. In 1986, having spent the winter season working with a construction crew in Key West while spending free time at the gym and the beach, I happened to be in peak condition and decided to compete in the International Mr. Leather Contest. Winning was the last thing I had in mind, and I look shell-shocked on the video recording of the event.

Carrying that title for a year meant that I learned a good deal about the gay male porn business. In a preliminary photo session for Falcon Studios, I fucked myself with a leather dildo as part of the "interview." Later, at the Falcon offices, sitting in the midst of a dozen silent screens running hard-core videos, I was offered magazine and film exposure. I was persistent about wage scales, contracts, and assurances of safe sex— and, being unsatisfied with the evasive response, I finally chose to model only once for an independent photographer. Dressed in minimal leather —boots, harness, and studded jock—I had the curious sensation of seeing myself on the cover of *Drummer* and in the pages of *The Advocate*. For nearly a year after, my mail included Polaroids and passionate requests from strangers.

For regular performers in gay porn, pornography itself rarely amounts to a decent income; rather, it often serves as advertising for prostitution. Depending where you look in this line of work, you will find honest professionals and sleazebags alike. As for my general aesthetic, ethical, and political view of porn and the sex industries, this remains essentially the same as when I wrote my essay in 1983. I would simply add that with the Supreme Court decision against gay privacy, with the grotesque Meese Commission on pornography, and with the continuing AIDS epidemic, I believe sex-affirmative free speech and action of all kinds is all the more worth preserving and protecting.

What Porn Did

by

JEFF WEINSTEIN

I want to tell you that I would have no sexual life if it weren't for pornography. I don't recall the title of the film, but I remember remembering it as the story of a young boy kidnapped by a thin, dark-haired young man, kidnapped across a border into a dirty town with oil tanks and alleys. I was seven. They were going to get him for doing that. The first erection was when they finally captured him, tied him up, beat him up for what he did. He was so resistant; his face was passive.

Who, which one of them, was I? Over and over I captured him, they captured me, I was taken across the border, I was taken back. Tell me, does anyone know the name of the movie? It may have been a politically motivated film. If you remember it after we leave tonight, please drop me a line, because I think it would be interesting to see it again.

At age eight or nine I saw attractive teenagers hanging around the torture room of Ripley's Believe It or Not. One asked me why the Iron Maiden was a maiden. He said that ruined it for him. At twelve I switched from going to Ripley's to going to the Metropolitan Museum, and then to the Museum of Modern Art: I stopped having erections in Manhattan.

Big Irish kids in Queens asked me to look up "intercourse" in the Webster's for them, and then went to the second-floor bathroom to show each other their fat, uncut cocks. I wouldn't go with them; what would they do to me? They never asked me to go, anyway. They were big, but so was the dictionary.

When I went to college, and someone told me Grove Press was *in*, I found, accidentally, the Marquis de Sade, for $1.75, with a blue cover. I opened it at random:

> Hercule, 26, very pretty, but also of a very mean character, the Duc's favorite; his prick measures eight and one-quarter inches around and 13 inches in length. Plentiful discharge.

A whole book of this! I couldn't believe it. I got a hard-on so fast I didn't know where to put it. Actually, there's a small danger I'll get hard even now, as I write, or now, as I read. I'll turn around.

I closed the book, afraid I would use it up. This was on the B & M Railroad from Waltham to Boston, and my face flushed uncontrollably.

Robert—he told me later—saw my red face, sat down, put his duffel coat over my legs, asked me if I thought de Sade was really serious, and felt the knob of my cock. He was older than I. A stain penetrated my twill pants, a stain I could feel but not see; I was so embarrassed. He asked me to get off at Porter Square with him; I said yes, almost left de Sade on the train, but something in me said the book will last longer than Robert will—although God knows I fell in love—so I ran back to grab it.

Robert was a prick, and he went to Harvard. However, he couldn't understand why this part was so erotic:

> At Fournier's establishment we had another curious article of furniture: a kind of toilet chair, provided with the usual hole and set against the wall; things were so arranged that a man could lie in such a way that while his body extended into the neighboring room, his shoulders passed through an opening and his head occupied the place usually reserved for the chamber pot.

How did he know then? I can't . . . there are no secrets, none.

> I had been appointed to the task, and kneeling between his legs, I sucked his prick as best I could throughout the operation.

They got a worker from the country to shit on his face, but orchestrated it, the writing and the thing itself, at such length that it went beyond the practical. "His fuck sprang down my throat the same moment the turd splashed upon his face." Turds splash!

Robert saw the class conflict of debasement because he was a red-diaper baby, but he thought it was foolish to be so excited about a text (a grad student said this). He had never fucked anyone in the ass because he was too fastidious.

Some people, I learned from firsthand experience, write much more filth and emotion than they can manage in real life. For others, like myself, I told Robert in a recent letter, it is just the other way around. Which should you prefer? I mean, really. . .

In graduate school I did a year's special project on pornography, after I had come out. This meant hanging around porn shops in downtown San Diego, near where Kathy lived with her first, cute husband. My friend X—this one had recently left her husband, a soon-to-be-famous journalist, so I can't use her name—decided to see if she could make a living outside of academia, so for $550 she wrote *The Naked Ballerina* under a pseudonym, "Karla Jules." The book, which contained realistic-sounding passages about thongs and forced postures, was an undeniable gem of fem-jep lust. ("Fem-jep" means *female in jeopardy*.) I don't know if I was more excited by the action or by the fact that it was the first book I personally knew the author of. It was reprinted over and over and became a best seller in that world, but "Karla" had signed a work-for-hire contract, and though the publisher made thousands of dollars on *The Naked Ballerina*, Karla got screwed, for $550.

I discovered the thrill of pretending I was doing work but really trying to get some cock. Standing by the plasticine-covered S/M magazines was the most efficient way. He and I would touch, and we'd go to the back room, where, depending on who pushed whom to the floor first, we'd suck on one another's long, butch dicks. We couldn't do that now.

After my first semester I rarely checked into the Lit Department, not even to pick up my mail. I set up a cot in the porn shop, which I called my office. I brought Dickens and the then-fashionable Lacan to read. It turned out I learned a good deal, understood that I was a born teacher, and dreamed about nothing but warm margaritas, the navy, and getting fucked: all for six units under a California State scholarship.

I learned that almost any pornography would get me hot; there didn't even have to be men in it. When Helen in *Helen and Desire* crawls at the feet of sailors, inducing them to piss on her, I got hot . . . oh, I guess the sailors were men, but I mean beyond that.

I learned that pornography is the great entrée into life, that fucking a lot of different people once is only a little different, imaginatively, from fucking one person differently a lot. It works both ways, too.

You also learn that context pushes the ambiguous object over into the realm of the highly desired. Here's one example. (THE SPEAKER HOLDS UP A RIDGED, BLACK-RUBBER BELT WITH METAL SNAPS.) What do you think this is?

> "You're damned certain no one's ever done anything to you here?"
> "But sir, what am I to do?"

"Hum . . . looks all right," mutters the brute, "bring it nearer."

I also believe, and am now in the process of trying to find out, that the perception of lust, even the actual experience of orgasm, is historically mediated—as is happiness. Love sits in another corner. After all, who thinks about love?

Pornography Without Power?

by

CHRIS CLARK

I like to look at naked men. I admit it. I have for a long time now. I liked it as a child when I'd play "I'll show you mine/You show me yours" with other boys. I liked it growing up seeing older men in locker rooms. I liked it in puberty, discovering my father's collection of *Playboy* and being fascinated with pictures of naked men in the "Sex in Cinema" features; or going to the library and looking through sex books or any book—art, theater, photography—that had a picture of a naked man. I liked it in my late teens, having girlfriends who knew I was gay buy *Playgirl* for us to look at. I like to look at naked men.

As a product of this desire to see naked men, I discovered pornography, specifically gay male pornography. This brought to light a whole new dimension to my pleasure, seeing naked men together, holding, touching, naked men being sexual together. I think I remember that first picture: two men embracing on a dock, no genitals visible, one man with one eye partially open, looking at the viewer. There were stories and real-life fantasies and occurrences, all for my pleasure. It and my masturbation viewing it, was an *affirmation* of my sexuality.

Yet, my pleasure was private! It had to be hidden. I had to sneak the porn into my house—not only was it pornography, "dirty" in itself, but it was *gay* porn! It became somewhat of an obsession. I would sneak it in with other magazines, with other packages, any way I could. When I widened my freedom by moving out on my own, I also removed the bars on my obsession—I became a collector.

At first, I collected whole magazines, and when that grew too bulky, I started cutting pictures out and putting them in collections—"My Favorite Porn"—then simply collecting the pictures in large plain envelopes. They were "my men," my sexuality.

Not coincidentally, my entrance into "gay culture" was through porn. Growing up in a small city, the only openly advertised public sex venue was a gay male porn movie house—complete with live nude dancers. (Until I went, I was never really sure whether it was for men or women —that's how "openly gay" it was.) Here I saw films of men having sex (doing things I didn't know existed or had only read about), and I saw men dancing naked, again for my pleasure. I felt my sexuality affirmed. How could I now take any position other than *for* that which first affirmed and then later confirmed my deviant sexuality?

> To gay men, the fear of sexuality, especially in the form of internalized self-hatred and self-disgust, is the most pernicious expression of sexism in our society. The first step toward personal communal liberation is unlearning those lessons of socialization which make our cocks and asses dirty. The acceptance of our bodies, the unhindered celebration of our sexuality and the act of loving other men spiritually, romantically and physically is the necessary first step toward liberation. Anything that helps to free our repressed selves —including pornography—has a positive value.

This is a radical statement. (It's from "Gay Porn—a Discussion," in *Achilles Heel*, a British anti-sexist men's magazine.) Pornography, like other expressions of sexuality, must be put into context, viewed through cultural, social, political and economic filters.

Many in the argument over porn seek to clarify the distinction between pornography and erotica. Though noble in purpose, such distinctions are themselves reflective of sexual preferences and social norms and biases. As Ellen Willis argues, it may simply become: "What turns me on is erotica, what turns you on is pornographic." To maintain a broad perspective, I use Ellen Willis' definition of pornography as "any image or description intended or used to arouse sexual desire," and follow her generalization that

> pornography is the return of the repressed, of feelings and fantasies driven underground by a culture that atomizes sexuality, defining love as a noble affair of the heart and mind, lust as a base animal urge centered in unmentionable organs. Prurience—the state of mind I associate with pornography—implies a sense of sex as forbidden, secretive pleasure, isolated from any emotional or social context.

It is here that gay male pornography and straight pornography overlap —a union rarely seen or addressed.

We are all affected by the social construction of gender and sexuality. Women, gay men and other sexual "minorities" and sub-cultures are oppressed. Straight men are forced, some with an unwillingness in spite of the many rewards, into the role of oppressor. This polarization of gender identity into female and male is what produces pornography. Three issues converge here: power, violence, and objectification. The three issues together form the basis of the anti-porn argument, and are also why I have some reservations about taking a pro-porn position.

Power is linked to socially defined sexuality in exactly the same way that aggression is linked to "maleness." Pornography as a product of male sexuality is thus a reflection of power issues. Power *can* be sexual and yet sexuality *can* be portrayed without power. Sex without power is often portrayed in gay porn where the relation between two partners has the possibility of gender equality. Sexual power is evident in most straight porn because of the imbalance of power implicit in the relations between men and women. To refute this distinction between gay and straight porn is itself homophobic; since gay men begin as gender-equals, the only way to conflate gay and straight porn is to label one participant as the passive-feminine role.

Power and violence are linked to sexuality in our culture and porn simply reflects this situation. As Gloria Steinem argues,

> It takes violence or the threat of it to maintain the unearned dominance of any group of human beings over another. Moreover, the threat must be the most persuasive wherever men and women come together intimately and are most in danger of recognizing each other's humanity.

However, though violence maintains dominance, and porn often depicts violence, attacking porn is not the answer. This is trying to cure the symptoms—pornography—and leaving the disease—our socialization into strictly dichotomous roles—to express itself elsewhere. Those opposing pornography are venting their rage at sexual oppression and violence on a by-product of the oppression.

My other reservation in taking a pro-porn position is also common to both straight and gay pornography: objectification. It is an implicit function of any representation of reality, a function of focus. Pornography is a representation of sexuality; it focuses intently on it, and thus objectifies it. I am victimized by this objectification because I want a link between my sexuality and my emotions. Pornography obscured that link even while affirming my sexuality. In my case, objectification manifested itself in promiscuity. Realizing this, I began to examine my objectification of sexual partners. I began to control the objectification and restore the link between sex and emotion. I see now how porn aided the construction of my sexuality; I also see, and can now control, the side-effects.

Arguments over pornography produce, from many positions, many solutions. The most visible, advocated by those against porn, is censorship or restriction of visibility of porn, such as legal ordinances against pornography. But Steinem reminds us that

> ... any societal definition of pornography in a male-dominated society ... probably would punish the wrong people. Freely chosen homosexual expression might be considered more "pornographic" than snuff movies, or contraceptive courses for teenagers more "obscene" than bondage. Furthermore, censorship in itself ... would drive pornography into more underground activity ...

This moralistic solution in a patriarchal society would reify the good girl/bad girl split for women, the repression of any "unacceptable" sexuality—i.e., that which is not heterosexual or male defined. Instead, I would suggest, with Deirdre English, that we "need, even more than women against pornography ... women pornographers—or eroticists, if that sounds better." The gay porn I've seen has been moving in this direction. Movies are focusing more on coming out and love relationships. Magazines are shifting toward more self-affirming stories and photo images. We need *more* porn addressing our oppression and affirming our sexuality. Let's join forces—those of us who are repressed by current norms—and create a new porn, a pornography without power, that glorifies the freedom to choose our own form of sexual expression.

Dialing for Sex

by

STEVE ABBOTT

It's a rainy Wednesday morning. You have the day off and feel bored, horny. Paging through the *Sentinel* (or any gay men's newspaper), you see phone sex ads where bathhouse ads used to be—eleven to be exact. "When one just is not enough!" teases a blue banner headline above four photos of attractive nude guys. "Only 95¢ . . . conference call . . . 976–BODS (not a recorded message)."

Staring at the phone I feel silly. I want to *see* a guy's eyes, face, how he moves his hands (80% of all communication lies in body language, psychologists say). If I'm calling someone I really like, I sometimes stare nervously at the phone for 20 minutes before dialing.

Like Dean, a guy I met last summer whose phone voice was hypnotic. Just as certain opera singers can hit a pitch that shatters glass, the timbre of Dean's voice automatically gave me a hard-on. Or was it how he'd start to murmur? Is language innately sexual, with some words carrying extra voltage? "Murmur," for instance, or "spank"? (All "sp" words turn me on actually—speak, spark, sperm.) If I heard Dean's voice on the phone now, I'd swoon.

So screwing my courage to the sticking place, to steal Shakespeare's metaphor, I dial 976–BODS. A scratchy, rapid-fire recorded message says, "Welcome to the gay conference line. You'll be connected to up to eight other guys. Start talking and enjoy."

"Hi," I begin hesitantly. "I'm Steve and I'm looking for someone. Is anyone there?" Dead silence. I babble on inanely a minute more before hanging up, feeling foolish, irritated, relieved. I hang up and smoke a cigarette.

Then my phone rings. Is BODS calling me back? No, it's Stan, a friend I can make a real date with. We chat, I relax, smoke another cigarette. When our conversation's over I return to the phone sex ads.

Some turn me off right away. Sleazeline offers truckers, bikers, B&D. On the opposite page a smaller ad catches my eye. Is that my heartthrob Lou Cass on the couch? "My girlfriend's gone and I'm horny," says the headline. So I dial 976–RODS. A young voice answers.

"I was on my way home from the gym when I see this hot punker get off the bus. He was carrying a skateboard and I could see he had a big, hard dick. He followed me home to my apartment and . . ."

A recorded message but the script's well written, actually believable, and the narrator gets breathy and excited as he builds up steam. I can imagine I'm right there . . .

Voyeurism lies at the heart of all good storytelling. You haven't really *had* an experience until you've shared it. So porn, like gossip, confirms our human identity. We need to exist like we need air to breathe because we're social animals. Repress it and it will pop up in your dreams. (What does Ed Meese dream about I wonder, or Jerry Falwell?)

. . . So I'm just getting into this hot story when an adult voice breaks in: "Ron's fantasies change with every call, so call back soon." Click. Silence.

Silence—there's the rub. When the State wants to break a person, they throw them into solitary confinement. When the New Right wants to break the gay community, they try to silence all our porn outlets. He who controls the airwaves (including phone lines) controls the nation. About 40% of the 976 numbers are for "adult services" and Pac Bell claims to get 100 complaints a month—mostly from parents. Phone sex calls generate about $12 million a year for the phone company and Ronald Thompson is suing Pac Bell for $10 million for corrupting his 12-year-old son, who molested a 4-year-old girl after listening to $50 worth of phone sex chatter.

Who can I sue for the contradictory sex messages that were stuffed into my head as a child: "Sex is bad—unless used to sell Coke or new cars. . . . Sex is playful, but should be carefully regulated and controlled. . . . Only the young are wild and sexy; only the old are wise and nurturing. . . . Homosexuality is an illness?" Can I sue the Church, the government, my parents?

I ask friends about their phone sex experience.

"I used to work for a phone sex outfit," Jeff tells me. "I like talking on the phone and I like talking dirty so it was great. But exploitative. I got $5 for every recording while my company got $35. Phone sex is safe but it's not healthy."

Not healthy because we're driven to it out of loneliness, or because it reflects our fear of real intimacy? Jeff doesn't say.

"I called the Connector," *Sentinel* rock critic Don Baird tells me with a laugh. "Every guy I talked to said he had eight inches." Marc Geller says it's great if you get the right message, but just when you spring a boner, your call is over, he laments.

Chris complains that his ex-lover ran up huge phone bills making 976 calls to NYC. "Some of the recorded messages are a real hoot," Chris says. "The conference calls are more interesting. You can listen in to other people before joining in. The hard part is getting the right guy to call you back."

I don't want to dump on anyone's pleasure, but what I wonder is how much real satisfaction phone sex gives. If I want to masturbate, I can come up with some pretty good fantasies on my own and to disembody the sexual experience by talking to strangers on the phone strikes me as the height of absurdity. And yet a lot of people seem to enjoy it. Are we becoming addicted to the tension of dissatisfaction?

"Intemperate language wreaks havoc on the heart," Matthew Arnold wrote in *Culture and Anarchy*. Intemperate dialing, it appears, does the same.

What Is To Be Done Now?

Pornography and Pride

by

VAN F. WHITE

I'm 59 years old, and I've known something about pornography for many years. When I was young, I worked for the Department of Economic Security, in public works, and in construction, and I remember the magazines and the conversations that the men had. They would look at the pictures and make derogatory remarks: "Boy, what I could do to that bitch." "Look at her—she can't get enough." I was a part of that at one time, listening and looking and thinking it was a laugh. But now my feelings have changed.

I'm a husband, the father of a daughter and a son, and seven years ago I became the first person of color ever elected to the city council of Minneapolis. I've learned a lot over the years about the way pornography affects people. I see the pornography stores in the neighborhoods of this city—they always seem to be put in the poorest of the communities—where black, Native American, Hispanic, and poor whites are living. But in the finer parts of the city you don't find them, and today—it's something we didn't have when I was a teenager. It's real now; they're using human beings. They're putting out magazines that show women in all kinds of degrading situations where they're smiling and apparently enjoying it as if saying, "This is what I'm about; this is all there is to me; I haven't any intelligence; my body is all that there is. . . ." And I see how pornography makes many men believe it. And it all makes me wonder, *Where in the hell are we going?*

I came up rather hard in this society. I'm not an innocent. I have seen the role models: the pimps, the prostitutes. And I remember that back in 1944, people participating in those activities would tell those of us who were young to do something different. "There are better things in life than this," they'd tell us. They were concerned about young people, and

Reprinted from *Essence*, September, 1984. Copyright © 1984 by ESSENCE Communications, Inc. Reprinted by permission.

that's my concern about young people today. You have to look back at those who are coming after you and provide a meaningful and viable future for them. I believe that's what life is all about.

In the fall of 1983, as chair of the Minneapolis City Council government operations committee, I conducted two days of public hearings on pornography. The council members were considering a civil rights approach to dealing with the injury of pornography to people's lives. And I was absolutely amazed at what I heard. For over 12 hours, I heard women testify about how men had used pornography to coerce them into sex acts; I heard a woman who had been gang-raped by men who had been using pornography; I heard a woman whose husband used a pornography magazine as a kind of handbook for how to tie her with ropes and then sexually assault her. And for the first time I began to think that pornography is something that downgrades women and keeps them in the position of chattel.

Hearing those horror stories made me think of times in the history of slavery in this country in terms of black women—how they were at the bottom of the pile, how they were treated like animals instead of human beings. As I listened to these victims of pornography testify, I heard young women describe how they felt about seeing other women in pornography in such degrading positions, how they felt about the way women's genitals and breasts are displayed and women's bodies are shown in compromising postures. And I thought about how during the time of slavery, black women would have their bodies examined, their teeth and limbs examined, their bodies checked out for breeding, checked out as you would check out an animal—and I thought: We've come a long way, haven't we?

Today we have an industry that grosses $8 billion a year showing women in the same kind of submissive and animalistic roles. A lot of housing could be provided for $8 billion, a lot of education, a lot of retraining. But as far as I know, the pornography industry puts nothing back into our society toward upgrading people's self-esteem. Instead, that industry is taking that away and saying, "This is all you really are as a woman—and as a man."

We have 30 million functional illiterates in our society, and many of them spend a lot of money to look at the visual communication in pornographic magazines. What's going to become of these people? Is this the only model of education they're going to have—that this is how women are?

I remember my mother telling me when I was 10, after my father died, that I was now the man of the family. She said, "Being a man doesn't mean not having feelings." Some people have mistaken my caring for people as a weakness; they don't recognize it as my strength. I try to pass on my feelings and my caring about people to my children, and show them that this is the way to be. I believe there are a lot of men in our society who are like me; they just never speak out.

So I want to say to men: Take a hard look at what is happening. Understand that there are women and children being degraded daily by pornographers. Many young women who are in search of a better life end up in the hands of pornographers—simply because they're young and their minds are searching—then some smooth turkey talks them into doing something, and the next thing you know, their self-esteem is on the ground and people are walking on it.

And to men who use pornography, men who will buy it, who will subscribe to it, all I can say is what I feel—and I feel it very truly: I understand what pornography can do; I understand it can be a thing that can arouse sexual prowess. But I know that pornography degrades men too, because by using pornography, by looking at other human beings in demeaning positions as a lower form of life, they are perpetuating the same kind of hatred that brings racism to society.

Just try to put yourself in that picture, in that position, and imagine how it feels.

Is Pornography Jerking You Around?

by

MEN AGAINST PORNOGRAPHY

Does Pornography Help You Have Sexual Intimacy?

For many men who begin to use pornography in their lives, it starts off as a kind of sex education. But what does pornography really teach about who you are inside and who you might really want to know intimately someday? How well does pornography really help you be close to someone?

Many men find in pornography a very artificial idea of what men and women are supposed to act like. Pornography says very little about what it means to be a loving human being—or what it means to be worthy of someone else's love.

Pornography, many men find, actually prevents intimacy between people. Even though it seems to "turn you on," it actually encourages you to "shut off" those feelings that help you feel really close to someone.

Sexual Honesty Begins with You

The more honest and self-aware you become about the role you have given pornography in your life, the more able you'll be to make decisions that you'll feel really good about. Just as you learn how certain foods or artificial stimulants can affect how you feel about yourself, so you can learn how pornography can influence your moods, your well-being, your self-esteem, and your ability to live fully. And if you feel it's jerking you around, you can begin to decide not to let it.

> WARNING: Habitual use of this product may be hazardous to your self-esteem and well-being.

What would you think if you saw that label on a pornographic magazine or video? Would you believe it?

Whether you use pornography regularly or only occasionally, it makes good sense to be aware of how it might be affecting you. You might be surprised.

Check Yourself Out

Here are some effects that pornography use can have on men. Not every man experiences all of them, but chances are there is at least one effect on this list that has happened to you:

☐ You become dissatisfied with your sexual partner's physical appearance or how they express themselves sexually.

☐ You become dependent on pornography in order to masturbate. You can't masturbate without it.

☐ You become dissatisfied with your own physical appearance and/or sexual expression.

☐ You need to remember images or scenes from pornography in order to have sex with someone.

☐ You withdraw into yourself or you become less outgoing—and therefore less likely to meet someone who you'd like to know better.

☐ You look at people's body parts a lot, especially the parts you look at most in pornography.

☐ You become attracted to people just because they remind you of people you have only seen in pornography.

☐ When you are having sex with someone, images or scenes you've seen in pornography "get in the way"—they come into your mind and won't go away, even if you want them to.

☐ You treat people the way you see people in pornography treated.

☐ You become more hostile or more aggressive toward other people in your life.

☐ You seek out more and more violent or degrading pornography in order to get the same sexual turn-on.

☐ You can't feel "turned on" without pornography.

What Makes You Feel Like Using Pornography?

Here's a good exercise for understanding more about yourself and the role you give to pornography in your life:

1. Think back to the last time you decided to use pornography— to get turned on or to masturbate. Try to remember how you felt. Do any of the words on this list describe how you felt *just before* you decided to use pornography?

tense	excited	nervous	calm
depressed	happy	lonely	angry
anxious	self-confident	up	horny
proud	relaxed	secretive	uptight
worthless	frustrated	in love	odd
well-liked	outgoing	withdrawn	restless

2. Is there any *pattern* in the feelings that you have just before you decide to use pornography? Pay attention to the types of feelings that prompt you to want to use pornography. Become aware of how and why you might be using pornography.

3. Again, think back to the last time you used pornography. Try to remember how you felt *afterward*. Compared with how you felt just before, did you feel . . .
   better?   worse?   about the same?

Why We Are "Men Against Pornography"

We want to help create sexual justice, and we believe that pornography stands in the way of women. We see pornography as a key element in the oppression of women. And we see that one way pornography works is by manipulating men's sexuality.

Many men have learned a lot from pornography about what sex is supposed to be, what women are supposed to be, and what we're supposed to be as men. Pornography gives men false ideas and expectations about women's sexual nature—that women want men to possess and dominate them. Pornography also encourages us to "get off" by putting women down, so it gives us a false notion of our own natures as well.

We know that lies can be very difficult to face if they also turn us on. But we know that sexual equality will never exist until men develop the skills and courage to challenge the lies that pornography makes us believe.

We want to help men confront what pornography really is—and what it really does. We want to encourage men to examine their sexual relationship to pornography. We want to enable and encourage men to become involved in the struggle to end sexual oppression.

Testing Freedom and Restraint

by

WILLIAM SIMON

Pornography almost invariably involves a conflation of conceptions of human sexuality and ideas regarding freedom and constraint, most often with a resultant distortion in the meanings of both. The discussion occasioned by the recent publication of the *Final Report of the Attorney General's Commission on Pornography* is no exception. The central question—Does exposure to sexually explicit materials lead to increases in dangerous or offensive sexual behavior?—was addressed, but little is added by this latest report that was not considered by the earlier commission, which published its conclusions in 1971.

The majority of the commissioners admit to a continuing lack of availability of credible scientific evidence of a direct link between exposure to such materials, including those containing representations of violent or bizarre sexual acts, and the subsequent commission of antisocial sexual acts. Their primary appeal, in their assertion of such a relationship, is to a commonsense view of the nature of the sexual as a powerful, innate drive—one that is expressive of dark, primordial and unconscionable appetites.

In their bland acceptance of a view of the production of sexual behavior as virtually unlike any other category of human behavior, the authors of the report find legitimating support in current folk wisdom ("an erect penis has no conscience"), the beliefs of many religious fundamentalists (sex as original sin and the devil's major weapon), the metaphorically enriched language of some Freudians (the mysterious and ignoble savagery of the id), and the equally enriched metaphors of current socio- and psychobiologists (the Maileresque emphasis given to "hungry seed"). Thus, despite the radical rightist commitments of the architects of the commission, the authors of the report come close to touching the intellectual and attitudinal mainstreams of the nation.

The assumed powers of the sexual are often assumed to magically carry over to representations of the sexual. The language and images of sexuality are seen as possessing most of the seductive and corrupting magic of the behavior itself or even more of such powers than the behavior itself. In the view of Lionel Abel, expressed in a 1978 issue of *Dissent*, one of the doyens of the academic neoconservative Left, "one of the most important effects of pornography is to trivialize the erotic." Despite Abel's failure to disclose what nontrivialized forms of the erotic might look like, he views this as a serious matter: "the trivialization of the erotic is also barbarous, for the barbarian may be described as the diminished man, one whose experience of life (and sex) has been attenuated."

Sharing this januslike view of the sexual as being capable of producing some undescribed elevations or leading to the depths of depravity, sociologist Cynthia Fuchs Epstein, in the same issue of *Dissent*, asserts: "I believe we should censor pornography that insults, defames, and encourages assault on people, men or women. I believe that words and pictures have power." Although lacking specifics, she can conclude that "there's something to be said for an ounce of prevention in matters of the psyche." Clearly, Epstein is not talking about the psyche in general, she is talking about sex. Here, too, is something of an attenuation of the human as it is represented as being permanently flawed, permanently at the mercy—or lack of mercy—of its biological origins.

Publication of the *Final Report* brings into dramatic focus the degree to which human sexuality has been allowed to maintain an intellectually privileged position from which, immune from our most general understanding of the determinants of human behavior, it can be invoked to justify the most broadly cast oppression of sexual minorities, the criminalization of relatively innocuous behaviors, and the persistence of the self-doubts and self-accusations that generations have been encouraged to inflict upon themselves. We cannot help but be struck by the insight, in the manner of Michel Foucault, into the political uses of the sexual as a metaphor that leads to continued practices of self-discipline and the acceptance of the deployments of power upon the body—practices encouraged by belief in the mythic forces that are alleged to inhabit real, if inarticulate, bodies.

More than encouraging repression of various kinds of explicit erotic representations, these arguments further encourage a dangerously pervasive paranoia. Set off against a profoundly exaggerated and cynically exploited drug epidemic, over-dramatized claims of missing children, as well as the exploitation of such legitimate issues as rape and the multiplying tragedy of AIDS—all somehow linked to sex—the pornography issue becomes an additional inducement to volunteer for, even demand, an internalized garrison state. It is as if the most dangerous enemies are within: it may be the next person we encounter, it may even be ourselves. More than nervously policing the walls of the society, there is increasing demand for the policing of its hallways and inner chambers.

At the same time, the issue of pornography becomes a testing ground for current concepts of freedom and constraint. It is suggested: Even if pornography does not demonstrably produce sex crimes, why run even the smallest risk over materials that for the most part serve no good purpose and are hardly in "good taste"? Thus a utilitarian test—a legalistic functionalism—is created that requires the "earning" of a right to freedom from constraint. Even within the bounds of such an implicit functionalism, a case can be made for a loss—even when only the most disturbing appearances of pornography are nominated for banishment from visibility. Even where the availability of such materials is of little direct consequence, nonavailability may be of substantial consequence. The presence of pornography, particularly in what is seen as its most vulgar and unattractive forms, is the continuing guarantee that all other uses and explorations of the sexual will not be impeded. The proscription on representations of the sexual inevitably casts a chilling effect upon all who would incorporate the sexual in their science, their art, or their lives.

Governmentally imposed suppression sustains a sexual landscape that continues to instruct successive generations in what has yet to be demonstrated: the inherent dangers of the sexual. This continued advertisement of the assumption of the inherent dangers of the sexual tends to create something of a self-fulfilling prophecy: rather than being what we might find most loathsome in others or ourselves, the sexual often becomes a matephor through which such self-loathing or loathing of others is expressed. Bigotries and brutalities expressed in erotic imagery, even when despised, are seen by the surrounding world as being more understandable than the noneroticized expressions of such feelings; there appears to be a persistent desire to appear plausible even when we abandon claims for rationality.

A second conflation of issues can be observed in the enthusiasm with which the authors of the recent report are willing to coopt the arguments of a feminist critique of pornography which, appearing in the mid-1970s, effectively reopened a debate that many hoped had been effectively muted by the conclusions of the earlier, 1971 commission. This was about the alleged characteristic of pornography—which until that point had been for all practical purposes an entirely male concern—to portray women in thoroughly sexist ways. As a result, it was viewed as encouraging men to sexually use and/or abuse women in degrading and hurtful ways, and to contribute to the persistence of sexist practices in other aspects of social life. Typical was Robin Morgan's sloganizing of the issue: pornography is the theory, rape the practice—a response that is as indifferent to the evidentiary beyond the anecdotal as it is to traditional distinctions between ideas and actions.

This approach, as in the original feminist critique, creates at least three problems. First, themes of the naturalness of the subordination and inferiority of women, as well as their "capacity" for finding pleasure in subordination, are abundantly present at all levels of our culture and diffusely embedded in most forms of institutionalized practice. The scripted practices of our major social institutions produce and reproduce the confirming imagery of the dependence and inferiority of women in the practices of everyday life. It is probable that, even were all such sexual representation to be banished from visibility, only the most defective of men would have difficulty in erotically enriching the existing scenarios of female subordination in which women and men continue to be instructed and which are still prevalent as mandated interpersonal scripts. While this does not excuse its appearance in the realm of the pornographic, it does require that we question the special attention paid to it. Pornography is not the ultimate citadel of sexism; at best, it is a shadow cast by more important, more affluent, and far more powerful institutions.

The approach of limiting the social and sociosexual abuse of women by the elimination of all representations of the sexual that are offensive to some appears to legitimate a more general strategy of solving social problems: solving them by banishing them from visibility. A strategy which, up until the mid-1960s, had been the society's basic strategy for managing public representations of the sexual. A set of practices, many should recall, that led to an impoverishing and alienating underground sexual culture and a public sexual culture in which the most marginal suggestion of the sexual—the kiss, the closed door—was suffused with obscene possibilities. That which explicitly is ordered to be invisible tends to appear everywhere and most often in the most unrealistically distorted guises.

What shall we do when the same strategy is applied—as it has been —to sexual minorities or the representation of fantasies of "unhealthy" political or religious preferences? The implicit naive social learning theory—that seeing leads to doing—would justify proscriptions of many kinds as essential to community well-being. This is bad politics feeding off of bad theory—either a barbarous theory or a theory of barbarous human psychology.

Denying the biological origins or fixity of sexual passions should not be taken to mean that the sexual can be self-consciously molded or shaped to fit a particular ideological or aesthetic paradigm. The sexual, like much else describing the human experience, tends to emerge from complex developmental processes. Many of the products of development, once in place, may be difficult or impossible to change or totally repress. This may be particularly true of the sexual, with its metaphoric richness often reflecting an equal richness of origins—some found in places of light and others in places of darkness. From Freud, in *Three Essays on the Theory of Sexuality* in 1905, to Stoller, in *Observing the Erotic Imagination* in 1986, we have been aware that the erotic is fed by experiences and memories of comfort as well as by experiences and memories of pain. The requirement that all public representations of the sexual conform to only one standard, either moral or aesthetic, necessarily engenders a potential sexual self-alienation that must constantly deepen in a social world rich with suggestive and accusatory silences and absences.

Only fanatics require that all moments, both awake and asleep, be fully consistent with the fullest expression of our ideals. This is particularly appropriate in the consideration of human sexuality, in which our ideals regarding the sexual may be incompatible at times or in part with the forms in which we learn sexual desire. Indeed, some may have learned that we do not seek intimacy in order to love, but love in order to know intimacy—to share both what we are as well as what we aspire to become. Some may have learned that the bedroom need not always serve as a showplace of ideological achievement, but that it can also be a playground and sometimes a theater.

The larger intellectual issue underlying the current discussion is the relationship between representations and behavior. Several years ago, Irving Kristol reminded us that a questionable logic was involved in asserting that certain kinds of representations had no power to do harm, while also asserting that other representations have the power to do good. I now believe that he was correct; no text, literary or visual, has any inherent powers. This is a difficult conclusion for someone who has spent most of his life involved with books and writing. I used to believe that as long as the libraries were preserved so would be the values that I cherish as part of my version of the human heritage. But it is possible that the current deconstructionist critique is valid; the context of reading, or viewing, the text may forever be a stranger to the context of authorship. Correspondingly, the intent of authorship can be only unpredictably related to the intent and subsequent uses of the reader, or viewer. John Dewey was correct: meaning is forever the captive of the context of the search for meaning.

It is possible that if *The Story of O* were to be required reading in every high school freshman literature class, the number of sexually sadistic women or men or sexually masochistic men or women would increase no more than the required reading of Marx in the high schools of Eastern Europe increases the number of women or men who share Marx's humanistic goals or his commitment to engaging in revolutionary activity in order to achieve those goals.

It is impossible for any society to completely control the context that is the individual's total intrapsychic life or even the context that is her or his immediate interpersonal environment. It is least possible in societies such as ours, which provide so many differentiated experiences and settings. We can, however, attempt to shape the larger social context— what might be termed the surrounding social landscape. A context overly fearful of the sexual in all its forms calls forth its sexual golems; to proclaim the fearfulness and ugliness of the sexual is to make it available for those seeking to objectify their fears and their ugliness. A context that makes of it a major test of social, moral, and gender competence, as we tend to, already makes of it a potentially solemn occasion. Reflecting that context, it already comes to us too often as a realm of silences, darkness, isolation, and danger, as well as a fear of multiple, sometimes contradictory failures.

In these terms, the current report will protect no one: it is a carrier of the worst of our inherited traditions. Nevertheless, it should not be ignored; nothing should be more immunizing than having it read by large numbers of people—hopefully by large numbers of people who have lost neither their sense of proportion nor their sense of humor.

The present discussion of pornography, like most earlier ones, tends to take place in either the context of an ongoing debate or the anticipation of such a debate. The central focus of the debate invariably is whether it is harmful or innocuous, and what are the public policy implications of that determination. Even matters of definition of pornography are typically couched in terms of strategic advantage within that debate. Rarely have we seen a discussion of the nature of pornography free the constraints of the polemical. While such extraordinarily dialogical encounters serve to clarify and sharpen attitudes, they rarely deepen our understanding. Nothing written in these reflections can claim exemption from this limitation.

I would be remiss if I did not attempt a few clarifying comments about my views of pornography not as an issue, but as a phenomena. While these observations are based upon my understanding of the available literature, they are also based upon a history of reading and viewing a great deal of such material—some of it outrageous, almost all of it vulgar, but, nonetheless, most often read or viewed with the pleasure of being sexually aroused. Sometimes this arousal inspired some kind of sexual activity, but often it culminated in only the not inconsiderable pleasures of merely experiencing sexual arousal, of experiencing myself as a sexual person.

While occasionally transcending its own limitations and approaching "serious art," pornography is inherently vulgar and immature. There should be nothing surprising about this. So are many other forms of

popular culture. The several genre of adventure fiction that involve outrageous displays of over-masculinized heroism or much of current romance and historical fiction, with their characteristic excess of emotion,
could be described this way. All such genre involve critical distortion of
reality and invite us to vicariously participate in behaviors that we could
not and, for the most part, would not perform in real life. Many of us,
perhaps regrettably, cannot or will not confine our consumption of the
media to our most refined levels of cultivation; rather, we bring to such
consumption large parts of our history of desires and history of pleasure
in desire.

I have often been suspicious of those with such refined taste that any
lapse into anything less than the highest forms of art prompts immediate
expressions of displeasure. I have friends who say they would rather read
the works of Dickens or Henry James than anything else. I am sure that
they are not pretending. Nor do I assume that this necessarily is a limitation or form of impairment. However, for many, histories of development make available or even require a greater eclecticism.

Pornography is admittedly a special case if only because the sexual has
special features. One of the intellectual costs of accepting the idea of a
sexual instinct, common to most conventional and scientific thinking, is
that we have been allowed to take the formation of sexual interest for
granted, most often averting our eyes from the very moments in which
the erotic is created and given content—that is, the moments in development when given persons, objects, locations, and actions are infused
with erotic possibility. For many, perhaps most, this occurs during adolescence. These earliest encounters with originating or adapting sexual
scripts become wholly predictive of subsequent sexual practices for very
few; for another few they become wholly irrelevant.

Pornography in its very immaturity taps and renews these relevancies.
That is why pornography is hardly ever read out-loud or enjoyed by
many in public places. Our embarrassment is double: first, the embarrassment at being seen responding to material that is so blatantly adolescent and, second, having to confront our own interest or capacity to
respond to what is so blatantly adolescent. The silence of the interior
dialogue is far less observant, less critical, kinder.

Almost universally in the Western tradition, our first understandings of
the sexual involve an awareness of its naughtiness and danger. I would
like to think that in recent years this has lessened, but I doubt it. This is
why so much of our initial intrapsychic experience with the sexual took
us to what can be called "the badlands of desire" or the "land of bad
desires." This is essentially the same psychic space in which other desires
and other constructions of the self were exiled upon being recognized as
being what the world did not expect or no longer expected. The history
of development does not always flow smoothly; for many of us it was of

necessity a history of abandonments and betrayals. This does not necessarily include only dreams of oedipally inspired murder and other forms of mayhem, but also the gestures and recognitions once vital to constructions of the self that in their day were as real to us as what followed.

If not originally infused with erotic significance, merely sharing the same space in the badlands of desire makes this larger history of wishes available and sometimes useful in the current sexual moment, a moment that is enriched by many implicit metonymies. Issues of power, justice, risk, failure, and humiliation or success and triumph make of the overt sexual moment a complex fabrication, however rigidly simplistic the ritualized performance. I will never be Superman; nor do I want to be. Similarly, I was not and can never be a superstud matching limitless and dangerous appeal with boundless vitality. That does not mean that I have stopped dreaming of being either.

"Insult" or "Injury" : Sex, Pornography, and Sexism

by

MICHAEL S. KIMMEL

The contemplation of ruins is a masculine specialty.
—Erik Erikson

The essays in this book confront the issue of pornography in men's lives. What role does pornography play in the shaping of male sexuality? How does it reflect or inform men's relationships with women? Is pornography, as D. H. Lawrence saw it, "an attempt to insult sex"—a reduction of sexual passion to machinelike disconnected body parts, or is it far more serious, a form of violence against women that inspires men to commit further violence and comforts men that such violence in women's lives is actually pleasurable to women? Is pornography a pathetic diminution of sexual pleasure, a self-help book for the sexually deprived or repressed, or is it a how-to manual of violence and abuse, a graphic illustration of misogyny? And what does pornography say about men's sexuality, about men's relationships with their own bodies, with the construction of men's desire?

The men in this book take different positions on these questions and propose different strategies of what, if anything, is to be done about it. Some demand that we confront pornography directly, politically; others suggest that we confront those who would define and proscribe our sexuality for us, whether they be pious fundamentalist moralizers or antiporn feminists crusading for politically correct sex. Other men suggest we simply lie back and enjoy it.

As I see it, men's confrontation with the issue of pornography revolves around four central themes: (1) the definition of pornography; (2) the relationship between pornography and sexuality; (3) the relationship between pornography and violence against women; and (4) the ways in which pornography shapes our relationships with other men. Here, I want to explore these themes, describe how editing this book has influenced my thinking, and suggest some lines for future thought.

I. The Futile Search for Definitions

The debate about pornography often begins with a quibbling over the definition of pornography—and too often it ends there as well, with each side comfortable with its particular definition. Perhaps the belief that we need a definition that will hold across all cases is one of the major barriers that prevents various groups from speaking with each other. While some search genuinely for definitions, others use a variety of strategies to protect what they find erotic or thrilling and to still find the grounds to sanctimoniously condemn what others find titillating. We are quite resourceful in the ways we invent moral arguments to condemn in others what we like for ourselves. The debate thus ends either in a relativistic stew, in which discussion stops abruptly when someone says, "Well, it depends on what you mean by pornography," or in that moralistic conundrum once sarcastically derided by Gloria Steinem: If I like it it's erotica, if you like it it's pornography.

I find these arguments about the definition of pornography both tedious and boring, an endless cycle of assertions which allow men to abdicate responsibility for confronting the politics of desire. The search for abstract definitions itself often freezes sexual imagery outside of its social context. But it is that context which determines sexual arousal, which permits the imaginative leap between a movie screen or centerfold and fantasies of sexual gratification. To speak of pornography in the abstract is to see it as more powerful than it really is. Pornography is most often nothing more than a collection of images, words, and pictures that are constructed to arouse men and, once aroused, to sustain that arousal through a masturbatory fantasy. Pornography is what pornography does: If men cannot masturbate to it, it is not pornography. Since the erotic and the pornographic are both so dependent upon context, finding one definition that will apply in all cases is both impossible and politically distracting. In particular, the search for definitions distracts us from the more pressing questions: Regardless of how pornography is defined, why do those images arouse us? What do those images actually portray? Would those images, if they were real, continue to arouse us? Why do men find those images sexy? What do the answers to these questions tell us about our sexuality?

II. Sexism and Sexual Repression: Food for Fantasy

Men's sexual fantasies are, in part, fueled by the two themes that frame the feminist debate about pornography: sexism and sexual repression. Why should we be surprised that these are often conflated in sexual fantasy? Sexist assumptions about women's sexuality permeate our culture, and men often hold utterly contradictory notions about women's sexuality (along with cultural icons that signify these bizarre notions). Women are seen simultaneously as passive and asexual (the "frigid prude") and insatiable and demanding (the *vagina dentata* that will devour men). These images confuse men and can often paralyse women, making their struggle to claim a vital sexuality a difficult and politically charged process.

Sexual repression also fuels men's lust. (This is, of course, true for women as well, although it is often expressed differently. Though much of this discussion of fantasy shaped by sexism and sexual repression holds also for women, I will continue to focus here only on men's fantasies.) Few men would say that they are having as much sex as they want. The norms of masculinity, after all, require that men should want sex all the time, and produce instant and eternally rigid erections on demand. These norms, though, contradict the social demand for sexual repression and the profoundly erotophobic thread that runs through our culture. As a culture, we abhor sex and are terrified by it, because we believe that the iconoclastic anarchy of the orgasm threatens all forms of authority —political, social, economic, and familial. And so we associate sexual yearnings with guilt or shame. And we simultaneously understand masculinity as the constant and irrepressible capacity for desire. (In part, this helps explain Freud's opposition of civilization and sexuality, and why, in a sexist culture, women's sexuality is constructed as passive so that they can control men's sexual drive.)

Sexual repression produces a world in which the nonsexual is constantly eroticized—in fantasy we recreate mentally what we have lost in real life. And sexist assumptions about women's sexuality provide the social context in which these fantasies take shape. Who but the sexually starved could listen to a twenty-second prerecorded message from a faceless woman over a telephone and be aroused? And in what context but sexism could her message be understood? In these prerecorded fantasies, the woman's voice has a lot to accomplish in twenty seconds: She must set a scene (nurse/patient, camping trip, etc.), express her intense need for sex with the listener, vocally simulate her arousal and orgasm while pleading for his orgasm, and finally close the encounter with gratitude for such frenzied pleasure and bid a fond farewell to her caller, inviting him to call again or call a different number "for a live girl." All this in twenty seconds! On the telephone! On tape! And still it turns men on. Easily.

Men's consistent complaint of sexual deprivation has no basis in biology, although it is comfortingly convenient to blame our hormones when we want sex. To always seek sex, to seek to sexualize relationships with women, to never refuse an offer of sex—these are crucial elements in the normative definition of masculinity. Sexual pleasure is rarely the goal in a sexual encounter; something far more important than mere pleasure is on the line: our sense of ourselves as men. Men's sense of sexual scarcity and an almost compulsive need for sex to confirm manhood feed one another, creating a self-perpetuating cycle of sexual deprivation and despair. And it makes men furious at women for doing what women are taught to do in our society: saying no. In our society, men being what men are "supposed to be" leads inevitably to conflict with women, who are being what they are "supposed to be."

Certainly, women say no for reasons other than gender conditioning; they may not be interested, or they may be angry at their partner for some reason. And certainly, men are also angry at women who are sexually voracious and fully claim sexual appetite. But, in general, this dynamic of men wanting and women refusing is established early in our adolescent sexual socialization and has important consequences for both male and female sexualities.

Men's consumption of pornography is, in part, fed by this strange combination of lust and rage. Pornography can sexualize that rage, and it can make sex look like revenge. That men may gain from pornography an acceptable vehicle to vent that rage is why many antiporn feminists claim that pornography leads to rape and sexual assault. Yet social scientists are not so sure. Sociologists Murray Strauss and Larry Baron found that the number of rapes was positively correlated with the consumption of soft-core pornography; the higher the number of copies of *Playboy* and *Penthouse* sold in a particular state, the higher the number of rapes. Instead of jumping to the obvious—and, it turns out, false—conclusion, these researchers also found that these two statistics were also positively related to the number of "men's" magazines, such as *Field and Stream* and *Popular Mechanics*, that were sold in those states. Shall we prohibit newsstands from carrying them? It turns out that the higher rates of magazine sales and rapes are both due to the higher percentage of younger men in those states. Researcher Edward Donnerstein and his associates make the social-scientific case clearest: Even "if every violent rapist we could find had a history of exposure to violent pornography, we would never be justified in assuming that these materials 'caused' their violent behavior." Pornography, then, is part of a larger question, having to do with the definition of masculinity in our society.

In their laboratory experiments on the effects of pornography on men's behavior and attitudes, various research teams have reached similar conclusions. Several found that repeated exposure to violent pornography did lead to the psychological numbing of sensitivity toward violence against women, and, at least initially, increased men's beliefs in myths about rape. Donnerstein, for example, found that "exposure to degrading pornography did result in more calloused beliefs about rape," and "may have negative effects on attitudes about women."

To understand these results, though, researchers have attempted to disentangle the violence and the sex contained in violent pornography. Here, the results are important. While nonviolent sexual images had no noticeable impact on either attitudes or behavior, images of violence against women alone, as well as violent pornography, had similar dele- terious effects on men's attitudes. Clearly, it is the violence, and not the sex, that is responsible. In lieu of the Meese Commission's "unwarranted extrapolation from the available research data," Donnerstein and his col- leagues have argued, "depictions of violence against women, whether or not in a sexually explicit context, should be the focus of concern." Sex- ualized violence is only one form of violence that may cause harm; if policy makers choose to single it out, it is, I believe, because of their discomfort with the sexuality contained in the images, not the violence.

The policy implications drawn from research on the impact of pornog- raphy square with parallel research on rape, as Nicholas Groth has stated in his conclusion to *Men Who Rape*: "It is not sexual arousal but the arousal of anger that leads to rape." He concludes that "pornography does not cause rape, banning it will not stop rape." But such assertions beg the question: Why are men so angry at women? Everywhere, men are in power, controlling virtually all the economic, political, and social institutions of society. And yet individual men do not feel powerful—far from it. Most men feel powerless and are often angry at women, who they perceive as having sexual power over them: the power to arouse them and to give or withhold sex. This fuels both sexual fantasies and the desire for revenge.

In this world of constructed perpetual male lust and feelings of power- lessness in the face of women's constructed denial of desire, pornography becomes almost a side issue to the problem of men's anger at women. In one particularly compelling interview in Timothy Beneke's fascinating book *Men on Rape*, a young stockboy in a large corporation describes his rage at women who work with him:

> Let's say I see a woman and she looks really pretty and really clean and sexy, and she's giving off very feminine, sexy vibes. I think 'Wow, I would love to make love to her,' but I know she's not interested. It's a tease. A lot of times a woman knows that she's looking really good and she'll use that and flaunt it, and it makes me feel like she's laughing at me and I feel *degraded*....
>
> If I were actually desperate enough to rape somebody, it would be from wanting the person, but also it would be a very spiteful thing, just being able to say 'I have power over you and I can do anything I want with you,' because really I feel *they* have power

over *me* just by their presence. Just the fact that they can come up to me and just melt me and make me feel like a dummy makes me want revenge. They have power over me so I want power over them.

If men can see women's beauty and sexuality as so injurious that they can fantasize about rape as a retaliation for harm already committed by women, is it also possible that pornographic fantasies draw from this same reservoir of men's anger? If so, it would seem that men's rage at women, and not its pornographic outlet, ought to be our chief concern.

III. The Pornographic Spectacle

Thinking about men's experiences of power and powerlessness has led me to wonder if one could find an arena for men that is equivalent to the representation of women in pornography. The issues of male sexuality and control seem too similar in gay male pornography, even though the gender equality of the participants fundamentally alters the politics of gay porn. To empathize with women's responses to their representation in pornography means to identify with what women say they feel. Is there an arena in which what happens to women in pornography happens to men?

My first thought was of body building. Here is a place where the body is transformed into an object of its own consumption, as the woman's idealized body is stripped of its history, its identity, its personality in pornography. The artificial purity of form can only hint at its capacity to act. The body as object is perfected, without concern for its interior life. Body building is as decontextualized as pornography, the process of self-reification, the transformation of the body into its own objectified false essence. Body building allows men to experience what English art critic John Berger writes in *Ways of Seeing* about the relation between women and men and seeing and being seen: "Men act and women appear. Men look at women. Women watch themselves being looked at. This determines not only most relations between men and women, but also the relation of women to themselves." Body building transforms men into "women," making men and their exaggerated—even distorted—expression of gender the object of the gaze.

But body building is too tame, too generous—here, the male body is presented only in its allusion to strength, hardness, muscles. These may *refer* to masculine virtues such as strength, bravery, and power, but body builders are the analogs to the soft-core idealized female pornographic image, or, in Berger's understanding, to the painting of the nude. Harder-core pornography is about the idealized female image turned against itself, becoming, in a sense, the rationale for its own violation.

Pornography is more like boxing and wrestling than it is like body building. The analogy with wrestling suggests the ways in which pornography is artifice, spectacle. The wrestler's body is exaggerated masculinity just as the pornographic body is highly exaggerated, with a persistent focus on size, motion, how long it lasts. Like much pornography, the wrestling match is a staged spectacle, not real fighting; it is highly ritualized and follows elaborate conventions and codes of behavior that are rarely transgressed. The bodies of wrestlers are often costumed in stylized caricatures of various versions of masculinity, which often use cultural signifiers of "evil" drawn from class-based or political struggles (the hillbilly, the motorcycle delinquent, the Indian warrior, the Russian strongman, the Arab shiek, the body builder). Like much pornography, the primary relationship within the spectacle is the wrestlers' relationship with the audience; they perform to be observed. And like a good deal of pornography, the intensity of the violence between the wrestlers is an elaborate construction. No one actually believes they're hurting one another; one watches wrestling for the sheer thrill of the spectacle, of the illusion.

The analogy between wrestling and pornography, though, breaks down in the face of hard-core pornography and violent pornography. The importance of the event-as-spectacle diminishes, and the "truth" of the interaction becomes a central feature. Boxing is no less a spectacle than wrestling, but the boxers' relationship to one another assumes a far more significant dimension. The boxers themselves are intensely attuned to one another; the viewer is more the privileged voyeur, being allowed to watch the most intense interaction imaginable between two men.

Like wrestling and body building, there is a fetishization of the boxer's body, though in boxing the "tale of the tape" often implies a relationship to masculine perfection and not simply the capacity to do violence or the exaggerated qualities of the wrestler. The bodies of boxers are perfect specimens of masculinity—hard, strong, muscular—and these bodies are then transformed into dangerous machines that will destroy you unless you destroy them first. Boxing involves the "deadly improvement of the human physique when it is turned into an implement of its own destruction," writes Garry Wills. Just as we might say that pornography is more about *being* fucked than it is about fucking, boxing, as Joyce Carol Oates comments in her slender literary discussion of the sport, "is about being hit rather than it is about hitting, just as it is about feeling pain, if not devastating psychological paralysis, more than it is about winning." But Oates only partially glimpses the relationship between boxing and pornography:

> Boxing as a public spectacle is akin to pornography: in each case the spectator is made a voyeur, distanced, yet presumably intimately involved, in an event that is not supposed to be happening

as it is happening. The pornographic "drama," though as fraudulent as professional wrestling, makes a claim for being about something absolutely serious, if not humanly profound: it is not so much about itself as about the violation of a taboo. . . . The obvious difference between boxing and pornography is that boxing, unlike pornography, is not theatrical. It is not, except in instances so rare as to be irrelevant, rehearsed or simulated. Its violation of the taboo against violence is open, explicit, ritualized and . . . *routine*— which gives boxing its uncanny air. Unlike pornography (and professional wrestling) it is altogether real: the blood shed, the damage suffered, the pain (usually suppressed or sublimated) are unfeigned.

Harder-core pornography resembles boxing in precisely the ways that boxing differs from wrestling. Hard-core pornography is *real* sex, just as boxing is real fighting. Each is a "real" event (people are actually having sex and boxers are actually hurting one another), and each is carefully proscribed by rules.

Boxing resembles pornography in another way. Each activity turns on a particular moment in the unfolding drama, each has a moment of transformation. In boxing, Oates writes, the "moment of visceral horror" is "that moment when one boxer loses control, cannot maintain his defense, begins to waver, falter, fall back, rock with his opponent's punches which he can no longer absorb; the moment in which the fight is turned around and in which an entire career, an entire life, may end." In this moment, the "defeat of one man is the triumph of the other." So too in pornography, where the pivotal moment is when the woman's resistance collapses against the irresistible passion of the man's aggressive advances, when she can no longer physically push against his embrace and melts into his passion, and thus discovers her own passion. This is the moment when she is still saying no but now obviously means yes, the moment when Rhett Butler gathers a kicking and struggling Scarlett O'Hara into his arms and carries her upstairs where, offscreen, he will have his way with her, despite her initial resistance (and to the swoons of audiences everywhere). This is the pornographic moment, the moment that barriers are trespassed, when taboos are demolished, when individual integrity is transgressed. This is the moment of his victory and her defeat.

(Some pornography does not illustrate a simple win-lose model of male-female interactions. By showing lustful women who want to have as much hot sex as men do, some pornography can provide a fantasy situation in which both man and woman "win," that is, each gets the terrific sex that each wants. Unfortunately, this model informs less than one might optimally hope; what appears to be the majority of pornographic images impose traditional punishments on women for claiming their desire. These are the consequences for sexual women in the pornographic fantasy—defeat, resignation, pain, and humiliation.)

Like boxing, the pornographic moment also requires verification by independent observing eyes. Each depends upon a specific representation to demonstrate its authenticity. For the boxing match, it is the first drawing of blood. A collective gasp from the crowd often accompanies that moment when the boxer's pain is registered as authentic by a visible mark. In pornography, the "wet shot" or the "cum shot" provides a narrative climax to the proceedings, simultaneously concluding that sexual episode for the man and providing the validation that the sex was authentic. That is why, in pornography, male ejaculation almost invariably occurs outside the woman, and often on her, as if to show that this was not a staged, simulated sexual encounter designed solely for the pleasure of the viewer, but real sex, in which the man had a real orgasm. (Of course, since external ejaculation is not presented as a form of birth control but rather as a stamp of authentication, the cum shot also reveals that even these "real" sex scenes are fully staged, and as constructed by artifice as the wrestling match.) The viewer can now choose to believe that the sex was also mutually pleasurable, since its authenticity was demonstrated. This may also reduce any attendant guilt he might feel about using pornography to masturbate. "You see, the people in the film liked it, so how bad can it be?"

The costs of authentic sex in pornography and fighting in boxing are often concealed in the role of spectator. In an intriguing essay in which he explains his decision to avoid viewing boxing matches, Garry Wills is reminded of St. Augustine, who, in *The Confessions*, describes his friend Alypius, who revels in watching gladiators. "At the sight of the blood," Augustine writes, "he took a sip of animality. Not turning away, but fixing his eyes on it, he drank deeper of the frenzies without realizing it, and taking complicit joy in the contest was inebriated by his delight in blood." The real harm, Augustine believed, was to the viewer, not to the participant; Alypius was "wounded deeper in the soul than the gladiator in his body."

It is true that a major difference between boxing and pornography is the gender of the participants. In violent heterosexual male pornography, it is the woman's body, in ideal form, that is violated, while boxing implies, by definition, the almost perfectly matched equality of the combatants, and certainly demands their gender equality. This is a difference on the surface only. The anger at women that propels men's pornographic fantasies stems, in part, from men's belief that women have all the power in male-female relations, especially since women have the power to reject them. As Susan Griffin noted in her book *Pornography and Silence*, pornographic fantasy is a revenge fantasy against women's perceived power, a fantasy that often turns women's power to say no into their inability to get enough. In boxing, two apparent equals enter the ring to find the physical dimension that will separate them, that will mark them as unequal. One emerges the champion, the other as chump. In pornography's reversal of real life, two gender *unequals* enter a scene in which the one in power (the woman) is put back in her place. They enter the ring in reversed positions, but emerge as masculine man and feminine woman.

Though I am only talking about a small band on the pornographic spectrum here—violent heterosexual male pornography—the analogy between boxing and this kind of pornography is instructive in that it exposes a partial truth of men's rage at women. It means that we must understand pornography as a real event, unstaged and unfeigned, involving real people engaged in a real activity for the pleasure of the spectator, at the same time as we understand pornography to be a staged spectacle, a fantasy world, an illusion. Women can be seen as the victims of pornography in the same way as boxers are victimized. But how can they be cast as victims if they chose to participate? "No one held a gun to their heads and said 'Do it,'" remains a facile ploy to avoid confronting the issue. Freedom of choice is illusion. How many working-class men would choose boxing in a world of truly free choices, in which they might just as easily become brain surgeons? And how many working-class women would choose to be pornographic film stars, or prostitutes, if they could just as easily become Supreme Court justices? (That's why it is always big news when an upper-class woman is "discovered" to have a double life as a porn star.) Of course, some women do choose to work in the sex industry as a challenge to the sexual repression and sexism they see in the world around them; these women see their work as liberatory, vital, and often feminist. Though their voices are important to hear, I doubt that they are in the majority.

IV. Pornography and Fantasy

To the spectator, pornography is less about the real lives of pornographic actresses than about the viewer's fantasies that their activities provide. Pornography provides a world of fantasy to the male viewer—a world of sexual plenty, a world in which women say no but really mean yes (or say yes in the first place), a world of complete sexual abandon, a world of absolute sexual freedom, a world in which gorgeous and sexy women are eager to have sex with us, a world in which we, and our partners, are always sexually satisfied. The pornographic utopia is a world of abundance, abandon, and autonomy—a world, in short, utterly unlike the one we inhabit. (I have often wondered if it is the world we would like to inhabit if only we could, or if that world is too threatening to attempt to call it into existence.) In our jobs, men's sense of autonomy and control has historically decreased. In the sexual marketplace, men feel vulnerable to women's power of rejection. Most men do not make enough money, have enough workplace control, or get enough sex. Many men feel themselves to be "feminized" in the workplace—-dependent, helpless, powerless. Most men don't feel especially good about themselves, living lives of "quiet desperation," as Ralph Waldo Emerson so compactly put it. Pornographic fantasy is a revenge against the real world of men's lives.

But fantasy is not created from nothing; at least in a limited sense, fantasy is a "recollection" of a world we have lost. It is a psychoanalytic truism that what we lose in reality we recreate in fantasy. Now what have men lost that we seek to retrieve and recreate in pornographic fantasy? At the individual level, we recreate our infancies, the sense of infantile omnipotence, when the entire universe revolved around the satisfaction of our desires and the sense that the world we inhabited was full of sexual pleasures. The world of infancy is an eroticized world, a world of tactile pleasures ministered to by adults, especially the mother. But childhood socialization demolishes this world of erotic omnipotence and introduces the child to a world of scarcity (no-saying), repression (toilet training, punishment), and dependency on the will of that adult woman who is the mother. The world of childhood may be the reverse of the infantile world, but it more closely resembles the world we come to know as adults. And who wouldn't want a temporary imaginary vacation from such a world?

This dramatic transition from infancy to childhood also helps to explain the strange ways in which the pornographic narrative is often constructed. Our commonsense assumption is that a man identifies with the male actor in the pornographic film. But so many pornographic movies, especially those that eventually lead to rape, bondage, sadomasochism, begin with a woman alone—walking home at night, waiting in a bar or on a streetcorner or in her home. Perhaps in this first scene, the male viewer identifies with the woman, in a similar way that he identifies as a child with his mother. The male actor's violation of the woman, in a rape scene for example, allows the male viewer a moment to make the symbolic leap from identification with the woman in the film to identification with the man. Just as the familial oedipal triangle is resolved by the young boy making the symbolic leap from identification with mother to identification with father, the pornographic film allows a similar leap. Masculinity, as socially constructed in our culture, is therefore confirmed.

At the collective, or social level, this transition in identification is also evident. "If readers are especially fond of tales of women objectified and abused under particular circumstances, we might ask ourselves to what

extent those readers feel themselves victimized under comparable conditions in their own immediate phenomenal worlds," is the way Lawrence
Rosenfield posed the question. It is "as if the moral degradation the
reader might feel in his daily life were being reified for him in bodily
terms."

The social world that men have lost is the world of economic autonomy and political community, a world in which individual men could
take pride in their work and share it among a community of neighbors
and friends. It is a world in which work contained some intrinsic meaning. And it is a male-dominated world, a world in which men's power
over women was challenged, if at all, with far less effectiveness and with
far fewer results. But male domination has been decreasing rapidly with
industrial progress. Women's advances into the economic and political
arenas, and their assertion of social rights, have eroded the power of
men over women dramatically. The lives of women have dramatically
changed from a century ago: Women often have careers; they vote, own
property, control their own reproductive lives. Although male violence
against women is still a very serious problem, women today are actually
subject to far *less* violence than they were in pre-industrial societies, in
which rape was commonplace (although often not labeled rape) and
women were freely traded among men as possessions. Is it an ironic
consequence of the *success* of feminism that men, in their fantasies, sometimes need to return to that earlier historical era in which their word was
law and their desire was the only desire that mattered? Ironically, those
conservatives who would like to return us to this world of unquestioned
male domination *in real life* are often the same people who would like to
suppress our access to *fantasy versions* of it in pornography.

It may be true that the advance of women's rights has been accompanied by an increase in pornographic images. (I say "accompanied" and
not "caused," because I want to be clear that if this is an unanticipated
consequence of feminism's success, I neither want to blame feminism for
it, nor suggest that the only way to eliminate pornography is to abandon
feminism. In fact, the increase in women's rights and the increase in
pornographic images may both be caused by the general historical increase in the rights of individuals for free expression.) Pornography provides a world without job pressures and full of material abundance, and
of eager, available women capable of acting on sexual desire as *men* understand it. But most men realize that these earlier worlds of unchallenged male domination—of infantile omnipotence and sexualized
control over the mother—are gone forever. Pornography may be a sexualized "Fantasy Island," an oasis where men can retreat from everyday
life's pressures, but it is not "Gilligan's Island," from which there is no
escape once stranded there. Men can return from the fantasy paradise of
pornography. And they do return.

Though it's impossible to demonstrate this empirically, I suspect that men who actually did live in those societies in which slavery existed did not have many erotic fantasies about slaves. White South Africans have only a small amount of pornography about Black South Africans. In part, the reality of domination may diminish a psychological need for fantasies about it. Conversely, the proliferation of fantasy may testify to the decline of the reality of domination. On the other hand, pornography may speak to men's *incapacity* to act as they would like. In societies in which economic, political, or social domination is so repressively enforced, men may retain the capacity to act sexually against the women of that subject population. The casual rape of colonized women is a form of sexual terrorism—one that serves sexism by keeping women down and serves the other forms of domination by acting as a vicious reminder of the dominated men's incapacity to protect "their" women.

Recent social developments may have also begun to disentangle sexual fantasy from the guilt and shame with which it has historically been linked. Today, much of the growth in the pornography industry is in video cassettes for home use, either as rentals or for purchase. According to a survey in *Adult Video News* in 1986, one of every five video cassettes are in the category "adult action," and more than fifteen hundred new hardcore X-rated titles hit the market each year. In 1986, approximately $500 million was generated by retail sales of pornographic cassettes, double the volume in the previous three years.

As pornography is emerging from the dank darkness of the seedy porno theater in dangerous and disreputable neighborhoods, and moving into the suburban living room or bedroom, it is also changing its gender. While men continue to be the overwhelming majority of consumers, some researchers estimate that up to twenty percent of all renters are women. And married and unmarried couples are increasingly choosing a video cassette together to rent for their evening's entertainment. The proprietor of my local video store tells me that it is increasingly common for couples to choose three or four cassettes for a weekend's viewing, including a cartoon feature or a Walt Disney or Steven Spielberg film for the children, a family drama for the entire family, and a pornographic film for the time after the children have gone to bed. As couples continue to rent pornographic videos together, the clandestine nature of sexual fantasy, the furtive pleasures taken guiltily, and always with the risk of being caught, may decline as well. Is it possible that heterosexual couples can begin to use pornography as an affirmation of their sexuality instead of as a confirmation of their dirty thoughts? In short, can straight couples use porn the way that many gay men use it?

The progressive disentangling of sexual fantasy from guilt may allow men to admit what has always been true about their relationships with pornography, but which the norms of masculinity have long prevented them from admitting: Many men use pornography as sex education. In the world of sexual repression and scarcity that men inhabit, many men —perhaps most men—are unsure of themselves as lovers, uncertain of their capacity to give and receive pleasure. Pornography has likely always been a furtive source of sex education; men will offer to try something new with their partner or ask their partner to try something new. It may be true that violent pornography could suggest to some viewers that violence against women is reasonable on the sexual menu. But even here it is more likely to end up with a suggestion of a little consensual S/M, and not necessarily in rape. Most consumers are more innocent, taking a couple of sexual positions or the sequencing of the sex as what are often called "marital aids." That couples are now renting and viewing films together should, one hopes, increase the mutuality and equality in this less furtive form of sexual information.

V. Confronting Pornography

None of these psychoanalytic or sociological explorations is intended to let men off the hook, to defend unquestioningly men's "right" to consume pornographic images, especially within the three to five percent of the pornography market that presents images of women tortured and raped. Pornography cannot but contribute to men's storehouse of sexual fantasies, and, as such, impoverishes our sexual imaginations even in the guise of expanding our repertoires. Men must think carefully about these images in which violence against women becomes the vehicle by which men experience sexual arousal. Even through fantasy, "any form of rejection, cruelty, and injustice inflicted upon any group of human beings by any other group of human beings dehumanizes the victims overtly, and in more subtle ways, dehumanizes the perpetrators," wrote Kenneth Clark. Master and slave are mutually depraved, though only the master maintains institutional outlets for his depravity.

But confronting the role of pornography in men's lives doesn't necessarily mean removing sexual fantasy or constraining men's desire and capacity to imagine a world unlike the one in which they live, to imagine a world of sexual plenty. Sexual scarcity and sexual repression feed the pornographic imagination just as sexism becomes the content of much fantasy. Paul Goodman seemed to have this in mind when he wrote that "when excellent human power is inhibited and condemned, it will reappear ugly and dangerous. The censorious attitude toward the magazines and pictures is part of the general censorious attitude that hampers ordinary sexuality and thereby heightens the need for satisfaction by means of the magazines and pictures [and] must lead to more virulent expressions, e.g., still less desirable pornography."

For men to "confront" pornography means neither repudiating sexual pleasure nor ignoring the content of our sexual imaginations. It will require that we listen carefully to women, that we take seriously their pain, anguish, confusion, and embarrassment about the content of our pornography. It will require that we listen when women tell us about the pain and terror of sexual victimization, as well as their exhilaration at their claiming of a sexuality. This is not easy; men are not very good listeners. We're not trained to listen to women, but trained to *not* listen, to screen out women's voices with the screaming of our own needs. It will mean, therefore, listening to our own sexual yearnings, unfulfilled and, perhaps, unfulfillable, and exploring the mechanisms that will allow us to empower ourselves, and create images that arouse us without depicting the punishment of others as the basis for that arousal. It will mean learning to speak with other men about what is sexy to us and what isn't, about how to separate the sex from the sexism. It will mean making political and personal alliances with other men—not in silent complicity with misogynist pornographers, but in open defiance of both sexual repression and sexist violence, and in loving support of a common struggle within and against a repressive culture.

Notes and References

The following material is the notes, references, and other source information that the authors of some of the essays in this book had included in their essays. I have left their notes as they wrote them.

Confessions of a Feminist Porn Watcher
Scott MacDonald

1. During my twenties and early thirties I would guess I went to porn films and/or arcades half a dozen times a year. In the past few years (I'm 40) I've gone less frequently; it probably works out to two or three times a year at most. I assume that some men frequent such places, while others go once or twice in a lifetime. I have no information on how often or seldom an "average" man pays to see pornography. I've not been conscious of specific changes in the situation presented in the films or the attitudes which are evident in them. I assume there has been some evolution in this regard, but my experiences have been too sporadic (and too surrounded by personal anxieties) for me to be able to formulate useful conclusions about this evolution.

2. In this sense, the porn narratives seem rather similar to those of George Méliès's films (the acting is roughly comparable, too!).

3. Once I've decided to go to a porn theater, I go immediately, without checking to see when the movies begin or end; as often as not, I arrive in the middle of a film. (This is true only when the theater in question runs shows continuously; when a theater runs only one or two shows a day, I usually postpone a decision about going until just long enough before the beginning of the show so that the decision can be followed by immediate action.) With very rare exceptions, I've always left before a show is over; after one film had led up to and past its most stimulating motifs, I've waited only long enough to calm down and not

leave the theater with a visible erection. I've never sat all the way through a double feature of porn films.

4. Recent "trash" and "punk" films—John Waters's *Multiple Maniacs, Pink Flamingos, Female Trouble, Desperate Living;* Beth and Scott B's *G-Man;* Robert Huot's *Dr. Faustus' Foot Fetish,* for example—have exploited a similar sense of aggressive amateurishness. In fact, since *G-Man* and *Dr. Faustus' Foot Fetish* are Super-8 films, they bring with them something of the feel of Super-8 porn loops.

5. The frequency of anal sex in porn films seems to confute this, at least if one assumes that anal sex is annoying and painful for most, or many, women. Yet, a decision not to press for fulfillment of such a desire because its fulfillment will cause pain doesn't necessarily eliminate the desire. I would guess that for many men the anal sex in porn films functions as a way of giving harmless vent to a desire they've decided not to pressure the real women in their lives about (harmless, that is, unless one assumes the women in the films feel they are being harmed, something I have no information about).

6. One recent attempt to assess porn's effects is Dolf Zillmann and Jennings Bryant's "Pornography, Sexual Callousness, and the Trivialization of Rape," *Journal of Communication* (Autumn 1982). Unfortunately, this study's central finding—"our investigation focused on sexual callousness toward women, demonstrating that massive exposure to standard pornographic materials devoid of coercion and aggression seem to promote... callousness (in particular, the trivialization of rape...."—is based on testing procedures and supported by assumptions which raise nagging questions. The study's conclusions are based on a test of the impact of pornography on students exposed in groups, in a college setting, to "massive," "intermediate," and "no" amounts of conventional, nonviolent pornographic film. But in real life, porn films are seen in a very particular environment, at least in most instances I know of: in a public/private context.

Pornography and Freedom
John Stoltenberg

1. Edward Baker, *Tricked into White Slavery* (South Laguna, Calif.: Publisher's Consultants, 1978), p. 132.

2. Samuel Mixer, *Bondage Fling* (Los Angeles: Sutton House Publishing Co., 1977), p. 103.

3. Eli Robeson. "Knife Point," *Folsom Magazine,* No. 2 (1981): 27.

4. See Andrea Dworkin and Catharine A. MacKinnon, *Pornography and Civil Rights: A New Day for Women's Equality* (published and distributed by Organizing Against Pornography, 734 East Lake Street, #300 West, Minneapolis, Minnesota 55407, 1985).

Pornography and Censorship
Fred Small

1. I confine my discussion to pornography aimed at heterosexual males because I am most familiar with it and most qualified to assess it.

2. Andrea Dworkin, address delivered at Boston University, April 3, 1985.

3. Dworkin, *op. cit.*

4. *Ibid.*

5. See Ellen Willis, "Feminism, Moralism, and Pornography," in Snitow *et al.*, eds., *Powers of Desire: The Politics of Sexuality* (New York: Monthly Review Press, 1983), p. 464; Carole S. Vance and Ann Bar Snitow, "Toward a Conversation About Sex in Feminism: A Modest Proposal," *Signs,* Vol. 10, No. 1 (Autumn 1984), pp. 128–129.

6. *Hustler* editor Larry Flynt's vicious and deliberately provocative stances on sex and politics lead to hideous images. The May 1985 issue contained the most disturbing image I saw in my survey of pornography: a staged photograph of a black "family" cannibalizing an infant, with this text: "FOOD FOR THOUGHT. Millions of poor Africans are starving to death every day while lunch and dinner may be staring them right in the face. We're not saying that cannibalism is the only solution to the continent's massive hunger problem— it's just an idea the natives may find easy to digest," P. 27. Because this image does not concern sex, it would not be covered by a Minneapolis-type ordinance.

7. See Gayle Rubin, "Censored: Antiporn Laws and Women's Liberation," *Gay Community News,* Dec. 22, 1984, p. 8, for a similar impression of porn inventory. I assume one can obtain violent materials through the mails or by a more thorough search.

8. The Pornography Resource Center cites a study indicating that "depictions of bondage, domination, and spanking" constitute 17.2 percent of *hardcore* pornographic magazine covers surveyed in New York City's Times Square. *Women Against Pornography Newsreport* (no date, no page), citing *American Journal of Psychiatry,* Vol. 139, No. 11, Nov. 1982, pp. 1493–1495.

9. See U.S. Bureau of the Census, *Statistical Abstract of the United States: 1985* (Washington, D.C.: 1984), p. 170; Edward J. Brown, Timothy J. Flanagan, and Maureen McLead, eds., *Sourcebook of Criminal Justice Statistics—1983* (Washington, D.C.: U.S. Department of Justice, Bureau of Justice Statistics, 1984), pp. 341–42.

Incest Pornography and the Problem of Fantasy
Jeffrey Masson

1. I would like to thank Tim Beneke for collecting the material, for inspiring me to think about its implications, and for help in writing this article, as well as for the example he set in his book *Men on Rape*, which made a deep impression on me long before I had met its author.

2. No doubt this will be disputed. I am not aware of any statistics on the readership of pornography, but every time I have been in a pornography store or even walked past one, I have never seen a woman in any of them. The statistics on the sexual abuse of children by women show a very small figure. See Diana Russell, *Sexual Exploitation: Rape, Child Sexual Abuse and Workplace Harassment* (Beverly Hills, Calif.: Sage, 1984).

3. Sylvia Fraser, *My Father's House: A Memoir of Incest and of Healing* (Toronto: Doubleday Canada, 1987), p. 220.

4. One can point to the inherent contradiction in claiming that incest is both normal, healthy, and instigated by the girl, and at the same time claiming that girls who do this are "insane." This turns reality upside down, because in fact girls who are coerced into incestuous relations are so miserable that they become, in the eyes of society, "insane." This should help us to reject the very term "insanity" and to see how psychiatry perpetrates and uses to its own advantage some of the same myths accepted by the pornographer.

5. I am not aware of any study of the readership of incest pornography. Nor do I know of any estimate of the actual number of copies of these books sold. I called one well-known publishing house that specializes in pornography and was told by the publisher that, although exact figures are not known, he would be surprised to learn that these books sell more than about five thousand copies. Most pornographers, he explained to me, are not interested in reading; they primarily use video, which is very big business indeed. Next in the hierarchy come magazines. Books are at the bottom of the list. On the other hand, it is illegal to sell visual child-pornography, whereas printed matter is protected under the First Amendment.

6. The question of causation in incest pornography is similar to the same question with respect to rape and violent pornography in general. Almost all researchers agree that exposure to aggressive pornography reinforces and strengthens already existing beliefs and values as these are evidenced, for example, in callous attitudes about violence toward women. See Edward Donnerstein, Daniel Linz, and Steven Penrod, *The Question of Pornography: Research Findings and Policy Implications* (New York: The Free Press, 1987); also, N. M.

Malamuth and E. Donnerstein, eds., *Pornography and Sexual Aggression* (Orlando, Fla.: Academic Press, 1984).

7. See Andrea Dworkin, "Against the Male Flood: Censorship, Pornography, and Equality," *Harvard Women's Law Journal* 8 (1985): 1–29; and Catharine MacKinnon, "Not a Moral Issue," *Yale Law and Policy Review* 2 (1984): 321–345.

8. *Harvard Woman's Law Journal* 8 (Spring 1985). Reprinted in the fine collection by Andrea Dworkin, *Letters from a War Zone: Writings 1976–1987* (London: Secker & Warburg, 1988).

9. See in particular Catharine MacKinnon's *Feminism Unmodified: Occasional Discourses on Life and Law* (Cambridge, Mass.: Harvard University Press, 1987).

10. *Final Report of the Attorney General's Commission on Pornography* (Washington, D.C., 1986).

11. Philip Nobile and Eric Nadler, *United States of America vs. Sex: How the Meese Commission Lied About Pornography* (New York: Minotaur Press, Ltd., a Penthouse International Company, 1986).

The Antidialectic of Pornography
Joel Kovel

1. It seems, however, that the terror of AIDS is driving sexuality, including its representation, back in the direction of the recent past; but this raises issues beyond this essay's scope.

2. George Bataille, *Erotism, Death and Sensuality*, trans. Mary Dalwood (San Francisco: City Lights, 1986), p. 12.

3. Freud, as we know, did not have a differentiated self-concept. The same dualism, however, informs his entire project, whether inscribed as the tension between id and ego, or pleasure and reality principles. We cannot take up the theoretical points here.

4. Again, this is not the place to take up the matter, but Freud's notion of primitive society, and hence of taboo, was subject to many ethnocentric distortions. Bataille's appears to be sounder, although his insistence upon the centrality of the ritual blood-sacrifice is more a projection backward of his own obsession that a genuine anthropologic statement.

5. See his *Thalassa, a Theory of Genitality* (New York: W. W. Norton, 1968).

6. I must set aside discussion of the enormous difficulties posed by Reich here. See my "Why Freud or Reich?", *Free Associations* 4 (January 1986): 80–99, for consideration of some of the issues. To cite only one of the problems: Although the Father of the sexual-liberation movement, Reich was explicitly and strongly

homophobic. Moreover, he had little use for representation as such, being always directed toward actual orgastic discharge in a heterosexual embrace.

7. This does not mean that everybody has to have an exuberant sex life—a proposition that would restore sexuality to the cruder objectifications of the therapeuts. It means, rather, that something akin to free speech must apply to sexuality in a worthwhile society. People must have the right to define and express their sexuality freely, a right, which exercised, could well lead to a freely chosen asceticism in the interests, say, of a religious calling.

8. Alan Soble, *Pornography: Marxism, Feminism and the Future of Sexuality* (New Haven: Yale University Press, 1986).

9. As in Blake's "May God us keep, from single vision and Newton's sleep."

10. Which can happen narcissistically, as well as in the eyes of an other.

11. Then again, this can be turned around once more, and the genital shaved to provide yet another reversal. The point is that the erotic inheres in the act of eternally recurrent coding—combined, it must always be born in mind, with real physical presence. Sexuality does not exist strictly in the mind any more than it exists at a reflex level.

12. I refer to the infamous "snuff" films, which are certainly very rare, but also to a more common mode exhibited in the raunchier porn shops, in which animals are sacrificed, for example, a chicken killed while being copulated with.

13. Another would be *Shoah*, which used entirely a different mode of representation. I add this point to remind us that the erotic is not an exclusive pathway to the truth about the human condition.

Intrusive Images and Subjectified Bodies:
Notes on Visual Heterosexual Porn
Timothy Beneke

1. I originally got the distinction between the authorized and the stolen from a conversation with Erving Goffman. I apply it somewhat differently in *Men on Rape* (New York: St. Martin's Press, 1982), pp. 23–29.

2. Erving Goffman, *Relations in Public* (New York: Harper and Row, 1971), p. 46.

3. See George Lakoff and Mark Johnson, *Metaphors We Live By* (Chicago: University of Chicago Press, 1980), for a fascinating exposition of this kind of linguistic analysis.

4. *Men on Rape* (New York: St. Martin's Press, 1982), pp. 59–60.

5. Ibid., pp. 54–55.

6. Ibid., pp. 42–44.

7. See *Men's Health*, 24 July 1987, pp. 41–46.

8. See Arlie Hochschild, *The Managed Heart* (Berkeley: University of California Press, 1983).

9. I am indebted to Melinda Vadas, "Could Pornography Subordinate Women?" *The Journal of Philosophy* 84(11) (September 1987), for stimulating me to think along these lines.

10. Susan Griffin, *Pornography and Silence* (New York: Harper & Row, 1981), p. 36.

11. Laura Lederer, ed., *Take Back the Night* (New York: William Morrow, 1980), p. 24.

12. John Berger, *Ways of Seeing* (Baltimore: Penguin, 1972), p. 54.

13. *Playboy's Women of the World* (Chicago: Playboy Press, 1985).

14. See Nancy Chodorow, *The Reproduction of Mothering* (Berkeley: University of California Press, 1978), and Dorothy Dinnerstein, *The Mermaid and the Minotaur* (New York: Harper & Row, 1976).

Eros Thanatized:
Pornography and Male Sexuality
Harry Brod

1. See author's comments, note 17.

2. Susan Brownmiller, *Against Our Will: Men, Women, and Rape* (New York: Simon & Schuster, 1975).

3. Jules Feiffer, *Hold Me* (New York: Signet, 1964).

4. Andy Metcalf and Paul Morrison, "Motorway Conversations," *Achilles Heel* 6 & 7 (November 1982): 20.

5. Susan Griffin, *Pornography and Silence: Culture's Revenge Against Nature* (New York: Harper & Row 1981), 117.

6. Michael Betzold, "How Pornography Shackles Men and Oppresses Women," in *For Men Against Sexism: A Book of Readings*, ed. Jon Snodgrass (Albion, CA: Times Change Press, 1977), 47.

7. Quoted in Herbert Marcuse, *Eros and Civilization: A Philosophical Inquiry into Freud* (Boston: Beacon Press, 1966), 226.

8. Rollo May, *Love and Will* (New York: W. W. Norton & Company, 1969; reprint, New York: Dell, 1974), 71–73. My attention was drawn to this passage

by Marc Feigen Fasteau's reference to a portion of it in *The Male Machine* (New York: McGraw-Hill, 1974), 24.

9. Sigmund Freud, *The Ego and the Id*, trans. Joan Riviere, ed. James Strachey (New York: W. W. Norton, 1962), 37.

10. Marcuse, 234.

11. Griffin, 97.

12. Marcuse, 227.

13. Jim Stodder, "Confessions of a Candy-Ass Roughneck," in *The Women Say, The Men Say: Women's Liberation and Men's Consciousness*, ed. Evelyn Shapiro and Barry M. Shapiro (New York: Dell, 1979), 44.

14. Bernie Zilbergeld, *Male Sexuality: A Guide to Sexual Fulfillment* (Boston and Toronto: Little, Brown and Company), 24–25.

15. Betzold, 46.

16. I am indebted here to D. P. Verene's *Sexual Love and Western Morality: A Philosophical Anthology* (New York: Harper & Row, 1972).

17. I now think this claim must be qualified. While I still endorse the analysis here of how pornography damages men on a personal, individual level, greater emphasis must be placed on pornography's contribution to men's political, collective power. See my "Pornography and the Alienation of Male Sexuality," *Social Theory and Practice* 14 (Fall 1988): 265–284, revised version forthcoming in *Men, Masculinity, and Social Theory*, ed. Jeff Hearn and David Morgan (London: Unwin Hyman, 1990).

18. John Stuart Mill, *The Subjection of Women* (London: Longman, Green, Reader, and Dyer, 1869; reprint, Cambridge, MA: MIT Press, 1970), 80–81.

19. Karl Marx, "Economic and Philosophic Manuscripts: Third Manuscript," in *Early Writings*, trans. and ed. T. B. Bottomore (New York: McGraw-Hill, 1964), 159–160.

20. Marx, 154.

21. Marx, 164–165.

22. Nikola Milich, "A Call to Memory," M.: *Gentle Men for Gender Justice* 8 (Spring 1982), 15. For other men's responses to sexual violence, see Timothy Beneke's *Men on Rape* (New York: St. Martin's Press, 1982). Beneke's account in his Introduction of the "pornographizing," men do to women insightfully complements the analysis presented here. See pp. 23-29.

23. Marx, 194.

Pornography, Sexual Callousness, and the Trivialization of Rape
Dolf Zillmann and Jennings Bryant

Notes

1. This research has been detailed elsewhere (28). It is of no concern here, however, because all assessment variations were balanced (i.e., were identical across treatment conditions) and hence could not explain any later treatment effects.

2. "F" denotes F rations from the analysis of variance; "p" denotes probabilities of such ratios or of comparisons between individual means by appropriate statistical tests following the initial analysis. In general, the smaller p, the more confidence can be placed into a differentiation or difference. However, $p = .05$ is commonly accepted as low enough for the attribution of a differentiation among several means, or a difference between two means, to the experimental manipulation rather than to chance.

References

1. Barry, K. *Female Sexual Slavery.* Englewood Cliffs, N.J.: Prentice-Hall, 1979.

2. Brownmiller, S. *Against Our Will: Men, Women and Rape.* New York: Simon & Schuster, 1975.

3. Bryant, J., R. A. Carveth, and D. Brown. "Television Viewing and Anxiety: An Experimental Examination." *Journal of Communication* 31(1), Winter 1981, pp. 106–119.

4. Clark, L. "Pornography's Challenge to Liberal Ideology." *Canadian Forum* 3, 1980, pp. 9–12.

5. Cline, V. B. "Another View: Pornography Effects, the State of the Art." In V. B. Cline (Ed.) *Where Do You Draw the Line?: An Exploration into Media Violence, Pornography, and Censorship.* Provo, Utah: Brigham Young University Press, 1974

6. Donnerstein, E., and L. Berkowitz. "Victim Reactions in Aggressive Erotic Films as a Factor in Violence Against Women." *Journal of Personality and Social Psychology* 41, 1981, pp. 710–724.

7. Eysenck, H. J. "Obscenity—Officially Speaking." *Penthouse* 4, 1972, pp. 69–76.

8. Eysenck, H. J. *Sex and Personality.* Austin: University of Texas Press, 1976.

9. Eysenck, H. J., and D. K. B. Nias. *Sex Violence and the Media*. New York: St. Martin's Press, 1978.

10. Feldman-Summers, S., and K. Lindner. "Perceptions of Victims and Defendants in Criminal Assault Cases." *Criminal Justice and Behavior* 3, 1976, pp. 135–149.

11. Gerbner, G., and L. Gross. "Living with Television: The Violence Profile." *Journal of Communication* 26(2), Spring 1976, pp. 173–199.

12. Hawkins, R. P., and S. Pingree. "Television's Influence on Social Reality." In D. Pearl, L. Bouthilet, and J. Lazar (Eds.) *Television and Behavior: Ten Years of Scientific Progress and Implications for the Eighties*, Vol. 2. Washington, D.C.: U.S. Government Printing Office, 1982.

13. Hite, S. *The Hite Report: A Nationwide Study on Female Sexuality*. New York: Macmillan, 1976

14. Hite, S. *The Hite Report on Male Sexuality*. New York: Knopf, 1981.

15. Hughes, D. A. (Ed.) *Perspectives on Pornography*. New York: St. Martin's Press, 1970.

16. Hunt, M. *Sexual Behavior in the 1970s*. New York: Dell, 1974

17. Longino, H. E. "Pornography, Oppression, and Freedom: A Closer Look." In L. Lederer (Ed.) *Take Back the Night: Women on Pornography*. New York: Morrow, 1980.

18. Malamuth, N. M., and J. V. P. Check. "The Effects of Mass Media Exposure on Acceptance of Violence Against Women: A Field Experiment." *Journal of Research in Personality* 15, 1981, pp. 436–446.

19. Mosher, D. L. "Sex Callousness Toward Women," In *Technical Report of the Commission on Obscenity and Pornography*, Vol. 8. Washington, D.C.: U.S. Government Printing Office, 1971.

20. Roberts, E. J. "Television and Sexual Learning in Childhood." In D. Pearl, L. Bouthilet, and J. Lazar (Eds.) *Television and Behavior: Ten Years of Scientific Progress and Implications for the Eighties*, Vol. 2. Washington, D.C.: U.S. Government Printing Office, 1982.

21. Rossi, P., R. Waite, C. Bose, and E. Berk. "The Seriousness of Crimes: Normative Structure and Individual Differences." *American Sociological Review* 39, 1974, pp. 224–237.

22. Russell, D. E. H. "Pornography and Violence: What Does the New Research Say?" In L. Lederer (Ed.) *Take Back the Night: Women on Pornography*. New York: Morrow, 1980.

23. Scroggs, J. "Penalties for Rape as a Function of Victim Provocativeness, Damage, and Resistance." *Journal of Applied Social Psychology* 6, 1976, pp. 360–368.

24. Steinem, G. "Erotica and Pornography: A Clear and Present Difference." In L. Lederer (Ed.) *Take Back the Night: Women on Pornography.* New York: Morrow, 1980.

25. Tannenbaum, P. H., and D. Zillmann. "Emotional Arousal in the Facilitation of Aggression Through Communication." In L. Berkowitz (Ed.) *Advances in Experimental Social Psychology,* Vol. 8. New York: Academic Press, 1975.

26. U.S. Government. *Report of the Commission on Obscenity and Pornography.* New York: Bantam, 1970.

27. U.S. Government. *Technical Report of Commission on Obscenity and Pornography* (8 vols.). Washington, D.C.: U.S. Government Printing Office, 1971.

28. Zillmann, D., and J. Bryant. "Effects of Massive Exposure to Pornography." In N. M. Malamuth and E. Donnerstein (Eds.) *Pornography and Sexual Aggression.* New York: Academic Press, in press.

29. Zillmann, D., J. Bryant, and R. A. Carveth. "The Effects of Erotica Featuring Sadomasochism and Bestiality on Motivated Intermale Aggression." *Personality and Social Psychology Bulletin* 7, 1981, pp. 153–159.

30. Zillmann, D., J. Bryant, P. W. Comisky, and N. J. Medoff. "Excitation and Hedonic Valence in the Effect of Erotica on Motivated Intermale Aggression." *European Journal of Social Psychology* 11, 1981, pp. 233–252.

References to Postcript

Banks, A. M. (1988, May 1). "Is Rape Sometimes OK?" *Providence Sunday Journal,* pp. A–1, A–29.

Brannigan, A. (1987). "Pornography and Behavior: Alternative Explanations." *Journal of Communication* 37, pp. 185–192.

Brannigan, A., and S. Goldenberg (1987). "The Study of Aggressive Pornography: The Vicissitudes of Relevance." *Critical Studies in Mass Communication* 4, pp. 262–283.

Check, J. V. P. (1985). *The Effects of Violent and Nonviolent Pornography.* Ottawa: Department of Justice for Canada.

Christensen, F. (1986). "Sexual Callousness Re-examined." *Journal of Communication* 36, pp. 174–188.

Christensen, F. (1987). "Effects of Pornography: The Debate Continues." *Journal of Communication* 37, pp. 186–188.

Linz, D., and E. Donnerstein (in press). "The Methods and Merits of Pornography Research." *Journal of Communication.*

Mosher, D. L., and R. D. Anderson (1986). "Macho Personality, Sexual Aggression, and Reactions to Guided Imagery of Realistic Rape." *Journal of Research in Personality* 20, pp. 77–94.

Mosher, D. L., and M. Sirkin (1984). "Measuring a Macho Personality Constellation." *Journal of Research in Personality* 18, pp. 150–163.

Zillmann, D. (1986). "Effects of Prolonged Consumption of Pornography." In E. P. Mulvey and J. L. Haugaard (Eds.), *Report of the Surgeon General's Workshop on Pornography and Public Health.* Washington, D.C.: U.S. Department of Health and Human Services, Office of the Surgeon General, pp. 98–135.

Mass Media, Sexual Violence, and Male Viewers: Current Theory and Research
Edward Donnerstein and Daniel Linz

Abel, G., Barlow, D., Blanchard, E., & Guild, D. (1977). The components of rapists' sexual arousal. *Archives of General Psychiatry, 34,* 395–403, 895–903.

Bandura, A. (1977). *Social learning theory.* Englewood Cliffs, NJ: Prentice-Hall.

Baron, R. A. (1977). *Human aggression.* New York: Plenum.

Baron, R. A. (1984). The control of human aggression: A strategy based on incompatible resonses. In R. Green & E. Donnerstein (Eds.), *Aggression: Theoretical and empirical reviews* (vol II). New York: Academic Press.

Baron, R. A., & Bell, P. A. (1977). Sexual arousal and aggression by males: Effects of type of erotic stimuli and prior provocation. *Journal of Personality and Social Psychology, 35,* 79–87.

Berkowitz, L. (1974). Some determinants of impulsive aggression: Role of mediated associations with reinforcements for aggression. *Psychological Review, 81,* 165–179.

Berkowitz, L. (1984). Some effects of thoughts on anti- and prosocial influences of media events: A Cognitive-neoassociation analysis. *Psychological Bulletin 95,* 410–427.

Brownmiller, S. (1975). *Against our will: Men, women and rape.* New York: Simon & Schuster.

Burstyn, V. (1985). *Women against censorship.* Manchester, NH: Salem House.

Burt, M. R. (1980). Cultural myths and supports for rape. *Journal of Personality and Social Psychology, 38,* 217–230.

Check, J. V. P., & Malamuth, N. (1983). Violent pornography, feminism, and social learning theory. *Aggressive Behavior, 9,* 106–107.

Check, J. V. P., & Malamuth, N. (in press). Can participation in pornography experiments have positive effects? *Journal of Sex Research.*

Cline, V. B (Ed.) (1974). *Where do you draw the line?* Salt Lake City, UT: Brigham Young University Press.

Dienstbier, R. A. (1977). Sex and violence: Can research have it both ways? *Journal of Communication, 27,* 176–188.

Donnerstein, E. (1980a). Pornography and violence against women. *Annals of the New York Academy of Sciences, 347,* 277–288.

Donnerstein, E. (1980b). Aggressive-erotica and violence against women. *Journal of Personality and Social Psychology, 39,* 269–277.

Donnerstein, E. (1983). Erotica and human aggression. In R. Geen & E. Donnerstein (Eds.), *Aggression: Theoretical and empirical reviews.* New York: Academic Press.

Donnerstein, E. (1984). Pornography: Its effect on violence against women. In N. Malamuth & E. Donnerstein (Eds.), *Pornography and sexual aggression.* Orlando, FL: Academic Press.

Donnerstein, E., & Barrett, G. (1978). The effects of erotic stimuli on male aggression toward females. *Journal of Personality and Social Psychology, 36,* 180–188.

Donnerstein, E., & Berkowitz, L. (1982). Victim reactions in aggressive-erotic films as a factor in violence against women. *Journal of Personality and Social Psychology, 41,* 710–724.

Donnerstein, E., & Berkowitz, L. (1985). *Role of aggressive and sexual images in violent pornography.* Manuscript submitted for publication.

Donnerstein, E., Donnerstein, M., & Evans, R. (1975). Erotic stimuli and aggression: Facilitation or inhibition? *Journal of Personality and Social Psychology, 32,* 237–244.

Donnerstein, E., & Hallam, J. (1978). Facilitating effects of erotica on aggression against women. *Journal of Personality and Social Psychology, 36,* 1270–1277.

Donnerstein, E., & Linz, D. (1984 January). Sexual violence in the media, a warning. *Psychology Today,* pp. 14–15.

Dworkin, A. (1985). Against the male flood: Censorship, pornography, and equality. *Harvard Women's Law Journal,* 8.

Frodi, A. (1977). Sexual arousal, situational restrictiveness, and aggressive behavior. *Journal of Research in Personality, 11,* 48–58.

Howard, J. L., Liptzin, M. B., & Reifler, C. B. (1973). Is pornography a problem? *Journal of Social Issues, 29,* 133–145.

Liebert, R. M., & Schwartzberg, N. S. (1977). Effects of mass media. *Annual Review of Psychology, 28,* 141–173.

Linza, D., Donnerstein, E., & Penrod, S. (1984). The effects of long-term exposure to filmed violence against women. *Journal of Communication, 34,* 130–147.

MacKinnon, C. A. (1985). Pornography, civil rights, and speech. *Harvard Civil Rights–Civil Liberty Law Review,* 20 (1).

Malamuth, N. (1981a). Rape proclivity among males. *Journal of Social Issues, 37,* 138–157.

Malamuth, N. (1981b). Rape fantasies as a function of exposure to violent-sexual stimuli. *Archives of Sexual Behavior, 10,* 33–47.

Malamuth, N. (1984). Aggression against women: Cultural and individual causes. In N. Malamuth & E. Donnerstein (Eds.), *Pornography and sexual aggression.* Orlando, FL: Academic Press.

Malamuth, N., Feshbach, S., & Jaffe, Y. (1977). Sexual arousal and aggression: Recent experiments and theoretical issues. *Journal of Social Issues, 37,* 110–133.

Malamuth, N. M., & Spinner, B. (1980). A longitudinal content analysis of sexual violence in the best-selling erotic magazines. *Journal of Sex Research, 16* (3), 116–237.

Malamuth, N., & Check, J. V. P. (1981). The effects of mass media exposure on acceptance of violence against women: A field experiment. *Journal of Research in Personality, 15,* 436–446.

Malamuth, N., & Check, J. V. P. (1983). Sexual arousal to rape depictions: Individual differences. *Journal of Abnormal Psychology, 92,* 55–67.

Malamuth, N., & Donnerstein, E. (1982). The effects of aggressive pornographic mass media stimuli. In L. Berkowitz (Ed.), *Advances in experimental social psychology* (vol. 15). New York: Academic Press.

Malamuth, N., & Donnerstein, E. (Eds.) (1983). *Pornography and sexual aggression*. New York: Academic Press.

Malamuth, N., Haber, S., & Feshbach, S. (1980). The sexual responsiveness of college students to rape depictions: Inhibitory and disinhibitory effects. *Journal of Research in Personality, 14,* 399–408.

Malamuth, N., Heim, M., & Feshbach, S. (1980). Sexual responsiveness of college students to rape depictions: Inhibitory and disinhibitory effects. *Journal of Personality and Social Psychology, 38,* 399–408.

Mann. J., Sidman, J., & Starr, S. (1971). Effects of erotic films on sexual behavior of married couples. In *Technical Report of the Commission on Obscenity and Pornography* (vol. 8). Washington, DC: Government Printing Office.

Meyer, T. (1972). The effects of viewing justified and unjustified real film violence on aggressive behavior. *Journal of Personality and Social Psychology, 23,* 21–29.

President's Commission on Obscenity and Pornography (vol. 8). Washington, DC: Government Printing Office. 1970.

Russ, J. (1985). *Magic mommas, trembling sisters, puritans and perverts*. New York: Crossing.

Scott, J. (1985). *Sexual violence in* Playboy *magazine: Longitudinal analysis*. Paper presented at the meeting of the American Society of Criminology.

The war against pornography. (1985, March 18). *Newsweek,* pp. 58–62, 65–67.

Wills, G. (1977, November). Measuring the impact of erotica. *Psychology Today,* pp. 30–34.

Zillmann, D. (1971). Excitation transfer in communication-mediated aggressive behavior. *Journal of Experimental Psychology, 7,* 419–433.

Zillmann, D. (1979). *Hostility and aggression*. Hillsdale, NJ: Erlbaum.

Zillmann, D. (1984). *Victimization of women through pornography*. Proposal to the National Science Foundation.

Zillmann, D., & Bryant, J. (1982). Pornography, sexual callousness, and the trivialization of rape. *Journal of Communication, 32,* 10–21.

Zillmann, D., & Bryant, J. (1984). Effects of massive exposure to pornography. In N. Malamuth & E. Donnerstein (Eds.), *Pornography and sexual aggression*. New York: Academic Press.

Zillmann, D., & Sapolsky, B. S. (1977). What mediates the effect of mild erotica on annoyance and hostile behavior in males? *Journal of Personality and Social Psychology, 35,* 587–596.

Legalized Pornography in Denmark
Berl Kutchinsky

Fisher, William. "Pornography, Erotica and Behavior: More Questions than Answers." Paper presented at the Fourteenth International Congress on Law and Mental Health, Montreal, Canada, June 1988.

Howard, James I.; Liptzin, Myron B.; and Reifler, Clifford B. "Is Pornography a Problem?" *Journal of Social Issues* 29 (1973): 133–45.

Kinsey, Alfred C.; Pomeroy, Wardell B.; Martin, Clyde E.; and Gebhard, Paul H. *Sexual Behavior in the Human Female*. Philadelphia and London: Saunders, 1953.

Kutchinsky, Berl. "Obscenity and Pornography: Behavioral Aspects." In *Encyclopedia of Crime and Justice*, vol. 3, edited by S. H. Kadish, p. 1077-1086. New York: Free Press, 1983.

Kutchinsky, Berl. "Pornography and Its Effects in Denmark and the United States: A Rejoinder and Beyond." In *Comparative Social Research*, vol. 8, edited by Richard F. Thomasson, pp. 301–330. Greenwich, Conn.: JAI Press, 1985.

Kutchinsky, Berl. "Deception and Propaganda." *Society* 24 (1987): 21–24.

Kutchinsky, Berl. "Pornography and Sexual Violence: The Criminological Evidence from Aggregate Data in Several Countries." Paper presented at the Fourteenth International Congress on Law and Mental Health, Montreal, Canada, June 1988.

Kutchinsky, Berl. *Law, Pornography and Crime: The Danish Experience*. New Haven: Yale University Press, forthcoming.

Lederer, Laura, ed. *Take Back the Night: Women on Pornography*. New York: William Morrow, 1980.

Linz, Daniel; Penrod, Steven D.; and Donnerstein, Edward. "The Attorney General's Commission on Pornography: The Gaps between 'Findings' and Facts." *American Bar Foundation Research Journal* (1987): 713–736.

Malamuth, Neal M., and Donnerstein, Edward, eds. *Pornography and Sexual Aggression*. New York: Academic Press, 1983.

Mann, Jay; Sidman, Jack; and Starr, Sheldon. "Evaluating Social Consequences of Erotic Films: An Experimental Approach." *Journal of Social Issues* 29 (1973): 113–131.

Marshall, W. L., and Barbaree, H. E. "A Behavioral View of Rape." *International Journal of Law and Psychiatry* 7 (1984): 51–57.

Pornography Report of the Penal Code Council ("The Danish Pornography Report"). Translated from Danish. In Gordon Schindler, ed. *A Report on Denmark's Legalized Pornography.* Torrance, Calif.: Banner Books, 1969.

Attorney General's Commission on Pornography, First Report, vol. 1 ("The Meese Report"). Washington, D.C.: U.S. Government Printing Office, 1986.

Report of the Commission on Obscenity and Pornography ("The Obscenity Report"). Washington, D.C.: U.S. Government Printing Office, 1970.

Report of the Committee on Obscenity and Film Censorship ("The Williams Report"). Cmnd. 7772. London: Her Majesty's Stationary Office, 1979.

Gays and the Propornography Movement:
Having the Hots for Sex Discrimination
John Stoltenberg

1. Lev. 18:22.

2. Laws of New Hampshire, 1805, p. 267.

3. For a discussion of woman-hating in gay male pornography, see Andrea Dworkin, *Pornography: Men Possessing Women* (New York: Perigee, 1981), pp. 36–45.

4. See Robin Ruth Linden et al., eds. *Against Sadomasochism: A Radical Feminist Analysis* (East Palo Alto, Calif.: Frog in the Well, 1983).

5. Typical personal-ad excerpts culled from *New York Native,* 24 February 1986, pp. 55–56. Portions in brackets spell out coded abbreviations in the original.

6. *Magazine & Bookseller,* July 1985, pp. 69–70.

7. Michael J Bowers, Attorney General of Georgia v. Michael Hardwick, 478 U.S. (October term, 1985).

8. See Vern Countryman, ed., *The Douglas Opinions* (New York: Random House, 1977), pp. 234–236.

9. In Paris Adult Theater I v. Slaton, 413 U.S. 49 (1973), paraphrasing Stanley, in an opinion written by Chief Justice Warren Burger.

10. Laurence H. Tribe et al., *Brief for Respondent,* Bowers v. Hardwick, 478 U.S., p. 16.

11. In a 1976 case Doe v. Commonwealth's Attorney, 425 U.S. 901 (1976), the high court flatly rejected a challenge to Virginia's sodomy law.

12. Tribe et al., p. 24.

Pornography Without Power?
Chris Clark

Deidre English, "Pornography and Male Rage," *Mother Jones*, 1982.

"Gay Porn—a Discussion," *Achilles Heel*, 1983.

Gloria Steinem, "Erotica vs. Pornography" in *Outrageous Acts and Everyday Rebellions* (New York: Holt, Rinehart and Winston, 1983).

Ellen Willis, "Feminism, Moralism and Pornography," *Village Voice*, 1979.

Contributors

STEVE ABBOTT writes frequently for *The Advocate*, *The Sentinel*, and other gay publications. He is currently a fiction editor for Crossing Press, and his most recent book is *View Askew: Postmodern Investigations* (Androgyne Press, 1989).

TIMOTHY BENEKE is the author of *Men on Rape*. He lives in Oakland, California, and works as a freelance writer. He has been speaking out against violence against women since 1980.

HARRY BROD, Visiting Associate Professor of Gender Studies and Philosophy at Kenyon College, is editor of *The Making of Masculinities: The New Men's Studies* (Unwin Hyman, 1987) and *A Mensch Among Men: Explorations in Jewish Masculinity* (Crossing Press, 1988).

JENNINGS BRYANT is Professor of Communication at the University of Alabama. He holds the Reagan Chair for Broadcasting.

ROBERT CHRISTGAU is a senior editor at *The Village Voice*, who writes mostly about rock and roll.

JULES FEIFFER is a cartoonist and a playwright. In 1986 he was awarded the Pulitzer Prize for editorial cartooning.

TODD GITLIN, professor of sociology and director of the mass communications program at the University of California, Berkeley, is author of *The Whole World Is Watching*, *Inside Prime Time*, and *The Sixties: Years of Hope, Days of Rage*, and editor of *Watching Television*.

RICHARD GOLDSTEIN is a senior editor at *The Village Voice*, where he currently writes a monthly column on sex. A collection of his journalism from the 1960s will be published by Unwin Hyman in 1989.

MICHAEL S. KIMMEL, a sociologist at the State University of New York at Stony

Brook, is a specialist in the study of gender and sexuality. His books include *Changing Men: New Directions in Research on Men and Masculinity* (Sage Publications, 1987), *Men's Lives* (Macmillan, 1989), and *Against the Tide: Pro-Feminist Men in America, 1775 to the Present* (Beacon, forthcoming). He is currently working with John Gagnon on *Gender and Desire*, which will be published by Basic Books.

JOEL KOVEL is Alger Hiss Professor of Social Studies at Bard College. His two most recent books are *The Radical Spirit* and *In Nicaragua*, both available through Columbia University Press.

BERL KUTCHINSKY is a professor at the Institute of Criminal Science at the University of Copenhagen. The results of his two decades of research on pornography and law are now available in English as *Law, Pornography and Crime: The Danish Experience* (Yale University Press).

DANIEL LINZ teaches in the department of communications at the University of California at Santa Barbara. He is the co-author of *The Question of Pornograpahy* (Free Press, 1987).

PHILLIP LOPATE is the author of, among others, *Bachelorhood, The Rug Merchant,* and *Confessions of Summer*. He teaches English and creative writing at the University of Houston.

SCOTT MACDONALD teaches film history and American literature at Utica College. He has written on film for *Film Quarterly, Afterimage, Cinema Journal, The Independent, Journal of Film and Video, October,* and other journals, and is the author of *A Critical Cinema* (University of California, 1988). The ideas in the essay included here are developed in "Interview with Lizzie Borden," *Feminist Studies* 15 (1989).

JEFFREY MASSON, a former psychoanalyst, is the author of *The Assault on Truth, A Dark Science: Women, Sexuality, and Psychiatry in the Nineteenth Century,* and the recent *Against Therapy: Emotional Tyranny and the Myth of Psychological Healing*. He is currently working on two books, one about psychiatry and the Holocaust, and *When Elephants Weep: the Question of Animal Emotions.*

DAVID MURA is the author of *A Male Grief: Notes on Pornography and Addiction* (Milkweed Editions) and *After We Lost Our Way* (E. P. Dutton), which won the 1988 National Poetry Series contest. His essays have appeared in *Partisan Review, The Threepenny Review, The Utne Reader,* and *The Graywolf Annual V: A Multicultural Reader.*

FRED SMALL is an activist songwriter whose compositions include "59¢," "The Hug," "Annie," and "Father Song." He is a former attorney.

ROBERT STAPLES is a professor of sociology at the University of California, San Francisco. He is the author of *Black Masculinity.*

DAVID STEINBERG has been active in the California and national men's movements for twelve years and has led numerous workshops on fathering and men's sexuality. He is the editor of *Erotic by Nature: A Celebration of Life, of Love, and of Our Wonderful Bodies* and the producer of the erotic theater review "A Celebration of Eros."

JOHN STOLTENBERG is the author of *Refusing to Be a Man: Essays on Sex and Justice* (Breitenbush Books). He is chair of the Task Group on Pornography of the National Organization for Changing Men and cofounder of Men Against Pornography in New York City.

SCOTT TUCKER is a writer in Philadelphia. He was the International Mr. Leather in 1986.

JEFF WEINSTEIN is senior editor and columnist at *The Village Voice*. His collected essays, *Learning to Eat*, were published recently by Sun & Moon Press.

PHILIP WEISS is a writer who lives in New York City.

BERNIE ZILBERGELD is a psychotherapist in Oakland, California. His well-known book, *Male Sexuality*, is currently being revised for a new edition.

DOLF ZILLMANN is professor of communication and psychology at the University of Alabama. He is also associate dean for graduate studies and research at that institution.